Starting Up Your Own Business

Expert Advice From the
U.S. Small Business Administration

Starting Up Your Own Business

Expert Advice From the
U.S. Small Business Administration

Compiled by Dr. G. Howard Poteet

LIBERTY HALL
PRESS™

LIBERTY HALL PRESS books are published by LIBERTY HALL PRESS an imprint of
McGraw-Hill, Inc. Its trademark, consisting of the words ''LIBERTY HALL PRESS''
and the portrayal of Benjamin Franklin, is registered in the United States Patent
and Trademark Office.

FIRST EDITION
THIRD PRINTING

© 1991 by LIBERTY HALL PRESS, an imprint of TAB BOOKS.

Library of Congress Cataloging-in-Publication Data

Starting up your own business : a collection of SBA articles / G.
Howard Poteet, editor.
    p.   cm.
Includes index.
ISBN 0-8306-3548-3
1. New business enterprises. I. Poteet, G. Howard.
HD62.5.S74   1990
658.1'141—dc20   90-40306
                                        CIP

For information about other McGraw-Hill materials,
call 1-800-2-MCGRAW in the U.S. In other countries
call your nearest McGraw-Hill office.

Vice President & Editorial Director: David J. Conti
Manuscript Editor: Susan L. Rockwell
Director of Production: Katherine G. Brown
Cover Design: Jaclyn J. Boone
Cover Illustration: E. Salem Krieger

Contents

Part I
How to Get Off to a Good Start

Part II
Developing an Effective Business Plan

Part III
Specific Business Plans

Part IV
Finding Money for Your Business

Part V
Establishing Financial Controls for Your Business

Part VI
How to Set Up Effective Security

Part VII
Using Computers to Improve Your Business

Part VIII
Developing New Products

Introduction

Would you like to start up your own business and make it a success? This book can help you do that even if you do not have a background in business or possess a degree in business administration. It will also help you if you do.

You will find it useful because it is a compilation of publications by the Small Business Administration that cover succinctly and precisely the nuts and bolts of starting a business. It provides practical help where the novice entrepreneur most often needs it.

For example, this book explains in detail how to find a suitable location or the most effective steps to follow in buying an established business.

As part of creating your effective business plan, you'll learn how to borrow and manage money in your business, and you'll discover the secrets of controlling the finances of your business.

But there's more. As your business gets underway, you'll make use of the information supplied by experts on making your business grow. Soon, your business will be thriving as you put their inside techniques and procedures into effect.

Then, as your business expands even more, you'll turn to the appropriate sections in the book for advice on such matters as maintaining security, using computers, and even how to find and develop new products.

As you can see, this step-by-step guide will take you through the critical stages of starting your business, breathing life into it, and making it grow into a successful enterprise.

But, what makes this book different from the others on the market is that the information it contains is written by the most highly qualified experts available. They have used their knowledge and experience to produce these articles under the direction of the United States Small Business Administration.

Established in 1953, the SBA has helped thousands of men and women start their own businesses through its aid, counsel, and assistance. In addition to working for the interests of small business operators in Congress, making loans to them, and assuring that they receive government contracts, the SBA has concentrated on improving the management skills through publications of information by carefully chosen authorities and specialists in business operation and management. These articles are the results of their efforts.

Look at the name of the writers of these articles and their academic and professional qualifications and you will see why their advice will be most useful to you. In short, this information can supply you with the equivalent of an MBA in practical business techniques.

Put their ideas, suggestions, and inside advice to work and make a success of your own business.

Part I
How to Get Off to a Good Start

Checklist for Going into Business
    Members of SCORE

Choosing a Retail Location
    Edited by SBA Staff Members
    Contributors to the text: Jeffrey P. Davidson
                            James R. Lowry
                            J. Ross McKeever
                            Frank H. Spink, Jr.

Evaluating Franchise Opportunities
    SBA Staff Members

How to Buy or Sell a Business
    John A. Johansen

Selecting the Legal Structure for Your Firm
    Antonio M. Olmi

INTRODUCTION

Owning a business is the dream of many Americans . . . starting that business converts your dream into reality. But, there is a gap between your dream and reality that can only be filled with careful planning. As a business owner, you will need a plan to avoid pitfalls, to achieve your goals and to build a profitable business.

The "Checklist for Going into Business" is a guide to help you prepare a comprehensive business plan and determine if your idea is feasible, to identify questions and problems you will face in converting your idea into reality and to prepare for starting your business.

Operating a successful small business will depend on:

— a practical plan with a solid foundation;
— dedication and willingness to sacrifice to reach your goal;
— technical skills; and,
— basic knowledge of management, finance, record keeping and market analyses.

As a new owner, you will need to master these skills and techniques if your business is to be successful.

IDENTIFY YOUR REASONS

As a first, and often overlooked step, ask yourself why you want to own your own business. Check each of the reasons that apply to you.

	YES
1. Freedom from the 9–5 daily work routine.	____
2. Being your own boss.	____
3. Doing what you want when you want to do it.	____
4. Improving your standard of living.	____
5. You are bored with your present job.	____

	YES
6. You have a product or service for which you feel there is a demand.	____

Some reasons are better than others, none are wrong; however, be aware that there are tradeoffs. For example, you can escape the 9-5 daily routine, but you may replace it with a 6 AM to 10 PM routine.

A SELF ANALYSIS

Going into business requires certain personal characteristics. This portion of the checklist deals with you—the individual. These questions require serious thought. Try to be objective. Remember, it is your future that is at stake!

Personal Characteristics

	YES	NO
1. Are you a leader?	____	____
2. Do you like to make your own decisions?	____	____
3. Do others turn to you for help in making decisions?	____	____
4. Do you enjoy competition?	____	____
5. Do you have will power and self discipline?	____	____
6. Do you plan ahead?	____	____
7. Do you like people?	____	____
8. Do you get along well with others?	____	____

Personal Conditions

This next group of questions, though brief, is vitally important to the success of your plan. It covers the physical, emotional and financial strains you will encounter in starting a new business.

	YES	NO
1. Are you aware that running your own business may require working 12–16 hours a day, six days a week, and maybe even Sundays and holidays?	____	____

YES NO

2. Do you have the physical stamina to handle the work load and schedule? ____ ____

3. Do you have the emotional strength to withstand the strain? ____ ____

4. Are you prepared, if needed, to temporarily lower your standard of living until your business is firmly established? ____ ____

5. Is your family prepared to go along with the strains they, too, must bear? ____ ____

6. Are you prepared to lose your savings? ____ ____

PERSONAL SKILLS AND EXPERIENCE

Certain skills and experience are critical to the success of a business. Since it is unlikely that you possess **all** the skills and experience needed, you'll need to hire personnel to supply those you lack. There are some basic and special skills you will need for your particular business.

By answering the following questions, you can identify the skills you possess and those you lack (your strengths and weaknesses).

YES NO

1. Do you know what basic skills you will need in order to have a successful business? ____ ____

2. Do you possess those skills? ____ ____

3. When hiring personnel, will you be able to determine if the applicants' skills meet the requirements for the positions you are filling? ____ ____

4. Have you ever worked in a managerial or supervisory capacity? ____ ____

5. Have you ever worked in a business similar to the one you want to start? ____ ____

6. Have you had any business training in school? ____ ____

7. If you discover you don't have the basic skills needed for your business, will you be willing to delay your plans until you've acquired the necessary skills? ____ ____

FINDING A NICHE

Small businesses range in size from a manufacturer with many employees and millions of dollars in equipment to the lone window washer with a bucket and a sponge. Obviously, the knowledge and skills required for these two extremes are far apart, but, for success, they have one thing in common—each has found a business niche and is filling it.

The most crucial problems you will face in your early planning will be to find your niche and determine the feasibility of your idea. "Get into the right business at the right time" is very good advice but following that advice may be difficult. Many entrepreneurs plunge into a business venture so blinded by the dream that they fail to thoroughly evaluate its potential.

Before you invest time, effort and money, the following exercise will help you separate sound ideas from those bearing a high potential for failure.

IS YOUR IDEA FEASIBLE?

1. Identify and briefly describe the business you plan to start.
   _____
   _____
   _____
   _____

2. Identify the product or service you plan to sell.
   _____

3. Does your product or service satisfy an unfilled need? Yes ____ No ____

4. Will your product or service serve an existing market in which demand exceeds supply? Yes ____ No ____

5. Will your product or service be competitive based on its quality, selection, price or location? Yes ____ No ____

Answering yes to any of these questions means you are on the right track; a negative answer means the road ahead could be rough.

MARKET ANALYSIS

For a small business to be successful, the owner must know the market. To learn the market, you must analyze it, a process that takes time and effort. You don't have to be a trained statistician to analyze the market place nor does the analysis have to be costly.

Analyzing the market is a way to gather facts about potential customers and to determine the demand for your product or service. The more information you gather, the greater your chances of capturing a segment of the market. Know the market before investing your time and money in any business venture.

These questions will help you collect the information necessary to analyze your market and determine if your product or service will sell.

	YES	NO
1. Do you know who your customers will be?	___	___
2. Do you understand their needs and desires?	___	___
3. Do you know where they live?	___	___
4. Will you be offering the kind of products or services that they will buy?	___	___
5. Will your prices be competitive in quality and value?	___	___
6. Will your promotional program be effective?	___	___
7. Do you understand how your business compares with your competitors?	___	___
8. Will your business be conveniently located for the people you plan to serve?	___	___
9. Will there be adequate parking facilities for the people you plan to serve?	___	___

This brief exercise will give you a good idea of the kind of market planning you need to do. An answer of "no" indicates a weakness in your plan so do your research until you can answer each question with a "yes."

PLANNING YOUR START-UP

So far, this checklist has helped you identify questions and problems you will face converting your idea into reality, and determining if your idea is feasible. Through self analysis you have learned of your personal qualifications and deficiencies, and through market analysis you have learned if there is a demand for your product or service.

The following questions are grouped according to function. They are designed to help you prepare for "Opening Day."

	YES	NO

Name and Legal Structure

1. Have you chosen a name for your business?	___	___
2. Have you chosen to operate as a sole proprietorship, partnership or corporation?	___	___

Your Business and the Law

A person in business is not expected to be a lawyer, but each business owner should have a basic knowledge of laws affecting the business. Here are some of the legal matters you should be acquainted with:

	YES	NO
1. Do you know which licenses and permits you may need to operate your business?	___	___
2. Do you know the business laws you will have to obey?	___	___
3. Do you have a lawyer who can advise you and help you with legal papers?	___	___
4. Are you aware of:		
— Occupational Safety and Health (OSHA) requirements?	___	___
— Regulations covering hazardous material?	___	___
— Local ordinances covering signs, snow removal, etc.?	___	___
— Federal Tax Code provisions pertaining to small business?	___	___
— Federal regulations on withholding taxes and Social Security?	___	___
— State Workmen's Compensation laws?	___	___

Protecting Your Business

It is becoming increasingly important that attention be given to security and insurance protection for your business. There are several areas that should be covered. Have you examined the following categories of risk protection?

	YES	NO
-- fire	____	____
— theft	____	____
— robbery	____	____
— vandalism	____	____
— accident liability	____	____

Discuss the types of coverage you will need and make a careful comparison of the rates and coverage with several insurance agents before making a final decision.

Business Premises and Location

	YES	NO
1. Have you found a suitable building in a location convenient for your customers?	____	____
2. Can the building be modified for your needs at a reasonable cost?	____	____
3. Have you considered renting or leasing with an option to buy?	____	____
4. Will you have a lawyer check the zoning regulations and lease?	____	____

Merchandise

	YES	NO
1. Have you decided what items you will sell or produce, or what service(s) you will provide?	____	____

	YES	NO
2. Have you made a Merchandise Plan based upon estimated sales, to determine the amount of inventory you will need to control purchases?	____	____
3. Have you found reliable suppliers who will assist in the start-up?	____	____
4. Have you compared the prices, quality and credit terms of suppliers?	____	____

Business Records

	YES	NO
1. Are you prepared to maintain complete records of sales, income and expenses, accounts payable and receivables?	____	____
2. Have you determined how to handle payroll records, tax reports and payments?	____	____
3. Do you know what financial reports should be prepared and how to prepare them?	____	____

FINANCES

A large number of small businesses fail each year. There are a number of reasons for these failures, but one of the main reasons is insufficient funds. Too many entrepreneurs try to start-up and operate a business without sufficient capital (money). To avoid this dilemma, you can review your situation by analyzing these three questions.

1. How much money do you have?

2. How much money will you need to start your business?

3. How much money will you need to stay in business?

Use the following chart to answer the first question:

CHART–1

PERSONAL FINANCIAL STATEMENT

—————————— , 19 ——

ASSETS   LIABILITIES

CASH ON HAND	———	ACCOUNTS PAYABLE	———
SAVINGS ACCOUNTS	———	NOTES PAYABLE	———
STOCKS, BONDS, SECURITIES	———	CONTRACTS PAYABLE	———
ACCOUNTS/NOTES RECEIVABLE	———	TAXES	———
REAL ESTATE	———	REAL ESTATE LOANS	———
LIFE INSURANCE (cash value)	———	OTHER LIABILITIES	———
AUTOMOBILE/OTHER VEHICLES	———		
OTHER LIQUID ASSETS	———		
TOTAL ASSETS	———	TOTAL LIABILITIES	———

NET WORTH (ASSETS MINUS LIABILITIES) ———

The next chart will help you answer the second question—How much money will you need to start your business? The chart is for a retail business—items will vary for service, construction and manufacturing firms.

CHART–2

START UP COST ESTIMATES

DECORATING, REMODELING	———
FIXTURES, EQUIPMENT	———
INSTALLING FIXTURES, EQUIPMENT	———
SERVICES, SUPPLIES	———
BEGINNING INVENTORY COST	———
LEGAL, PROFESSIONAL FEES	———
LICENSES, PERMITS	———
TELEPHONE UTILITY DEPOSITS	———
INSURANCE	———
SIGNS	———
ADVERTISING FOR OPENING	———
UNANTICIPATED EXPENSES	———
TOTAL START-UP COSTS	———

The answer to the third question (How much money will you need to stay in business?) must be divided into two parts—immediate costs and future costs.

From the moment the door to your new business opens, a certain amount of income will undoubtedly come in. However, this income should not be projected in your operating expenses. You will need enough money available to cover costs for at least the first three months of operation. Chart 3 will help you project your operating expenses on a monthly basis.

CHART–3

EXPENSES FOR ONE MONTH

Your living costs   _____

Employee Wages   _____

Rent   _____

Advertising   _____

Supplies   _____

Utilities   _____

Insurance   _____

Taxes   _____

Maintenance   _____

Delivery/Transportation   _____

Miscellaneous   _____

         TOTAL   _____

Now multiply the total of Chart 3 by three. This is the amount of cash you will need to cover operating expenses for three months. Deposit this amount in a savings account before opening your business. Use it only for those purposes listed in the above chart because this money will insure that you will be able to continue in business during the crucial early stages.

By adding the total start-up costs (Chart–2) to the total expenses for three months (three times the total cost on Chart–3,) you can learn what the estimated costs will be to start-up and operate your business for three months. By subtracting the totals of Charts–2 and 3 from the cash available (Chart–1), you can determine the amount of additional financing you may need, if any.

Now, you will need to estimate your operating expenses for the first year after start-up. Chart–4 is used for this estimation.

The first step in determining your annual expenses is to estimate your sales volume month by month. Be sure to consider seasonal trends that may affect your business when estimating the sales volume. Information on seasonal sales patterns and typical operating ratios can be secured from your trade associations.

{NOTE: The relationships between amounts of capital that you invest, levels of sales, each of the cost categories, the number of times that you will sell your inventory (turnover) and many other items form "financial ratios." These ratios provide you with extremely valuable checkpoints before it's too late to make adjustments. In the reference section of your local library are publications such as "The Almanac of Business and Industrial Financial Ratios," as a source of ratios to compare your performance with that of other, similar businesses.

For thorough explanations of these ratios and how to use them follow up on the sources of help and information mentioned at the end of this publication.}

Next, determine the cost of goods that will be sold to produce your expected sales. The cost of goods sold or the operating ratio is expressed in dollars and as a percentage of the sales. After determining the operating ratio, estimate the expenses necessary to achieve your anticipated sales.

As you prepare Chart 4, understand that you are looking for the percent of total sales that each item represents. Fill out each month's column in dollars, total them in the far right column, and then divide each item into the total net sales to produce the operating ratios (cost of goods sold to sales, rent to sales). Now, fill in Chart 4.

PROJECTED PROFIT/LOSS

	%	J	F	M	A	M	J	J	A	S	O	N	D	Total
Total net sales														
Cost, goods sold														
Gross														
Controllable expense														
Salaries/wages														
Payroll taxes														
Legal/Accounting														
Advertising														
Automobile														
Office supplies														
Dues/Subscriptions														
Telephone														
Utilities														
Miscellaneous														
Total Con. Exp.														
Fixed Expenses														
Rent														
Depreciation														
Insurance														
Licenses/Permits														
Taxes														
Loan Payments														
Total Fixed Exp.														
Total Expenses														
Net profit/Loss (before tax)														

AFTER START-UP

The primary source of revenue in your business will be from sales but your sales will vary from month to month because of seasonal patterns and other factors. So it is important to determine if your monthly sales will produce enough income to pay each month's bills.

An estimated cash flow projection (Chart-5) will show if the monthly cash balance is going to be subject to such factors as:

— failure to recognize seasonal trends,

— excessive cash taken from the business for living expenses;

— too rapid expansion, and

— slow collection of accounts if credit is extended to customers.

Use the following to build a worksheet to help you with this problem. In this example, all sales are made for cash.

CHART-5

ESTIMATED CASH FLOW FORECAST

	Jan.	Feb.	Mar.	Apr.	May	Jun.	(etc.)
Cash in bank (1st of MO.)							
Petty cash (1st of MO.)							
Total cash (1st of MO.)							
Anticipated cash sales							
Total receipts							
Total cash & receipts							
Disbursements for MO. (rent, loan payments, utilities, wages, etc.)							
Cash Balance (End of Month)							

CONCLUSION

Beyond a doubt, preparing an adequate business plan is the most important step in starting a new business. A comprehensive business plan will be your guide to managing a successful business. **The business plan is paramount to your success.** It must contain all the pertinent information about your business; it must be well written, factual, and organized in a logical sequence. Moreover, it should not contain any statements that cannot be supported.

If you have carefully answered all the questions on this checklist and completed all the worksheets, you have seriously thought about your goal. But . . . there may be some things you may feel you need to know more about.

Owning and running a business is a continuous learning process. Research your idea and do as much as you can yourself, but don't hesitate to seek help from people who can tell you what you need to know.

SCORE (Service Corps of Retired Executives, a nation-wide volunteer organization of retired business executives and professionals) is a good place to start. Information and assistance is also available from trade associations, Chambers of Commerce, community colleges, universities and Small Business Development Centers.

INFORMATION IS POWER!

Make it your business to know what business information is available, where to get it and most importantly, how to use it. Sources of information include:

• U. S. Small Business Administration (SBA)

  — SBA District Offices

  — Small Business Development Centers (SBDCs)

  — Service Corps of Retired Executives (SCORE)

  — Small Business Institutes (SBIs)

Also, you may request a free Directory of Business Development Publications from your local SBA office or the Answer Desk.

OTHER SOURCES:

- State Economic Development Agencies

- Chambers of Commerce

- Local Colleges

- The Library

- Manufacturers and suppliers of small business technologies and products.

GOOD LUCK!

Summary

The choice of a store location has a profound effect on the entire business life of a retail operation. A bad choice may all but guarantee failure, a good choice success.

This Aid takes up site selection criteria, such as retail compatibility and zoning, that the small store owner-manager must consider after making basic economic, demographic, and traffic analyses. It offers questions the retailer must ask (and find answers to) before making the all important choice of store location.

This publication was edited by SBA staff members. Contributors to the text were **Jeffrey P. Davidson**, Management Consultant, The EMAY Corporation, Washington, D.C.; **James R. Lowry**, Head, Department of Marketing, College of Business, Ball State University, Muncie, Indiana; and **J. Ross McKeever** and **Frank H. Spink, Jr.**, the Urban Land Institute, Washington, D.C.

The first step in choosing a retail business location takes place in your head. Before you do anything else, define your type of business in the broadest terms and determine your long term objectives. Write them down. This exercise will help you later in choosing a retail location.

In picking a store site, many store owners believe that it's enough to learn about the demographics ("people information" like age, income, family size, etc.) of the population, about the kind of competition they'll be facing, and about traffic patterns in the area they're considering. Beyond a doubt these factors are basic to all retail location analysis.

Once you've spotted a tentative location using these factors, however, you've only done half the job. Before you make a commitment to moving in and setting up, you must carefully check several more aspects of the location to help insure your satisfaction with—and most importantly your success at—the site you've chosen.

Factors to be Considered

Three factors confront you as an owner-manager in choosing a location: selection of a city; choice of an area or type of location within a city; and identification of a specific site.

If you are going to *relocate in another city*, naturally you consider the following factors:

Size of the city's trading area.
Population and population trends in the trading area.
Total purchasing power and the distribution of the purchasing power.
Total retail trade potential for different lines of trade.
Number, size, and quality of competition.
Progressiveness of competition.

In choosing an *area or type of location* within a city you evaluate factors such as:

Customer attraction power of the particular store and the shopping district.
Quantitative and qualitative nature of competitive stores.
Availability of access routes to the stores.
Nature of zoning regulations.
Direction of the area expansion.
General appearance of the area.

Pinpointing the *specific site* is particularly important. In central and secondary business districts, small stores depend upon the traffic created by large stores. Large stores in turn depend on attracting customers from the existing flow of traffic. (However, where sales depend on nearby residents, selecting the trading area is more important than picking the specific site.) Obviously, you want to know about the following factors when choosing a specific site:

Adequacy and potential of traffic passing the site.
Ability of the site to intercept traffic en route from one place to another.
Complementary nature of the adjacent stores.
Adequacy of parking.
Vulnerability of the site to unfriendly competition.
Cost of the site.

Types of Consumer Goods

Another factor that affects site selection is the customers' *view* of the goods sold by a store. Consumers tend to group products into three major categories: convenience, shopping, and specialty goods.

Convenience goods usually mean low unit price, purchased frequently, little selling effort, bought by habit, and sold in numerous outlets. Examples: candy bars, cigarettes, and milk.

For stores handling *convenience goods*, the quanitity of traffic is most important. The corner of an intersection which offers two distinct traffic streams and a large window display area is usually a better site than the middle of a block. Downtown convenience goods stores, such as low-priced, ready-to-wear stores and drugstores, have a limited ability to generate their own traffic. In merchandising convenience goods, it is easier to build the store within the traffic than the traffic within the store. Convenience goods are often purchased on impulse in easily accessible stores.

In addition, the greater the automobile traffic, the greater the sales of convenience goods for catering to the drive-in traffic. For the drive-in store selling low-priced convenience goods, the volume of traffic passing the site is a most important factor in making a site decision. The consumer purchases these goods frequently and wants them to be readily available. Consumers are reminded when passing a convenience goods store that he or she needs a particular item.

If consumers must make a special trip to purchase such convenience staple goods as food and drug items, they want the store to be close to home. One study of foodstore purchases in the central city area revealed that nearly 70 percent of the women patronized stores within one to five blocks of their homes. Another study of foodstores indicated that for suburban locations the majority of customers lived within three miles of the stores, while the maximum trading area was five miles. For rural locations, the majority of consumers lived within a ten minute drive to the store, with the maximum trading area within a twenty minute drive.

Shopping goods usually mean high unit price, purchased infrequently, more intensive selling effort usually required on the part of the store owner, price and features compared, and sold in selectively franchised outlets. Examples: men's suits, automobiles, and furniture.

For stores handling *shopping goods*, the quality of the traffic is more important. While convenience goods are purchased by nearly everyone, certain kinds of shopping goods are purchased by only certain segments of shoppers. Moreover, it is sometimes the character of the retail establishment rather than its type of goods that governs the selection of a site. For example, a conventional men's wear store should be in a downtown location close to a traffic generator like a department store. On the other hand, a discount store handling menswear would prefer an accessible highway location.

In many cases, buyers of shopping goods like to compare the items in several stores by traveling only a minimum distance. As a result stores offering complementary items tend to locate close to one another. An excellent site for a shopping goods store is next to a department store or between two large department stores where traffic flows between them. Another good site is one between a major parking area and a department store.

A retailer dealing in shopping goods can have a much wider trading area. Without a heavily trafficked location—but with the help of adequate promotion—this more expensive type of store can generate its own traffic. In this case, a location with low traffic density but easy accessibility from a residential area is a satisfactory site. The consumer buys these goods infrequently and deliberately plans these purchases. Consumers are willing to travel some distance to make shopping comparisons.

If you offer shopping goods, however, you should not locate too far away from your potential customers. One study of a discount department store showed that 79.6 percent of the shoppers lived within five miles of the store and another 16.1 percent lived within a ten-mile radius. The magnitude of the trading area for a shopping goods store can be determined by a customer survey, automobile license checks, sales slips, charge account records, store deliveries, and the extent of local newspaper circulation.

Specialty goods usually mean high unit price, although price is not a purchase consideration, bought infrequently, requires a special effort on the part of the customer to make the purchase, no substitutes considered, and sold in exclusively franchised outlets. Examples: precious jewelry, expensive perfume, fine furs, and so on, of specific brands or name labels.

Specialty goods are often sought by consumers who are already "sold" on the product, brand, or both. Stores catering to this type of consumer may use isolated locations because they generate their own consumer traffic.

Stores carrying specialty goods that are complementary to certain other kinds of shopping goods may desire to locate close to the shopping goods stores. In general, the specialty goods retailer should locate in the type of neighborhood where the adjacent stores and other establishments are compatible with his or her operation.

Retail Compatibility

How important is retail compatibility? For a small retail store in its first year of operation, with limited funds for advertising and promoting, **retail compatibility can be the most important factor** in the survival of the store.

Will you be located next to businesses that will generate traffic for your store? Or will you be located near businesses that may clash with yours?

For example, if you offer shopping goods, the best location is near other stores carrying shopping goods. Conversely, locating your shopping goods store in a convenience goods area or center is not recommended.

Take a look at shopping centers in your area. Invariably, you'll find a clothing or shoe store — in trouble — in an otherwise convience goods shopping center.

On the other hand, with the advent of the mall and regional shopping center, shopping goods and convenience goods outlets may now be found co-existing easily under the same roof. In this situation, it is still important to be located in a section of the shopping complex that is conducive to what you're selling. For example, a pet store should not be located immediately adjacent to a restaurant, dress shop, or salon. You would want to locate a gift shop near places like department stores, theaters, restaurants—in short, any place where lines of patrons may form, giving potential customers several minutes to look in the gift shop's display windows.

Merchants' Associations

Most first time business owners have no idea how effective a strong merchant's association can be in promoting and maintaining the business in a given area. Always find out about the merchant's association. The presence of an effective merchants' association can strengthen your business and save you money through group advertising programs, group insurance plans, and collective security measures.

A strong merchants association can accomplish through group strength what an individual store owner couldn't even dream of. Some associations have induced city planners to add highway exits near their shopping center. Other have lobbied for—and received—funds from cities to remodel their shopping centers, including extension of parking lots, refacing of buildings, and installation of better lighting.

Merchants' associations can be particularly effective in promoting of stores using common themes or events and during holiday seasons. The collective draw from these promotions is usually several times that which a single retailer could have mustered.

How can you determine if the retail location you're considering has the benefit of an effective merchants' association? Ask other store owners in the area. Find out:

How many members the association has;

Who the officers are;
How often the group meets;
What the yearly dues are; and
What specifically, it has accomplished in the last 12 months.

Ask to see a copy of the last meeting's minutes. Determine what percentage of the members were in attendance.

What if there is no merchants' association? Generally (though not always) a shopping area or center with no merchants' association, or an ineffective one, is on the decline. You'll probably see extensive litter or debris in the area, vacant stores, a parking lot in need of repair, and similar symptoms. You should shun locations with these warning signs. With a little on-site investigation, they're easy to avoid.

Responsiveness of the Landlord

Directly related to the appearance of a retail location is the responsiveness of the landlord to the individual merchant's needs. Unfortunately, some landlords of retail business properties actually hinder the operation of their tenants' businesses. They are often, in fact, responsible for the demise of their properties.

By restricting the placement and size of signs, by foregoing or ignoring needed maintenance and repairs, by renting adjacent retail spaces to incompatible — or worse, directly competing — businesses, landlords may cripple a retailer's attempts to increase business.

Sometimes landlords lack the funds to maintain their properties. Rather than continuing to "invest" in their holdings by maintaining a proper appearance for their buildings and supporting their tenants, they try to "squeeze" the property for whatever they can get.

To find out if a landlord is responsive to the needs of the retail tenants talk to the tenants before you commit to moving in yourself. Ask them: 1) Does the landlord return calls in a reasonable period and send service people quickly? 2) Is it necessary to nag the landlord just to get routine maintenance taken care of? 3) Does the landlord just collect the rent and disappear, or is he or she sympathetic to the needs of the tenants? 4) Does the landlord have any policies that hamper marketing innovations?

In addition to speaking with current tenants, talk to previous tenants of the location you have in mind. You'll probably come up with a lot of helpful information. Find out what businesses they were in and why they left. Did they fail or just move? What support or hinderances did the landlord provide? If the opportunity presented itself, would they be retail tenants of this landlord again?

Zoning and Planning

Your town's zoning commission will be happy to provide you with the latest "mapping" of the retail location and surrounding areas that you are considering. Here are some questions to consider:

Are there restrictions that will limit or hamper your operations?

Will construction or changes in city traffic or new highways present barriers to your store?

Will any competitive advantages you currently find at the location you're considering be diminished by zoning changes that will be advantageous for competitors or even allow new competitors to enter your trade area?

Most zoning boards, along with economic/regional development committees, plan several years in advance. They can probably provide you with valuable insights to help you decide among tentative retail locations.

Leases

Directly related to zoning is your intended length of stay and your lease agreement. Before you enter into any rigid lease agreement, you must get information on future zoning plans and decide how long you wish to remain at the location under consideration:

Do you plan to operate the business in your first location indefinitely or have you set a given number of years as a limit?

If your business is successful, will you be able to expand at this location?

Is your lease flexible, so that you have an option to renew after a specified number of years? (On the other hand, is the lease of limited duration so, if need be, you may seek another location?)

Study the proposed lease agreement carefully. Get advice from your lawyer or other experts. Does the agreement:

Peg rent to sales volume (with a definite ceiling) or is rent merely fixed?

Protect you as well as the property owner?

Put in writing the promises the property owner has made about repairs, construction and reconstruction, decorating, alteration, and maintenance?

Contain prohibitions against subleasing?

Consider these factors *before* you settle on a location.

Other Considerations

A host of other considerations have varying importance in choosing a retail location, depending on your line of business. The following questions, while they certainly don't exhaust all possibilities, may help you decide on a retail location:

How much retail, office, storage or workroom space do you need?

Is parking space available and adequate?

Do you require special lighting, heating or cooling, or other installations?

Will your advertising expenses be much higher if you choose a relatively remote location?

Is the area served by public transportation?

Can the area serve as a source of supply of employees?

Is there adequate fire and police protection?

Will sanitation or utility supply be a problem?

Is exterior lighting in the area adequate to attract evening shoppers and make them feel safe?

Are customer restroom facilities available?

Is the store easily accessible?

Does the store have awnings or decks to provide shelter during bad weather?

Will crime insurance be prohibitively expensive?

Do you plan to provide pick up or delivery?

Is the trade area heavily dependent on seasonal business?

Is the location convenient to where you live?

Do the people you want for customers live nearby?

Is the population density of the area sufficient?

Shopping Centers

Shopping centers are distinctly different from the other two major locations—that is, downtown and local business strips. The shopping center building is pre-planned as a merchandising unit for interplay among tenants. Its site is deliberately selected by the developer for easy access to pull customers from a trade area. It has on-site parking as a common feature of the layout. The amount of parking space is directly related to the retail area.

Customers like the shopping center's convenience. They drive in, park, and walk to their destination in relative safety and speed. Some shopping centers also provide weather protection and most provide an atmosphere created for shopping comfort. For the customer, the shopping center has great appeal.

For the merchant making a decision whether or not to locate in a shopping center, these "plus" characteristics must be related to the limitations placed upon you as a tenant. In a shopping center, a tenant is part of a merchant team. As such, you must pay your pro rata share of the budget for the team effort. You must keep store hours, light your windows, and place your signs within established rules.

What Are Your Chances?

Whether or not a small retailer can get into a particular shopping center depends on the market and management. A small shopping center may need only one children's shoe store, for example, while a regional center may expect enough business for several. The management aspect is simple to state: Developers and owners of shopping centers look for successful retailers.

In finding tenants whose line of goods will meet the needs of the desired market, the developer-owner first signs on a prestige merchant as the lead tenant. Then, the developer selects other types of stores that will complement each other. In this way, a "tenant mix" offers a varied array of merchandise. Thus, the center's competitive strength is bolstered against other centers as well as supplying the market area's needs.

To finance a center, the developer needs major leases from companies with strong credit ratings. The developer's own lenders favor tenant rosters that include the triple-A ratings of national chains. However, local merchants with good business records and proven understanding of the local markets have a good chance of being considered by a shopping center developer.

But even so, a small independent retailer can sometimes play "hard to get." When most spaces are filled, the developer may need **you** to help fill the rest of them.

If you are considering a shopping center for a first-store venture you may have trouble. Your financial backing and merchandising experience may be unproved to the owner-developer. Your problem is to convince the developer that the new store has a reasonable chance of success and will help the "tenant mix."

What Can the Center Do for You?

Suppose that the owner-developer of a shopping center asks you to be a tenant. In considering the offer, you would need to make sure of what you can do in the center. What rules will there be on your operation? In exchange for the rules, what will the center do for you?

Even more important, you must consider the trade area, the location of your competition, and the location of your space in the center. These factors help to determine how much business you can expect to do in the center.

In a Neighborhood Shopping Center, the leading tenant is a supermarket or drug store. The typical leasable space is 50,000 square feet but may range from 30,000 to 100,000 square feet. The typical site area is from 3 to 10 acres. The minimum trade population is 2,500 to 40,000.

In a Community Shopping Center, the leading tenant is a variety/junior department store or discount department store. The typical leasable space is 150,000 square feet but may range from 100,000 to 300,000 square feet. The typical site area is 10 to 30 acres. The minimum trade population is 40,000 to 150,000.

In a Regional Shopping Center, the leading tenant is one or more full-line department stores. The typical leasable space is 400,000 square feet with a range from 300,000 to more than 1,000,000 square feet. The typical site area is 30 to 50 acres. The minimum trade population is 150,000 or more. When the regional center exceeds 750,000 square feet and includes three or more department stores, it becomes a SUPER-REGIONAL CENTER.

The Center's Location. In examining the center's location, look for answers to questions such as these:

Can you hold old customers and attract new ones?

Would the center offer the best sales volume potential for your kind of merchandise?

Can you benefit enough from the center's access to a market? If so, can you produce the appeal that will make the center's customers come to your store?

Can you deal with your logical competition?

To help answer such questions, you need to check out: (1) the trade area and its growth prospects; (2) the general income level in the trade area; (3) the number of households; and (4) the share of various age groups in the population. If your line is clothes for young women, for example, you would not want to locate in a center whose market area contains a high percentage of retired persons.

Make your own analysis of the market which the developer expects to reach. In this respect, money for professional help is well spent, especially when the research indicates that the center is not right for your type of operation.

Your Space. Determine where your space will be. Your location in the center is important. Do you need to be in the main flow of customers as they pass between the stores with the greatest customer pull? Who will be your neighbors? What will be their effect on your sales?

How much space is also important. Using your experience, you can determine the amount of space you will need to handle the sales volume you expect to have in the shopping center. And, of course, the amount of space will determine your rent. Many merchants need to rethink their space requirements when locating in a shopping center. Rents are typically much higher and, therefore, space must be used very efficiently.

"Total Rent"-In most non-shopping center locations, rent is a fixed amount which has no relationship to sales volume. In shopping centers the "rent" is usually stated as a minimum guaranteed rent per square foot of leased area against a percentage. Typically, while this is between 5 and 7 percent of gross sales, it varies by type of business and other factors. This means that if the rents as calculated by the percentage of sales is higher than the guaranteed rent, the higher amount is the rent. If it is lower than the guaranteed rent, then the guaranteed rent is the amount paid.

But this guarantee is not the end. In addition, you may have to pay dues to the center's merchant association. You may have to pay for maintenance of common areas. Consider your rent, then, in terms of "total rent." If, and when, this "total rent" is more than your present rent, your space in the center, of course, will have to draw sales enough to justify the added cost.

Finishing Out. Generally, the owner furnishes the bare space. You do the "finishing out" at your own expense. In completing your store to suit your needs, you pay for light fixtures, counters, shelves, painting, floor coverings. In addition, you may have to install your own heating and cooling units. (Your lease should be long enough to pay out your "finishing out" expense.)

An innovation is the "tenant allowance." By this system, landlords provide a cost allowance towards completion of space. It is for store fronts, ceiling treatment, and wall coverings. The allowance is a percentage of their cost and is spelled out in a dollar amount in the lease.

Some developers help tenants plan store fronts, exterior signs, and interior color schemes. They provide this service to insure store fronts that add to the center's image rather than subtracting from it.

Types of Shopping Centers

Because each planned shopping center is built around a major tenant, centers are classed, in part, according to this leading tenant. According to tenant makeup and size, there are three types: neighborhood, community, and regional.

Neighborhood. The supermarket or the drugstore is the leading tenant in a neighborhood center. This type is the smallest in size among shopping centers. It caters to the convenience needs of a neighborhood.

Community. Variety, junior department stores, or discount department stores lead in the next bigger type - the community center. Here, you find room also for more specialty shops, need for wider price ranges, for greater style assortments, and for more impulse-sale items. In recent years the community center has also been designed around the home improvement department store which combine hardware, lumber, electrical, plumbing, flooring, building materials, garden supplies, and a variety of other goods under one roof. The shops that are grouped around this type of anchor tend to be similar in character and may include custom kitchen and bath shops, upholstery, bedding, drapery, and other such shops. While this type of center tends to meet the Community Shopping Center definition as to floor area and site size, its market may be more like a regional center.

Regional. The department store, with its prestige, is the leader in the regional center - the largest type of shopping center. When you find that a second or third department store is also locating in such a center, you will know the site has been selected to draw from the widest possible market area. Super-Regional centers have been developed with as many as 5 department stores. You will find, too, that the smaller tenants are picked to offer a range of goods and services approaching the appeal once found only downtown.

The latest development in regional shopping centers is the enclosed mall. This type of center is designed to shut out the weather and to serve a larger trade area than other regional centers. Customers enjoy the open store fronts, the easy entrance, and the "all-weather" shopping. Tenants enjoy more center-wide promotions because of weather control.

An enclosed air-conditioned mall enables you to merchandise the full width of your store. The whole store becomes a display area, eliminating window backing and expensive display settings. You can rely on sliding doors or an overhead open drop grill for locking up the store.

If you are considering a mall, you should weigh the benefits against costs. At the outset, it may be difficult to measure savings, such as the elimination of store fronts, against costs, for example the cost for heating and air-conditioning in the enclosed mall.

Specialty Theme Shopping Centers. In addition to the three major categories of shopping centers new types of centers are evolving that have been called specialty or theme centers. In general these centers do not have a major anchor tenant. There is a greater percentage of restaurants and specialty food stores, the other stores tend to be highly specialized with more imported goods, custom crafted goods, designer clothes etc. Also a greater number of the merchants are independents. Unusual and interesting architectural design is a normal characteristic and frequently a tourist market rather than a resident market exists.

How to Make a Traffic Count

First of all, be sure you need a traffic count. Although knowledge of the volume and character of passing traffic is always useful, in certain cases a traffic survey may not really make any difference. Other selection factors involved may be so significant that the outcome of a traffic study will have relatively little bearing on your decision. When the other selection factors, such as parking, operating costs, or location of competitors, become less important and data on traffic flow becomes dominant, then a count is needed. Once you have determined that you really need a traffic count, the general objective is to count the passing traffic—both pedestrian and vehicular—that would constitute potential customers who would probably be attracted into your type of store. To evaluate the traffic available to competitors, you may desire to conduct traffic counts at their sites, too.

Data from a traffic count should not only show how many people pass by but generally indicate what kinds of people they are. Analysis of the characteristics of the passing traffic often reveals patterns and variations not readily apparent from casual observation.

For counting purposes, the passing traffic is divided into different classifications according to the characteristics of the customers who would patronize your type of business. Whereas a drugstore is interested in the total volume of passing traffic, a men's clothing store is obviously more concerned with the amount of male traffic, especially men between the ages of sixteen and sixty-five.

It is also important to classify passing traffic by its reasons for passing. A woman on the way to a beauty salon is probably a poor prospect for a paint store, but she may be a good prospect for a drugstore. The hours at which individuals go by are often an indication of their purpose. In the early morning hours people are generally on their way to work. In the late afternoon these same people are usually going home from work. When one chain organization estimates the number of potential women customers, it considers women passing a site between 10 a.m. and 5 p.m. to be the serious shoppers.

Evaluation of the financial bracket of passersby is also significant. Out of 100 women passing a prospective location for an exclusive dress shop, only ten may appear to have the income to patronize the shop. Of course, the greater your experience in a particular retail trade, the more accurately you can estimate the number of your potential customers. To determine what proportion of the passing traffic represents your potential shoppers, some of the pedestrians should be interviewed about the origin of their trip, their destination, and the stores in which they plan to shop. This sort of information can provide you with a better estimate of the number of potential customers.

In summary, the qualitative information gathered about the passing traffic should include counting the individuals who seem to possess the characteristics appropriate to the desired clientele, judging their reasons for using that route, and calculating their ability to buy.

Pedestrian Traffic Count

In making a pedestrian count you must decide: *who* is to be counted; *where* the count should take place; and *when* the count should be made. In considering *who* is to be counted, determine what types of people should be included. For example, the study might count all men presumed to be between sixteen and sixty-five. The directions should be completely clear as to the individuals to be counted so the counters will be consistent and the total figure will reflect the traffic flow.

As previously indicated, it is frequently desirable to divide the pedestrian traffic into classes. Quite often separate counts of men and women and certain age categories are wanted. A trial run will indicate if there are any difficulties in identifying those to be counted or in placing them into various groupings.

You next determine the specific place *where* the count is to be taken. You decide whether all the traffic near the site should be counted or only the traffic passing directly in front of the site. Remember that if all the pedestrians passing through an area are counted, there is the possibility of double counting. Since a person must both enter and leave an area, it is important that each person be counted only once—either when entering or when leaving. Therefore, it is essential that the counter consistently counts at the same location.

When the count should be taken is influenced by the season, month, week, day, and hour. For example, during the summer season there is generally an increased flow of traffic on the shady side of the street. During a holiday period such as the month before Christmas or the week before Easter, traffic is denser than it is regularly. The patronage of a store varies by day of the week, too. Store traffic usually increased during the latter part of a week. In some communities, on factory paydays and days when social security checks are received, certain locations experience heavier than normal traffic.

The day of the week and the time of day should represent a normal period for traffic flow. Pedestrian flow accelerates around noon as office workers go out for lunch. Generally more customers enter a downtown store between 10 a.m. and noon and between 1 p.m. and 3 p.m. than at any other time. Local custom or other factors, however, may cause a variation in these expected traffic patterns.

After you choose the day that has normal traffic flow, the day should be divided into half-hour and hourly intervals. Traffic should be counted and recorded for each half-hour period of a store's customary operating hours. If it is not feasible to count the traffic for each half-hour interval, the traffic flow can be sampled. Traffic in representative half-hour periods in the morning, noon, afternoon, and evening can be counted.

Estimate of Store Sales

Data from a pedestrian traffic survey can give you information on whether or not the site would generate a profitable volume for your store. A retailer with some past experience in the same merchandise line for which a store is planned can make a reasonable estimate of sales volume if the following information is available (in lieu of past personal experience, the trade association for your type of business may be of help):

Characteristics of individuals who are most likely to be store customers (from pedestrian interviews).
Number of such individuals passing the site during store hours (from traffic counts).
Proportion of passersby who will enter the store (from pedestrian interviews).
Proportion of those entering who will become purchasers (from pedestrian interviews).
Amount of the average transaction (from past experience, trade associations, and trade publications).

One retailer divides the people who pass a given site into three categories: those who enter a store; those who, after looking at the windows, may become customers; and those who pass without entering or looking. Owing to prior experience, this retailer is able to estimate from the percentage falling into each classification not only the number who will make purchases but also how much the average purchase will be. If, out of 1,000 passersby each day, five percent enter (fifty) and each spends an average of $8 ($400), a store at that site which operates 300 days a year will have an annual sales volume of $120,000.

Automobile Traffic Count

A growing number of retail firms depend on drive-in traffic for their sales. Both the quantity and quality of automotive traffic can be analyzed in the same way as pedestrian traffic. For the major streets in urban areas, either the city engineer, the planning commission, the State highway department, or an outdoor advertising company may be able to provide you with data on traffic flows. However, you may need to modify this information to suit your special needs. For example, you should supplement data relating to total count of vehicles passing the site with actual observation in order to evaluate such influences on traffic as commercial vehicles, changing of shifts at nearby factories, through highway traffic, and increased flow caused by special events or activities.

Help in Choosing a Location

Choosing a retail location is, at best, a risky undertaking. Considering the consequences of choosing a location that proves to be unsuitable, it pays to get as much assistance as possible.

The local chamber of commerce in a city of more than 125,000 usually has a division devoted primarily to assisting budding owner-managers in finding suitable locations for their businesses. This is a free service that suprisingly few people take advantage of.

The U.S. Small Business Administration (SBA) has field offices located throughout the country. SBA field offices can provide free counseling assistance, literature, and information to help you select a retail site. (See your local directory under "U.S. Government.")

You may wish to hire a consultant to analyze two or three locations that you have selected. It costs less if you provide the consultant with preselected potential locations than to have him or her initate an open-ended search for a location. The business school of a nearby college or university may also be able to provide help.

Other sources of information on potential locations include bankers and lawyers, who may have been in position to have observed over an extended period of time many locations where other clients previously did business. Realtors can also provide information on location. Remember though, their compensation is based upon commissions for renting property.

Locate in Haste, Repent at Leisure

Selection of a retail location requires time and careful consideration. It should not be done in haste just to coincide, say, with a loan approval. If you haven't found a suitable location, don't plan to open until you're sure you've got what you want. Put your plans on hold, don't just settle for a location you hope might work out. A few months' delay is only a minor setback compared to the massive—often fatal—problems that occur from operating a retail business in a poor location.

Summary

Although the success rate for franchisee-owned businesses is significantly better than for many other start-up businesses, success is not guaranteed. One of the biggest mistakes that you can make is to be in a hurry to get into business. If you shortcut your evaluation of a potential business, you might neglect to consider other franchises that are more suitable for you. Don't be "pressured" into a franchise that is not right for you. Although most franchises are managed by reputable individuals, as in all industries, some are not. Also, some franchises could be poorly managed and financially weak.

This AID is designed to assist you in investigating your options. Questions needed to adequately evaluate the business, the franchisor, the franchise package, and yourself are included.

What is Franchising?

A franchise is a legal and commercial relationship between the owner of a trademark, service mark, trade name, or advertising symbol and an individual or group seeking the right to use that identification in a business. The franchise governs the method for conducting business between the two parties. While forms of franchising have been in use since the Civil War, enormous growth has occurred more recently. By the end of 1985, 500,000 establishments in 50 industries will achieve gross sales of over half a trillion dollars and employ 5.6 million full and part-time workers. Industries that rely on franchised business to distribute their products and services touch every aspect of life from automobile sales and real estate to fast foods and tax preparation.

In the simplest form, a franchisor owns the right to a name or trademark and sells that right to a franchisee. This is known as "product/trade name franchising." In the more complex form, "business format franchising," a broader and ongoing relationship exists between the two parties. Business format franchises often provide a full range of services, including site selection, training, product supply, marketing plans, and even financing. Generally, a franchisee sells goods or services supplied by the franchisor or sells goods or services that meet the franchisor's quality standards.

Benefits of a Franchise

There are a number of aspects to the franchising method that appeal to prospective business owners. Easy access to an established product as well as a proven method of marketing reduces the many risks of opening a business. In fact, Small Business Administration and Department of Commerce statistics show a significantly lower failure rate for franchisee-owned businesses than for other business start-ups. The franchisee purchases, along with a trademark, the experience and expertise of the franchisor's organization. However, a franchise does not ensure easy success. If you are not prepared for the total commitment of time, energy, and financial resources that any business requires, this is the point at which you should stop.

Investigate Your Options

As in all major business decisions, nothing substitutes for thorough investigation, planning, and analysis of your options. This AID is designed to help you set up a systematic program to analyze the possibilities and pitfalls of the franchised business you are considering. Use the questions below to guide your research and cover all the bases. Read the full AID before you begin to gather the information you will need.

Sources of Information

You will need at least the following sources of information as well as experienced professional advice:

1. **A directory of franchisors,** such as the *Franchise Opportunities Handbook* (published by the U.S. Department of Commerce and available from The Superintendent of Documents, U.S. Government Printing Office, Washington, D.C. 20402). Others are available at your library.

2. **The disclosure document.** A Federal Trade Commission rule requires that franchise and business opportunity sellers provide certain information to help you in your decision. The FTC rule requires the franchisor to provide you a detailed disclosure document at least ten days before you pay any money or legally commit yourself to a purchase. This document includes 20 important items of information, such as:

- Names, addresses, and telephone numbers of other purchasers

- A fully-audited financial statement of the seller

- The background and experience of the key executives

- The cost required to start and maintain the business

- The responsibilities you and the seller will share once you buy

3. **Current franchisees.** Talk to other owners and ask them about their experiences regarding earnings claims and information in the Disclosure Document. Be certain that you talk to franchisees and not company-owned outlets.

4. **Other references.** You should get more information and publications from the U.S. Small Business Administration, the Federal Trade Commission, the Better Business Bureau, the local Chamber of Commerce and associations, such as the International Franchise Association (1025 Connecticut Ave., N.W., Washington, D.C. 20036).

5. **Professional advice.** Finally, unless you have had considerable business experience and legal training, you need a lawyer, an accountant, and a business advisor to counsel you and go over the Disclosure Document and proposed contract. Remember, the money and time you spend before it's too late may save you from a major loss on a bad investment.

What is the business?

Determine whether the business would be a successful venture apart from the benefits offered by a franchise.

1. Is the product or service offered new or proven? Is the product one for which you have a solid background? Do you feel strong motivation for producing the product or providing the service?

2. Does the product meet a local demand? Is there a proven market?

3. What is the competition?

4. If the product requires servicing, who bears the responsibilities covered by warrantees and guarantees? The franchisee? The franchisor? If neither, are service facilities available?

5. What reputation does the product enjoy?

6. Are suppliers available? What reputation do they enjoy?

Who is the franchisor?

Visit at least one of the firm's franchisees, observe the operation, and talk to the owner. You need to determine reputation, stability, and financial strength of the franchisor.

1. How long has the franchisor been in the industry? How long has the firm granted franchises?

2. How many franchises are there? How many in your area?

3. Examine the attitude of the franchisor toward you. Is the firm concerned about your qualifications? Are you being rushed to sign the agreement? Does the firm seem interested in a long-term relationship or does that interest end with the initial fee?

4. What is the current financial condition of the franchisor?

5. Who are the principal officers, owners, and management staff? What is their background?

6. Compare promises with the documentation. Be certain that the sales presentation is realistic and that major promises are written in the contract. Be alert for exaggerated claims and pressure tactics.

7. Verify earnings claims and compare them with other business opportunities. Treat your money like any other investment. Does the franchise offer the return you require? You may want to look at a different opportunity.

8. What is the legal history of the franchisor? Have any of the executives been involved in criminal or civil actions? Are any litigations pending and do they involve any restrictions on trade that affect the franchise?

What is the Franchise Package?

Bring all of your information and resources together as you examine the contract. Think carefully about the level of independence you will maintain as a franchise. How comprehensive are the operating controls? Be very clear about the full costs of purchasing the franchise. Involve your attorney, accountant, and business advisor as you examine these questions.

1. What is the full initial cost? What does it cover?

- Licensing fee?

- Land purchase or lease?

- Building construction or renovation?
- Equipment?
- Training?
- Starting inventory?
- Promotional fees?
- Use of operations manuals?

2. What continuing costs are related to the franchisor?

- Royalties?
- Ongoing training?
- Cooperative Advertising fees?
- Insurance?
- Interest on financing?

3. Are you required to purchase supplies from the franchisor? Are the prices competitive with other suppliers?

4. What, if any, restrictions apply to competition with other franchisees?

5. What are the terms covering renewal rights? Reselling the franchise?

Again, use your professional support to examine all of these questions. Some of the contract terms may be negotiable. Find out before you sign; otherwise, it will be too late.

Personal Assessment

Finally, an examination of your own skills, abilities, and experience is perhaps your most important step. Determine exactly what you want out of life and what you are willing to sacrifice to achieve your goals. Be honest, rigorous, and specific. Ask yourself:

Am I qualified for this field?

- Physically?
- By experience?
- By education?
- By learning capacity?
- Financially?

Ask yourself about the effects of this decision on your family. How will this new life style affect them? Do they understand the risks and sacrifices, and will they support your efforts? Beginning a franchise business is a major decision that does not ensure easy success. However, an informed commitment of time, energy, and money by you and your family can lead to an exciting and profitable venture.

Summary

The decision to buy or sell a business requires careful consideration of the many factors involved. If you are a seller, these factors include preparing your business for sale and finding buyers. If you are a buyer, they include pricing and financing your purchase.

This **Aid** presents an outline to buying and selling factors as well as the necessary procedures for structuring transactions, negotiations and settlements.

1. Making The Decision To Buy Or To Sell A Business

The Decision to Sell

Business owners choose to sell for a variety of reasons:

1. **Retirement.**
2. **Partnership dispute.**
3. **Diminished interest in the business due to boredom or frustration.**
4. **Illness or death of one of the principals.**
5. **Sales and earnings have plateaued because the company lacks the working capital or management resources to grow.**
6. **Losing money.**

Selling a business is different than selling any other asset one owns, because a business is more than an income earning asset. It is a lifestyle as well. Therefore, the decision to part with it can be emotional. Personal ambitions should be weighed against economic consequences to achieve a properly balanced decision to sell or not to sell.

It is said that timing is everything, and certainly that old axiom is true as applied to the decision to sell a business. Intelligent business owners carefully plan out the decision to sell. They recognize that a business should be sold only after proper preparation and not because of sudden personal frustration or a short-term downturn in business.

The Decision to Buy

It is imperative that a potential business buyer carefully think through his motives for considering the purchase of a business and his criteria in selecting one. A buyer should consider his experience—both vocational and avocational—what he is good at and what he enjoys. If a buyer is interested in a business that has a product or service that is outside his area of expertise, then he should make certain that key employees will stay on after the change in ownership or that similar expertise can be hired.

It is equally important that a buyer identify the desired location(s) and the amount of money willing to be invested. If the money to be used is not in liquid form, the buyer should assess what the realistic possibilities are of obtaining the funds from outside sources. One should also decide on the size of the business in terms of sales, profits, and the number of employees.

It is important to determine if the desired business is to be one that is profitable and stable or one that is losing money and in need of new management. The more profitable and stable a business, the more it is likely to cost.

2. Preparing The Business For Sale

Nearly every privately-held business is operated in a manner that minimizes the seller's tax liability. Unfortunately, the same operating techniques and accounting practices that minimize tax liability also minimize the value of a business. As a result, there is often a conflict between running a business the way an owner wants and preparing the business for sale. Although it is possible to reconstruct financial statements to reflect the actual operating performance of the business, this process may also put the owner in a position of having to pay back income taxes and penalties. Therefore, plans to sell a business should be made years in advance of the actual sale. This will permit the time required to make necessary changes in accounting practices that demonstrate a 3 to 5 year track record of maximum profits.

Audited statements are the best type of financial statements because they are most easily verified by the buyer. However, it is not uncommon for a business's financial statements to be reviewed or compiled. Good financial statements don't eliminate the need for making the business aesthetically pleasing. The business should be clean, the inventory current, and the equipment in good working order.

Next, a valuation report should be prepared. The valuation report eliminates guesswork and the painful trial and error method of pricing that so many owners rely on. All too often, they arbitrarily decide on an excessive price for the business and then go to the expense and effort of developing prospective buyers, only to be unable to strike a deal. It is only after gradually lowering the price and repeating this folly several times that they learn what their business is really worth. Having a professionally prepared appraisal eliminates this problem.

Finally, a business presentation package should be prepared. All facets of the business should be addressed in this document. They include:

1. A history of the business.
2. A description of how the business operates.
3. A description of the facilities.
4. A discussion of suppliers.
5. A review of marketing practices.
6. A description of the competition.
7. A review of personnel including an organizational chart, description of job responsibilities, rates of pay, and willingness of key employees to stay on after the sale.
8. Identification of the owners.
9. Explanation of insurance coverages.
10. Discussion of any pending legal matters or contingent liabilities.
11. A compendium of 3 to 5 years' financial statements.

3. Finding Buyers And Sellers

The first step is to find a business to buy or find a buyer for the business.

Print Advertising

Business opportunity classified ads are a viable way to advertise a business for sale. Many ads are placed by intermediaries (business brokers or merger and acquisition specialists), but some are placed directly by business owners. The larger local newspapers are the best source of such ads for smaller, privately-held businesses. Sundays are generally the most popular days for these ads.

Larger, privately-held businesses (so-called 'middle-market' companies) are more likely to be advertised in the *Wall Street Journal* on Thursdays. The *Wall Street Journal* produces several different regional editions of their paper. Businesses for sale in any one edition are most likely to be located in that region. Middle-market businesses may also appear in other publications. First Maryland National Bank's *First List* is one such publication, available by subscription only and published on a quarterly basis.

Business opportunity ads, whether for small or large businesses, usually describe the business in several short phrases, keeping its identity anonymous, and list a phone number to call or post office box for reply. The ad should be worded to demonstrate the business's best qualities, (both financial and non-financial) and many include a qualifying statement describing the kind of cash investment or experience required. A telephone

number in the ad will draw more responses than a post office box number, but may not permit the anonymity of a post office box.

Trade Sources

Trade sources can be a viable source of information on businesses for sale. Key people within an industry or in companies on the periphery of the industry, such as suppliers, often know when businesses come up for sale and may be aware of potential buyers. Every industry has a trade association and trade association publications can do a good job of communicating the sale of a business in their industry. If a seller thinks a buyer is likely to come from the same industry, the trade association's publications department should be contacted to see if classified advertising is permitted.

Intermediaries

Business opportunity intermediaries generally can be divided into two groups, 1) business brokers and 2) merger and acquisition specialists. The differences between these two groups are subtle, but in general, business brokers primarily handle the smaller businesses, and merger and acquisition specialists handle the larger middle-market companies. Both groups usually ask for a contract with a 180 day or more exclusive right to sell the business.

Business brokers charge a fee usually amounting to 10% of the purchase price. Merger and acquisition specialists also charge fees, although often the fee is well under 10% since the transactions they work on are much larger. Often, a good merger and acquisition specialist receives a portion of the fee in advance, paid as either a flat fee or an hourly fee. In exchange, the intermediary performs some tangible service such as preparing a presentation package for prospective buyers and a valuation report. Although it is sometimes paid by the buyer, it is more common for the seller to pay the intermediary's fee.

An experienced intermediary can offer assistance in (1) pricing the business, (2) setting the terms, (3) compiling a comprehensive presentation package, (4) professionally marketing the business, (5) screening potential buyers, (6) negotiating and evaluating offers, (7) making certain that proper legal steps are taken. The result can be a considerable saving of the business owner's or business buyer's time and effort.

4. Evaluating The Business

The first step a buyer must take in evaluating a business for sale is that of reviewing its history and the way it operates. It is important to learn how the business was started, how its mission may have changed since its inception and what past events have occurred to shape its current form. A buyer should understand the business's methods of acquiring and serving its customers and how the functions of sales, marketing, finance and operations interrelate. General information about the industry can be obtained from trade associations.

The business's financial statements, operating documents, and practices should be reviewed. A summary of the items to be reviewed follows.

Balance Sheet

Accounts Receivable

1. Obtain an accounts receivable aging schedule and determine if there is concentration among a few accounts.
2. Determine the reasons for all overdue accounts.
3. Find out if any amounts are in dispute.
4. Are any of the accounts pledged as collateral?
5. Is the reserve for bad debt sufficient and how was it established?
6. Review the business's credit policy.

Inventory

1. Make sure the inventory is determined by physical count and divided by finished goods, work in progress and raw materials.
2. Assess the method of valuation and why it was used. (LIFO, FIFO, etc.).
3. Determine the age and condition of the inventory.
4. How is damaged or obsolete inventory valued?
5. Is the amount of inventory sufficient to operate efficiently and for how long?
6. Should an appraisal be obtained?

Marketable Securities

1. Obtain a list of marketable securities.
2. How are the securities valued?
3. Determine the fair market value of the securities.
4. Are any securities restricted or pledged?
5. Should the portfolio be sold or exchanged?

Real Estate

1. Obtain a schedule of real estate owned.
2. Determine the condition and age of the real estate.
3. Establish the fair market value of each of the buildings and land.
4. Should appraisals be obtained?
5. Are repairs or improvements required?
6. Are maintenance costs reasonable?
7. Do any of the principals have a financial interest in the company(s) that perform(s) the maintenance?

8. Is the real estate required to operate the business efficiently?
9. How is the real estate financed?
10. Are the mortgages assumable?
11. Will additional real estate be required in the near future?
12. Is the real estate adequately insured?

Machinery and Equipment

1. Obtain a schedule of machinery and equipment owned and leased.
2. Determine the condition and age of the machinery and equipment and the frequency of maintenance.
3. Identify the equipment and machinery that is state-of-the-art.
4. Identify the machinery and equipment that is obsolete.
5. Identify the machinery and equipment that is used in compliance with EPA or OSHA standards and determine if additional equipment and machinery is needed to comply.
6. Should an appraisal be obtained?
7. Will immediate repairs be required and at what cost?

Accounts Payable

1. Obtain a schedule of accounts payable and determine if there is concentration among a few accounts.
2. Determine the age of the amounts due.
3. Identify all amounts in dispute and determine the reason.
4. Review transactions to determine undisclosed and contingent liabilities.

Accrued Liabilities

1. Obtain a schedule of accrued liabilities.
2. Determine the accounting treatment of:
   —unpaid wages at the end of the period
   —accrued vacation pay
   —accrued sick leave
   —payroll taxes due and payable
   —accrued Federal income taxes
   —other accruals
3. Search for unrecorded accrued liabilities

Notes Payable and Mortgages Payable

1. Obtain a schedule of notes payable and mortgages payable.
2. Identify the reason for indebtedness.
3. Determine terms and payment schedule.
4. Will the acquisition accelerate the note or mortgage or is there a prepayment penalty?

5. Determine if there are any balloon payments to be made and the amounts and dates due.
6. Are the notes or mortgages assumable?

Income Statement

The potential earning power of the business should be analyzed by reviewing profit and loss statements for the past 3 to 5 years. It is important to substantiate financial information by reviewing the business's federal and state tax returns. The business's earning power is a function of more than bottom line profits or losses. The owner's salary and fringe benefits, non-cash expenses, and non-recurring expenses should also be calculated.

Financial Ratios

While analyzing the balance sheet and the income statement, sales and operating ratios should be calculated in order to point out areas requiring further study. Key ratios are the current ratio, quick ratio, accounts receivable turnover, inventory turnover and sales/accounts receivable. The significance of these ratios, the methods for calculating them, and industry averages are available through *Dun & Bradstreet* and *Robert Morris Associates*. Look for trends in the ratios over the past 3 to 5 years.

Leases

1. What is the remaining term of the lease?
2. Are there any option periods, and if so, is the option exercised only by the choice of the tenant?
3. Is there a percent of sales clause?
4. What additional fees (such as a common area maintenance or merchants association dues) are paid over and above the base rent?
5. Is the tenant or landlord responsible for maintaining the roof and the heating and air conditioning system?
6. Is there a periodic rent increase called for to adjust the rent for changes in the consumer price index or for an increase in real estate tax assessments?
7. Is there a demolition clause?
8. Under what terms and conditions will the landlord permit an assumption or extension of the existing lease?

Personnel

1. What are the job responsibilities, rates of pay, and benefits of each employee?
2. What is each employee's tenure?
3. What is the level of each employee's skill in their position and are they employed under an employment contract?
4. Will key employees stay after the business is purchased?

5. Are any employees part of a union, or is any union organizing effort likely?

Marketing

1. Are any of the products proprietary?
2. Describe any new upcoming products and projected sales.
3. What is the business's geographic market area?
4. What is the business's percentage of market share?
5. What are the business's competitive advantages?
6. What are the business's annual marketing expenditures?

Patents

A list of trade names, trademarks, logos, copyrights and patents should be obtained, noting the period of time remaining before each expires.

Taxes

1. Are FICA, unemployment, and sales tax payments current?
2. What was the date and the outcome of the last IRS audit?

Legal Issues

1. Are there any suits now or soon to commence?
2. What OSHA and EPA requirements must be met and are they currently being met?
3. Are all state registration requirements and regulations being met?
4. Are all local zoning requirements being met?
5. Review the articles of incorporation, minute books, bylaws, and/or partnership agreements.
6. What are the classes of stock and the restrictions of each, if any?
7. Has any stock been cancelled or repurchased?
8. Is the business a franchise? If so, review the franchise agreement.

Competitors

1. Who are the business's competitors?
2. What is their market share?
3. What are each competitor's competitive advantages and disadvantages?

. . . .

All the factors identified in this section on evaluating a business have to be carefully scrutinized and weighed. Some factors will have a positive influence on the decision to buy. Others will have a negative influence. Seek out professional assistance if help is needed in interpreting the significance of the information. The important thing is to obtain all the information needed to make a decision. In most instances, all of the business records should be made available to the buyer. In some cases however, certain information may be withheld until a bona fide offer, contingent upon obtaining that information, has been made. If important information is unreasonably withheld, the likelihood of making the transaction work diminishes.

5. Financing The Purchase

A buyer's source of financing depends in part on the size of the business being purchased. The vast majority of businesses (and particularly the smaller businesses) are purchased with a significant portion of the purchase price financed by the owner. The buyer, however, still must make a down payment and be sure that adequate working capital sources are available.

If the funds needed for the down payment are not readily available, the buyer must look for financing from an outside source. To grant such financing, an institutional lender is almost certain to require personal collateral for the loan as well as a compendium of financial and operating data of the business to be acquired. It is rare indeed to be granted a loan to purchase a smaller, privately-held business when the loan is secured only by the assets of the business. The most attractive types of personal collateral from the lender's point of view are real estate, marketable securities and cash value of life insurance. In addition to personal collateral, it must also be demonstrated to the lender that the buyer is of good character, has a clear source of repayment, and has a good business plan. The most common sources for such loans are financial institutions such as banks and consumer finance companies.

The chances of obtaining outside financing improve as the size of the business being acquired increases. Not only does the willingness of the lender to participate in the transaction increase, the number of potential lenders increases as well. Banks, insurance companies, commercial finance companies and venture capital companies all may be interested in lending money for an acquisition of some size. Again, the borrower must be of good character, have a clear source of repayment and have a good business plan.

Lenders for larger transactions may or may not require personal collateral from the purchaser; however, they will require a personal guarantee. Collateral for larger loans generally will consist of a first lien security interest in the tangible assets of the business such as accounts receivable, inventory, equipment and real estate. The lender will set loan conditions and restrictions regarding certain activities of the business. In the

case of insurance companies and venture capitalists, the lender may insist on an equity position in the business and a role in major management decisions. Insurance companies typically only participate in transactions above $10 million. Commercial finance companies make loans on much the same basis as banks. While the interest rate such companies charge is usually higher than that charged by a bank, they are often willing to take more risk.

It is rare for a privately-held business to be acquired without leveraging the business's assets in some manner, pledging them as collateral for a loan made either by the owner of the business or an outside lender. The owner has a strong incentive to provide financing if he feels it is necessary to get the price he wants for the business and has confidence in the buyer. An outside lender must be convinced that the loan's risk of failure is minimal and represents a profitable transaction. Institutional lenders are generally conservative and concentrate rate primarily on repayment. To obtain outside financing it is important to be well prepared and have the information that a lender needs to make a decision. This data should be submitted in the form of a loan proposal and should contain the following items:

1. Purpose of the loan
2. Amount required
3. Term desired
4. Source of repayment
5. Collateral available
6. History and nature of the business
7. Age, experience and education of management
8. Key advisors
9. Product
10. Market area and method of distribution
11. Major customers
12. Suppliers
13. Competition
14. Facilities
15. Employees and unions
16. Three years of business financial statements
17. Three years of business tax returns
18. Current personal financial statement
19. Proforma business income statement, balance sheet and cash budget (for at least three years)

In instances where obtaining bank financing on a stand-alone basis is not possible, a SBA guarantee or underwriting by a state or municipal economic development agency may be available.

6. Pricing The Business

Determining the value of a business is the part of the buy-sell transaction most fraught with potential for differences of opinion. Buyers and sellers usually do not share the same perspective. Each has a distinct rationale, and that rationale may be based on logic or emotion.

The buyer may believe that the purchase will create synergy or an economy of scale because of the way the business will be operated under new ownership. The buyer may also see the business as an especially good lifestyle fit. These factors are likely to increase the amount of money a buyer is willing to pay for a business. The seller may have a greater than normal desire to sell due to financial difficulties or the death or illness of the owner or a member of the owner's family.

For the transaction to come to conclusion, both parties must be satisfied with the price and be able to understand how it was determined.

Factors That Determine Value

The topic of business evaluation is so complex that any explanation short of an entire book does not do it justice. The process takes into account many, many variables and requires that a number of assumptions be made. Shannon Pratt,* a noted business valuation expert, names six of the most important factors:

1. Recent profit history.
2. General condition of the company (such as condition of facilities, completeness and accuracy of books and records, morale and so on).
3. Market demand for the particular type of business.
4. Economic conditions (especially cost and availability of capital and any economic factors that directly affect the business).
5. Ability to transfer goodwill or other intangible values to a new owner.
6. Future profit potential.

The six factors named above determine the fair market value. However, businesses rarely change hands at fair market value. The reason is that three other factors often come into play in arriving at an agreed upon price. Pratt identifies them as follows:

1. Special circumstances of the particular buyer and seller.
2. Tradeoff between cash and terms.
3. Relative tax consequences for the buyer and seller, which depend on how the transaction is structured.

The definition of fair market value is the price at which property would change hands between a willing buyer and a willing seller, both being adequately informed of all material facts and neither being compelled to buy or

---

* Shannon Pratt, *Valuing Small Businesses and Professional Practices* (Homewood, Illinois, Dow-Jones Irwin 1986.)

to sell. In the market place, buyer and seller are nearly always acting under different levels of compulsion.

Rule-of-Thumb Formulas

The rule for using rule-of-thumb formulas for pricing a business is don't use them. The problem with rule-of-thumb formulas is that they address few of the factors that impact a business's value. They rely on a 'one size fits all' approach when, in fact, no two businesses are identical.

Rule-of-thumb formulas do, however, provide a quick means of establishing whether a price for a certain business is "in the ballpark." Formulas exist for many businesses. They are normally calculated as a percentage of either sales or asset values, or a combination of both.

Comparables

Using comparable sales as a means of valuing a business has the same inherent flaw as rule-of-thumb formulas. Rarely if ever are two businesses truly comparable. However, businesses in the same industry do have some characteristics in common, and a careful contrasting may allow a conclusion to be drawn about a range of value.

Balance Sheet Methods of Valuation

This approach calls for the assets of the business to be valued. It is most often used when the business being valued generates earnings primarily from its assets rather than the contributions of its employees or when the cost of starting a business and getting revenues past the break-even point doesn't greatly exceed the value of the business's assets.

There are a number of balance sheet methods of valuation including book value, adjusted book value, and liquidation value. Each has its proper application. The most useful balance sheet method is the adjusted book value method. This method calls for the adjustment of each asset's book value to equal the cost of replacing that asset in its current condition. The total of the adjusted asset values is then offset against the sum of the liabilities to arrive at the adjusted book value.

Adjustments are frequently made to the book values of the following items:

Accounts Receivable—often adjusted down to reflect the lack of collectability of some receivables.

Inventory—usually adjusted down since it may be difficult to sell off all of the inventory at cost.

Real Estate—frequently adjusted up since it has often appreciated in value since it was placed in service.

Furniture, Fixtures, and Equipment—adjusted up if those items in service (probably more than a few years) have been depreciated below their market value, or adjusted down if the items have become obsolete.

Income Statement Methods of Valuation

Although a balance sheet formula is sometimes the most accurate means to value a business, it is more common to use an income statement method. Income statement methods are most concerned with the profits or cash flow produced by the business's assets. One of the more frequently used methods is the discounted future cash flow method. This method calls for the future cash flows (before taxes and before debt service) of the business to be calculated using the 4-step formula below.

Step #1

The historical cash flows are a good basis from which to project future cash flows. Cash flows are computed to include the following:

1. The net profit or loss of the business.
2. The owner's salary (in excess of an equivalent manager's compensation).
3. Discretionary Benefits paid the owner (such as automobile allowance, travel expenses, personal insurance and entertainment).
4. Interest (unless the buyer will be assuming the interest payment).
5. Non-Recurring Expenses (such as non-recurring legal fees).
6. Non-Cash Expenses (such as depreciation and amortization).
7. Equipment Replacements or Additions. (This figure should be deducted from the other numbers since it represents an expense the buyer will incur in generating future cash flows).

While the future cash flows may be projected out for a number of years, for many small businesses it is not possible to project very far into the future before the projections become meaningless. Even with somewhat larger and more substantial businesses, it is difficult to project cash flows for more than 5 years.

Step #2

Once the future cash flows have been projected, they must be discounted back to their present value. This is done by selecting a reasonable rate of return or capitalization rate for the buyer's investment. The selected rate of return varies substantially from one business to the next and is largely a function of risk. The lower the risk

associated with an investment in a business, the lower the rate of return that is required. The rate of return required is usually in the 20–50% range and, for most businesses, it is in the 30–40% range. The present value of the future cash flows can then be determined by using a financial calculator or a set of present value tables that are available in most book stores. The following example demonstrates how the conversion is made with a 40% rate of return.

Year	Projected Cash Flow	Discount Factor *	Present Value	
Year 1	$360	.714	$257	
Year 2	$383	.510	$195	
Year 3	$397	.364	$145	
Year 4	$413	.260	$107	
Year 5	$438	.186	$ 81	
			$785	Total**

* — Based on 40% rate of return. The discount factor declines in each succeeding year.

** — Present value of the sum of discounted projected cash flows. This figure is added to the residual value of the business to arrive at the total value of the business.

Step #3

One more calculation must now be done—the residual value of the business. The residual value is the present value of the business's estimated net worth at the end of the period of projected cash flows (in this example, at the end of five years). This is calculated by adding the current net worth of the business and future annual additions to the net worth. The annual additions are defined as the sum of each year's after-tax earnings, assuming no dividends are paid to stockholders. These additions are added to the current net worth, and that total is discounted to its present value to yield the residual value.

Step #4

The residual value is added to the present value sum of the projected future cash flows previously computed to arrive at a price for the business. An example follows.

	After Tax Income	
Year 1	$125	
Year 2	$131	
Year 3	$138	
Year 4	$144	
Year 5	$152	
Total Additions to net worth		$690
Current net worth		$910
Total net worth		$1600
Residual Value (1600 ×.186)		$298***

*** — Multiplying the total net worth by the discount factor used in the final year of projected cash flows yields the residual value. Adding the residual value of $298 to the present value sum of projected cash flows of $785 yields a value for the business of $1,083.

Although this formula is widely used, it cannot be applied in this simplistic form to arrive at a definitive value conclusion. It fails to address issues such as the buyer's working capital investment, the terms of the transaction, or the valuing of assets like real estate which may not be needed to produce the projected cash flows. However, it is useful in establishing a price range for negotiation purposes.

7. The Role of Advisors

A variety of resources are available for those buyers and sellers wanting to obtain professional advice. These resources include business owners in the industry, Small Business Administration counselors, industry consultants, professional intermediaries, business valuation experts, accountants and attorneys. Each of these resources can be of assistance and each has its limitations.

Business owners, SBA counselors, consultants, and intermediaries are the best source of industry information and operating suggestions. SBA, SCORE (Service Corp of Retired Executives) or ACE (Active Corp of Executives) counselors provide their services free of charge and can be reached through local SBA offices. Business owners may be able to give free advice, and they are often the best source of information. No one knows more about an industry than someone who is successfully running a business in that industry.

Business valuation experts can independently appraise a business's value. Bear in mind, however, that they rely on the representations of the seller. They render a conditional opinion based on the assumption that the financial statements are accurate and complete. They will attempt to independently verify only certain information.

Accountants are best used to perform an audit (if one is needed), help interpret financial statements, or provide advice in structuring the transaction to minimize tax consequences for the buyer and seller.

Probably the most often consulted advisor in the purchase or sale of a business is an attorney. Attorneys are asked to do everything from assessing the viability of a business and appraising its value to negotiating the purchase price and preparing the necessary documents. Attorneys, however, cannot assess the viability of a business undertaking. That is something only the buyer and seller can do. Attorneys also generally cannot value a business, but they can occasionally help negotiate a price between buyer and seller. The involvement of an attorney (or any individual other than the principals) can, however, strain the lines of communication between buyer and seller, so they should be allowed into the negotiation process only after careful consideration.

The primary function of an attorney is to prepare the purchase and sale documents as negotiated by the parties. It should include reasonable and balanced protections for both parties. Experience and reputation are important criteria when selecting an attorney. The attorney chosen should have experience handling similar transactions. It may make sense to choose one attorney to represent both buyer and seller. This avoids the adversarial relationship that opposing attorneys often adopt and improves the odds of successfully completing the transaction. It also eliminates some of the emotion in the negotiation process, improves the lines of communication between the parties, expedites completion of the deal and is less expensive.

8. Structuring The Transaction

Tax and other consequences of the structure of a transaction have an important effect on the overall value of the transaction to the principals. Each type of structure carries with it different tax consequences for the buyer and seller. The type of corporation owned by the seller (regular corporation or S corporation), the size and date of the transaction, and the type of consideration paid may all have a bearing on the tax consequences. Since tax law is constantly changing, it is important to seek legal and tax advice in determining the best way to structure the purchase or sale.

Asset Versus Stock Transactions

The purchase and sale of a business can be structured in either of two basic formats: (1) the purchase of the stock of the seller's corporation, or (2) the purchase of the assets of the seller's business.

—Asset Transactions—

In an asset transaction, the assets to be acquired are specified in the contract. Practices vary from industry to industry but, in general, all the assets of the business except cash and accounts receivable and none of the liabilities of the business convey to the buyer. The seller uses the proceeds from the sale to liquidate all short term and long term liabilities. This means that the buyer purchases all of the business's equipment, furniture, fixtures, inventory, trademarks, tradenames, goodwill and other intangible assets.

An asset transaction generally favors the buyer. The buyer acquires a new cost basis in the assets which may allow a larger depreciation deduction to be taken. The seller must pay taxes on the difference between his basis in the assets and the price paid by the buyer for the business.

The buyer may also prefer an asset transaction for liability reasons. By purchasing assets, the buyer may avoid the possibility of becoming liable for any of the seller's corporation's undisclosed or unknown liabilities. The most common liabilities of this type are federal and state income taxes, payroll withholding taxes and legal actions.

—Stock Transactions—

Stock transactions generally call for all of the assets and liabilities of the seller's corporation and the stock of the corporation to be transferred to the buyer. In some cases, the buyer and seller may choose to exclude certain assets or liabilities from being conveyed. The seller must pay taxes on the difference between the seller's basis in the stock and the price paid by the buyer for the stock.

Sometimes stock deals are more expedient for both parties. Stock transactions provide for continuity in relationships with suppliers. They also preclude the necessity of obtaining a lease assignment when the lease is held only in the name of the corporation and when there is no provision in the lease calling for an assignment in the event of a change in the controlling interest of the corporation. The risk of inheriting undisclosed debts of the seller in a stock transaction can be minimized by providing for the right of offset to future payments due the seller.

In choosing to structure a deal as a stock transaction, the seller should be aware that the U.S. Supreme Court has ruled that the sale of the stock of a closely held corporation falls under the umbrella of federal securities laws. This places a greater burden on the seller in a stock transaction to fully disclose all material information about the business. Failure to do so opens the seller up to the risk of securities fraud litigation.

Installment Sales

It is rare for a privately-held business to change hands for an all-cash price. Almost all transactions are structured as installment contracts which provide for the seller to receive some cash, but for the bulk of the purchase price to be owner financed. For smaller privately-held businesses, the down payment often ranges from 10% to 40% of the selling price and the buyer executes a promissory note (secured by the assets of the business only) for the balance. Such notes are typically for a period of 3–15 years at an interest rate that varies with the prime rate but is most often 9–12%. The payments required to retire the debt service should not exceed 25–50% of the discretionary cash flow as calculated in the section on "*Pricing the Business.*"

Leveraged Buyouts

Just as in an installment sale, a leveraged buyout uses the assets of the business to collateralize a loan to buy the business. The difference is that the buyer in a leveraged buyout typically invests little or no money, and the loan is obtained from a lending institution.

This type of purchase is best suited to asset rich businesses. A business that lacks the assets needed for a completely leveraged buyout may be able to put together a partially leveraged buyout. In this structure, the seller finances part of the transaction and is secured by a second lien security interest in the assets. Because leveraged buyouts place a greater debt burden on the company than do other types of financing, buyer and seller must take a close look at the business's ability to service the debt.

Earn-Outs

An earn-out is a method of paying for a business that helps bridge the gap between the positions of the buyer and seller with respect to price. An earn-out can be calculated as a percentage of sales, gross profit, net profit or other figure. It is not uncommon to establish a floor or ceiling for the earn-out.

Earn-outs do not preclude the payment of a portion of the purchase price in cash or installment notes. Rather, they are normally paid in addition to other forms of payment. Because the payment of money to the seller under the provisions of the earn-out is predicated on the performance of the business, it is important that the seller continue to operate the business through the period of the earn-out.

Stock Exchanges

In some instances a business owner may want to accept the stock of a purchasing corporation in payment for the business. Typically, the stock he receives (if it is the stock of a publicly-held company) may not be resold for two years. If the stock may not be freely traded, it is not as valuable as freely traded stock, and its value should be discounted to allow for this lack of marketability.

There is an advantage to the seller in this kind of transaction. Taxes incurred by the seller on the gain from the sale of the business are deferred until the acquired stock is eventually sold. This kind of transaction is termed a tax-free exchange by the IRS. There are several tests that must be met to qualify for this tax treatment.Check with a competent accountant or tax attorney or request a ruling from the IRS Reorganization Branch in Washington, D.C.

9. Negotiation

The art of negotiation plays an important role in buying or selling a business. Differences of opinion are inherent in the negotiation process and only realistic negotiators can find creative solutions to such differences. Businesses change hands most easily when the parties assume a non-adversarial posture. It is imperative that the parties know the issues that are important to one another. Each should understand the other's position on these issues.

Price is just one aspect of the transaction to be negotiated. Terms are just as important, particularly the period of time over which the debt is to be repaid and the allocation for tax purposes of the purchase price.

Sellers naturally have the upper hand in negotiations since they best know the business. A seller should make full use of that advantage. A buyer should minimize the seller's advantage by learning as much as possible about the business. The section in this booklet entitled *"Evaluating the Business"* identifies the key areas to be studied.

It is important to do more than study the business to prepare for negotiations. The parties must both understand each other's motivation for wanting to buy or sell the business, and each other's plans after transition takes place. They must also understand why the other party has taken a certain position on an issue.

Developing a working strategy means each party must not only know the other's position, they must develop their own position as well. They should prepare in writing a list of reasons that validate their position. They should also think through possible weaknesses in their reasoning. In this way, each can anticipate and respond to the objections the other party may raise.

Buyers should request that the seller not negotiate with other buyers while the specifics of the offer are being negotiated. Sellers, on the other hand, are advantaged when they can negotiate with more than one buyer at a time. The most important thing in negotiations is to be able to see things from the other party's perspective.

This eliminates much of the difficulty of reaching agreement and keeps the parties from wasting time.

10. Making And Evaluating Offers

Making the Offer

Before making an offer, a buyer will typically investigate a number of businesses. At some point in the investigation process, it may be necessary to sign a confidentiality agreement and show the seller a personal financial statement. A confidentiality agreement pledges that the buyer will not divulge any information about the business to anyone other than immediate advisors.

A buyer should determine a range of value for the business. An appraisal of the business as is can be used to establish a pricing floor. A pricing ceiling can be established by using an appraisal that capitalizes projected future cash flows under new management.

A buyer should have access to all records needed to prepare an offer. If some information is lacking, the buyer must make a decision to either discontinue the transaction or make an offer contingent on receiving and approving the withheld information. The nature and amount of withheld information determines which course of action to take.

An offer may take the form of a purchase and sale agreement or a letter of intent. Purchase and sale agreements are usually binding on the parties while a letter of intent is often non-binding. The latter is more often used with larger businesses.

Regardless of which form of the agreement is used, it should contain the following:

1. Total price to be offered.
2. Components of the price (amount of security deposit and down payment, amount of bank debt, amount of seller financed debt).
3. A list of all liabilities and assets that are being purchased. The minimum amount of accounts receivable to be collected and the maximum amount of accounts payable to be assumed may be specified.
4. The operating condition of equipment at settlement.
5. The right to offset the purchase price in the amount of any undisclosed liabilities that come due after settlement and in the amount of any variance in inventory from that stated in the agreement.
6. A provision that the business will be able to pass all necessary inspections.

7. A provision calling for compliance with the Bulk Transfer provisions of the Uniform Commercial Code. (This does not apply to sales of the stock of the corporation.)

8. Warranties of clear and marketable title, validity and assumability of existing contracts if any, tax liability limitations, legal liability limitations and other appropriate warranties.

9. A provision (where appropriate) to make the sale conditional on lease assignment, verification of financial statements, transfer of licenses, obtaining financing or other provisions.

10. A provision for any appropriate prorations such as rent, utilities, wages and prepaid expenses.

11. A non-competition convenant. This document is sometimes part of the purchase and sale agreement and is sometimes a separate exhibit to the purchase and sale agreement.

12. Allocation of the purchase price.

13. Restrictions on how the business is to be operated until settlement.

14. A date for settlement.

The purchase and sale agreement is a complex document and it is a good idea to get professional help in its drafting.

Evaluating the Offer

The seller should look for all the same provisions in an offer that were enumerated in the section on making the offer. The types of offers a seller is likely to receive depend in some measure on the size of the business. A seller should ask for a resume and financial statement from an individual buyer and an annual report if the buyer is another company. Find out what attributes the buyer brings. Sometimes, a buyer with a commitment to the work ethic is all that is needed. In other cases, successful related work experience may be important. If the acquiror is another company, look for the logic behind the acquisition. Perhaps some kind of synergy or an economy of scale is created. A buyer should prepare and show the seller a post-acquisition business plan.

One final note—carefully study offers to determine what assets and liabilities are being purchased. An offer for the assets of a business may be worth considerably less than an offer for its stock even though the price offered for the assets is higher.

11. Closing The Transaction

Meeting Conditions of Sale

After buyer and seller have entered into a binding contract, there may be several conditions to be met before the sale may be closed. Such conditions often address issues like assignment of the lease, verification of financial statements, transfer of licenses, or obtaining financing. There is usually a date set for meeting the conditions of sale. If a condition is not met within the specified time frame, the agreement is invalidated.

Types of Settlements

Business settlements or closings, as they are also called, are usually done in one of two ways.

1. An attorney performs settlement. In this procedure, the attorney for the buyer, or an independent attorney acting on behalf of both buyer and seller, draws up the necessary documents for settlement. Buyer and seller meet with the settlement attorney at a predetermined time (after all conditions of sale have been met). Documents are signed at the meeting by buyer and seller.

A good settlement attorney is also a good problem solver. He can help find creative ways to resolve differences of opinion. The settlement attorney holds money in escrow and disburses it when all the appropriate documents are signed.

2. Escrow. In an escrow settlement, the money to be deposited, bill of sale and other documents are placed in the hands of a neutral third party or escrow agent. The escrow agent is usually an escrow company or the escrow department of a financial institution. Buyer and seller sign escrow instructions that name the conditions to be met before completion of the sale. Once all conditions are met, the escrow agent disburses previously executed documents and disburses funds. There usually is no formal final meeting at which the signing of the documents takes place. Buyer and seller usually sign them independently of one another.

Regardless of whether escrow or a settlement attorney is used, requirements of the bulk sales act must be met if the assets (not the stock of the corporation) of the business are being sold. This law calls for the business's suppliers to be notified of the impending sale. The supplier must respond within the allowed time frame if money is owed by the seller. A lien search is also performed by the attorney or escrow agent. This determines if any liens against the business's assets have been filed in the records of the local courthouse.

Documents

A number of documents are required to close a transaction. The purchase and sale agreement is the basic document from which all the documents used to close the transaction are created. The documents most often used in closing a transaction are described below. Other documents not described below may also be needed depending on the particulars of the transaction.

Settlement Sheet: Shows, as of the date of settlement, the various costs and adjustments to be paid by or credited to each party. It is signed by buyer and seller.

Escrow Agreement: Is used only for escrow settlements. It is a set of instructions signed by buyer and seller in advance of settlement that sets forth the conditions of escrow, the responsibilities of the escrow agent, and the requirements to be met for the release of escrowed funds and documents.

Bill of Sale: Describes the physical assets being transferred and identifies the amount of consideration paid for those assets. It must always be signed by the seller and is often also signed by the buyer.

Promissory Note: Used only in an installment sale, it shows the principal amount and terms of repayment of the debt by the buyer to the seller. It specifies remedies for the seller in the event of default by the buyer. It is signed by the buyer and the buyer often must personally guarantee the debt.

Security Agreement: Creates the security interest in the assets pledged by the buyer to secure the promissory note and underlying debt. It also sets forth the terms under which the buyer agrees to operate those assets which constitute collateral. It is used only in an installment sale. It is signed by both parties.

Financing Statement: Creates a public record of the security interest in the collateral and therefore notifies third parties that certain assets are encumbered by a lien to secure the existing debt. The cost to record the financing statement varies by jurisdiction. It is used only in installment sales. It is signed by buyer and seller.

Covenant not to compete: Protects the buyer and his investment from immediate competition by the seller in his market area for a limited amount of time. The scope of this document must be reasonable in order for it to be legally enforceable. The covenant not to compete is sometimes included as a part of the purchase and sale agreement and is sometimes written as a separate document. It is signed by both parties. It is not required in every transaction.

Employment Agreement: Specifies the nature of services to be performed by the seller, the amount of compensation, the amount of time per week or per month the services are to be performed, the duration of the agreement and often a method for discontinuing the agreement before its completion. Employment agreements are not required in all transactions, but they are used with great frequency. It is not uncommon that the seller remain involved with the business for periods of as little as a week or as much as several years. The length of time depends on the complexity of the business and the experience of the buyer. For periods of more than 2–4 weeks, the seller is often compensated for his services. It is signed by both the buyer and the seller.

Contingent Liabilities

Contingent liabilities must be taken into account and provided for when a business is sold. They most often occur because of pending tax payments, unresolved lawsuits or anticipated but uncertain costs of meeting regulatory requirements. Contingent liabilities can be handled by escrowing a portion of the funds earmarked for disbursement to the seller. The sum escrowed then can be used to pay off the liability as it comes due. Any remaining money can then be disbursed to the seller.

Summary

There are many reasons today for owner-managers of small businesses to look at the legal structure of their firms. The changing tax laws and fluctuating availability of capital are just two situations which require alert managers to review what legal structures best meets their needs.

All forms of business organization have advantages and disadvantages. This Aid **seeks to briefly identify them for the owner-manager who wants to know "what question to ask" when seeking the proper professional advice.**

If you were to make an analogy between starting a business and playing a card game, you might say, "The game is just for fun, but business is business." Well, you would be right. But let's consider some important similarities.

The game requires skill, strategy, planning, and, most important, a thorough knowledge of the rules. Going into business requires skill (the knowledge of your craft or trade), and it also requires strategy and planning. Most important, to be sucessful in business, you must understand the rules (or the laws) by which you must conduct your business. All planning and strategy must consider the multitude of local, state, and federal laws and business practices that govern the operation of the business.

Before you enter the complex arena of business and the myriad of laws which influence your freedom of choice and mobility of action, you must first choose the legal structure for your business that will best suit your needs and the needs of your particular business. In order to intelligently select the legal structure for your business, you must ask yourself, "What are my alternatives?" So, let's now look at the nature of various legal business structures.

There are three principal kinds of business structures: the proprietorship, the partnership, and the corporation. Each has certain general advantages and disadvantages, but they must all be weighted to reflect your specific circumstances, goals, and needs. The sole proprietorship is the first firm we'll consider.

The Sole Proprietorship

The sole proprietorship is usually defined as a business which is owned and operated by one person. To establish a sole proprietorship, you need only obtain whatever licenses you need and begin operations.

Hence, it is the most widespread form of small business organization.

Advantages of the Sole Proprietorship

Ease of formation. There is less formality and fewer legal restrictions associated with establishing a sole proprietorship. It needs little or no governmental approval and is usually less expensive than a partnership or corporation.

Sole ownership of profits. The proprietor is not required to share profits with anyone.

Control and decision making vested in one owner. There are no co-owners or partners to consult. (Except possibly your spouse.)

Flexibility. Management is able to respond quickly to business needs in the form of day to day management decisions as governed by various laws and good sense.

Relative freedom from government control and special taxation.

Disadvantages of the Sole Proprietor

Unlimited liability. The individual proprietor is responsible for the full amount of business debts which may exceed the proprietor's total investment. This liability extends to all the proprietor's assets, such as house and car. Additional problems of liability, such as physical loss or personal injury, may be lessened by obtaining proper insurance coverage.

Unstable business life. The enterprise may be crippled or terminated upon illness or death of the owner.

Less available capital, ordinarily, than in other types of business organizations.

Relative difficulty in obtaining long-term financing.

Relatively limited viewpoint and experience. This is more often the case with one owner than with several.

NOTE: A small business owner might very well select the sole proprietorship to begin with. Later, if the owner succeeds and feels the need, he or she can form a partnership or corporation.

The Partnership

The Uniform Partnership Act, adopted by many states, defines a partnership as "an association of two or more persons to carry on as co-owners of a business for profit." Though not specifically required by the Act, written Articles of Partnership are customarily executed. These articles outline the contribution by the partners into the business (whether financial, material or managerial) and generally delineate the roles of the partners in the business relationship. The following are example articles typically contained in a partnership agreement:

Name, Purpose, Domicile

Duration of Agreement

Character of Partners (general or limited, active or silent)

Contributions by Partners (at inception, at later date)

Business Expenses (how handled)

Authority (individual partner authority in conduct of business)

Separate Debts

Books, Records, and Method of Accounting

Division of Profits and Losses

Draws or Salaries

Rights of Continuing Partner

Death of a Partner (dissolution and winding up)

Employee Management

Release of Debts

Sale of Partnership Interest

Arbitration

Additions, Alterations, or Modifications of Partnership Agreement

Settlements of Disputes

Required and Prohibited Acts

Absence and Disability

Some of the characteristics that distinguish a partnership from other forms of business organization are the limited life of a partnership, unlimited liability of at least one partner, co-ownership of the assets, mutual agency, share of management, and share in partnership profits.

Kinds of Partners

Ostensible Partner. Active and known as a partner.

Active Partner. May or may not be ostensible as well.

Secret Partner. Active but not known or held out as a partner.

Dormant Partner. Inactive and not known or held out as a partner.

Silent Partner. Inactive (but may be known to be a partner).

Nominal Partner (Partner by Estoppel). Not a true partner in any sense, not being a party to the partnership agreement. However, a nominal partner holds him or herself out as a partner, or permits others to make such representation by the use of his/her name or otherwise. Therefore, a nominal partner is liable as if he or she were a partner to third persons who have given credit to the actual or supposed truth of such representation.

Subpartner. One who, not being a member of the partnership, contracts with one of the partners in reference to participation in the interest of such partner in the firm's business and profits.

Limited or Special Partner. Assuming compliance with the statutory formalities, the limited partner risks only his or her agreed investment in the business. As long as he or she does not participate in the management and control of the enterprise or in the conduct of its business, the limited partner is generally not subject to the same liabilities as a general partner.

Advantages of the Partnership

Ease of formation. Legal informalities and expenses are few compared with the requirements for creation of a corporation.

Direct rewards. Partners are motivated to apply their best abilities by direct sharing of the profits.

Growth and performance facilitated. In a partnership, it is often possible to obtain more capital and a better range of skills than in a sole proprietorship.

Flexibility. A partnership may be relatively more flexible in the decision making process than in a corporation. But, it may be less so than in a sole proprietorship.

Relative freedom from government control and special taxation.

Disadvantages of a Partnership

Unlimited liability of at least one partner. Insurance considerations such as those mentioned in the proprietorship section apply here also.

Unstable life. Elimination of any partner constitutes automatic dissolution of partnership. However, operation of the business can continue based on the right of survivorship and possible creation of a new partnership. Partnership insurance might be considered.

Relative difficulty in obtaining large sums of capital. This is particularly true of long term financing when compared to a corporation. However, by using individual partners' assets, opportunities are probably greater than in a proprietorship.

Firm bound by the acts of just one partner as agent.

Difficulty of disposing of partnership interest. The buying out of a partner may be difficult unless specifically arranged for in the written agreement.

The Corporation

The corporation is by far the most complex of the three business structures. For the purpose of this *Aid*, we shall discuss only the general characteristics of the corporation, not its intricacies.

As defined by Chief Justice Marshall's famous decision in 1819, a corporation "is an artificial being, invisible, intangible, and existing only in contemplation of the law." In other words, a corporation is a distinct legal entity, distinct from the individuals who own it.

Formation of the Corporation

A corporation usually is formed by the authority of a state government. Corporations which do business in more than one state must comply with the Federal laws regarding interstate commerce and with the state laws, which may vary considerably.

The procedure ordinarily required to form a corporation is that, first, subscriptions for capital stock must be taken and a tentative organization created. Then, approval must be obtained from the Secretary of State in the state in which the corporation is to be formed. This approval is in the form of a charter for the corporation, stating the powers and limitations of the particular enterprise.

Advantages of the Corporation

Limitations of the stockholder's liability to a fixed amount of investment. However, do not confuse corporate liability with appropriate liability insurance considerations.

Ownership is readily transferable.

Separate legal existence.

Stability and relative permanence of existence. For example, in the case of illness, death, or other cause for loss of a principal (officer or owner), the corporation continues to exist and do business.

Relative ease of securing capital in large amounts and from many investors. Capital may be acquired through the issuance of various stocks and long term bonds. There is relative ease in securing long term financing from lending institutions by taking advantage of corporate assets and often personal assets of stockholders and principals of guarantors. (Personal guarantees are very often required by lenders.)

Delegated authority. Centralized control is secured when owners delegate authority to hired managers, although they are often one and the same.

The ability of the corporation to draw on the expertise and skills of more than one individual.

Disadvantages of the Corporation

Activities limited by the charter and by various laws. However, some states do allow very broad charters.

Manipulation. Minority stockholders are sometimes exploited.

Extensive government regulations and required local, state, and federal reports.

Less incentive if manager does not share in profits.

Expense of forming a corporation.

Double tax - income tax on corporate net income (profit) and on individual salary and dividends.*

*You should be aware, also, of the possibility of selecting subchapter S status (IRC 1371-1379). The purpose of subchapter S is to permit a "small business corporation" to have its income taxed to the shareholders as if the corporation were a partnership. One objective is to overcome the double tax feature of our system of taxing corporate income and stockholder dividends. Another purpose is to permit the shareholders to have the benefit of offsetting business losses incurred by the corporation against the income of the shareholders.

Among the conditions for the making and maintenance of subchapter S election are that the corporation have ten or fewer shareholders, all of whom are individuals or estates, that there be no nonresident alien shareholders, that there be only one class of outstanding stock, that all shareholders consent to the election, and that a specific portion of the corporation's receipts be derived from active business rather than enumerated passive investments. No limit is placed on the size of the corporation's income and assets.

In summary, review the following eight questions:

1. What is the size of the risk? That is, what is the amount of the investors' liability for debts and taxes?

2. What would the continuity (life) of the firm be if something happened to the principal or principals?

3. What legal structure would insure the greatest adaptability of administration for the firm?

4. What is the influence of applicable laws?

5. What are the possibilities of attracting additional capital?

6. What are the needs for and possibilities of attracting additional expertise?

7. What are the costs and procedures in starting?

8. What is the ultimate goal and purpose of the enterprise, and which legal structure can best serve its purposes?

The small business owner is required to wear many hats, but none can be expected to be a lawyer, certified public accountant, marketing specialist, production engineer, environmental specialist, etc. Therefore, you should get the facts before making decisions. When necessary and if possible, you should also get professional counsel to help you avoid misunderstanding technical or legal issues and avoid making bad decisions and false starts that require backtracking and added expense. This is especially true when you are deciding what legal form to adopt. This *Aid* has presented an introduction to the options and guidelines for selecting the best legal structure for your business.

Part II
Developing an Effective Business Plan

Introduction

Homework has taken on new meaning for more than 10 million Americans. The drive for economic self-sufficiency has motivated large numbers of persons to market their skills and talents for profit from home. More than 400,000 persons launched home enterprises in 1985. Our increasingly service oriented economy offers a widening spectrum of opportunities for customized and personalized small business growth.

Though untrained entrepreneurs have traditionally had a high rate of failure, small businesses can be profitable. Success in small home based business is not an accident. It requires both skills in a service or product area and acquisition of management and attitudinal competencies.

The purpose of this SBA Management Aid is to help you take stock of your interests, aptitudes and skills. Many people have good business ideas but not everyone has what it takes to succeed. If you are convinced that a profitable home business is attainable, this Management Aid will provide step by step guidance in development of the basic written business plan.

Information Gathering

A helpful tool for use in determining if you are ready to take the risks of a home based business operation is the SBA Publication #MA 2.016, *Checklist for Going Into Business*. It will help you focus on the basic steps in information gathering and business planning.

While the reasons for the rapid growth of home based business operations may vary from the need to supplement family income with a few hundred dollars all the way to a sophisticated technical consulting service billing hundreds of thousands of dollars, there are many common characteristics and challenges to be considered in launching most home based businesses, regardless of size. Some tasks are universal to all small business startups, while others are unique to a home base.

Careful planning, based on the experience of the author, and on interviews with dozens of home based operators over the past decade indicate that special planning is required to research legal and tax issues, proper space utilization and to establish time management discipline. Inadequate or careless attention to development of a detailed business plan can be costly for you and your family in terms of lost time, wasted talent and disappearing dollars.

The Entrepreneurial Personality

A variety of experts have documented research that indicates that successful small business entrepreneurs, whether male or female, have some common characteristics. How do you measure up? On this checklist, write a "Y" if you believe the statement describes you; an "N" if it doesn't; and a "U" if you can't decide:

____ I have a strong desire to be my own boss.

____ Win, lose or draw, I want to be master of my own financial destiny.

____ I have significant specialized business ability based on both my education and my experience.

____ I have an ability to conceptualize the whole of a business; not just its individual parts, but how they relate to each other.

____ I develop an inherent sense of what is "right" for a business and have the courage to pursue it.

____ One or both of my parents were entrepreneurs; calculated risk-taking runs in the family.

____ My life is characterized by a willingness and capacity to persevere.

____ I possess a high level of energy, sustainable over long hours to make the business successful.

While not every successful home based business owner starts with a "Y" answer to all of these questions, three or four "N"'s and "U"'s should be sufficient reason for you to stop and give second thought to going it alone. Many proprietors who sense entrepreneurial deficiencies seek extra training and support their limitations with help from a skilled team of business advisors such as accountants, bankers and attorneys.

Selecting A Business

Perhaps you have already decided what your home based business will be. You know how you will serve your market and with what. If not, but you are determined to establish a home based source of income, then you need to decide exactly what business you will enter. A logical first step for the undecided is to list potential areas of personal background, special training, educational and job experience, and special interests that could be developed into a business. Review the following list of activities which have proven marketable for others. On a scale of "0" (no interest or strength) to 10 (maximum interest or strength) indicate the potential for you and a total score for each activity:

	My Level of Interest	Personal Strength	Market Strength	Total Points
Personal services				
—house cleaning				
—babysitting				
—tutoring				
—secretarial				
—catering				
—direct mail				
Handicrafts				
—needle work				
—ceramics				
—jewelry design				
—upholstering				
Artistic work				
—painting				
—photography				
—prints				
—wire sculpture				
—engraving				
Repair services				
—small appliances				
—furniture				
—clothing				
—TV and radio				
—automotive				
Instruction skills				
—languages				
—math				
—gourmet cooking				
—music				
—home repairs				
Mail order ideas				
—product sales				
—repairs				
—business service				
Seasonal products				
—foodstuffs				
—clothing				
—gift items.				
Party sales				
—cookware				
—plants				
—plastic goods				
—cosmetics				
Your own ideas				

For other ideas, check your local public library for one or more of the publications listed in the Resource Section of this Management Aid.

SCORING

0 to 10	Almost a sure loser
11 to 15	Reconsider, but proceed with caution
16 to 20	Some potential here, worth further study
21 to 25	Probably a winner, if you answered correctly
26 to 30	How can you lose?

This checklist should give you a good idea of the kind of a business that would suit you best and why.

Time Management

For both the novice and the experienced business person planning a small home based enterprise, an early concern requiring self-evaluation is Time Management.

It is very difficult for some people to make and keep work schedules even in the disciplined setting of an employer's office. At home, as your own boss, the problem can be much greater. To determine how much time you can devote to your business, begin by drafting a weekly task timetable listing all current and potential responsibilities and the blocks of time required for each. When and how can business responsibilities be added without undue physical or mental stress on you and your family? Potential conflicts must be faced and resolved at the outset and as they occur. Otherwise, your business can become a nightmare. During the first year of operation, continue to chart, post and checkoff tasks on a daily, weekly, monthly basis.

Distractions and excuses for procrastination abound. It is important to keep both a planning and an operating log. These tools will help avoid oversights and provide vital information when memory fails. To improve the quality of home work time, consider installation of a separate telephone line for the business and attach an answering machine to take messages when you do not wish to be distracted or are away from home. A business line has the added advantage of allowing you to have a business listing in the phone book and, if you wish to buy it, an ad in the classified directory.

Is A Home Based Business Site Workable?

- Where in the home will the business be located?
- What adjustments to living arrangements will be required?
- What will be the cost of changes?
- How will your family react?
- What will the neighbors think?

It will be important to set aside a specific work area. For example, more than one fledgling business ledger has gone up in smoke, been chewed by the family dog, or thrown out with the trash when business records were not kept separate from family papers. Ready access to business records during work hours is essential, but they must be protected.

Check the reasons below for and against working at home that apply to you. List any additional drawbacks or obstacles to operating this business at home.

Pros	Cons
Lower startup costs	Isolation
Lower fixed costs	Space limitations
Tax benefits	Zoning
Lifestyle flexibility	Security concerns
No commuting	Household interference

Note that changes in personal habits will be required. Examples:

- Self discipline to keep TV off while working.
- Limiting personal telephone calls in length and number.
- Diligence in meeting work deadlines when no one is checking

Ask family members to comment on pros and cons. Their concerns may require reconsideration of some specifics.

Is A Home Based Business Site Allowable?

Now you will want to investigate potential legal and community problems associated with operating the business from home. You should gather, read and digest specialized information concerning federal, state, county and municipal laws and regulations concerning home based business operations.

Check first! Get the facts in writing. Keep a topical file for future reference. Some facts and forms will be needed for your business plan. There may be limitations enforced that can make your planned business impossible or require expensive modifications to your property.

Items to be investigated, recorded and studied are:

TO DO   DONE

TO DO	DONE	
_____	_____	county or city zoning code restrictions
_____	_____	necessary permits and licenses for operation
_____	_____	state and local laws and codes regarding zoning
_____	_____	deed or lease restrictions such as covenants and restrictive conditions of purchase
_____	_____	parking and customer access; deliveries
_____	_____	sanitation, traffic and noise codes
_____	_____	signs and advertising
_____	_____	state and federal code requirements for space, ventilation, heat and light
_____	_____	limitations on the number and types of workers If not, check with the local Chamber of Commerce office
_____	_____	reservations that neighbors may have about a business next to or near them

Here are some ways to collect your information. Call or visit the zoning office at county headquarters or city hall. In some localities the city or county Office of Economic Development has print materials available to pinpoint key "code", items affecting home based business.

Even in rural areas, the era of unlimited free enterprise is over. Although the decision makers may be in the state capital or in a distant regional office of a federal agency, check before investing in inventory, equipment or marketing programs. If in doubt call the state office of Industrial Development or the nearest SBA district office. In some states the county agent or home demonstration agent will have helpful information concerning rural or farm business development.

To cover the income tax rules regarding a home based business, be sure to secure the IRS Publication #587, *BUSINESS USE OF YOUR HOME*.

Is The Home Based Business Site Insurable?

In addition to community investigations, contact your insurance company or agent. It is almost certain that significant changes will be required in your coverage and limits when you start a home based business. When you have written a good description of your business, call your agent for help in insuring you properly against new hazards resulting from your business operations such as:

- fire, theft and casualty damage to inventories and equipment
- business interruption coverage
- fidelity bonds for employees
- liability for customers, vendors and others visiting the business
- workmen's compensation
- group health and life insurance
- product liability coverage if you make and/or sell a product; workmanship liability for services
- business use of vehicle coverage

Overall Home Site Evaluation

After you have gathered as much information as seems practical you may wish to evaluate a home based site vs. one or more other nearby locations. Here's a handy checklist. Using the "0" to "10" scale, grade these vital factors:

Factors To Consider

	Grades For Each Factor	
	Home	Other
1. Customer convenience	_____	_____
2. Availability of merchandise or raw materials	_____	_____
3. Nearby competition	_____	_____
4. Transportation availability and rates	_____	_____
5. Quality and quantity of employees available	_____	_____
6. Availability of parking facilities	_____	_____
7. Adequacy of utilities (sewer, water, power, gas)	_____	_____
8. Traffic flow	_____	_____
9. Tax burden	_____	_____
10. Quality of police and fire services	_____	_____
11. Environmental factors	_____	_____
12. Physical suitability of building	_____	_____
13. Provision for future expansion	_____	_____
14. Vendor delivery access	_____	_____
15. Personal convenience	_____	_____
16. Cost of operation	_____	_____
17. Other factors including how big can you get without moving	_____	_____
Totals	_____	_____

The greater the difference between the totals of the two columns, the clearer your decision should be. In the space below, write out what your decision and the reasons that support it.

Decision:_____

_____

_____

_____

_____

Writing The Business Plan

Now that your research and plan development is nearing completion, it is time to move into action. If you are still in favor of going ahead, it is time to take several specific steps. The key one is to organize your dream scheme into a business plan.

What is it?

- Is written by the home based business owner with outside help as needed
- Is accurate and concise as a result of careful study
- Explains how the business will function in the marketplace
- Clearly depicts its operational characteristics
- Details how it will be financed
- Outlines how it will be managed
- Is the management and financial "blueprint" for startup and profitable operation
- Serves as a prospectus for potential investors and lenders

Why create it?

- The process of putting the business plan together, including the thought that you put in before writing it, forces you to take an objective , critical, unemotional look at your entire business proposal
- The finished written plan is an operational tool which, when properly used, will help you manage your business and work toward its success
- The completed business plan is a means for communicating your ideas to others and provides the basis for your financing your business

Who should write it?

- The home based owner to the extent possible

- Seek assistance in weak areas, such as:
  - accounting
  - insurance
  - capital requirements
  - operational forecasting
  - tax and legal requirements

When should a Business Plan be used?

- To make crucial startup decisions
- To reassure lenders or backers
- To measure operational progress
- To test planning assumptions
- As a basis for adjusting forecasts
- To anticipate ongoing capital and cash requirements
- As the benchmark for good operational management

Proposed Outline For Home Based Business Plan

This outline is suggested for a small proprietorship or family business. Shape it to fit your unique needs. For more complex manufacturing or franchise operations see the Resource Section for other options.

Part I. — Business Organization

Cover Page:

    A. Business Name:

    _____

    Street Address:

    _____

    Mailing Address

    _____

    Telephone number:

    _____

    Owner(s) Name(s):

    _____

Inside Pages:

    B. Business Form:

    _____

    (proprietorship, partnership, corporation)
    If incorporated

    _____

    (state of incorporation)

Include copies of key subsidiary documents in an appendix. Remember even partnerships require written agreements of terms and conditions to avoid later conflicts, and to establish legal entities and equities. Corporations require charters, articles of incorporation and by-laws.

48 ◆ *The Business Plan for Homebased Business*

Part II. — Business Purpose and Function

In this section write an accurate yet, concise description of the business. Describe the business you plan to start in narrative form.

What is the principal activity? Be specific. Give product and/or service description(s):
- retail sales?
- manufacturing?
- service?
- other?

How will it be started?
- a new startup
- the expansion of an existing business
- purchase of a going business
- a franchise operation
- actual or projected start up date

Why will it succeed? Promote your idea!
- how and why this business will be successful.
- what is unique about your business
- what is its market "niche"

What is your experience in this business? If you have a current resume of your career, include it in an appendix and reference it here. Otherwise write a narrative here and include a resume in the finished product. If you lack specific experience, detail how you plan to gain it, such as training, apprenticeship or working with partners who have experience.

_____
_____
_____
_____
_____
_____
_____
_____
_____
_____
_____
_____

The Marketing Plan

The marketing plan is the core of your business rationale. To develop a consistent sales growth a home based business person must become knowledgeable about the market. To demonstrate your understanding, this section of the home based business plan should seek to concisely answer several basic questions:

Who is your market?

- Describe the profile of your typical customer
  Age_____
  Male, female, both_____
  How many in family_____
  Annual Family Income_____
  Location_____
  Buying patterns_____
  Reason to buy from you_____
  Other_____

- Geographically describe your trading area: (i.e. county, state, national, etc.)
  _____
  _____

- Economically describe your trading area: (single family, average earnings, number of children, etc.)
  _____
  _____

How large is the market?

- Total units or dollars _____
- Growing____ Steady____ Decreasing____
- If growing, annual growth rate_____

Who is your competition? No small business operates in a vacuum. Get to know and respect the competition. Target your marketing plans. Identify direct competitors (both in terms of geography and product lines), and those who are similar or marginally comparative. Begin by listing names, addresses and products or services. Detail briefly but concisely the following information concerning each of your competitors:

- Who are the nearest ones?
- How are their businesses similar or competitive to yours?
- Do you have a unique "niche"? Describe it.
- How will your service or product be better or more saleable than your competitors?
- Are their businesses growing? Stable? Declining? Why?
- What can be learned from observing their operations and/or talking to their present or former clients?
- Will you have competitive advantages or disadvantages by operating from home? Be honest!

Remember, your business can become more profitable by adopting the good competitive practices and by avoiding their errors.

To help you evaluate how successful your product or service will be, go down the following list of standard characteristics (you may want to add more from your knowledge of your field) and make a candid evaluation of your competitive "edge." On a scale of "0" (theirs puts mine to shame) to 10 (mine puts their to shame) indicate the potential for you and a total score:

FEATURE

Price	_____
Performance	_____
Durability	_____
Versatility	_____
Speed/accuracy	_____
Ease of operation or use	_____
Ease of maintenance or repair	_____
Ease or cost of installation	_____
Size or weight or color	_____
Appearance or styling or packaging	_____
Total Points	_____

A Total Points score of less than 60 indicates that you might reconsider the viability of your product or service and/or think about how you can improve it. Over 80 points indicates a clear competitive edge.

What percent of the market will you penetrate?

1. estimate the market in total units or dollars

_____

2. estimate your planned volume

_____

3. amount your volume will add to total market

_____

4. subtract 3 from 2

_____

Line 4 represents the amount of your planned volume that must be taken away from the competition.

What pricing and sales terms are you planning? The primary consideration in pricing a product or service is the value that it represents to the customer. If, on the previous checklist of features, your product is truly ahead of the field, you can command a premium price. On the other hand, if it is a "me too" product, you may have to "buy" a share of the market to get your foothold and then try to move price up later. This is always risky and difficult. One rule will always hold: ultimately, the market will set the price. If your selling price does not exceed your costs and expenses by the margin necessary to keep your business healthy, you will fail. Know your competitors pricing policies. Send a friend to comparison shop. Is there discounting? Special sales? Price leaders? Make some "blind" phone calls. Detail your pricing policy:

_____

_____

_____

What is your sales plan? Describe how you will sell, dis-

tribute and or service what you sell? Be specific. Below are outlined some common practices:

Direct sales by telephone or in person. The tremendous growth of individual sales representatives who sell by party bookings, door to door, and through distribution of call back promotional campaigns suggests that careful research is required to be profitable.

Mail Order

Specialized markets for leisure time or unique products have grown as more two income families find less time to shop. Be aware of recent mail order legislation and regulation.

Franchising

a. You may decide to either buy into someone else's franchise as a franchisee or

b. Create your own franchise operation that sells rights to specific territories or product lines to others. Each will require further legal, financial, and marketing research.

An excellent starting point if you are considering franchise involvement is the SBA Publication #MA 7.007, **Evaluating Franchising Opportunities.** The International Franchise Association also publishes a number of valuable aids in this field.

Distributors
You may decide to work as a local or regional distributor for several different product lines.

Outline your sales plan below:

_____

_____

_____

What is your advertising plan? Each product or service will need its own advertising strategy as part of the total business marketing plan. Before developing an advertising campaign for your business plan, take time to review a few basic assumptions. By definition, advertising is any form of paid, non-personal promotion that communicates with a large number of potential customers at the same time. The purpose of advertising is to inform, persuade and remind customers about your company's products or services. Every advertising activity should have specific goals. Common examples are:

- To bring in sales orders or contracts
- To promote special events such as sales, business openings, new products
- To bring in requests for estimates or for a sales representative to call
- A special goal at the outset may be to use special me-

dia to establish yourself even before startup and to get potential customer "feedback."

These might include one or more of the following:

- Purchase and distribution of business cards to potential clients
- Posting notices on free bulletin boards in area supermarkets or office complexes
- A telephone survey of potential clients to alert them to your startup plans.

To assist in determining what types of advertising are appropriate and within company budget projections, it will be necessary to carefully review your customer profile. From this review, establish a clear statement of advertising goals. Write down what you want your advertising to accomplish:

_____
_____
_____
_____

The next step will be to develop answers to the following crucial questions:

Q. What should be said about the business and how should it be stated?

A. _____

Q. What media should be used?

A. _____
_____

Q. How much can be afforded?

A. _____
_____

Q. How can the advertising program be implemented?

A. _____
_____

Q. How can its effectiveness be measured?

A. _____
_____

The basic criteria for selecting specific types of media will include concise answers to the following:

- **Trading Area** — Do you plan to serve or sell to an industrial market, a national market, a neighborhood or specialized market? Describe yours: _____

- **Customer Type** — What does your potential customer read or listen to? Where? How often? What image does the media you are considering suggest? Does it fit your customer? Describe your customer: _____
_____

- **Budget Restrictions** — How will the amount of money you have to spend limit the media you can use? How can you spread your budget out over a year to give a repetitive, continuous message? While you may have to spend more at the start, a good ongoing guideleine is that advertising should not exceed one or two percent of sales. Set forth how much you are willing to invest in advertising in the first year:

  $_____

Break into months or quarters:

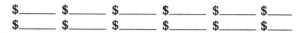

$_____ $_____ $_____ $_____ $_____ $_____
$_____ $_____ $_____ $_____ $_____ $_____

- **Continuity of Message** — How will the type of product or service, customer profile and seasonal buying patterns affect your choice of media and the frequency with which you advertise? Explain your message here: _____
_____
_____

- **Past Performance** — What is the track record for use of the medium you are considering for your type of business? What do your competitors use? What does your trade association suggest? Enter appropriate comments here: _____
_____

For more on media selection and creating your advertising plan, see SBA publication #MA4.018, *PLAN YOUR ADVERTISING BUDGET.*

Management Plan

Who will do what? Be sure to include four basic sets of information:

1. State a personal history of principals and related work, hobby or volunteer experience (include formal resumes in Appendix)

2. List and describe specific duties and responsibilities of each

3. List benefits and other forms of compensation for each

4. Identify other professional resources available to the business: Example: Accountant, lawyer, insurance broker, banker, etc. Describe relationship of each to business: Example: "accountant available on part time hourly basis, as needed, initial agreement calls for services not to exceed x hours per month at $ xx.xx per hour."

To make this section graphically clear, start with a simple organizational chart that lists specific tasks and shows, *who* (type of person is more important than individual name other than for principals) will do *what* indicated by arrows, work flow and lines of responsibility and/or communications. Consider the following examples:

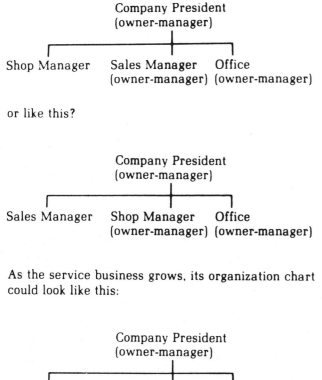

or like this?

As the service business grows, its organization chart could look like this:

Concisely answer the following questions:

Q. What are your personnel needs now?

A. 1._____
   2._____
   3._____
   4._____

Q. What skills must each key person have?

A. 1._____
   2._____
   3._____
   4._____

Q. Are the people needed available? Name them, indicate full or part time and salary rates:

A. 1._____
   2._____
   3._____
   4._____

Detail a proposed work schedule by week, and month for at least the first year.

Calculate total salaries, wages, fringe benefits and payroll taxes for each month of the first year:

	Compensation	Fringe Benefits	Payroll Taxes
1st Mo.	$_____	$_____	$_____
2nd Mo.	$_____	$_____	$_____
3rd Mo.	$_____	$_____	$_____
4th Mo.	$_____	$_____	$_____
5th Mo.	$_____	$_____	$_____
6th Mo.	$_____	$_____	$_____
7th Mo.	$_____	$_____	$_____
8th Mo.	$_____	$_____	$_____
9th Mo.	$_____	$_____	$_____
10th Mo.	$_____	$_____	$_____
11th Mo.	$_____	$_____	$_____
12th Mo.	$_____	$_____	$_____
Full Yr.	$_____	$_____	$_____

If you have identified any gaps in personnel skills, state how these will be overcome by training, purchase of outside services, or subcontracting. Check with the nearest state employment service office for assistance. Write your plan:

_____
_____
_____
_____

What is your banking plan?
What will be the location and type of bank accounts opened for the business. A word of caution, keep business accounts separate from personal or family accounts. These vital records will be necessary for future tax and accounting purposes. Describe your banking plan:_____
_____
_____
_____

How Is Your Credit Rating?

There may be several partial answers to this question. All will be of importance to the future of the business. First, what is your personal history of paying debts? Just to be safe, purchase a copy of your personal credit record from the local credit bureau for a small fee and make sure that it is accurate. Look in the classified telephone directory under "Credit Reporting Agencies."

To establish a credit rating, it is necessary to secure credit with a number of businesses and to use it. Your rating will be based upon your record for paying for goods and services based upon the agreed terms. If your prior credit rating is poor, discuss with your lawyer, accountant and banker options for improvement before seeking and being refused business credit.

Operational Plans Summary

The purpose of this section is to summarize from previous sections, the various operations of your business and link them to the finance section of your business plan. In addition you will want to summarize the advantages and disadvantages of a home based business operation. Refer to your earlier checklist. Write your summary here:

_____
_____
_____
_____
_____
_____
_____
_____
_____
_____
_____

The Financial Plan

Clearly the most critical section of your Business Plan Document is the Financial Plan. In formulating this part of the planning document, you will establish vital schedules that will guide the financial health of your business through the troubled waters of the first year and beyond.

Before going into the details of building the Financial Plan, it is important to realize that some basic knowledge of accounting is essential to the productive management of your business. If you are like most home business owners, you probably have a deep and abiding interest in the product or services that you sell or intend to sell. You like to do what you do, and it is even more fulfilling that you are making money doing it. There is nothing wrong with that. Your conviction that what you are doing or making is worthwhile is vitally important to success. Nonetheless, the income of a coach who takes the greatest pride in producing a winning team will largely depend on someone keeping score of the wins and losses.

The business owner is no different. Your product or service may improve the condition of mankind for generations to come, but, unless you have access to an unlimited bankroll, you will fail if you don't make a profit. If you don't know what's going on in your business, you are not in a very good position to assure its profitability.

Most home based businesses will use the "cash" method of accounting with a system of recordkeeping that may be little more than a carefully annotated checkbook in which is recorded all receipts and all expenditures, backed up by a few forms of original entry (invoices, receipts, cash tickets, etc.) For a Sole Proprietorship, the business form assumed by this Management Aid, the very minimum of recorded information is that required to accurately complete the federal Internal Revenue Service Form 1040, Schedule C. Other business types (partnerships, joint ventures, corporations) have similar requirements but use different tax forms.

If your business is, or will be, larger than just a small supplement to family income, you will need a something more sophisticated. Stationery stores can provide you with several packaged small business accounting systems complete with simple journals and ledgers and detailed instructions in understandable language.

Should you feel that your accounting knowledge is so rudimentary that you will need professional assistance to establish your accounting system, the classified section of your telephone directory can lead you to a number of small business services that offer a complete range of accounting services. You can buy as much as you need, from a simple "peg-board" system all the way to computerized accounting, tax return service, and monthly profitablity consultation. Rates are reasonable for the services rendered and an investigative consultation will usually be free. Look under the heading, "Business Consultants", and make some calls. Be sure to let them know the size of your business so you get to the ones who specialize in home based operations. Many of them are home-based entreprenuers themselves and know what you will be going through.

Let's start by looking at the makeup of the Financial Plan for the business.

The Financial Plan includes the following:

1. **Financial Planning Assumptions** — these are short statements of the conditions under which you plan to operate.
   - Market health _____
   - Date of startup_____
   - Sales buildup ($)_____
   - Gross profit margin_____
   - Equipment, furniture and fixtures required_____
   _____
   - Payroll and other key expenses that will impact the financial plan _____

2. **Operational Plan — Profit and Loss Projection —** this is prepared for the first year, broken into twelve individual months. It should become your first year's Budget. See Exhibits A & A-1.

3. **Source of Funds Schedule** — this shows the source(s) of your funds to capitalize the business and how they will be distributed among your fixed assets and working capital.

4. **Pro Forma Balance Sheet** — "Pro forma" refers to

the fact that the balance sheet is before the fact, not actual. This form displays Assets, Liabilities and Equity of the business. This will indicate how much Investment will be required by the business and how much of it will be used as Working Capital in its operation.

5. **Cash Flow Projection** — this will forecast the flow of cash into and out of your business through the year. It helps you plan for staged purchasing, high volume months and slow periods.

Creating the Profit and Loss Projection

Refer to Exhibits A & A-1. Create a wide sheet of analysis paper with a three inch wide column at the extreme left and thirteen narrow columns across the page. Write at the top of the first page the planned name of your business. On the second line of the heading, write "Profit and Loss Projection". On the third line, write "First Year".

Then, note the headings on Exhibit A and copy them onto your 13-column sheet. If startup is indefinite, just write "Month #1", Month #2", etc. Column 13 should be headed "Total Year".

In the wide, unnumbered column on the left of your 13-column sheet, copy the headings from the similar area on Exhibit A. Then follow the example set by Exhibit A and list all of the other components of your income, cost and expense structure. You may add or delete specific lines of expense to suit your business plan. Guard against consolidating too many types of expense under one account lest you lose control of the components. At the same time, don't try to break down expenses so discretely that accounting becomes a nuisance instead of a management tool. Once again, Exhibit A provides ample detail for most home based businesses.

Now, in the small column just to the left of the first monthly column, you will want to note which of the items in the left-hand column are to be estimated on a monthly (M) or a yearly (Y) basis. Items such as Sales, Cost of Sales and Variable Expenses will be estimated monthly based on planned volume and seasonal or other estimated fluctuations. Fixed Expenses can usually be estimated on an yearly basis and divided by twelve to arrive at even monthly values. The "M" and "Y" designations will be used later to distinguish between variable and fixed expense.

Depreciation allowances for Fixed Assets such as production equipment, office furniture and machines, vehicles, etc. will be calculated from the Source of Funds Schedule.

Exhibit A-1 describes line by line how the values on the Profit and Loss Projection are developed. Use this as your guide.

Source of Funds Schedule

To create this schedule, you will need to create a list of all of the Assets that you intend to use in your business, how much investment each will require and the source of funds to capitalize them. A sample of such a list is shown below:

ASSET	COST	SOURCE OF FUNDS
Cash	$ 2,500	Personal savings
Accounts Receivable	3,000	From profits
Inventory	2,000	Vendor Credit
Pickup truck	5,000	Currently owned
Packaging machine	10,000	Installment purchase
Office desk and chair	300	Currently owned
Calculator	75	Personal cash
Electric Typewriter*	500	Personal savings

   *A note about office equipment: although this Management Aid has been written for a broad audience of home based business operators, those who plan enterprises which produce printed products or a large volume of correspondence should consider an electronic word processor as a great time saver. Test use or rent two or more brands that appear to meet your needs and select the one with which you feel most comfortable. Don't be afraid to ask others who have had to make this decision for advice. Compatability of your system with those of potential typesetting services or printers should be of high consideration. If you are not quite sure, consider renting or leasing the equipment until you are. Service contracts on such complex electronic gear are usually a good insurance policy.

   Before you leave your Source of Funds Schedule, indicate the number of months (years x 12) of useful life for depreciable fixed assets. (In the example, the pickup truck, the packaging machine and the furniture and office equipment would be depreciable.) Generally, any individual item of equipment, furniture, fixtures, vehicles, etc., costing over $100 should be depreciated. For more information on allowances for depreciation, you can get free publications and assistance from your local Internal Revenue Service office. Divide the cost of each fixed asset item by the number of months over which it will be depreciated. You will need this data to enter as monthly depreciation on your Profit and Loss Projection. All of the data on the Source of Funds Schedule will be needed to create the Balance Sheet.

Creating the Pro Forma Balance Sheet

Refer to Exhibit B. This is a Balance Sheet form. There are a number of variations of this form and you may find it prudent to ask your banker for the form that the bank uses for small business. It will make it easier for them to evaluate the health of your business. Use Exhibit B to get started and transfer the data to your preferred form later. Accompanying Exhibit B is Exhibit B-1 which describes line by line how to develop the Balance Sheet.

Even though you may plan to stage the purchase of some assets through the year, for the purposes of this pro forma Balance Sheet, assume that all assets will be provided at the startup.

Cash Flow Projection

An important subsidiary schedule to your financial plan is a monthly Cash Flow Projection. Prudent business management practice is to keep no more cash in the business than is needed to operate it and to protect it from catastrophe. In most small businesses, the problem is rarely one of having too much cash. A Cash Flow Projection is made to advise management of the amount of cash that is going to be absorbed by the operation of the business and compares it against the amount that will be available.

SBA has created an excellent form for this purpose and it is shown as Exhibit C. Your projection should be prepared on 13-column analysis paper to allow for a twelve month projection. Exhibit C-1 represents a line by line description and explanation of the components of the Cash Flow Projection which provides a step-by-step method of preparation.

Outside Sources of Assistance

The U.S. Small Business Administration's Office of Business Development programs are extensive and diversified. They include free individual counseling, courses, conferences, workshops, problem clinics, and a wide range of publications. Counseling is provided through community based organizations such as:

SCORE and **ACE** which help small business owners solve their operating problems through a one-on-one relationship. Counseling is not limited to small businesses that have a problem. It is available as well to managers of successful firms who wish to review their objectives and long-range plans for expansion and diversification.

SMALL BUSINESS INSTITUTES (SBIs) which have been organized through SBA on over 500 university and college campuses as another way to help small business. At each SBI, senior and graduate students at schools of business ad-ministration, and their faculty advisors, provide on-site management counseling. Students are guided by the faculty advisors and SBA management assistance experts and receive academic credit for their work, and

SMALL BUSINESS DEVELOPMENT CENTERS (SBDCs) which draw from resources of local, state and federal government programs, the private sector, and university facilities to provide managerial and technical help, research studies, and other types of specialized assistance of value to small business. These university based centers provide individual counseling and practical training for small business owners.

BUSINESS MANAGEMENT TRAINING programs are co-sponsored by SBA in cooperation with educational institutions, Chambers of Commerce, and trade associations. *Courses* generally take place in the evening and last from six to eight weeks. In addition, *conferences* covering such subjects as working capital, business forecasting, and marketing are held for established businesses on a regular basis. SBA conducts, *Pre-Business Workshops*, dealing with finance, marketing assistance, types of business organizations, and business site selection, for prospective business owners. *Clinics* that focus on particular problems of small firms in specific industrial categories are held on an as-needed basis.

A Final Word

In completing this Management Aid, you have put in a great deal of time and effort. You should now have all of the elements needed to present as simple or sophisticated a prospectus for your enterprise as you desire. More important, you have created the management tools to guide you in your venture. Once the business opens its doors, you will be inundated by the details, problems, challenges and joys of going it alone. It will be difficult to hold to your course through the rough seas ahead, but don't forget this "chartbook", it will see you through to "Port Profit." It should be a living document, referred to regularly, massaged constantly, and revised to reflect your experience. Begin a planning cycle that expands this first year plan into one that spans three or five years out. Update it at regular intervals. Set your goals and live by them. Your success is in your hands. Good planning and good execution!

Resources

Atkinson, Wm. *Working at Home: Is It for You?* Dow Jones-Irwin, 1985. 162p. (HD62.7.A85 1985)

Behr, Marion. *Women Working Home: The Homebased Business Guide and Directory.* 2nd edition. Edison, N.J., WWH Press, 1983. (HD6072.6.U5B44 1983)

Brabec, Barbara. *Homemade Money: The Definitive Guide To Success in a Home Business.* Betterway Pubins., 1984. 272p.

Davidson, Peter. *Earn Money at Home: Over 100 Ideas for Businesses Requiring Little or No Capital.* McGraw-Hill, 1981. 326p. (HD69.N3D37)

Delany, George. *The #1 Home Business Book.* Liberty Publ. Co., 1981. 169p. (HD8036.D44)

Edwards, Paul and Sarah. *Working From Home.* Jeremy Tarcher Inc., 1985.

Feldstein, Stuart. *Home, Inc.: How to Start and Operate a Successful Business From Your Home.* Grosset & Dunlap, 1981. 249p. (HD8036.F45 1981)

Hewes, Jeremy J. *Worksheads: Living and Working in the Same Place.* Dolphin Books, 1981. 165p. (HD8037.U5H44)

Kishel, Gregory. *Dollars on Your Doorstep: The Complete Guide to Homebased Businesses.* Wiley, 1984. 183p. (HD62.7.K575 1984)

Lieberoff, Allen J. *Climb Your Own Ladder: 101 Home Businesses That Can Make You Wealthy.* Simon & Schuster, 1982. 242p. (HD2341.L49 1983)

Rice, Frederick H. *Starting a Home-Based Business,* University of Vermont. SBDC/DVES Burlington, VT., 1985.

Scott, Robert. *Office at Home.* Charles Scribner's Sons, 1985. 373p. (HF5547.5.S38 1985)

Tepper, Terri. *The New Entrepreneurs: Women Working From Home.* Universe Books, 1980. 238p. (HF5500.3.U54T46)

Waymon, Lynn. *Starting and Managing a Business from Your Home.* U.S. Small Business Administration, Starting and Managing Series, Vol. 2, Washington, D.C., 1986.

EXHIBIT A

OPERATING PLAN FORECAST (Profit and Loss Projection)												
		Month 1			Month 2–12			Totals				
Revenue (sales)	Ind %	Estimate	Actual	%	Estimate	Actual	%	Estimate	%	Actual	%	
Total Revenue (sales)												
Cost of Sales												
Total Cost of Sales												
Gross Profit												
Expenses												
Salary expense: Sales people, office and other												
Payroll Expenses (taxes, etc.)												
Outside Services												
Supplies (office and operating)												
Repairs and Maintenance												
Advertising												
Car, Delivery and Travel												
Accounting and Legal												
Rent												
Telephone												
Utilities												
Insurance												
Taxes (real estate, etc)												
Interest												
Depreciation												
Other Expenses (specify each)												
Miscellaneous (unspecified)												
Total Expenses												
Net Profit												

SBA FORM 1099 (4–82) SOP: 60 10 1   Present stock may be used until exhausted

EXHIBIT A1

PROFIT AND LOSS PROJECTION

The profit and loss statement (P&L) is valuable as a planning tool and as a key management tool to help control operations to reach business goals. It enables the owner/manager to develop a "preview" of the amount of profit, or loss, generated each month, and for the business year — based on reasonable predictions of monthly levels of sales, costs, and expenses. The owner/manager can compare the year's expected profits or losses against the profit goals and needs established for the business. A completed P&L statement allows the owner/manager to compare actual figures with the monthly projections, and to take steps to correct any problems.

REVENUE (Sales)

- List the departments within the business, e.g., assume your business is appliance sales and service: New appliances, used ones, parts, in-shop service, on-site service.
- In the "Estimate" columns, enter a reasonable projection of monthly sales for each department of the business. Include cash and on-account sales. In the "Actual" columns, enter the actual sales for the month as they become available.
- Exclude from the Revenue section any revenue that is not strictly related to the business.

COST OF SALES

- Cite costs by department of the business, as above.
- In the "Estimate" columns enter the cost of sales estimated for each month for each department. For product inventory, calculate the cost of the goods sold for each department (beginning inventory plus purchases and transportation costs during the month, minus the inventory). Enter "Actual" costs when known each month.

Gross Profits — Subtract the total cost of sales from the total revenue.

EXPENSES

- *Salary Expenses:* Base pay plus overtime.
- *Payroll Expenses:* Include paid vacations, sick leave, health insurance, unemployment insurance, social security taxes.
- *Outside Services:* Include costs of subcontracts, overflow work farmed out, special or one-time services.
- *Supplies:* Services and items purchased for use in the business, not for resale.
- *Repairs and Maintenance:* Regular maintenance and repair, including periodic large expenditures such as painting or decorating.
- *Advertising:* Include desired sales volume, and yellow pages expenses, e.g.
- *Car, Delivery and Travel:* Include charges if personal car used in business, including parking, tolls, buying trips, etc.
- *Accounting and Legal:* Outside professional services.
- *Rent:* List only real estate used in the business.
- *Telephone:* Self-explanatory.
- *Utilities:* Water, heat, light, etc.
- *Insurance:* Fire or liability on property or products, workmen's compensation.
- *Taxes* (real estate, etc.): Inventory, sales, excise tax, others.
- *Interest:* Self-explanatory.
- *Depreciation:* Amortization of capital assets.
- *Other Expenses* (specify each): e.g., tools, leased equipment.
- *Miscellaneous* (unspecified): Small expenditures without separate accounts.

Net Profit — To find net profit, subtract total expenses from gross profit.

EXHIBIT B

Company Name

① **BALANCE SHEET**

As of (current date)

② **ASSETS**		**LIABILITIES**		⑦
Current Assets		**Current Liabilities**		
Cash	$_____	Accounts payable	$_____	
Accounts receivable $_____		Short-term notes	$_____	
less allowance for		Current portion		
doubtful accounts $_____		of long-term notes	$_____	
Net realizable value	$_____	Interest payable	$_____	
Inventory	$_____	Taxes payable	$_____	
Temporary investments	$_____	Accrued payroll	$_____	
Prepaid expenses	$_____	Total Current Liabilities	$_____	⑧
③ Total Current Assets	$_____	**Long-Term Liabilities**		
Long-Term Investments		Notes payable	$_____	
(detailed list)	$_____	Total Long-Term Liabilities	$_____	⑨
④ Total Investments	$_____	**TOTAL LIABILITIES**	$_____	⑦
Fixed Assets		**EQUITY**		
Land	$_____	Total Owner's Equity		
Buildings: $_____ at		(proprietorship)	$_____	
cost, less accumulated		or		
depreciation of $_____		(Name's) Equity	$_____	
Net book value	$_____	(Name's) Equity	$_____	
Equipment: $_____ at		(partnership)		
cost, less accumulated		Total Partners' Equity	$_____	⑩
depreciation of $_____		or		
Net book value	$_____	Shareholders' Equity		
Furniture/Fixtures: $_____ at		(corporation)		
cost, less accumulated		Capital stock	$_____	
depreciation of $_____		Capital paid-in in excess		
Net book value	$_____	of par	$_____	
Autos/Trucks: $_____ at		Retained earnings	$_____	
cost, less accumulated		Total Shareholders' Equity	$_____	
depreciation of $_____		**TOTAL LIABILITIES**		
Net book value	$_____	**AND EQUITY**	$_____	⑪
⑤ Total Net Fixed Assets	$_____	**RECONCILEMENT OF EQUITY**		
Other Assets		**As of (current date)**		
(detailed list)	$_____	Equity at beginning of period	$_____	
⑥ Total Other Assets	$_____	Plus: Net income (or Minus: Net		
② **TOTAL ASSETS**	$_____	loss) after taxes	$_____	
		Plus: Additional capital contributions		
		(investments by owner(s) or stock		
		purchases by shareholders)	$_____	
		Less: Total deductions (withdrawals		
		by owner(s) or dividends to		
		shareholders)	$_____	
		Equality as shown on current		
		Balance Sheet	$_____	⑫

Source: "Understanding Financial Statements," _Small Business Reporter_, Copyright © Bank of America NT & SA, 1980.

EXHIBIT B1

Sample Blank Balance Sheet

The following text covers the essential elements of a Balance Sheet. Figures used to compile the Balance Sheet are taken from the previous and current Balance Sheet as well as the current **Income Statement** (or **Profit & Loss Statement**). The report is usually attached to the Balance Sheet.

1. **Heading** — The legal name of the business, the type of statement, and the day, month, and year. Must be shown at the top of the report.

2. **Assets** — Anything of value that is owned or legally due the business. Total assets include all **net realizable** and **net book** (also **net carrying**) values. Net realizable and net book values are amounts derived by substracting any estimated allowances for doubtful accounts, depreciation, and reductions of future service — such as amortization of a premium during the term of an insurance policy — from the acquisition price of assets.

3. **Current Assets** — Cash and resources that can be converted into cash within 12 months of the date of the Balance Sheet (or during one established cycle of operations). Besides cash (money on hand and demand deposits in the bank, e.g., checking accounts and regular savings accounts), resources include:

   Accounts Receivable — The amounts due from customers in payment for merchandise or services.

   Inventory — Includes raw materials on hand, work in process, and all finished goods either manufactured or purchased for resale.

   Temporary Investments — Interest- or dividend-yielding holdings expected to be converted into cash within a year. Also called marketable securities or short-term investments, they include stocks and bonds, certificates of deposit, and time deposit savings accounts. List on the Balance Sheet at either their cost or market value, whichever is less.

   Prepaid Expenses — Goods, benefits, or services a business buys or rents in advance of use. Examples are office supplies, insurance protection, and floor space.

4. **Long-Term Investments** — Also called long-term assets. They are holdings the business intends to keep for at least a year and that typically yield interest or dividends. Included are stocks, bonds, and savings accounts earmarked for special purposes.

5. **Fixed Assets** — Fixed assets, frequently called plant and equipment, are the resources a business owns or acquires for use in operations and does not intend for resale. Land is listed at its original purchase price, with no allowance for appreciation or depreciation. Other fixed assets are listed at cost, less depreciation. Fixed assets may be leased. Depending on the leasing arrangement, both the value and the liability of the leased property may need to be listed on the Balance Sheet.

6. **Other Assets** — Resources not listed with any of the above assets. Examples include tangibles such as outdated equipment salable to the scrap yard, and intangibles such as trademarks.

7. **Liabilities** — All monetary obligations of a business and all claims creditors have on its assets.

8. **Current Liabilities** — All debts and obligations payable within 12 months or within one cycle of operations. Typically they are:

   Accounts Payable — Amounts owed to suppliers for goods and services purchased in connection with business operations.

Short-Term Notes — The balance of principal due to pay off short-term debt for borrowed funds.

Current Portion of Long-Term Notes — Current amount due of total balance on notes whose terms exceed 12 months.

Interest Payable — Any accrued fees due for use of both short- and long-term borrowed capital and credit extended to the business.

Taxes Payable — Amounts estimated by an accountant to have been incurred during the accounting period.

Accured Payroll — Salaries and wages currently owned.

9. **Long-Term Liabilities** — Notes, contract payments, or mortgage payments due over a period exceeding 12 months or one cycle of operations. They are listed by outstanding balance, less the current portion due.

10. **Equity** — Also called **net worth.** Equity is the claim of the owner(s) on the assets of the business. In a proprietorship or partnership, equity is each owner's original investment plus any earnings after withdrawals.

    In a corporation, the owners are the shareholders. The corporation's equity is the sum of contributions plus earnings retained after paying dividends.

11. **Total Liabilities and Equity** — The sum of these two amounts must always match that for Total Assets.

12. **Reconcilement of Equity** — Used for proprietorships and partnerships, this report reconciles the equity shown on the current Balance Sheet. It records equity at the beginning of the accounting period and details additions to or subtractions from this amount made during the period. Typically, additions and subtractions are net income or loss and owner contributions and/or deductions.

    For corporations, the same type of report is called the **Statement of Retained Earnings.** It lists increases or decreases in this accumulated net income since the beginning of the current period.

Source: Extracted from "Understanding Financial Statements," *Small Business Reporter,* Copyright © Bank of America NT & SA 1980.

MONTHLY CASH FLOW PROJECTION

EXHIBIT C

YEAR MONTH	Pre-Start-up Position		1		2-12		TOTAL Columns 1–12		
	Estimate	Actual	Estimate	Actual	Estimate	Actual	Estimate	Actual	
1. CASH ON HAND (Beginning of month)									1.
2. CASH RECEIPTS (a) Cash Sales									2. (a)
(b) Collections from Credit Accounts									(b)
(c) Loan or Other Cash injection (Specify)									(c)
3. TOTAL CASH RECEIPTS (2a+2b+2c=3)									3.
4. TOTAL CASH AVAILABLE (Before cash out) (1+3)									4.
5. CASH PAID OUT (a) Purchases (Merchandise)									5. (a)
(b) Gross Wages (Excludes withdrawals)									(b)
(c) Payroll Expenses (Taxes, etc.)									(c)
(d) Outside Services									(d)
(e) Supplies (Office and operating)									(e)
(f) Repairs and Maintenance									(f)
(g) Advertising									(g)
(h) Car, Delivery, and Travel									(h)
(i) Accounting and Legal									(i)
(j) Rent									(j)
(k) Telephone									(k)
(l) Utilities									(l)
(m) Insurance									(m)
(n) Taxes (Real estate, etc.)									(n)
(o) Interest									(o)
(p) Other Expenses (Specify each)									(p)
(q) Miscellaneous (Unspecified)									(q)
(r) Subtotal									(r)
(s) Loan Principal Payment									(s)
(t) Capital Purchases (Specify)									(t)
(u) Other Start-up Costs									(u)
(v) Reserve and/or Excrow (Specify)									(v)
(w) Owner's Withdrawal									(w)
6. TOTAL CASH PAID OUT (Total 5a thru 5w)									6.
7. CASH POSITION (End of month) (4 minus 6)									7.
ESSENTIAL OPERATING DATA (Non-cash flow information) A. Sales Volume (Dollars)									A.
B. Accounts Receivable (End of month)									B.
C. Bad Debt (End of month)									C.
D. Inventory on Hand (End of month)									D.
E. Accounts Payable (End of month)									E.
F. Depreciation									F.

SBA FORM 1100 (8-75) REF: SOP 60 10 1

EXHIBIT C1

1. CASH ON HAND (Beginning of month)	Cash on hand same as (7), Cash Position Previous Month
2. CASH RECEIPTS	
(a) Cash Sales	All cash sales. Omit credit sales unless cash is actually received.
(b) Collections from Credit Accounts	Amount to be expected from all credit accounts.
(c) Loan or Other Cash Injection	Indicate here all cash injections not shown in 2(a) or 2(b) above. See "A" of "Analysis"
3. TOTAL CASH RECEIPTS (2a+2b+2c=3)	Self-explanatory
4. TOTAL CASH AVAILABLE (Before cash out) (1+3)	Self-explanatory
5. CASH PAID OUT	
(a) Purchases (Merchandise)	Merchandise for resale or for use in product (paid for in current month)
(b) Gross Wages (Excludes withdrawals)	Base pay plus overtime (if any)
(c) Payroll Expenses (Taxes, etc.)	Include paid vacations, paid sick leave, health insurance, unemployment insurance, etc. (this might be 10 to 45% OF 5(b)
(d) Outside Services	This could include outside labor and/or material for specialized or overflow work, including subcontracting
(e) Supplies (Office and operating)	Items purchased for use in the business (not for resale)
(f) Repairs and Maintenance	Include periodic large expenditures such as painting or decorating
(g) Advertising	This amount should be adequate to maintain sales volume–include telephone book yellow page cost
(h) Car, Delivery, and Travel	If personal car is used, charge in this column–include parking
(i) Accounting and Legal	Outside services, including, for example, bookkeeping
(j) Rent	Real estate only (See 5(p) for other rentals)
(k) Telephone	Self-explanatory
(l) Utilities	Water, heat, light, and/or power
(m) Insurance	Coverages on business property and products e.g. fire, liability; also workman's compensation, fidelity, etc. Exclude "executive" life (include in "5w")
(n) Taxes (Real estate, etc.)	Plus inventory tax–sales tax–excise tax, if applicable
(o) Interest	Remember to add interest on loan as it is injected (See 2(c) above)
(p) Other Expenses (Specify each)	Unexpected expenditures may be included here as a safety factor
	Equipment expenses during the month should be included here (Non-capital equipment)
	When equipment is rented or leased, record payments here
(q) Miscellaneous (Unspecified)	Small expenditures for which separate accounts would not be practical
(r) Subtotal	This subtotal indicates cash out for operating costs
(s) Loan Principal Payment	Include payment on all loans, including vehicle and equipment purchases on time payment
(t) Capital Purchases (Specify)	Non-expensed (depreciable) expenditures such as equipment, building, vehicle purchases, and leasehold improvements
(u) Other Start-up Costs	Expenses incurred prior to first month projection and paid for after the "start-up" position
(v) Reserve and/or Escrow (Specify)	Example: Insurance, tax, or equipment escrow to reduce impact of large periodic payments
(w) Owner's Withdrawal	Should include payment for such things as owner's income tax, social security, health insurance, "executive" life insurance premiums, etc.
6. TOTAL CASH PAID OUT (Total 5a thru 5w)	Self-explanatory
7. CASH POSITION (End of month) (4-6)	Enter this amount in (1) Cash on Hand following month–See "A" of "Analysis"
ESSENTIAL OPERATING DATA (Non-cash flow information)	This is basic information necessary for proper planning and for proper cash projection. In conjunction with this data, the cash flow can be evolved and shown in the above form.
A. Sales Volume (Dollars)	This is a very important figure and should be estimated carefully, taking into account size of facility and employee output as well as realistic anticipated sales (Actual sales performed–not orders received)
B. Accounts Receivable (End of month)	Previous unpaid credit sales plus current month's credit sales, less amounts received current month (deduct "C" below)
C. Bad Debt (End of month)	Bad debts should be subtracted from (B) in the month anticipated
D. Inventory on Hand (End of month)	Last month's inventory plus merchandise received and/or manufactured current month minus amount sold current month
E. Accounts Payable (End of month)	Previous month's payable plus current month's payable minus amount paid during month
F. Depreciation	Established by your accountant, or value of all your equipment divided by useful life (in months) as allowed by Internal Revenue Service

SBA FORM 1100 (8-75)

Summary

Many authorities on business management identify five functions of management: planning, organizing, directing, controlling, and coordinating. The planning and controlling functions often get less attention from owner-managers of small business than they should. One way to strengthen both of these functions is through effective goal setting.

Long range goals for sales, profits, competitive position, development of people, and industrial relations must be established. Then, goals are set for the current year which will lead towards the accomplishment of the long range goals.

This Aid presents Management by Objectives to the owner-manager of a small manufacturing company for use in this type of planning and goal setting. MBO includes goal setting by all managers down to the first level of supervision. Their goals are tied to those of the company.

Traditionally, people have worked according to job descriptions that list the *activities* of the job. The Management by Objectives (MBO) approach, on the other hand, stresses *results*.

Let's look at an example. Suppose that you have a credit manager and that his or her job description simply says that the credit manager supervises the credit operations of the company. The activities of the credit manager are then listed. Under MBO, the credit manager could have five or six goals covering important aspects of the work. One goal might be to increase credit sales enough to support a 15 percent increase in sales.

The traditional job description for a personnel specialist might include language about conducting the recruiting program for your company. Under MBO, the specialist's work might be covered in five or six goals—one which could be "recruit five new employees in specified categories by July 1."

Thus, MBO looks for results, not activities. With MBO, you view the job in terms of what it should achieve. Activity is never the essential element. It is merely an intermediate step leading to the desired result.

What Business Am I In?

In making long range plans, the first question you ought to think about is "what business am I in?" Is the definition you have of your business right for today's market?

Are there emerging customer needs that will require a changed definition of your business next year?

For example, one owner-manager's business was making metal trash cans. When sales began to fall off, the owner was forced to reexamine the business. To regain lost sales and continue to grow the owner redefined the product as metal containers and developed a marketing plan for that product.

How you view your business will provide the framework for your planning with respect to markets, product development, buildings and equipment, financial needs, and staff size.

Your long range objectives for your business will be the cornerstone in the MBO program for your company. At a minimum, they must be clearly communicated to your managers; however, for a truly vital program your managers should have a part in formulating these long range goals. Your managers will base their short range goals on these objectives. If they have had a role in establishing the long range objectives, they will be more committed to achieving them.

The Complete MBO Program

Management by Objectives may be used in all kinds of organizations. But not everyone has had the same degree of success in using this concept. From examining those MBO programs that failed, it is clear that the programs were incomplete.

The minimum requirements for an MBO program are:

1. Each manager's job includes five to ten goals expressed in specific, measurable terms.

2. Each manager reporting to you proposes his or her goals to you in writing. When you both agree on each goal, a final written statement of the goal is prepared.

3. Each goal consists of the statement of the goal, how it will be measured, and the work steps necessary to complete it.

4. Results are systematically determined at regular intervals (at least quarterly) and compared with the goals.

5. When progress towards goals is not in accordance with your plans, problems are identified and corrective action is taken.

6. Goals at each level of management are related to the level above and the level below.

Goal Setting

Goals for each of your managers are the crucial element in any MBO system. Goals at middle levels of management must be consistent with those at top levels. Goals of first line supervisors must relate to those at middle levels. Goals prepared by the manager responsible for certain steps in a large processing operation must tie in with those of managers responsible for other steps in the processing. And all goals must relate to and support your long range objectives for the company.

When all these goals are consistent, then an MBO system will be developed. Until then, there will be many like the middle manager of a research and development company who exclaimed in a seminar, "How can I set my goals when I don't know where top management wants to go?"

Each manager will probably find between five and eight goals enough to cover those aspects of the job crucial to successful performance. These are the elements which you will use to judge his or her performance. Of course, other duties which do not fall into the above goals should not be neglected. But they are of secondary importance.

When you first start your MBO program, your managers will undergo a learning period. They must learn how to prepare a goal which will make them stretch but is not beyond their capabilities. They must learn to develop ways to effectively measure their performance. They must learn to anticipate real problems which threaten the achievement of the goals and then take steps to cope with the problems.

During this learning period, your managers should first set a few goals. Then as they learn how to develop and achieve goals, the coverage and number of goals can be extended.

The Miniature Work Plan

Your managers may find the miniature work plan useful. On this work plan the manager can show each of the major work steps (subgoals) necessary to reach the goal. Then, if each work step is performed by the indicated date, the goal will be reached when the last work step is completed.

You may also use this form to discuss goals with your manager. By looking at this form, you can see not only the goal but also the plan for reaching that goal. This will allow you to ask questions about the work steps and anticipated problems, as well as to question how the goal will be measured. By pointing out the relationship between the manager's goal and your goal, you'll be helping each of your managers to understand how his/her goals relate to those of the company.

A Manager's Goal

Instructions for Completing Form

Management by Objectives provides for the establishment of four to ten goals by each manager. You should set up goals in each of several important areas in your job. You might try to establish at least one in each of these categories: Regular, Problem Solving, Innovative, and Development. By following this approach you will be more likely to see the full range of possibilities open to you through goal setting.

Develop each goal as a miniature work plan. The steps that follow will result in goals which are complete and useful to both you and your boss.

Goal (Be specific and concise)
_____

Measurement (The bench mark that tells you that you have achieved the goal, should be expressed in quantitative terms)
_____

Major Problems Anticipated
_____
_____

Work Steps (List three or four most essential steps, give completion dates for each)
_____
_____
_____

Superior's Goal (Give goal at next higher level to which your goal relates)
_____

Whenever a problem is listed on the work plan, the manager should include a work step to deal with it. For example, suppose the head of your supply department set a goal to deliver all packages within one day of when they were received. He thought he might have difficulty in getting his people to follow the new procedures. So, he included a work step to teach these procedures before the new program went into effect.

Kinds of Goals

When your managers begin to set their goals, they may want to know what areas are suitable for goal setting. What are the really important aspects of their jobs rather than that part which is most visible to them? How can they be sure that their program is balanced for the long haul, rather than just reacting to immediate, pressing problems? How can they set goals which are most likely to help them control their jobs?

It might be useful for them to have a classification of goals that suggests areas of opportunity. Generally, each manager should have between five and eight goals. One or two goals in each of these areas should be helpful:

1. Regular work goals.

2. Problem solving goals.

3. Innovative goals.

4. Development goals.

Regular work refers to those activities which make up the major part of the manager's responsibilities. The head of production would be primarily concerned with the amount, quality, and efficiency of production. The head of marketing would be primarily concerned with developing and conducting the market research and sales programs. Each manager should be able to find opportunities to operate more efficiently, to improve the quality of the product or service, and to expand the total amount produced or marketed.

Problem solving goals will give your managers an opportunity to define their major problems. Then, they may set a goal to eliminate each one. There is no danger of anyone ever running out of problems. New problems or new versions of old problems always seem to replace those overcome.

Innovative goals may be viewed the same way. A goal for innovation may apply to an actual problem. But, some innovation may not deal with a problem. For example, the head of building management sets a goal to invigorate the employee suggestion program by putting five suggestions into effect during the next four months. There was no specific problem to be solved, the manager was just trying to do the best job possible.

The development goal recognizes how important the development of your employees is to your business. Your managers can be encouraged to develop their people just as they are to produce more effectively. Every manager must be to some extent a teacher and coach; each manager must plan for the employees' continued growth in both technical areas and in working together effectively.

By asking your managers to set at least one goal in the four areas listed above, you may open their eyes to possibilities they had not seen before. The goal setting process can be a very useful educational step, even for those who are primarily specialists.

Progress Reports

An MBO program without provision for regular reports on progress is worthless. That is why some articles and books on MBO call the concept MBO/R. The "R" refers to results. Nothing is accomplished by setting goals or objectives unless the program calls for a regular review of progress towards results.

A large organization issued nearly 100 pages of goals prepared by many of its managers. Most of the goals were well developed. The document was very impressive. But there was absolutely no provision for a reporting system of any kind. It is easy to imagine the reaction of those who set goals for the first year when they were asked the following year to draw up new goals.

A monthly or quarterly review of progress towards goals will help you determine where progress is below expectations. For example, suppose that one of your goals calls for a reduction of overtime by 50 percent this year, and the first quarter reduction is only 15 percent. A special effort must be exerted in the succeeding quarters to regain the lost ground or the goal will not be achieved by the end of the year. When progress is below expectations, the problem or problems holding back progress should be identified and assigned to someone, usually the manager, for resolution. Make these assignments part of the company MBO files so that responsibility for correcting the problem areas cannot be evaded.

Perfomance Evaluation

You will have to evaluate the performance of every person working for you in some way, either formally or informally. When your managers are working to achieve a full set of five to eight goals, their ability to get results on each goal can be a good, objective measure of performance.

Traditional performance evaluation systems have been strongly criticized because they deal with subjective matters such as leadership qualities, rather than the more objective measure of results. Evaluating performance by MBO, while objective, is a complex task, which must be undertaken with care by someone who fully understands MBO. Failure to reach goals can be a result of setting the wrong objectives in the first place, the existence of organizational restrictions not taken into account, inadequate or improper measures of goal achievement, personal failure, or a combination of factors.

Installing MBO

When installing an MBO program, many owner-managers have found it best to start by asking their managers to define their jobs. What are their major responsibilities? Then, for each responsibility, the manager and the boss decide how they will measure performance in terms of results.

The result of this exercise may surprise you. Often managers and their bosses do not even agree on the manager's major responsibilities. Also, you may find that no one is performing some of the functions that you consider important.

As the owner-manager, you must appreciate what the system will do. You have to show interest in the concept from the beginning. You have to set the example for your subordinate managers, if the MBO system is to be a success.

The education of your managers may be a formidable task. They have probably thought in terms of specific functions—managing a sales department, directing a credit office—rather than in terms of goals which contribute to the organization.

It might be best to start with a seminar of six to nine hours in a classroom. This ought to be enough to introduce MBO to the managers who will be setting goals. Either you or a consultant might conduct the seminar. (If you choose a consultant, be sure that you are there for the entire seminar.)

Provide enough time so that your managers can express their doubts, reservations or opposition to MBO. It is best to get their feelings out into the open as soon as possible. Other participants can help them deal with their concerns.

A very useful part of such a seminar is the preparation of an actual goal by each participant. In small group sessions, your managers can help each other by reviewing work plans and offering suggestions to improve each other's plans.

Working with goal setting, periodic review of goals, and other aspects of MBO will be a learning experience for most managers. If they set annual goals, it may take three to four years before good results from this new system of managing appear. MBO may look simple on the surface, but it requires experience and skill to make it work effectively.

Threats to the MBO System

Not all MBO programs are successful. Some of the leading reasons why past programs failed to reach their potential are:

1. Top management did not get involved.

2. Corporate objectives were inadequate.

3. MBO was installed as a crash program.

4. It was difficult to learn the system because the nature of MBO was not taught.

It is hard to get people to think in terms of results rather than activities relating to their work. However, it can be done. The sequence of steps one owner-manager uses may not work for another. It is often an individual matter. Results are what count.

If you feel that you are ready to introduce MBO to your company, why not set this as a goal for yourself. Turn back and follow through with the work plan. List your goal, measurement, anticipated problems, and the work steps necessary to get your company managing by objectives.

Introduction

This brochure will help you develop a Strategic Plan for your small business by:

- Taking advantage of your company's strengths,

- Eliminating or reducing its weaknesses,

- Capitalizing on opportunities and emerging trends,

- Taking defensive steps to reduce threats facing your business,

- Bringing together all the resources of your company and directing them toward specific goals in areas like Sales growth, Profit, Productivity and Service and

- Prioritizing and documenting all the things your company wants to accomplish over the next 3–5 years, allocating resources, and assigning responsibilities to be certain they get done.

Is Strategic Planning Really Necessary?

"My business is very small. Do you think I really need to develop a plan like this?"

The best response to this question is, "Only if you want to stay in business and prosper."

Times change so rapidly and running a business is so complex these days that owner-managers can easily find things getting out of control if adequate planning and control are not utilized. And competition seems to be getting tougher all the time. In most cases, small businesses find themselves competing with much larger companies—ones that know the benefits of long range planning and practice it. From a defensive standpoint, it is important that you employ the same concepts to your operation.

"Steering a business by financial controls alone is not enough."[1] The small business owner needs more than a budget to manage the future direction of his company.

Through Strategic Planning, you can get employees in all areas of your business pulling in the same direction and sharing the same vision that you have for the future of your business. At the same time, plans of this type enable you to act and react quickly to market opportunities and problems.

You can also use your plan to communicate with bankers who often do not understand the nature of your business. Bankers need to be convinced that your company is in control of its future before they will lay their money on the line. A comprehensive plan aimed at sustained growth in sales and earnings can be very convincing.

A plan is also very helpful in dealings with your suppliers, advertisers, attorney, accountant, auditor, investors, and/or business consultants.

What is Strategic Planning?

Ask ten people for a definition of Strategic Planning and you will probably receive ten different answers. But, most will agree that it relates to the overall direction of the company.

Every company exists for a purpose. That purpose is its "mission," and all the things it does are generally directed toward fulfilling that mission.

Strategic planning is a process by which key people in an organization can:

- Define or redefine the company's mission,

- Assess its current situation,

- Decide what they want the business to look like in say 3–5 years and

- Map out a course to bring the company from where it is now to where they want it to be, recognizing its

    —Strengths

    —Weaknesses

    —Opportunities, and

    —Threats

[1]"Uses and Misuses of Strategic Planning"; Daniel H. Gray; Harvard Business Review; January-February, 1986.

When done properly, a strategic planning is a simple, creative, and flexible process that works well for a small business, a way to replace separate marketing, operational, financial, and/or budgeting plans with one comprehensive plan.

Let's take a closer look at the process itself.

Step 1—Analysis of Current Situation: External Factors

The process begins with an assessment of the current situation in which the business finds itself. Those areas that predominantly relate to external factors impacting on the company are usually examined first. In most cases, it makes sense to divide your analysis into groupings. For example:

- National Economic Outlook

- Local or Regional Economic Outlook

- Industry Outlook

This part of the analysis should begin early, at least a quarter or so before you begin the formal planning process. By making a folder for each of the preceding outlook areas, you can begin to collect information for later analysis. Among the common sources of information to consider are:

- The Wall Street Journal

- The New York Times

- Business Week

- Industry Periodicals

- United States Department of Commerce (especially for the 12 leading economic indicators).

- Federal Reserve Banks

- Local Industry Associations

- Local Chambers of Commerce

- The Public Library

After data is collected, its present and future impact can be assessed. For example, slow housing starts, weak retail auto sales, reductions in real disposable personal income, and increasing levels of unemployment would signal reduced future demand for goods and services.

After preparing a written, concise assessment of the impact of these external factors and sharing it with key people in your organization, you are ready to begin the next phase of your planning effort.

The Planning Session

After preparing a concise, written assessment of the external environment, you are ready to gather together key people in your organization for a marathon planning session. These should include owners and key people in the organization (sales, service, finance, processing, manufacturing, etc.).

It is essential that all effective areas of the company be represented. In that way, you will reveal the company's strengths, opportunities, weaknesses and threats and all areas of the company will be more likely to "buy into" the goals eventually set. Strategic planning is most successful when it is a participative process.

For the process to be most effective, an energized environment must be created. One that is free of interruptions and distractions. To get the creative juices flowing, it is usually best to get away from the business premises. A hotel meeting room where coffee and lunches can be brought in is usually sufficient. For many businesses the process takes two full days, so you may want to accomplish it over a weekend.

The sessions will function best if they are structured. The following is a proven technique:

- Appoint someone to be the facilitator of the group. It should be someone impartial and not so locked into his/her own ideas that he or she cannot see potential merit in the ideas of others,

- Agree in advance that creativity is desirable so no idea brought up at the session will be immediately discarded as impractical or undesirable. (Sometimes impractical or impossible suggestions can "spark" other extremely positive ideas),

• Appoint someone who can capture the essence of what the group agrees to and write it down,

• Equip the room with a flip chart and bring a sufficient number of felt tip markers,

• Bring masking tape and/or thumb tacks for use in tacking up the flip chart pages around the walls of the room as needed and

• Follow an agenda. The one shown on Exhibit I, has been proven very effective.

After the meeting's opening comments, review of the session's procedures, and report on the external environment, you are ready to begin what is perhaps the most important part of the process—S.W.O.T. analysis.

Analysis of Strengths, Weaknesses, Opportunities, and Threats

Here the facilitator divides the flip chart page into two sections by drawing a vertical line down the middle and heading the page as follows:

STRENGTHS & WEAKNESSES
OPPORTUNITY & THREATS

Then the facilitator asks anyone in the room to identify a strength, weakness, opportunity or threat for any area of the company. He or she explains that eventually these areas will be addressed in the goal setting portion of the session.

Each SWOT is written very concisely on the flip chart. Everyone is asked to identify any SWOT's they can think of. The process can be accomplished by starting with one person and going around the room in a clockwise fashion. By announcing this technique, you put everyone on guard that when their turn comes up, a response is expected. This rapidly creates a "charged" atmosphere. No one wants to feel foolish in front of a group, so they will listen carefully to what is said and think hard about a number of possible responses they may use when their turn comes up.

Most companies have several SWOT's designed to impact on their ability to:

• Increase Revenues,

• Improve Financial Condition (Profitability, Liquidity, Solvency, Credit and Collections Policies, Etc.),

• Keep pace with the Competition,

• Improve Efficiency, Productivity and Service,

• Capitalize on Emerging Trends,

• Improve Labor Relations, Human Resource Development and Training (Personnel Issues: Salary Administration, Job Descriptions, Benefits, Personnel Manuals, Etc.),

• Improve Internal Communications,

• Improve Distributor or Supplier Relationships,

• Improve Public Relations, Advertising, Promotions, Etc.,

• Improve or Enhance Products and Services,

• Capitalize on their Physical Facilities (Location, Capacity, Layout, Parking, Costs, Etc.) Improve or Enhance their Insurance Coverage,

• Function at Peak Efficiency with their current Organizational Structure,

• Get the most out of their Present Legal Structure and

• Arrange for the orderly Retirement and Transfer of Ownership and Control of Senior Owners to Junior Owners or Potential Owners

The facilitator should be certain that all SWOT's are recorded on the chart. If someone's description of a SWOT is so complex that it cannot be recorded concisely, ask that person to describe it in no more than five words.

As pages of the flip chart become full, tack them up around the room where everyone can see them. They will be used again later on.

When the facilitator has gone around the room several times and every conceivable SWOT has been identified, the group is ready to attack the next phase of the planning session.

Development of "Mission" Statement

An organization's Mission Statement (usually no more than one or two sentences) describes the purpose of the organization. It is aimed at enabling all members of the organization to share the same view of the company's goals and philosophy.

The mission statement describes the business you are in. It typically speaks to:

- Reason the organization exists,

- Products and services offered,

- Clientele served,

- Nature and geographic marketing territory of the business and

- Areas of specialization

Every organization needs a mission statement and many require one for every business unit that is part of their organization.

The facilitator should lead the group in establishing (or redefining) its mission statement in view of the changes discussed earlier regarding their external environment, and the SWOT's they have discussed.

Let's take a look at some sample Mission Statements—

- "The Johnson Corporation of Ohio is dedicated to maintaining its position as a leader in providing quality insurance and financial service products to businesses and individuals through a staff of highly trained people sharing a tradition of integrity and service to its clients."

- "Budget Travel provides economical vacation travel and related services to customers in the greater Chicago area, who expect efficient, problem-free travel arrangements at a low cost."

- "Our goal is simply stated. We want to be the best service organization in the world."—IBM

- "Whitefield Markets" goal is to be the lowest cost provider of quality foods and groceries in the West Orange area."

- "Velvet Green Nurseries" goal is to provide a full range of high quality wholesale and retail nursery products to professional landscapers and discriminating homeowners."

- "Smith Packing Company's mission is to be the lowest cost producer of pork products in Delaware."

Identification and Analysis of Key Results Areas (KRA's)

The next phase of the planning session is to identify and analyze your company's key results areas. Most companies have from 8–15 key results areas where the organization must achieve success for it to grow and prosper. The company's objective and tactics can be grouped into these key areas, making it easier to process, prioritize, allocate resources, and coordinate with other areas.

The facilitator should lead the group in identifying key results areas for their business. Many of the areas mentioned earlier in the SWOT analysis section of this booklet (Increase Revenues, Improve Financial Condition, etc) will often become the KRA's for a company.

Establish Strategic Objectives

After each Key Results Area is agreed upon, the next phase of the session is to establish strategic objectives for each KRA. Usually there will be one or two strategic objectives for each KRA, but occasionally there can be more. As with all objectives, it is important to make them as quantifiable as possible.

Example:

Key Results Area: Increase Revenues
Strategy Statement: Increase Revenues from new customers, expanded sales to existing customers, acquisition of other related businesses, opening new branches, marketing new products/services, investment income and inflation to achieve:

$_____ in Revenues by Dec. 31, 19_____
$_____ in Revenues by Dec. 31, 19_____
$_____ in Revenues by Dec. 31, 19_____
$_____ in Revenues by Dec. 31, 19_____
$_____ in Revenues by Dec. 31, 19_____

Example:

Key Results Area: Improve Financial Condition
Strategy Statement: Establish and maintain a financial condition sufficient to support planned growth
through achieving liquidity, solvency and profitability as follows:

19_____ 19_____ 19_____ 19_____ 19_____

Liquidity—
Achieve a work-
ing capital posi-
tion of

Solvency—
Achieve net worth
of

Profitability—
Achieve pre tax
profit margins as
follows

Establish Tactical Objectives

After Strategic Objectives are established for each KRA,
you are ready to establish tactical objectives to support each
strategic objective. Eventually you will prioritize these tactical objectives, assign responsibilities and agree to target
dates for completion.

An easy way to do this is to go back to the pages of ideas
from the SWOT analysis (they should still be tacked up on
the walls of the room) and use them to facilitate the process.
Group each idea shown on the SWOT analysis into one of
the Key Results Area categories. For example, say the flip
chart pages identified 12 SWOT's that could either positively or negatively impact on KRA #1 "Increase Revenues."
Use those SWOT's to develop tactics for the Increase

Revenues strategy. Strengths and Opportunities can be
capitalized upon by establishing tactics to get the most
from them.

Weaknesses and Threats can be reduced or eliminated by
establishing tactics to deal with them.

Tactical objectives are specific objectives, usually of a short
term nature, aimed at supporting the strategic objective. For
example, if your strategic objective is to Increase Revenues,
some tactical objectives might be to:

- Produce and market a new product (take advantage
  of an opportunity),

- Develop and market a new service (take advantage of
  an opportunity),

- Identify a specific market you have been successful
  with and develop a target marketing plan to penetrate that market (capitalize on a strength),

- Retain sales staff or replace weak sales staff (correct
  a weakness),

- Revise traffic flow of store or change displays, signs,
  etc. (correct a weakness or capitalize on a strength),

- Change marketing or advertising theme (take advantage of an opportunity),

- Establish a sales campaign with meaningful incen-
  tives (take advantage of an opportunity) or

- Change salary program for sales people from fixed
  salary to variable salary based on their sales (correct
  a weakness)

After you have established tactics to address each SWOT
and have categorized all of the SWOT's, you are ready to
proceed with the next phase of the process.

Integration of Budgeting into Strategic Plan

The strategies and tactics agreed to will impact on revenue
and expenses to differing degrees and at different times,

depending on implementation dates. The group needs to consider the potential impact of each objective on both revenues and expenses so that they can eventually be prioritized and reflected in future budgets.

When this has been completed you are ready to prioritize your objectives.

Prioritizing Objectives, Assigning Responsibilities and Establishing Target Dates

It is important that you resist the temptation to set extremely ambitious target dates for your objectives. In most cases, the tactics you have agreed on need to be accomplished by people who already have a full day's work with no time to spare. Each employee must be given sufficient time to achieve the specific objectives assigned to him or her, or the plan will quickly be viewed as impossible to accomplish and will relegate itself to uselessness.

When assigning a tactic, let the recipient tell the group how long it will take and accept that target date, if at all possible.

After prioritizing all the objectives, assigning responsibilities and agreeing to target dates for each, you are ready to discuss business plan coordination and monitoring.

Business Plan Coordination and Monitoring

For maximum sustained results, an overall coordinator for the Business Plan must be appointed. That person should be responsible for bringing together the various pieces of the business plan into one comprehensive plan and for monitoring the continuing process of following the plan.

Exhibit II displays a suggested format for the Business Plan and Exhibits III and IV are examples of the two primary forms used for recording strategic and tactical objectives.

Exhibit III is completed for each key strategy area. It displays the key strategic objectives and all the supporting tactical objectives. It also provides the name of the person responsible and the agreed upon target date, with a section for comments on the status of each objective.

Exhibit IV is an Individual Objective/Summary Status Report. This form enables the individual to keep track of the status of each objective he or she is responsible for and report monthly to the business plan coordinator.

The monitoring process should be made as simple as possible. Each month, the business plan coordinator collects the updated individual objective summary/status reports from employees and makes certain that all objectives in the plan have been accounted for. He or she makes note of shortfalls, needs for reforecasts or meetings to be called, and documents progress in a brief memo to all business plan recipients. For example:

- "At the end of April, we are on target or ahead of plan in all but 2 tactical objectives. The attached individual objectives status reports describe the status of every objective."

- "Where a shortfall exists, I have highlighted the shortfall and made notation of the actions being taken."

- "Overall we are well on our way towards achieving our major objectives."

When this procedure has been discussed with the group, agreement should be reached on when the written Business Plan should be completed and ready for use.

The method of communicating the content of the plan to all employees should also be discussed.

Why Business Plans Fail

No treatment of this subject would be completed without mention of the fact that some business plans fail—and for good reasons.

The major reasons some fail are:

- Some plans are constructed around incorrectly defined strategies.

• Some do not have detailed implementation plans with tasks, schedules and responsibilities.

• Some plans do not state goals in quantifiable terms.

• In some plans, the process used to develop the plan did not allow all individuals to share a common view of the organization's future and how to get there.

The process described in this booklet is aimed at avoiding these pitfalls and has been proven effective with small businesses.

EXHIBIT I
Strategic Planning Session: Agenda

Dates:

Location:

Facilitator:

Scribe:

Day I

TIME	TOPIC	RESPONSIBILITY
8:00–8:05	Opening Comments	President
8:05–8:15	Review Agenda Review Procedures for Session Review Roles of Facilitator and Scribe	Facilitator
8:15–8:30	Review completed analysis of External Environment	Preparer of Analysis
8:30–10:00	*SWOT Analysis Part I* Round table discussion aimed at identifying and documenting on the flip chart, all of the company's Strengths, Opportunities, Weaknesses and Threats	Facilitator and Group
10:00–10:15	Coffee Break	
10:15–12:00	*SWOT Analysis—Part II* Continuance of SWOT analysis	Facilitator and Group
12:00–12:45	Lunch	
12:45–2:30	Develop or redefine "Mission Statement" for organization (statement of purpose)	Facilitator and Group

2:30–2:45	Coffee and soft drink break	
2:45–3:30	Analysis and identification of Key Results Areas (areas in which the company must achieve significant results in order to achieve the kind of revenues and profits desired)	Facilitator and Group
3:30–5:00	Establish Strategic Objectives Within each Key Results Area establish a small number of strategic objectives (objectives that are descriptive of a condition you want to achieve)	Facilitator and Group
5:00–6:30	Dinner	

Day II

8:00–8:05	Opening Comments	President
8:05–8:15	Review of where group left off	Facilitator
8:15–10:00	Establishing Tactical Objectives to address SWOT's—Part I	Facilitator and Group
10:00–10:15	Coffee Break	
10:15–12:00	Establishing Tactical Objectives to address SWOT's—Part II	Facilitator and Group
12:00–12:45	Lunch	
12:45–1:45	Integration of Budgeting Process into the strategic plan	Facilitator and Group
1:45–2:00	Coffee and soft drink break	
2:00–4:00	Prioritizing objectives, assignment of responsibilities and establishment of target dates	Facilitator and Group
4:00–4:30	Discussion of Business Plan Coordination and Monitoring (Includes discussion of Business Plan format and appointment of Business Plan Coordinator who will handle monitoring and keep everyone advised when shortfalls or reforecast situations arise.)	Facilitator and Group
4:30–4:45	Agreement on timing of written report and method of communicating the plan to all employees of the organization	Facilitator and Group
4:45–5:00	Closing Comments	President

EXHIBIT II
Business Plan Format

• Cover

• Table of Contents

• Mission Statement

•Summary of Key Strategies

• Objectives, Responsibilities and Targets

  –For (enter Key Strategy Area #1)

  –For (enter Key Strategy Area #2)

  –For (enter Key Strategy Area #3)

  –For (enter Key Strategy Area #4)

  –For (enter Key Strategy Area #5)

  –For (enter Key Strategy Area #6)

  –For (enter Key Strategy Area #7)

  –For (enter Key Strategy Area #8)

  –For (enter Key Strategy Area #9)

  –For (enter Key Strategy Area #10)

  –For (enter Key Strategy Area #11)

  –For (enter Key Strategy Area #12)

• Individual Objectives Summaries/Status Reports

  –For (enter Employee's Name)

  –For (enter Employee's Name)

  –For (enter Employee's Name)

  –For (enter Employee's Name)

  –For (enter Employee's Name)

  –For (enter Employee's Name)

  –For (enter Employee's Name)

  –For (enter Employee's Name)

EXHIBIT III

Objectives/Responsibilities & Targets

Key Strategy Area:

Strategy Statement:

TACTICAL OBJECTIVES	RESPONSIBILITY	TARGET DATE	STATUS

EXHIBIT IV

<u>Individual Objectives Summary/Status Report for   (Employee)</u>

TACTICAL OBJECTIVES	KEY STRATEGY AREA	TARGET DATE	STATUS

SUMMARY

This *Aid* provides an overview of business owners' life insurance needs that typically are not considered until after the death of one of the business' principal owners or shareholders. It has specific alternatives for your consideration when planning for the future of your business. It outlines how business life insurance applies to various business situations. Additionally, this *Aid* demonstrates the benefits of the insurance for the surviving heirs and the estate of a deceased owner, as well as its being a means of paying retirement income and insurance premiun during the owner's life.

Life insurance can provide significant amounts of cash to help employees and family members cushion the financial impact of the death or retirement of the owner-manager of a sole proprietorship, partnership or a closely-held corporation. It can also help attract and retain valuable employees.

This brochure discusses life insurance needs of small business owners and how business life insurance applies to their situations.

The small business owner usually depends on the business as the source of family income, a personal investment vehicle and the major portion of his/her estate. Generally, many of the assets of the sole proprietor, partner or close corporation stockholder are tied up in the business. So, if it fails, financial hardships may well follow unless certain steps are taken.

The personal insurance needs of the business owner are closely related to his/her business interest. The business can provide a portion of the cash needed by surviving heirs and the estate of a deceased owner, as well as a means of paying retirement income and insurance premiums during the owner's lifetime.

Problems at Death of a Sole Proprietor

The personal skills, reputation, and management ability of the sole proprietor help to make the business successful. Without these human life values the business is worth only the liquidation value of the tangible assets.

The sole proprietor's personal and business assets are one and the same. When death occurs, the loss can become a financial disaster to the proprietor's estate and fatal to the business. The business which was producing a good living for the owner and family would become a defunct business. Once representing the major portion of the sole proprietor's estate, the family is left with only the auction price value of the business.

Possible Actions

Family continuation of the business

The business may be transferred to a capable family member as a gift through provisions in the proprietor's will or by a sale provided through a prearranged purchase agreement effective at death.

Cash is needed to offset losses to the business caused by the owner's death, to equalize the value of bequests made to other family members if the transfer is a gift, and to provide the sale price if the transfer is through sale.

New owner

If the buyer is a key employee, competitor, or other person, the business may be transferred at death, pursuant to a prearranged sale agreement.

However, cash is needed to provide a "business continuation fund" to meet expenses and perhaps to offset losses until the business adjusts to the new management.

Liquidation

If future management is not available, then the business must be liquidated.

Cash is needed to offset the difference between the business' going-concern value and its auction-block liquidation value to provide a fund for income replacement to the family and to pay outstanding business debts.

The least expensive and only sure way to provide the cash at the instant it is needed is through life insurance on the sole proprietor's life.

Sole Proprietor's Life Insurance Plan

Family continuation of the business

Life insurance:

Insured: the sole proprietor.

Applicant and owner: usually the sole proprietor but sometimes a beneficiary who has funds to pay the premium.

Beneficiary: those for whom the insurance proceeds are intended: the new owner (for the insurance to provide the business "shock fund" and sale price), family members (for the insurance to provide the equalization fund).

Sole proprietor's will: If the family member is to receive the business as a gift, this should be provided for in the will. Distribution in the will to other heirs may also be provided, keeping in mind any other life insurance proceeds they may receive.

Family buy-out: A binding buy and sell agreement, funded with life insurance, entered into by the sole proprietor and purchasing heir.

New Owner

Life insurance:

Insured: the sole proprietor.

Applicant and owner: the buyer.

Beneficiary: the buyer.

Buy-out agreement: A binding buy and sell agreement, funded with life insurance, should be entered into by the sole proprietor and the purchaser. Because a sole proprietorship is not a separate legal entity, the business assets may be titled in the sole proprietor's name, or jointly with his/her spouse. The business property should therefore be specifically described in the agreement, and the document signed by the spouse, the sole proprietor, and the purchaser.

Sole proprietor's will: The executor of the estate should be bound to sell the business to the named buyer and, when payment is received, directed to cooperate with the purchaser to effectuate the transfer of the business assets.

Liquidation

Life insurance:

Insured: the sole proprietor.

Applicant and owner: usually the sole proprietor but sometimes the spouse or other heir who pays the premiums.

Beneficiary: those for whom the insurance proceeds are intended.

Sole proprietor's will: The executor of the estate should be authorized to liquidate the business.

Problems at Death of a Partner

Unless there is a written agreement to the contrary, the death of a partner automatically dissolves the firm.

In the absence of an agreement to the contrary, surviving partners have no right to buy the deceased's partnership interest.

• Surviving partners cannot assume the goodwill or take over the assets without consent of the deceased's estate.

• If the deceased was in debt to the partnership, the estate must settle the account in full and in cash.

The surviving partners act as liquidating trustees.

• They have exclusive possession of firm property but no right to carry on the business. If the business is continued, the surviving partners must share all profits with the deceased's estate and are liable for all losses.

• They must convert everything into cash at the best price obtainable.

• They must make an accounting to the deceased's estate and divide the proceeds with the estate.

• They must liquidate themselves out of their business and income.

Possible Actions

Liquidation, arranged after death

If the surviving partner and deceased's heirs do nothing, the business is liquidated, resulting in "auction price" value for the salable assets. It may receive nothing for goodwill. This is a disastrous solution for both the dead partner's family and the surviving partners. It means termination of jobs for the surviving partners and employees.

Reorganization, arranged after death

The surviving partners may attempt to reorganize the partnership by:

• Taking the heirs into the partnership. But if heirs are incapable of working, the survivors must do all the work and share the profits.

• Accepting a new partner picked by heirs. But that person may lack ability or be unacceptable to the survivor(s). Also, the heirs may not receive a "going concern" value for their interest.

• Selling the surviving partner(s') interest to the heirs. It may take time to agree on a price and the heirs may have difficulty raising the funds. Also, besides being unemployed, the surviving partner(s) may have to accept poorly secured installment payments.

• Buying out the heirs. For both parties, agreeing on a fair price after a partner's death and making certain funds are available to consummate the deal present difficulties.

Reorganization, arranged before death

Buy and sell agreements

Buy and sell agreements funded with life insurance should be entered into while all partners are alive.

Determine the funding medium by applying for the insurance before the buy and sell agreement is finalized; the availability and price of life insurance can be determined as well as whether some other method of funding will be necessary.

The partners should be able to make a fairly accurate estimate of the value of the partnership, so proper amounts of insurance can be requested. The amount of the insurance proceeds often serves as the minimum purchase price or the amount of the down payment, if less than the full purchase price.

Each partner may be the applicant, owner and beneficiary of insurance on the life of each of the other associates. Or the partnership, as an entity, may be the applicant, owner and beneficiary of insurance on the lives of each partner.

Before the buy and sell agreement is in final form, have an accountant help you determine the current value of each partner's interest and how its value is to be reestablished from time to time.

Enter into a binding buy and sell agreement

Have an attorney draft the agreement which typically will include:

- A commitment by each partner not to dispose of the interest during his/her lifetime without first offering it at the agreed sale price to an associate (or directly to the partnership).

- A commitment by each associate (or the partnership) to buy a deceased's interest, and to bind each partner's own estate to sell at death.

- A commitment as to the purchase price (or a means of determining the price) and method of making the payment(s).

- A commitment as to the method of funding the agreed purchase price.

Partners' Life Insurance Plan

Life insurance:

Insured: each partner.

Applicant and owner: the buyer(s) of the partnership interest (co-partners or the partnership itself).

Beneficiary: the buyer(s) of the partnership interest (co-partners or the partnership itself).

Problems at Death of a Stockholder

The death of a stockholder who has been active in the operation of a closely-held corporation allows the business entity to continue its *legal* structure, but not its *personal* structure. The interests of the heirs of the deceased inevitably come in conflict with the interests of the surviving associates.

Surviving stockholders want business growth through reinvestment of profits. They continue to receive income through tax-deductible salaries and employee fringe benefits. The deceased's family wants immediate withdrawal of profits to provide continuing income, through non-deductible dividends.

Possible Solutions

Retention of stock by the heirs

The deceased's family may retain the stock interest. If the heirs have a majority interest, they may choose to become personally involved in management in order to receive income. Or, they may choose to remain inactive, elect a new board of directors and force the company to pay dividends.

In either case, the surviving stockholders may lose a voice in management and possibly their jobs, while the deceased's family may become heirs to a business on the brink of failure.

If the heirs have a minority interest and are not employed by the surviving associates, their only means of receiving an income from the corporation will be through dividends. But, the surviving stockholders can not afford to have much, if anything, paid as "double-taxed" dividends. This will result in a dissatisfied group of minority stockholders, who may become an intolerable nuisance factor.

Sale of stock by the heirs, arranged after death

After the death of a stockholder, the deceased's family or estate may offer to sell the stock interest to the surviving stockholders. The price the family thinks is reasonable may be exorbitant to the other stockholders.

Even if they can agree on a price, the buyers may have neither available cash nor the ability borrow the needed funds. Thus, the deceased's heirs may have to accept installment payments.

An outside buyer may be interested only in a majority interest. Any purchase offer of a minority interest will likely be less than the proportionate full value of the business as a "going concern."

The heirs may end up with less than the fair price, and the surviving stockholders may have a new associate who may be neither a capable employee nor a compatible member of the management team.

Sale of stock by the heirs, arranged before death

While all interested parties are alive, they can enter into a binding buy and sell agreement funded with life insurance.

When a death occurs:

- The deceased's heirs immediately receive a fair price in cash for the deceased's interest in the corporation.

- The surviving stockholders immediately have the cash to pay the agreed price and become sole owners of the business.

- Both parties benefit equally under the plan.

Stockholder's buy and sell agreement

Determine the funding medium:

Life insurance is the least expensive and only sure means of immediately guaranteeing cash when needed at the time of death. It should be applied for on the life of each stockholder. The amount can be determined by agreement of the associates as to the value of the business.

Applications should be submitted immediately so the availability and price of life insurance can be known prior to the attorney's drafting of the purchase and sale agreement.

The applicant, owner and beneficiary of a policy on the life of a stockholder should be the purchaser of that stockholder's stock. When few stockholders are involved, each may agree to purchase a pro-rata portion of the stock owned by each of the other shareholders. Or they may prefer to have the corporation be the purchaser of a deceased's entire stock interest. (Caution—If the stockholders are members of the same primary family group, other than brothers and sisters, careful legal and tax counseling is necessary to avoid adverse tax consequences if the corporation is to be the purchaser.)

Establish the purchase price

An accountant and/or lawyer can assist the stockholders in establishing fair and equitable current values and a means of determining how these valuations should be adjusted in the future.

These values must be determined prior to completion of the buy and sell agreement. If they are not in line with the amounts of life insurance which have been purchased, changes may have to be made to the insurance.

Enter into a binding buy and sell agreement

A lawyer will advise the stockholders whether to choose a cross purchase or a stock redemption plan and will prepare the necessary agreements. Under a cross purchase plan, each stockholder agrees to purchase a portion of an associate's stock interest. Under a stock redemption plan, the corporation agrees to purchase each stockholder's interest.

The provisions of a typical agreement to purchase stock of a close corporation generally include:

- A commitment by each stockholder not to dispose of the stock interest during his/her lifetime without first offering it, at the agreed sale price, to an associate, or to the corporation itself.

- A commitment by each stockholder (or the corporation) to buy the shares of a deceased stockholder and to bind his/her own estate to sell at death.

- A commitment as to the purchase price (or a means of determining the price) and method of making the payment(s).

- A commitment as to the method of funding the agreed purchases.

Stockholder's Life Insurance Plan

Life insurance:

Insured: each stockholder.

Applicant and owner: the buyer(s) of the stock (the co-stockholder(s) or the corporation).

Beneficiary: the buyer(s) of the stock (the co-stockholder(s) or the corporation).

Key Employee Insurance

Fire losses to buildings, or equipment breakdowns, may never occur, are seldom total, and usually can be repaired or replaced. Death loss is always total, and only people can replace people.

How to Offset the Loss of a Key Employee

It is impossible to provide an exact replacement of a deceased key person. The most effective offset to the value of the lost services is CASH, immediately available to the business.

- To offset losses during the readjustment period and keep it running.
- To retain good credit standing.
- To assure customers and suppliers that the company will continue as usual.
- To retire loans, mortgages, bonds, etc.
- To attract and train a successor.
- To continue paying salaries.
- To carry out ongoing plans for expansion and new developments.

Life insurance is the most economical and effective means of providing cash because:

- during life, the cash values constitute an increasing liquid tax-sheltered reserve, available to help meet any financial need of the business.
- at death, the full cash proceeds are immediately available. These funds are received completely free of income tax, even though the proceeds normally exceed the premiums by a substantial amount.

Key Employee Life Insurance Plan

There is no set formula to establish the value of each key individual. However, the following are some general guidelines:

- The capitalized value of that portion of the company's profits attributable to such person.
- The costs of replacing the key employee.
- Two to five times the key person's annual salary.

The business (employer, if a Sole Proprietorship) is the applicant, owner and beneficiary of an insurance policy on the life of the key individual. No form of agreement is necessary between the business and key employee except the individual's consent to be insured, evidenced by signing the application. Thus, the business has complete flexibility to use the policy: the cash values during life, the proceeds after death.

Though the primary purpose for the insurance is to indemnify the business for its loss of the key worker's human life value at death, the policy may also:

- Provide funds for sudden emergencies or unexpected opportunities.
- Bolster the credit standing of the company.
- Serve as collateral for confidential policy loans at a guaranteed interest rate.
- Provide funds which the corporation could use for the insured's retirement or for the family if the key person dies.

Life insurance:

Insured: the key person.

Applicant and owner: the employer.

Beneficiary: the employer.

Deferred Supplemental Compensation

A non-qualified Deferred Compensation Plan is an agreement made by an employer, backed by the good faith and credit of the concern, to pay an employee amounts at a date specified in the future in lieu of current salary increases which would be subject to current income tax or supplemental to normal salary. Payments normally commence at the employee's retirement but also may be made if the employee becomes disabled or dies. In consideration of such promised payments, the employee usually agrees to continue employment until retirement, and during retirement to be available as a consultant to the firm and refrain from competitive activity.

Deferred Supplemental Compensation Plan

The employer and employee enter into a written contract prepared by an attorney.

The employer generally agrees:

- To employ the executive at an agreed-upon current salary rate.

- To pay the employee a specified additional deferred salary for a certain number of years or lifetime, commencing at a stated retirement date, or in the event of preretirement, death or disability.

- To continue payments to the employee's beneficiary for a certain number of years if death occurs after retirement, but before receipt of all stipulated payments.

- To pay a death benefit (specified single sum or installment payments) to the spouse, if the executive dies before retirement.

- To pay the executive a certain salary for an agreed-upon period of time in event of total disability prior to retirement (normally funded through a Disability Income policy).

The executive generally agrees:

- To remain in the employ of the business for an agreed-upon number of years.

- To provide the company with occasional consulting or advising services during retirement.

- To refrain from providing service to any competitor during retirement.

A life insurance policy assures the company of the funds it will need to pay the promised benefits. The life of the executive is insured for an amount at least sufficient to provide the business with its deductible after-tax cost of the death or retirement payments. The business is the applicant, owner and beneficiary of the *life* insurance policy.

A *disability* income policy for the appropriate amount is provided to the employee with premiums paid by the employer.

Income Tax Aspects of the Deferred Compensation Plan

Premium payments made by the business for the life insurance policy are *not* deductible; disability income insurance premiums *are* deductible.

The employee incurs no current income tax on the amount of compensation deferred nor on the employer's premium payments for the insurance policies.

The cash value of the life policy accrues tax free to the business.

Proceeds of the life policy are received tax free by the business at the death of the insured. Benefits under the *disability* income policy are tax-reportable by the employee when and as received.

Deferred Compensation benefits for normal retirement or death are deductible by the business as they are paid to the employee or the employee's beneficiaries. Retirement and/or death benefits are taxable to the recipient only when and as received (usually at a lower rate than that of the employee prior to retirement or death). Disability benefits are paid directly to the employee by the insurance company, hence are not deductible by the employer. (Instead, the premium payments are deductible.)

Life Insurance:	Disability Income Insurance:
Insured: the employee	the employee
Applicant and owner: the employer	the employee
Beneficiary: the employer	the employee

Family Death Benefit

This is a plan under which an employer agrees to make one or more payments, at the death of a key employee (usually if death occurs during active employment), to the deceased's family (usually the surviving spouse and/or children). In effect, it is a supplemental compensation plan which offers no retirement or disability payments for the employee, but instead defers all payments until after the employee's death. It is often called a Death Benefit Only (DBO) plan.

Death Benefit Only Plan

One or more employees are selected to participate in the plan. The employer offers the plan to each selected person, individually.

Usually, a plan provides a continuation of a specified portion of the employee's salary for a specified number of years, in event of the employee's death prior to retirement. If desired, the death benefit can be made in installments or in one sum. Moreover, benefits may be payable whenever death occurs, during active employment or retirement.

The employee agrees to be the insured in a life insurance policy owned and paid for by the employer. The amount of insurance purchased is at least equal to the employer's after-tax deductible cost of the death benefit payments. In

most plans, the life insurance equals or exceeds the employer's total before-tax payments to the employee's family, thus providing sufficient tax free funds to cover not only the tax deductible payments to the family but most or all of the premiums paid for the insurance, and to allow for benefit increases that are tied to salary increases.

Income Tax Aspects of the Plan

- premium payments made by the employer are not a deductible business expense.
- The insured employee incurs no income tax as a result of the plan.
- Policy cash value increases are accrued tax free to the employer-owner of the policy.
- The policy death proceeds are received free of income tax by the employer-beneficiary.

Payments made by the employer to the deceased's family are deductible as paid (so long as they are not unusually generous if paid to the families of substantial stockholder-employees).

The benefits are included as taxable income of the recipient as received. (Usually, the deceased's spouse is in a relatively low tax bracket and the payments are made over a period of several years to reduce the income tax which would otherwise result if the total payment were received in one sum.)

Life Insurance:

Insured: the employee.

Applicant and owner: the employer.

Beneficiary: the employer.

Split Dollar

Split dollar insurance is an attractive plan for any employee needing assistance in paying life insurance premiums and for employers who wish to provide, at little or no cost, a fringe benefit to selected employees.

A split dollar life insurance plan provides an employer with the advantages of an employee benefit plan by being:

- Made available to those key employees individually selected by the employer, thus increasing the attractiveness of employment and reducing turnover.

- Tailored to the individual needs of each participant according to the employer's desires.

- Started, continued and discontinued with no government approval required.

- A tax-sheltered accumulating fund (the policy cash values) which is available for business needs and emergencies.

- One of very few fringe benefit plans under which a large part or all of the employer's costs are recovered.

The split dollar method of paying for life insurance is very attractive to selected (including stockholder-employee) participants because it:

- Provides a substantial amount of insurance at a lower cost than if paid for from personal after-tax income.

- Can become a self-completing plan in event of disability, through the addition of the waiver of premium provision.

- Allows the insured to acquire the entire life insurance policy in event of plan or employee termination prior to death.

- Can be arranged so the proceeds are not included in the insured's taxable estate at death. (Special provisions may be required if the insured is the majority stockholder of a corporation.)

- Can be expanded, at the employer's option, into a plan which provides deductible retirement benefits.

Split Dollar Plan

Because of the substantial amounts that may be involved, it is preferable to spell out the rights and obligations of the employer, employee and beneficiary in writing.

There are two basic systems of arranging split dollar life insurance policies:

- **Collateral Assignment Method.** The *insured* (or sometimes a third party spouse, child or trust) applies for, owns, pays the premiums, and names the beneficiary of the life insurance policy. Part (or often all) of the premiums is loaned to the insured (or other policy owner) by the employer.

  The policy owner (normally the insured employee) collaterally assigns the policy to the employer as security for the premium amounts advanced by the employer.

- **Endorsement Method.** The *employer* applies for, owns, and pays the premiums of the life insurance policy, and the employee (or sometimes a third party) pays to the employer an agreed upon portion of the premium, if any.

  The employer is the beneficiary of an agreed upon portion of the death proceeds (usually the total employer contributions or—if greater—the cash value) and the other party to the agreement (usually the insured employee, but sometimes a third party) has the right to designate a beneficiary for the balance.

  The employer and selected employee determine the form and amount of insurance, plus the split of premium payments and split of death benefit. The insurance is applied for and the employee provides evidence of his/her insurability. The split dollar agreement is signed by both parties. (If the collateral assignment method is used, the policy owner signs a collateral assignment and promissory notes to the employer for the amount of premium advances).

Income Tax Aspects of the Plan

In the case of employer-employee related split dollar plans, the employer's premium contributions are not a deductible expense, but the proceeds paid at death to the business are received free of income tax. The employee receives a current taxable economic benefit from the plan. This economic benefit is the annual value of the employee's death benefit, measured by the term cost of the protection, reduced by any employee premium payment. The death proceeds paid to the employee's beneficiary are received income tax free.

Life Insurance:

Party:	Collateral Assignment	Endorsement
Insured:	the employee.	the employee.
Applicant and owner:	the employee (or third party).	the employer.
Premium payer:	the employee (or third party) with loans from the employer.	the employer with contributions from employee (or third party).
Beneficiary:	the employer of a predetermined portion; the employee's (or third party's) beneficiary for the balance.	

Selective Protection (Bonus) Plan

A Selective Protection Plan is an informal employee benefit arrangement between an employer and one or more selected employees. The employer pays part or all of the premiums for a life insurance policy written on the life of the employee. The insured employee has all ownership rights to the contract. No government approval is required. The employer decides who is to be included and what insurance benefits are to be provided. Each payment, as made by the employer to the plan, is fully tax deductible as a business expense.

Income Tax Aspects of the Plan

- Premiums paid by the employer are deducted, for income tax purposes, as a regular business expense.

- The employee's reportable income is increased by the amount of the employer's premium contribution, similar to cash bonus. Thus, the employee's cost is the income tax on the employer's premium payments, plus any additional premiums paid by the employee.

- Cash value increases of the policy are not subject to current income tax, even though they are owned by and available to the employee.

- Death benefits paid to an employee's beneficiary are received free of income tax.

- Policy proceeds withdrawn by the employee during life are received income tax free to the extent of total premiums paid (both the employer's and any employee premiums).

Life insurance:

Insured: the employee.

Applicant and owner: the employee.

Beneficiary: as selected by the employee.

Premium payer: employer alone or employer and employee. As with any transaction involving legal or tax considerations, no irrevocable steps should be taken without legal, tax and insurance counsel.

Part III
Specific Business Plans

Business Plan for Small Construction Firms
SBA Staff Members
Office of Management Assistance

Business Plan for Small Manufacturers
SBA Staff Members
Office of Management Assistance

Business Plan for Small Service Firms
SBA Staff Members
Office of Management Assistance

Business Plan for Retailers
SBA Staff Members
Office of Management Assistance

Summary

A business plan can provide the owner-manager or prospective owner-manager of a small construction firm with a pathway to profit. This *Aid* is designed to help an owner-manager in drawing up a business plan.

In building a pathway to profit you need to consider the following questions: What business am I in? What do I sell? Where is my market? Who will buy? Who is my competition? What is my sales strategy? How much money is needed to operate my firm? How will I get the work done? What management controls are needed? How can they be carried out? When should I revise my plan? Where can I go for help?

No one can answer such questions for you. As the owner-manager you have to answer them and draw up *your* business plan. The pages of this *Aid* are a combination of text and workspaces so you can write in the information you gather in developing *your* business plan—a logical progression from a commonsense starting point to a commonsense ending point.

A Note On Using This Aid

It takes time and energy and patience to draw up a satisfactory business plan. Use this *Aid* to get your ideas and the supporting facts down on paper. And, above all, make changes in your plan on these pages as that plan unfolds and you see the need for changes.

Bear in mind that anything you leave out of the picture will create an additional cost, or drain on your money, when it unexpectedly crops up later on. If you leave out or ignore too many items, your business is headed for disaster.

Keep in mind, too, that your final goal is to put your plan into action. More will be said about this step near the end of this *Aid*.

What's In This For Me?

The hammer, trowel, pliers, and wrench are well known tools of the construction industry. They have their various uses and are needed to get the work done. Management is another tool that the owner-manager of a construction firm must use. Each job must be planned and organized if the firm is to run smoothly and efficiently. The business plan will help you increase your skill as a manager.

Because of the diversification in the construction industry, you may be engaged in residential, commercial, or industrial construction. You may be either a general or specialty contractor. But, the same basic managerial skills are needed. This plan will serve as a guide to the various areas that you as a manager will be concerned with. As you work through this plan, adapt it to your own particular needs.

When complete, your business plan will help guide your daily business activities. When you know where you want to go, it is easier to plan what you must do to get there. Also, the business plan can serve as a communications device which will orient key employees, suppliers, bankers, and whoever else needs to know about your goals and your operations.

Whether you are just thinking about starting your own firm or have already started, the business plan can help you. As your skill as a manager increases so will the number of jobs you can effectively control. The careful completion of this plan may point out your limitations. This is important. To be a successful contractor you must not only know your business thoroughly, but must also know your limitations and seek professional advice in these areas.

Why Am I In Business?

Most contractors are in business to make money and be their own boss. Very important reasons. But, don't forget, no one is likely to stay in business unless you also satisfy a consumer need at a competitive price. Profit is the reward for satisfying consumer needs in a competitive economy.

In the first years of business, your profits may seem like a small return for the long hours, hard work, and responsibility of being the boss. But there are other rewards associated with having your own business. For example, you may find satisfaction in helping to put groceries on your employees' tables. Or, maybe your satisfaction will come from building a business you can pass on to your children.

Why are you in business? _____

_____

_____

What Business Am I In?

At first glance this may seem like a rather silly question. You may say, "If there is one thing I'm sure of, it's what business I'm in." But wait. Let's look further into the question. Suppose you say, "I build houses." Are you a speculative or custom builder? Are you a remodeler? Are you a subcontractor? Can you schedule a complete job and make money? By planning according to this decision, you should realize the value of this type of thinking in dollars.

Consider this example. Bob Rogers* started a small construction business shortly after World War II. Because of Mr. Rogers' skill and talent for design, he directed all his activity toward building taverns. There was enough call for this type of building to keep him and his crew busy until the early 60's. Then sales began to fall off.

By moving his shop to smaller quarter with less overhead and by laying off half his crew, he was able to maintain his business to his satisfaction the rest of his life. After his death, his son examined the situation and decided that he wasn't really in the business of building commercial bars. He was in the business of custom finishing.

Today his business is prospering. He is building cabinets and small bars for private homes. His company also does other finishing work which requires the craftsmanship his crew is capable of.
In the space below, state what business you're really in.

_____

_____

What are your reasons for this opinion? _____

_____

_____

Marketing

When you have decided what sort of construction business you're really in, you have made your first marketing decision. Now, in order to sell your service or product, you must face other marketing decisions.

Your marketing objective is to find enough jobs at the right times to provide a *profitable continuity* for your business. Your job starts must be coordinated to eliminate the down time between jobs. In other words, you want to get enough jobs, starting at the right times, to keep from being broke between jobs.

Unless an individual can come up with enough ideas to keep a crew working 12 months a year, maybe he or she is not ready for a construction business.

*All names in *Aids* are fictitious.

Where Is Your Market?

Describe your market area in terms of customer profile (age, school needs, income, and so on) and geography. For example, if you are a custom builder, you may decide to build homes in the $80,000 to $130,000 price range. This would mean that your customers will have to have incomes in the middle to upper-middle class ranges. You may also decide that you can profitable build these homes on the owner's lot if it is located within a radius of 30 miles from your office. (The significance of a customer profile is that it will help you narrow your advertising to those media that will reach the potential customer you have profiled.) In the space below describe your market in terms of customer profile and geography.

My Product   Types of Customers   Location of Customers

_____   _____   _____

_____   _____   _____

Now that you have described what you want in terms of customer and location, what is it about your operation that will make these people want to buy your service? For instance, quality work, competitive prices, guaranteed completion dates, effective advertising, unique design, and so on.

Write your answer here. _____

_____

_____

Advertising

You have determined what it is you're marketing, who is going to buy it, and why they're going to buy it. Now you have to decide on the best way to tell your prospective customers about your product.

What should your advertising tell prospective customers? _____

_____

What form should your advertising take? Ask the local media (newspapers, radio and television stations, and printers of direct mail pieces) for information about their services and the results they offer for your money.

How you spend advertising money is your decision, but don't fall into the trap that snares many advertisers. As one consultant describes this pitfall: It is amazing the way many business managers consider themselves experts on advertising copy and media selection without any experience in these areas.

The following workblock should be useful in determining what advertising is needed to sell your construction service.

Form of Advertising	Size of Audience	Frequency of Use	Cost of A single ad	Estimated Cost
_____	_____	_____	x $ _____	= $ _____
_____	_____	_____	x $ _____	= $ _____
_____	_____	_____	x $ _____	= $ _____
_____	_____	_____	x $ _____	= $ _____
			Total $	_____

Competition

The competition in the construction industry often results in low profit margins. However, if you are just starting or are a relatively small firm, this does not put you at a disadvantage. The smaller firm can often compete with the bigger outfit because of lower overhead expense. For example, your office may be in your home, saving that expense. You can often work right out of your truck, saving the expense of a field office.

Competition is largely price competition, although a good reputation for quality and efficiency is beneficial. But, the result of any competition is a high failure rate for poor planners and poor performers. This points out the need for careful planning, particulary in the areas of estimating and bidding.

In order to see what you are up against competition-wise, answer the following questions so you can plan accordingly.

Who will be your major competitors?_____

_____

How will you compete against them?_____

_____

Sales Strategy

The market for the construction industry is unique in many ways. As a contractor you will find your market to be dependent on such variables as the state of the economy, local employment stability, the seasonality of the work, labor relations, good subcontractors and interest rates. Also, as a contractor, you will find that you are unavoidably dependent on others, such as customers or financing institutions for payment, and other contractors for performance of their work. You will also want to take your cash flow into consideration when you estimate and bid on a job. The money must come in time to meet your own obligations.

Estimating

Whether an owner-manager in the construction business succeeds—makes a profit or not—depends to a great extent on bidding practices. Therefore, you must make careful and complete estimates.

Many of the more successful contractors attribute their success to their estimating procedures. They build the job on paper before they submit a bid. In doing this, they break the job down into work units and pieces of material. Then, they assign a cost to each item. The total of these costs will be the direct construction cost. You must also figure on the indirect costs of a job. For instance, you will have overhead expenses such as the cost of maintaining your office, trucks, license fees, and so on. The estimate should also consider any interest charges you will pay on money you borrow to get the job under way. You have insurance fees to pay, surety bond premiums, travel expenses, advertising costs, office salaries, lawyer's fees, and so on. These must also be paid out of your gross income.

Trade associations, as one of their services, often provide their members with a package of business forms. The cost estimate form would be included in this package. The obvious advantage in using these forms is that they are specifically designed for the particular trade.

Regardless of what estimate form you use, it should include such headings as "activity," "material," "labor," "subcontracts," and "estimated cost." And it should have areas for direct construction costs, indirect construction costs, overhead, and profit.

In addition, a column for the actual cost compared to the estimated cost of a specific work item will make this form an invaluable record. Here you would have a handy reference to evaluate the profitability of a job after it is complete. It would show you where your estimate was high or low, and enable you to adjust future bids on similar projects. This added column will also be necessary when it comes time for your financial accounting.

Bidding

Your decision to bid or not to bid on a particular job should be determined by several factors. First, do you have the capacity to complete the job on schedule and according to specifications. Beware of overextending yourself out of business. You have to operate within your known capabilities. On any job, you must follow all the details of the work yourself, or find competent supervision.

Bonding

The practice of bonding has been a traditional way of life for anyone engaged in contract construction. Bonding companies provide bonds for a certain percentage of the contract price. There are three main types of bonds:

(1) Bid bonds assure that the bidder is prepared to perform the work according to the terms of the contract if successful in the bid.

(2) Performance bonds assure completion of the job according to plans and specifications.

(3) Payment bonds assure anyone dealing with the bonded contractor that they will be paid.

The effect that bonding companies have had on contractors is evident in the area of competition. The customer, by requiring that the contractor is bonded, is more or less assured of adequate completion of the job. Therefore, contractors are compared on a basis of price. Also, banks are often more lenient to bonded contractors.

Bonding companies usually require the contractor to have proven experience and the organizational financial capacity to complete the project. This can be a real stumbing block to the new construction firm.

With the widespread use of bonding requirements, the competition that is generated often leads the inexperienced contractor to submit bids that are unrealistically low. One or two such mistakes often can spell bankruptcy.

Will you need bonding _____ often, _____ occasionally, _____ seldom?

Where will you get your bond?_____
_____

What will the terms be? _____
_____

The Small Business Administration has a surety bond program designed to help small and emerging contractors who might have previously been unable to get bonding. SBA is authorized to guarantee up to 90 percent of losses incurred under bid, payment, or performance bonds on contracts up to $500,000. Application for this assistance is available from any SBA field office.

Planning the Work

When your marketing efforts result in jobs to be done, the problem becomes one of production. How will you plan the work so that the job gets done on time?

No matter how you plan the work, your plan should assist you in two specific ways: (1) it should help you maintain your production schedule, and (2) it should allow you to adjust production to meet changed conditions, such as bad weather.

In planning the work, keep in mind two things: (1) the timing of starts, and (2) the timing of the various steps in the construction of your company. If you have sufficient help and sufficient supervisory personnel, it will be possible for you to engage in as many projects as you can *control*. The size and nature of the job must be considered here also.

The timing of the steps of constructions (the work scheduling) will show the various operations in sequence and assign a working day designation to each with a space for the calendar day designation. Several operations may be in progress simultaneously. Such a work schedule will show at a glance whether the work is progressing at the right time. Many companies offer commercial scheduling boards designed for this purpose.

Below is a partial work schedule to demonstrate how yours may be set up. Note that there is a column that can be filled in with either a solid mark or an "X" to indicate either partial or completed work. When you look at a particular calendar day, an "X" next to it would indicate that you're on schedule. An open square indicates a delay. Here, then, is a convenient way to see trouble spots that are causing delays and it gives you an opportunity to take corrective action.

Working Day

Activity	Start	Finish	Calendar Day	Complete
1. Layout	1	1	15	⊠
2. Foundation Forms	1	2	16	⊠
3. Foundation Pour	3	3	19	◩

(indicates ¾ complete)

You should save your work schedules. They will form the basis for future estimates. For example, if you are estimating a particular job, you have information on the steps of production, an indication of what materials you'll need and when you'll need them, an indication of how long the job will take, and any peculiarities that may affect the completion of the job. When you consider all these things, you'll be more likely to submit an accurate bid.

By carefully keeping such records, you will also have an indication of how many workers you will need. Perhaps, if the work falls behind schedule, you may need to bring more workers to the job to assure scheduled completion and avoid a possibly larger financial loss from penalization, if that is called for in your contract. Also, such records will give you an indication of the organizational structure you may need for your firm.

Getting the Work Done

If your firm is going to run efficiently, you will need organization. Organization is essential because as your company grows you will not be able to do all the work. You have to delegate work, responsibility, and authority. The organization chart is a useful device in getting this done. It shows quite clearly who is responsible for the major activities of your business.

At first, many construction companies are one man shows. It is up to the owner to do almost everything. In this case the organization chart might look something like this:

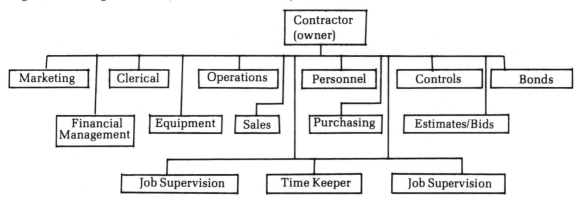

As the company grows, perhaps specialists are added, such as an engineer/estimator, an office manager, and a general superintendent. The organization chart then begins to look something like this:

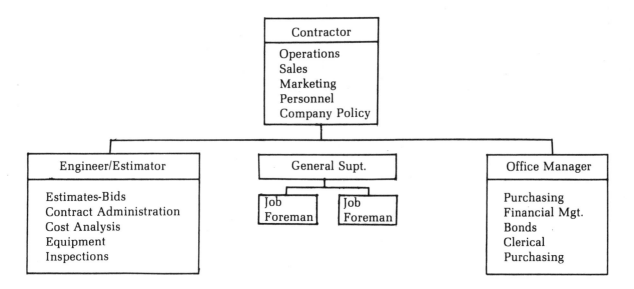

Often, people with complementary experience and skills, such as work experience and office experience will form a partnership. The organization chart will look like this:

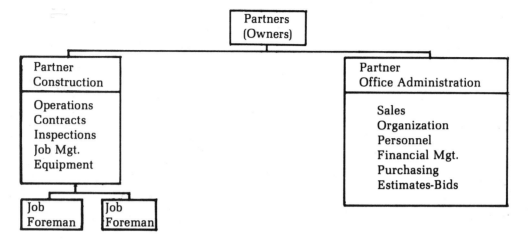

Draw an organization chart for your company.

What are Your Personnel Requirements?

Will you carry a permanent crew or hire workers as the need arises? _____

Will you use union or nonunion labor? _____

How many workers will you need? _____

What is the hourly rate you will pay? _____

What will fringe benefits cost? _____

Will you supervise the work yourself or hire a foreman?

If you hire a foreman, what will this salary be? _____

Will you need clerical help? _____ What will it cost? __

_____

Equipment

What special equipment will you need (assuming that your work force will supply their own hand tools)?

Equipment	Rent	Buy	Your Cost
_____	_____	_____	$ _____
_____	_____	_____	$ _____
_____	_____	_____	$ _____
_____	_____	_____	$ _____
_____	_____	_____	$ _____

Will you need an office or use your home? _____

_____

If you will need an office, what will the rent and other expenses cost? _____
_____
_____
_____

Put Your Plan Into Dollars

Just as with the other aspects of managing a construction business, the basic unit of financial management is the job. The financial aspects of a job must be planned as carefully as the actual construction. The payment for each job must cover the direct and indirect construction costs as well as the allocated share of overhead.

Accounting requirements will vary from company to company and from trade to trade. Your accountant will help you set up the accounting system which will best meet your needs.

However, you must make the overall plans yourself. You must develop the goals necessary to guide and manage your business. This overview will prove invaluable in establishing a good working relationship with your banker (or other lender) and bonding company.

In your financial planning, the first consideration is where the dollars will come from. In dollars, how much business (sales) will you be able to do in the next 12 months? $ _____

Expenses

In connection with annual sales volume, you need to think about expenses. For example, if you plan to do $100,000 worth of work, how much will it cost you to do this amount of business? And even more important, what will be left over as profit at the end of the year?

Profit is your pay. Even if you pay yourself a salary for living expenses, your business must make a profit if it is to continue year after year and pay back the money and time you invest in it. Profit helps your firm to be strong—to have a financial reserve for any lean periods.

The "Expenses Worksheet" is designed to help you figure your yearly expenses. To use this worksheet, you need to get one set of figures—the operating ratios for your line of business. If you don't have these figures, check with the trade association which serves your area of the construction industry.

Matching Money and Expenses

After you have planned for your month to month expenses, the next question is: Will there be enough money coming in to meet these expenses and to sustain your company in the event that there is down time until your next job?

The cash forecast is a management tool which can eliminate much of the anxiety that can plague you during lean month. Use the worksheet "Estimated Cash Forecast," or ask your accountant to use it, to estimate

the amounts of cash that you expect to flow through
your business during the next 12 months.

Remember that the expenses of buying the materials and
supplies for a particular job may occur a month or two
before a payment is made. The "Estimated Cash
Forecast" should show this.

Estimated Cash Forecast	**Jan**	**Feb**	**Mar**	**Apr**	**May**	**Jun**	**Jul**	**Aug**	**Sep**	**Oct**	**Nov**	**Dec**
Expected Available Cash												
Cash Balance												
Expected Receipts												
Job A												
Job B												
Job C												
Bank Loans												
Total Expected Cash												
Expected Cash Requirements												
Job A												
Job B												
Job C												
Equipment Payments												
Taxes												
Insurance (including surety bond payments)												
Overhead												
Loan Repayments												
Total Cash Required												
Cash Balance												
Total Loans Due to Bank												

Expenses Worksheet

	Sample Figures for Specialty Contractors*	% of Your Sales	Your Annual Sales Dollar	Your Dollars Jan	Your Dollars Feb	Your Dollars Mar	Your Dollars Apr	Your Dollars May	Your Dollars Jun	Your Dollars Jul	Your Dollars Aug	Your Dollars Sep	Your Dollars Oct	Your Dollars Nov	Your Dollars Dec
Sales		100.00%													
Cost of Sales		44.45													
Gross Profit		55.55													
Controllable expenses															
Outside labor		1.15													
Operating supplies		2.34													
Gross wages		22.78													
Repairs and maintenance		.59													
Advertising		1.12													
Car and delivery		2.04													
Bad debts		.03													
Administrative and legal		.48													
Miscellaneous expenses		1.03													
Total controllable expenses		31.56													
Fixed expenses															
Rent		1.00													
Utilities		1.41													
Insurance		1.16													
Taxes and licenses		.85													
Depreciation		.10													
		1.65													
Total fixed expenses		6.18													
Total expenses		37.74													
Net profit (before income tax)		17.81													

*These percentages are taken from *Barometer of Small Business,* Accounting Corporation of America. These figures are presented only as a sample and refer to specialty contractors with an annual gross volume between $50,000 and $200,000. The percentages vary from one business to another.

Is Additional Money Needed?

In your planning you may find periods when you will be short of cash. For example, when you start a job you will need materials and supplies. Perhaps it may be a month or two before your first payment. What do you do in the interim if trade credit will not completely satisfy your cash needs?

Your bank may be able to help with a short term loan. If a banker is to lend you money on either a short or long term, he or she will want to know whether your company's financial condition is weak or strong. The bank officer will ask to see a balance sheet.

A blank balance sheet is included. Even if you don't need to borrow, use it. Or, have your accountant use it to draw the "picture" of your firm's financial condition. Moreover, if you don't need to borrow money, you may want to show your plan to the bank that handles your company's account. It is never too early to build good relations with your banker. For the time may come when you will have to borrow.

Current Balance Sheet
for
(name of your firm)

as of _____
      (date)

Assets

Current Assets $_____
  Cash $_____
  Receivables $_____
  Cost of jobs in progress $_____
  Inventories of supplies and tools $_____
    Total Current Assets $_____
Fixed Assets $_____
Other Assets $_____
Total Assets $_____

Liabilities

Current Liabilities
  Notes payable $_____
  Accounts payable $_____
  Miscellaneous current liabilities $_____
    Total Current Liabilities $_____
Equipment Contracts $_____
Owner's equity $_____
Total Liabilities $_____

Control and Feedback

To make your plan work you will need feedback at the various stages of your management process. When you approach a job as a manager, you will need to plan the job, direct the job, and control the job. Throughout this process, you will need adequate financing. Thus, the management controls you set up should supply you with the information you need to keep your operation "on the money."

During the planning stage, you will need to carefully calculate your bid estimate. To direct the job, you will need your job cost analysis to make sure that the job is going to make a profit. And, to control the job, your forces must be organized. This requires the organized production of any given job (work schedule), competent personnel, and your personal follow-up to insure efficient performance.

Is Your Plan Workable?

Now that you've planned this far, step back and take a look at your plan. It is realistic? Can you do enough business to make a living.

Now is the time to revise your plan if it isn't workable, not after you've invested your time and money. If you feel that some revisions are needed before you start your own business, then make them. Go back to the cash flow and adjust the figures. Better, show your plan to someone who has not had a hand in making out your business plan. Your banker, contact man at SBA, or any outside advisor may be able to point out your strong points which if emphasized could turn into dollars.

If you have strong doubts about your business or your ability to run it, it might be better to delay going into business until you feel as comfortable with the tools of management as you are with the tools of your trade.

Keeping Your Plan Up To Date

How many people in this world can predict the future? Very few indeed! You can expect things to change. You can expect circumstances to be different from what you expected. This is only natural. The difference between successful and unsuccessful planning is often only the ability to keep alert and watch for changes. Stay on top of changing conditions and adjust your plan accordingly.

In order to adjust your plan to account for changes, an owner-manager must:

1. Be alert to the changes that come about in your industry, your market, and in your customers.

2. Check your plan against these changes.

3. Determine what revisions, if any, are needed in your plan.

Whatever methods you use to keep up with changing conditions is up to you. Once a month or so, go over your plan. See whether it needs adjusting. If revisions are needed, make then and put them into action.

Put Your Plan Into Action

When your plan is as near on target as possible, you are ready to put it into action. Keep in mind that action is the difference between a plan and a dream. If a plan is not acted upon, it is of no more value than a pleasant dream that evaporates over the breakfast coffee.

The first action step would be acquiring enough capital to get started. Do you already have the money? Will you borrow it from friends, relatives, or a bank? Where and when will you hire competent employees?

What else needs to be done? Look for positive action steps that will get your business rolling. For example, where and how will you get whatever licenses you need to be a contractor? (These requirements differ from state to state. A summary of licensing, prequalification, and tax information may be found in *Summary of State Regulation and Taxes Affecting General Contractors*, published annually by the American Insurance Association.)

In the following space, list the things that you must do to get your business off the drawing board and into action. Give each item a date so that it can be done at the right time.

Action   *Completion Date*

_____   _____

_____   _____

_____   _____

Summary

A business plan can provide the owner-manager or prospective owner-manger of a small manufacturing firm with a pathway to profit. This _publication_ is designed to help an owner-manager in drawing up a business plan.

In building a pathway to profit you need to consider the following questions: What business am I in? What goods do I sell? Where is my market? Who will buy? Who is my competition? What is my sales strategy? What merchandising methods will I use? How much money is needed to operate my company? How will I get the work done? What management controls are needed? How can they be carried out? When should I revise my plan? Where can I go for help?

No one can answer such questions for you. As the owner-manager you have to answer them and draw up your business plan. The pages of this _publication_ are a combination of text and workspaces so you can write in the information you gather in developing your business plan—a logical progression from a commonsense starting point to a commonsense ending point.

A Note on Using This Publication

It takes time and energy and patience to draw up a satisfactory business plan. Use this publication to get your ideas and the supporting facts down on paper. And, above all, make changes in your plan on these pages as that plan unfolds and you see the need for changes.

Bear in mind that anything you leave out of the picture will create an additional cost, or drain on your money, when it unexpectedly crops up later on. If you leave out or ignore enough items, your business is headed for disaster.

Keep in mind, too, that your final goal is to put your plan into action. More will be said about this step near the end of this publication.

What's in This for Me?

Time was when an individual could start a small business and prosper provided you were strong enough to work long hours and had the knack for selling for more than the raw materials or product cost. Small stores, grist mills, livery stables, and blacksmith shops sprang up in many crossroad communities as Americans applied their energy and native intelligence to settling the continent.

Today this native intelligence is still important. But by itself the common sense for which Americans are famous will not insure success in a small business. Technology, the marketplace, and even people themselves have become more complicated than they were 100, or even 25, years ago.

Common sense must be combined with new techniques in order to succeed in the space age. Just as one would not think of launching a manned space capsule without a flight plan, so one should not think of launching a new small manufacturing business without a business plan.

A business plan is an exciting new tool that you can use to plot a "course" for your company. Such a plan is a logical progression from a commonsense starting point to a commonsense ending point.

To build a business plan for your company, an owner-manager needs only to think and react as a manager to questions such as: What product is to be manufactured? How can it best be made? What will it cost me? Who will buy the product? What profit can I make?

Why Am I in Business?

If you're like most business people, you're in business to make money and be your own boss. But, few business people would be able to say that those are the only reasons. The money that you will make from your business will seldom seem like enough for all the long hours, hard work, and responsibility that go along with being the boss.

Then, why do so many stay in business?

This is hardly the time for philosophy. If you're starting or expanding a business, you have enough to think about. But, whether or not you even think about it, the way you operate your business will reflect your "business philosophy."

Consider this. An owner-manager inspects a production run and finds a minor defect. Even though in nine out of ten cases the user of the product would not notice the defect, the owner decides to scrap the entire run.

What does this tell you? It shows that he (or she) gets an important reward from doing what is the right thing—in this case, providing a quality product.

The purpose of this section is not to play down the importance of making a profit. Profits are important. They will keep your business going and attract additional capital into your business. But you should be aware that there are other rewards and responsibilities associated with having your own business.

In your planning, you might give some thought to your responsibilities to employees, community, stockholders, customers, product, and profit. Jot these down. Later, when you've lined-up your management team, discuss this subject with them. This type of group thinking will help everyone, including yourself, understand the basic purposes for each day's work.

Even though you won't advertise it throughout your market, the way you operate your business will reflect your business philosophy.

What Business Am I in?

In making your business plan, the next question to consider is: What business am I really in? At first reading, this question may seem silly. "If there is one thing I know," you say to yourself, "it is what business I'm in." But hold on. Some owner-managers go broke and others waste their savings because they are confused about the business they are really in.

The experience of an old line manufacturing company provides an example of dealing with the question: What business am I really in? In the early years of this century, the founder of the company had no trouble answering the question. As he put it, "I make and sell metal trash cans." This answer held true for his son until the mid-1950's when sales began to drop off. After much thought, the son decided he was in the container business.

Based on this answer, the company dropped several of its lines of metal trash cans. modified other lines, and introduced new products, such as shipping cartons used by other manufacturers and Government agencies.

What business am I in? (Write your answer here) _____

_____

Asking questions like: What does my product do for my customer? Why? When? Where? How? What doesn't it do? What should it do later but doesn't now? can lead to the ultimate conclusion of what business you're in and possibly direct you to new lines of products or enterprises.

Marketing

When you have decided what business you're really in, you have just made your first marketing decision. Now you must face other marketing considerations.

Successful marketing starts with you, the owner-manager. You have to know your product, your market, your customers, and your competition.

Before you plan production, you have to decide who your market is, where it is, why they will buy your product, whether it is a growth or static market, if there are any seasonal aspects of the market, and what percentage of the market you will shoot for in the first, second, and third year of operation. Your production goals and plans must be based on and be responsive to this kind of fact finding (market feasibility and research).

The narrative and work blocks that follow are designed to help you work out a marketing plan. Your objective is to determine what needs to be done to bring in sales dollars.

In some directories, marketing information is listed according to the Standard Industrial Classification (SIC) of the product and industry. The SIC classifies firms by the type of activity they're engaged in, and it is used to promote the uniformity and comparability of statisical data relating to market research. When you begin your market research, you may find it useful to have already classified your products according to this code. (The Standard Industrial Classification Manual is available for sale from the Superintendent of Documents, U.S. Government Printing Office, Washington , D.C. 20402. It may also be available at your local library.)

Product	SIC No.
1. _____	_____
2. _____	_____

Market Area. Where and to whom are you going to sell your product? Describe the market area you will serve in terms of geography and customer profile:

_____

Who Are Your Competitors? List your principal competitors selling in your market area, estimate their percentage of market penetration and dollar sales in that market, and estimate their potential loss of sales as a result of your entry into the market.

Name of Competitor and Location	% Share of Market	Estimated Sales	Estimated Sales Loss Because of You
1. _____	_____	$ _____	_____
2. _____	_____	$ _____	_____
3. _____	_____	$ _____	_____

How Do You Rate Your Competition? Try to find out the strengths and weaknesses of each competitor. Then write your opinion of each of your principal competitors, their principal products, facilities, marketing characteristics, and new product development or adaptability to changing market conditions.

_____

Have any of your competitors recently closed operations or have they withdrawn from your market area? (State reasons if you know them):

_____

Advantages Over Competitors. On what basis will you be able to capture your projected share of the market? Below is a list of characteristics which may indicate the advantages your product(s) enjoy over those offered by competitors. Indicate those advantages by placing a check in the proper space. If there is more than one competitor, you may want to make more than one checklist. Atttach these to the worksheet.

Analyze each characteristic. For example, a higher price may not be a disadvantage if the product is of higher quality than your competitor's. You may want to make a more detailed analysis than is presented here. If you wish to spell out the specifics of each characteristic and explain where your product is disadvantaged and how this will be overcome, attach it to this worksheet. Also, the unique characteristics of your product can be the basis for advertising and sales promotion.

Remember, the more extensive your planning, the more your business plan will help you.

Product(s)	Product No.1	Product No.2
Price	( )	( )
Performance	( )	( )

Product(s)	Product No. 1	Product No. 2
Durability	( )	( )
Versatility	( )	( )
Speed or accuracy	( )	( )
Ease of operation or use	( )	( )
Ease of maintenance or repair	( )	( )
Ease or cost of installation	( )	( )
Size or weight	( )	( )
Styling or appearance	( )	( )
Other characteristics not listed:		
_____	( )	( )
_____	( )	( )

What, if anything, is unique about your product? _____

_____

_____

Distribution. How will you get your product to the ultimate consumer? Will you sell it directly through your own sales organization or indirectly through manufacturer's agents, brokers, wholesalers, and so on? Use the blank to write a brief statement of your method of distribution and manner of sales:

_____

What will this method of distribution cost you? _____

_____

Do you plan to use special marketing, sales, or merchandising techniques? Describe them here: _____

_____

List your customers by name, the total amount they buy from you, and the amount they spend for each of your products.

Names of Principle Customers	Total Purchasing Volume	By Products	% of Your Sales
_____	_____	_____	_____

Market Trends. What has been the sales trend in your market area for your principal product(s) over the last 5 years? What do you expect it to be 5 years from now? You should indicate the source of your data and the basis of your projections.* Industry and product statistics are usually indicated in dollars. Units, such as numbers of customers, numbers of items sold, etc, may be used, but also relate your sales to dollars.

Product	Source of Data	Sales 5 Years Ago	Current Sales	Projected Sales in 5 Years
1. ____	____	____	____	____
2. ____	____	____	____	____

*This is a marketing research problem. It will require you to do some digging in order to come up with a market projection. Trade associations will probably be your most helpful source of information. The Bureau of Census publishes a great deal of useful statistics.

List the name and address of trade associations which serve your industry and indicate whether or not you are a member.

_____

List the name and address of other organizations, governmental agencies, industry associations, etc., from which you intend to obtain management, technical, economic, or other types of information and assistance.

_____

Share of the Market. What percentage of total sales in your market area do you expect to obtain for your products after your facility is in full operation?

Products or Products Category	Local Market (%)	Total Market (%)
_____	_____	_____

Sales Volume. What sales volume do you expect to reach with your products?

	Total Sales	Product(s) 1	Product(s) 2
First Year	$_____	$_____	$_____
Units	_____	_____	_____
Second Year	$_____	$_____	$_____
Units	_____	_____	_____
Third Year	$_____	$_____	$_____
Units	_____	_____	_____

Production

Production is the work that goes on in a factory that results in a product. In making your business plan, you have to consider all the activities that are involved in turning raw materials into finished products. The work blocks which follow are designed to help you determine what production facilities and equipment you need.

Manufacturing Operations. List the basic operations, for example, cut and sew, machine and assemble, etc., which are needed in order to make your product.

_____

_____

Raw Materials. What raw materials or components will you need, and where will you get them?

Material/ Component	Source	Price	Comments (location, delivery, financing, etc.)
_____	____	$ ____	_____
_____	____	$ ____	_____

What amount of raw materials and/or components will you need to stock? _____

_____

Are there any special considerations concerning the storage requirements of your raw material? For example, will you use chemicals which can only be stored for a short time before they lose their potency?

_____

_____

Equipment. List the equipment needed to perform the manufacturing operations. Indicate whether you will rent or buy the equipment and the cost to you.

Equipment	Buy	Rent	Your Cost
_____	____	____	_____
_____	____	____	_____
_____	____	____	_____

Your equipment facilities, and method of operation must comply with the Occupational Safety and Health

Act of 1970. You may obtain a copy of *Standards for General Industry* from the Superintendent of Documents, U.S. Government Printing Office, Washington, D.C. 20402, or a field office of the Occupational Safety and Health Administration.

Labor Skills. List the labor skills needed to run the equipment:

Skill Classification	Number of Persons Needed	Pay Rate	Availability
_____	_____	_____	_____

List the indirect labor (for example, material handlers, stockmen, janitors, and so on) that is needed to keep the plant operating:

Skill Classification	Number of Persons Needed	Pay Rate	Availability
_____	_____	_____	_____
_____	_____	_____	_____

If persons with these skills are not already on your payroll, where will you get them?

_____

Space. How much space will you need to make the product? Include restrooms, storage for raw material and for finished products, and employee parking facilities if appropriate. Are there any local ordinances you must comply with?

_____

_____

Do you own this space?   Yes _____   No _____

Will you buy this space?   Yes _____   No _____

Will you lease this space?   Yes _____   No _____

How much will it cost you?   _____

Overhead. List the overhead items which will be needed in addition to indirect labor and include their cost. Examples are: tools, supplies, utilities, office help, telephone, payroll taxes, holidays, vacations, and salaries for your key people (sales manager, plant manager, and foreman).

_____

How Much Money is Needed?

Money is a tool you can use to make your plan work. Money is also a measuring device. You will measure your plan in terms of dollars; and outsiders, such as bankers and other lenders, will do the same.

When you determine how much money is needed to start (or expand) your business, you can decide whether or not to move ahead. If the cost is greater than the profits which the business can make, there are two things to consider. Many businesses do not show a profit until the second or third year of operation. If this looks like the case with your business, you will need the plans and financial reserves to carry you through this period. On the other hand, maybe you would be better off putting your money into stocks, bonds, or other reliable investments rather than taking on the time consuming job of managing a small business.

Like most businesses, your new business or expansion will require a loan. The burden of proof in borrowing money is upon the borrower. You have to show the banker or other lender how the borrowed money will be spent. Even more important, the lender needs to know how and when you will repay the loan.

To determine whether or not your plan is economically feasible, you need to pull together three sets of figures:

(1) Expected sales and expense figures for 12 months.
(2) Cash flow figures for 12 months.
(3) Current balance sheet figures.

Then visit your banker. Remember, your banker or lender is your friend, not your enemy. So, meet regularly. Share all the information and data you possess. If the lender is ready to help you, he (or she) needs to know not only your strengths but also your weaknesses.

Expected Sales and Expenses Figures. To determine whether or not your business can make its way in the market place, you should estimate your sales and expenses for 12 months. The form which follows is designed to help you in this task.

Cash Flow Figures. Estimates of future sales will not pay an owner-manager's bills. Cash must flow into the business at the proper times if bills are to be paid and a profit realized at the end of the year. To determine whether your projected sales and expenses figures are realistic, you should prepare a cash flow forecast for the 12 months covered by your estimates of sales and expenses.

The forms that follow were designed to help you estimate your cash situation and to get the appropriate figures on paper.

Projected Statement of Sales and Expenses for One Year

	Total	Jan	Feb	Mar	Apr	May	Jun	Jul	Aug	Sep	Oct	Nov	Dec
A. Net Sales													
B. Cost of Goods Sold													
1. Raw Materials													
2. Direct Labor													
3. Manufacturing Overhead													
Indirect Labor													
Factory Heat, Light, and Power													
Insurance and Taxes													
Depreciation													
C. Gross Margin (Subtract B from A)													
D. Selling and Administrative Expenses													
4. Salaries and Commissions													
5. Advertising Expenses													
6. Miscellaneous Expenses													
E. Net Operating Profit (Subtract D from C)													
F. Interest Expense													
G. Net Profit before Taxes (Subtract F from E)													
H. Estimated Income Tax													
I. Net Profit after Income Tax (Subtract H from G)													

Estimated Cash Forecast

	Jan	Feb	Mar	Apr	May	Jun	Jul	Aug	Sep	Oct	Nov	Dec
(1) Cash in Bank (Start of Month)												
(2) Petty Cash (Start of Month)												
(3) Total Cash (add (1) and (2))												
(4) Expected Accounts Receivable												
(5) Other Money Expected												
(6) Total Receipts (add (4) and (5))												
(7) Total Cash and Receipts (add (3) and (6))												
(8) All Disbursements (for month)												
(9) Cash Balance at End of Month in Bank Account and Petty Cash (subtract (8) from (7)*												

*This balance is your starting cash balance for the next month.

Current Balance Sheet Figures. A balance sheet shows the financial conditions of a business as of a certain date. It lists what a business has, what it owes, and the investment of the owner. A balance sheet enables you to see at a glance your assets and liabilities.

Use the blanks below to draw up a current balance sheet for your company.

Current Balance Sheet

For

_____

(name of your company)

as of

_____

(date)

Assets

Current Assets

| | | | **Liabilities** | | |

Current Assets / **Current Liabilites**

Cash $ _____

Accounts Receivable $ _____

Inventory   _____

Fixed Assets

Land $ _____

Building $ _____

Equipment   _____

    Total   _____

Less

Depreciation   _____ $ _____

Total   ═══════════

Liabilities

Current Liabilites

Accounts Payable $ _____

Accrued Expenses   _____

Short Term Loans   _____

Fixed Liabilities

Long Term Loan $ _____

Mortgage   _____

Net Worth $ _____

Total $ ═══════════

Getting the Work Done

Your manufacturing business is only part way home when you have planned your marketing and production. Organization is needed if your plant is to produce what you expect it to produce.

Organization is essential because you as the owner-manager probably cannot do all the work.

You'll have to delegate work, responsibility, and authority. A helpful tool in getting this done is the organization chart. It shows at a glance who is responsible for the major activities of a business. However, no matter how your operation is organized, keep control of the financial management. Examples are given here to help you in preparing an organization chart for your business.

In the beginning, the president of the small manufacturing company probably does everything.

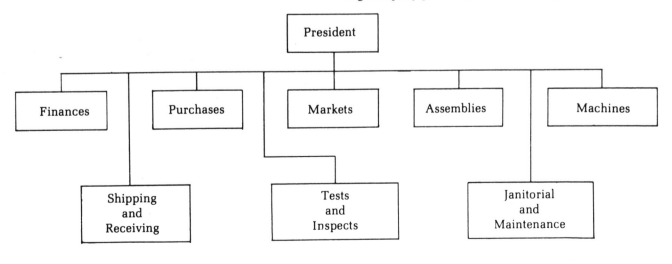

As the company grows to perhaps 50-100 employees, the organization may begin to look something like the chart below.

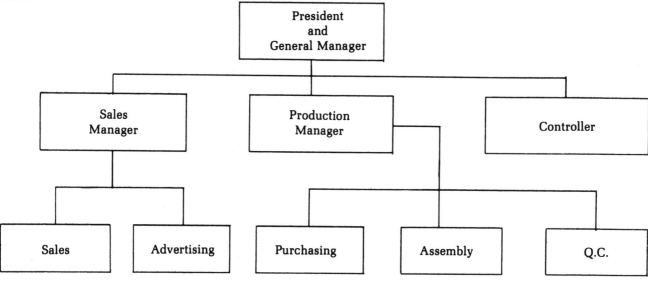

In the space that follows or on a separate piece of paper, draw an organization chart for your business.

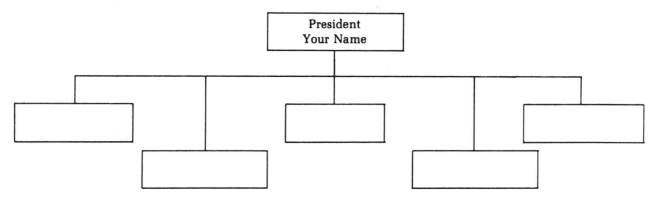

It is important that you recognize your weaknesses early in the game and plan to get assistance wherever you need it. This may be done by using consultants on an as-needed basis, by hiring the needed personnel, or by retaining a lawyer and accountant.

The workblock below lists some of the areas you may want to consider. Adapt it to your needs and indicate who will take care of the various functions. (One name may appear more than once.)

Manufacturing _____

Marketing _____

Research and
Technical Backup _____

Accounting _____

Legal _____

Insurance _____

Other:

_____ _____

_____ _____

_____ _____

_____ _____

Making Your Plan Work

To make your plan work you will need feedback. For example, the year end profit and loss (income) statement shows whether your business made a profit or loss for the past 12 months.

But you can't wait 12 months for the score. To keep your plan on target you need readings at frequent intervals. A profit and loss statement at the end of each month or at the end of each quarter is one type of frequent feedback. However, the P and L may be more of a *loss* than a profit statement if you rely only on it. In addition, your cash flow projection must be continuously updated and revised as necessary. You must set up management controls which will help you to insure that the right things are being done from day to day and from week to week.

The management control system which you set up should give you precise information on: inventory, production, quality, sales, collection of accounts receivable, and disbursements. The simpler the system, the better. Its purpose is to give you and your key people current information in time to correct deviations from approved policies. procedures, or practices. You are after facts with emphasis on trouble spots.

Inventory Control. The purpose of controlling inventory is to provide maximum service to your customers. Your aim should be to achieve a rapid turnover on your inventory, the fewer dollars you tie up in raw materials inventory and in finished goods inventory, the better. Or, saying it in reverse, the faster you get back your investment in raw materials and finished goods inventory, the faster you can reinvest your capital to meet additional consumer needs.

In setting up inventory controls, keep in mind that the cost of the inventory is not your only cost. There are inventory costs, such as the cost of purchasing, the cost of keeping inventory records, and the cost of receiving and storing raw materials.

Production. In preparing this business plan, you have estimated the cost figures for your manufacturing operation. Use these figures as the basis for standards against which you can measure your day-to-day operations to make sure that the clock does not nibble away at profits. These standards will help you to keep machine time, labor man-hours, process time, delay time, and down time within your projected cost figures. Periodic production reports will allow you to keep your finger on potential drains on your profits and should also provide feedback on your overhead expense.

Quality Control. Poorly made products cause a company to lose customers. In addition, when a product fails to perform satisfactorily, shipments are held up, inventory is increased, and a severe financial strain can result. Moreover, when quality is poor, it's a good bet that waste and spoilage on the production line are greater than they should be. The details—checkpoints, reports, and so on—of your quality control system will depend on your type of production system. In working out these details, keep in mind that their purpose is to answer one question: What needs to be done to see that the work is done right the first time? Will you have to do extensive quality control on raw materials? This is an added expense you must consider.

Sales. To keep on top of sales, you will need answers to questions, such as: How many sales were made? What was the dollar amount? What products were sold? At what price? What delivery dates were promised? What credit terms were given to customers?

It is also important that you set up an effective collection system for "accounts receivable," so that you don't tie up your capital in aging accounts.

Disbursements. Your management controls should also give you information about the dollars your company pays out. In checking on your bills, you do not want to be penny-wise and pound-foolish. You need to know that major items, such as paying bills on time to get the supplier's discount, are being handled according to your policies. Your review system should also give you the opportunity to make judgments on the use of funds. In this manner, you can be on top of emergencies as well as routine situations. Your system should also keep you aware that tax monies, such as payroll income tax deductions, are set aside and paid out at the proper time.

Break Even. Break-even analysis is a management control device because the break-even point shows about how much you must sell under given conditons in order to just cover your costs with NO profit and NO loss.

In preparing to start or expand a manufacturing business you should determine at what approximate level of sales a new product will pay for itself and begin to bring in a profit.

Profit depends on sales volume, selling price, and costs. So, to figure your break-even point, first separate your fixed costs, such as rent or depreciation allowance, from your variable costs per unit, such as direct labor and materials.

The formula is

$$\text{break-even volume} = \frac{\text{total fixed costs}}{\text{selling price} - \text{variable cost per unit}}$$

For example, Ajax Plastics has determined its fixed costs to be $100,000 and variable costs to be $50 per unit. If the selling price per unit is $100, then Ajax's break-even volume is

$$\text{break-even volume} = \frac{\$100,000}{\$100 - \$50} = 2000 \text{ units}$$

Earlier you estimated your expected sales for each product and total sales. Compute the break-even point for each.

Product 1:_____ Product 2:_____ Total Sales: _____

Keeping Your Plan Up to Date

The best made business plan gets out of date because conditions change. Sometimes the change is within your company, for example, several of your skilled operators quit their jobs. Sometimes the change is with customers. Their desires and tastes shift. For example, a new idea can sweep the country in six months and die overnight. Sometimes the change is technological as when new raw materials and components are put on the market.

In order to adjust a business plan to account for such changes, an owner-manager must:

(1) Be alert to the changes that come about in your company, in your industry, in your market, and in your community.

(2) Check your plan against these changes.

(3) Determine what revisions, if any, are needed in your plan.

You may be able to delegate parts of this work. For example, you might assign your shop foreman the task of watching for technical changes as reported in trade journals for your industry. Or you might expect your sales manager to keep you abreast of significant changes that occur in your markets.

But you cannot delegate the hardest part of this work. You cannot delegate the decisions as to what revision will be made in your plan. As owner-manager you have to make those judgments on an on-going basis.

When judgments are wrong, cut your losses as soon as possible and learn from the experience. The mental anguish caused by wrong judgments is part of the price you pay for being your own boss. You get your rewards from the satisfaction and profits that result from correct judgments.

Sometimes, serious problems can be anticipated and a course of action planned. For example, what if sales are 25 percent lower than you anticipated, or costs are 10 percent higher? You have prepared what you consider a reasonable budget. It might be a good idea to prepare a ''problem budget,'' based on either lower sales, higher costs, or a combination of the two.

You will also have to exercise caution if your sales are higher than you anticipated. The growth in sales may only be temporary. Plan your expansion. New equipment and additional personnel could prove to be crippling if sales return to a previous lower level.

Keep in mind that few owner-managers are right 100 percent of the time. They can improve their batting average by operating with a business plan and by keeping that plan up to date.

Summary

A business plan can provide the owner-manager or prospective owner-manager of a small service firm with a pathway to profit. This Aid **is designed to help an owner-manager in drawing up a business plan.**

In building a pathway to profit you need to consider the following questions: What business am I in? What services do I provide? Where is my market? Who will buy? Who is my competition? What is my sales strategy? What merchandising methods will I use? How much money is needed to operate my firm? How will I get the work done? What management controls are needed? How can they be carried out? When should I revise my plan? Where can I go for help? And many more.

No one can answer such questions for you. As the owner-manager you have to answer them and draw up your business plan. The pages of this Aid **are a combination of text and workspaces so you can write in the information you gather in developing your business plan—a logical progression from a commonsense starting point to commonsense ending point.**

A Note on Using this Aid

It takes time and energy and patience to draw up a satisfactory business plan. Use this **Aid** to get your ideas and the supporting facts down on paper. And, above all, make changes in your plan on these pages as that plan unfolds and you see the need for changes.

Bear in mind that anything you leave out of the picture will create an additional cost, or drain on your money, when it crops up later on. If you leave out or ignore enough items, your business is headed for disaster.

Keep in mind, too, that your final goal is to put your plan into action. More will be said about this near the end of this **Aid.**

What's in this for Me?

You may be thinking: Why should I spend my time drawing up a business plan? What's in it for me? If you've never drawn up a plan, you are right in wanting to hear about the possible benefits **before** you do your work.

A business plan offers at least four benefits. You may find others as you make and use such a plan. The four are:

(1) The first, and most important, benefit is that a plan gives you a path to follow. A plan makes the future what you want it to be. A plan with goals and action steps allows you to guide your business through turbulent economic seas and into harbors of your choice. The alternative is drifting into "any old port in a storm."

(2) A plan makes it easy to let your banker in on the action. By reading, or hearing, the details of your plan he will have real insight into your situation if he is to lend you money.

(3) A plan can be a communications tool when you need to orient sales personnel, suppliers, and others about your operations and goals.

(4) A plan can help you develop as a manager. It can give you practice in thinking about competitive conditions, promotional opportunities, and situations that seem to be advantageous to your business. Such practice over a period of time can help increase an owner-manager's ability to make judgments.

Why am I in Business?

Many enterprising Americans are drawn into starting their own business by the possibilities of making money and being their own boss. But the long hours, hard work, and responsibilities of being the boss quickly dispel any preconceived glamor.

Profit is the reward for satisfying consumer needs. But, it must be worked for. Sometimes a new business might need two years before it shows a profit. So where, then, are reasons for having your own business?

Every small business owner-manager will have his or her own individual reasons for being in business. For some, satisfaction comes from serving their community. They take pride in serving their neighbors and giving them quality work which they stand behind. For others, their business offers them a chance to contribute to their employees' financial security.

There are as many rewards and reasons for being in business as there are business owners. Why are you in business?

_____

_____

_____

_____

What Business am I in?

In making your business plan, the first question to consider is: What business am I really in? At the first reading this question may seem silly. "If there is one thing I know," you say to yourself, "it is what business I'm in." But hold on. Some owner-managers go broke and others waste their savings because they are confused about the business they are in.

The changeover of barbershops from cutting hair to styling hair is one example of thinking about what business you're really in.

Consider this example, also. Joe Riley* had a small radio and tv store. He thought of his business as a retail store though he also serviced and repaired anything he sold. As his suburb grew, appliance stores emerged and cut heavily into his sales. However, there was an increased call for quality repair work.

When Mr. Riley considered his situation, he decided that he was in the repair business. As a result of thinking about what business he was really in, he profitably built up his repair business and has a contract to take care of the servicing and repair business for one of the appliance stores.

Decide what business you are in and write your answer in the following spaces. To help you decide, think of the answers to questions such as: What inventory of parts and materials must you keep on hand? What services do you offer? What services do people ask for that you do not offer? What is it you are trying to do better, more of, or differently from your competitors?

_____

_____

_____

_____

Marketing

When you have decided what business you're in, you have made your first marketing decision. Now you are ready for other important considerations.

Successful marketing starts with the owner-manager. You have to know your service and the needs of your customers.

*All names in **Aids** are fictitious.

The narrative and work blocks that follow are designed to help you work out a marketing plan for your firm. The blocks are divided into three sections:

Section One—Determining the Sales Potential
Section Two—Attracting Customers
Section Three—Selling to Customers

Section One—Determining the Sales Potential

In the service business, your sales potential will depend on the area you serve. That is, how many customers in this area will need your services? Will your customers be industrial, commercial, consumer, or all of these?

When picking a site to locate your business, consider the nature of your service. If you pick up and deliver, you will want a site where the travel time will be low and you may later install a radio dispatch system. Or, if the customer must come to your place of business, the site must be conveniently located and easy to find.

You must pick the site that offers the best possibilities of being profitable. The following questions will help you think through this problem.

In selecting an area to serve, consider the following:

population and its growth potential
income, age, occupation of population
number of competitive services in and around your proposed location
local ordinances and zoning regulations
type of trading area (commercial, industrial, residential, seasonal)

For additional help in choosing an area, you might try the local chamber of commerce and the manufacturer and distributor of any equipment and supplies you will be using.

You will want to consider the next list of questions in picking the specific site for your business.

Will the customer come to your place of business?
How much space do you need?
Will you want to expand later on?
Do you need any special features required in lighting, heating, ventilation?
Is parking available?
Is public transportation available?

Is the location conducive to drop-in customers?
Will you pick up and deliver?
Will travel time be excessive?
Will you prorate travel time to service call?
Would a location close to an expressway or main artery cut down on travel time?
If you choose a remote location, will savings in rent offset the inconvenience?
If you choose a remote location, will you have to pay as much as you save in rent for advertising to make your service known?
If you choose a remote location, will the customer be able to readily locate your business?
Will the supply of labor be adequate and the necessary skills available?
What are the zoning regulations of the area?
Will there be adequate fire and police protection?
Will crime insurance be needed and be available at a reasonable rate?

I plan to locate in _____ because

_____

_____

_____

_____

Is the area in which you plan to locate supported by a strong economic base? For example, are nearby industries working full time? Only part time? Did any industries go out of business in the past several months? Are new industries scheduled to open in the next several months?

Write your opinion of the area's economic base and your reason for that opinion here. _____

_____

_____

Will you build? _____ What are the terms of the loan

or mortgage?_____

_____

_____

Will you rent?_____ What are the terms of the lease?__

_____

_____

Is the building attractive?_____ In good repair?_____

Will it need remodeling?_____Cost of remodeling

$_____ What services does the landlord provide?____

_____

What is the competition in the area you have picked?

The number of firms that handle my service_____

Does the area appear to be saturated?_____

How many of these firms look prosperous?_____

Do they have any apparent advantages over you?_____

How many look as though they're barely getting by?____

How many similar services went out of business in this area last year?_____

Can you find out why they failed?_____

How many new services opened up in the last year?_____

How much do your competitors charge for your service? _____

Which firm or firms in the area will be your biggest

competition? _____

List the reasons for your opinion here._____

_____

_____

_____

Section Two—Attracting Customers

When you have a location in mind, you should work through another aspect of marketing. How will you attract customers to your business? How will you pull customers away from your competition?

It is in working with this aspect of marketing that many small service firms find competitive advantages. The ideas which they develop are as good, and often better, than those which large companies develop with hired brains. The workblocks that follow are designed to help you think about image, pricing, customer service policies, and advertising.

Image. Whether you like it or not, your service business is going to have an image. The way people think of your firm will be influenced by the way you conduct your business. If people come to your place of business for your service, the cleanliness of the floors, the manner in which they are treated, and the quality of your work will help form your image. If you take your service to the customer, the conduct of your employees will influence your image. Pleasant, prompt, and courteous service before and **after** the sale will help make satisfied customers your best form of advertising.

Thus, you can control your image. Whatever image you seek to develop, it should be concrete enough to promote in your advertising. For example, "service with a smile" is an often used image.

Write out what image you want customers to have of your business.

_____

_____

_____

Pricing. In setting prices for your service, there are four main elements you must consider:

(1) Materials and supplies
(2) Labor and operating expenses
(3) Planned profit
(4) Competition

Further along in this **Aid** you will have the opportunity to figure out the specifics of materials, supplies, labor, and operating expenses. From there you may want the assistance of your accountant in developing a price structure that will not only be fair to the customer, but also fair to yourself. This means that not only must you cover all expenses but also allow enough margin to pay yourself a salary.

One other thing to consider. Will you offer credit?____ Most businesses use a credit card system. These credit costs have to come from somewhere. Plan for them. If

you use a credit card system, what will it cost you? _____ Can you add to your prices to absorb this cost?_____

Some trade associations have a schedule for service charges. It would be a good idea to check with the trade association for your line of business. Their figures will make a good yardstick to make sure your prices are competitive.

And, of course, your prices must be competitive. You've already found out your competitors' prices. Keep these in mind when you are working with your accountant. If you will not be able to make an adequate return, now is the time to find it out.

Customer Service Policies. Customers expect certain services or conveniences, for example, parking. These services may be free to the customer, but not to you. If you do provide parking, you either pay for your own lot or pick up your part of the cost of a lot which you share with other businesses. Since these conveniences will be an expense, plan for them.

List the services that your competitors provide customers.

_____

_____

_____

_____

Now list the services that you will provide your customers.

Service	Estimated Cost
_____	$_____
_____	$_____
_____	$_____
_____	$_____

Advertising. In this section on attracting customers, advertising was saved until last because you have to have something to say before advertising can be effective. When you have an image, price range, and customer services, you are ready to **tell** prospective customers why they should use your services.

When the money you can spend on advertising is

limited, it is vital that your advertising be on target. Before you can think about how much money you can afford for advertising, take time to determine what jobs you want advertising to do for your business. The work blanks that follow should be helpful to your thinking.

The strong points about my service business are_____

_____

My service business is different from my competition in

the following ways_____

_____

My advertising should tell customers and prospective

customers the following facts about my business and

services _____

_____

When you have these facts in mind, you now need to determine who you are going to tell it to. Your advertising needs to be aimed at a target audience—those people who are most likely to use your services. In the space below, describe your customers in terms of age, sex, occupation, and whatever else is necessary depending on the nature of your business. This is your customer profile. For example, an auto repair business may have a customer profile of "male and female automobile owners, 18 years old and above." Thus, for this repair business, anyone over 18 who owns a car is likely to need its service.

The customer profile for my business is_____

_____

Now you are ready to think about the form your advertising should take and its cost. You are looking for the most effective means to tell your story to those most likely to use your service. Ask the local media (newspapers, radio and television, and printers of direct mail pieces) for information about the services and the results they offer for your money.

How you spend advertising money is your decision, but don't fall into the trap that snares many advertisers As one consultant describes this pitfall: It is amazing the way many managers consider themselves experts on advertising copy and media selection without any experience in these areas.

The following blanks should be useful in determining what advertising is needed to sell your strong points to prospective customers.

Form of Advertising	Size of Audience	Frequency of Use	Cost of A Single Ad	Estimated Cost
_____	_____	_____	× $ _____	= $ _____
_____	_____	_____	× $ _____	= $ _____
_____	_____	_____	× $ _____	= $ _____
_____	_____	_____	× $ _____	= $ _____
			Total	$ _____

When you have a figure on what your advertising for the next 12 months will cost, check it against what similar stores spend. Advertising expense is one of the operating ratios (expenses as a percentage of sales) which trade associations and other organizations gather. If your estimated cost for advertising is substantially higher than this average for your line of service, take a second look. No single expense item should be allowed to get way out of line if you want to make a profit. Your task in determining how much to spend for advertising comes down to: How much can I afford to spend and still do the job that needs to be done?

Section Three—Selling to Customers

To complete your work on marketing, you need to think about what you want to happen after you get a customer. Your goal is to provide your service, satisfy customers, and put money into the cash register.

One-time customers can't do the job. You need repeat customers to build a profitable annual sales volume. When someone returns for your service, it is probably because he was satisfied by his previous experience. Satisfied customers are the best form of advertising.

If you previously decided to work only for cash, take a hard look at your decision. Americans like to buy on credit. Often a credit card, or other system of credit and collections, is needed to attract and hold customers.

Based on this description and the dollar amount of business you indicated that you intend to do this year, fill in the following workblocks.

Fixtures and Equipment. No matter whether or not customers will come to your place of business, there will be certain equipment and furniture you will need in your place of business which will allow you to perform your service. List that equipment and its cost to you here.

Parts and Materials. You will probably need some kind of parts or materials to provide your service. List them and their cost to you in the following workblock.

Type of Equipment	Number Needed	×	Unit Cost	=	Cost
_____	_____		$ _____		$ _____
_____	_____		$ _____		$ _____
_____	_____		$ _____		$ _____
_____	_____		$ _____		$ _____
_____	_____		$ _____		$ _____

Item	Amount Needed For 12 months	Unit Cost	Cost
_____	_____	$ _____	$ _____
_____	_____	$ _____	$ _____
_____	_____	$ _____	$ _____
_____	_____	$ _____	$ _____
_____	_____	$ _____	$ _____

I plan to buy parts and materials from:

Name of Item	Name of Supplier	Address of Supplier	Discount Offered	Delivery Time*	Freight Costs**	Fill-in Policy***
_____	_____	_____	_____	_____	_____	_____
_____	_____	_____	_____	_____	_____	_____
_____	_____	_____	_____	_____	_____	_____
_____	_____	_____	_____	_____	_____	_____
_____	_____	_____	_____	_____	_____	_____
_____	_____	_____	_____	_____	_____	_____
_____	_____	_____	_____	_____	_____	_____
_____	_____	_____	_____	_____	_____	_____
_____	_____	_____	_____	_____	_____	_____
_____	_____	_____	_____	_____	_____	_____
_____	_____	_____	_____	_____	_____	_____
_____	_____	_____	_____	_____	_____	_____

* How many days or weeks does it take the supplier to deliver the parts and materials to you?

** Who pays? You, the buyer? The supplier? (This cost can be a big expense item.)

*** What is the supplier's policy on fill-in orders? That is, do you have to buy a gross, a dozen, or only 2 or 3 items? How long does it take to deliver to you?

Before you make any supply arrangements, examine the supplier's obsolescence policy. This can be a vital factor in service parts purchasing. You should also look at the supplier's warranty policy.

Now that you have determined the parts and materials you'll need, you should think about the type of stock control system you'll use. A stock control system should enable you to determine what needs to be ordered on the basis of: (1) what is on hand, (2) what is on order, (3) what has been used. (Some trade associations and suppliers provide systems to members and customers.)

When you have decided on a system for stock control, estimate its cost. My system for stock control will cost me $_____ for the first year.

Overhead. List the overhead items which will be needed. Examples are: rent, utilities, office help, insurance, interest, telephone, postage, accountant, payroll taxes, and licenses or other local taxes. If you plan to hire others to help you manage, their salaries should be listed as overhead.

_____

_____

_____

_____

_____

_____

_____

_____

_____

Getting the Work Done

An important step in setting up your business is to find and hire capable employees. Then you must train them to work together to get the job done. Obviously, organization is needed if your business is to produce what you expect it to produce, namely profits.

Organization is essential because you as the owner-manager cannot do all the work. As your organization grows, you have to **delegate work, responsibility and authority.** A helpful tool in getting this done is the organization chart. It shows at a glance who is responsible for the major activities of a business. Examples are given here to help you in preparing an organization chart for your business.

An organization chart for a small service business will reflect the fact that the owner-manager does most of the managing. For example, an organization chart for a small service business might look like this:

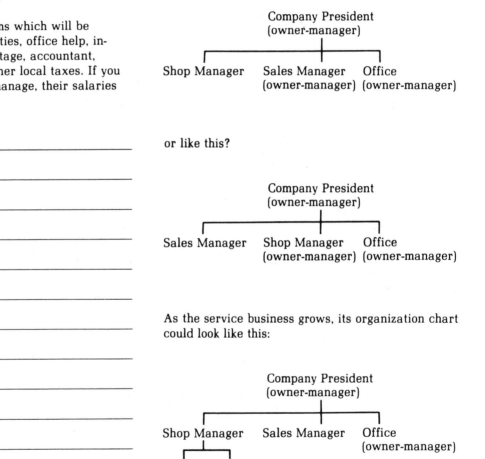

or like this?

As the service business grows, its organization chart could look like this:

In the space below, draw up an organization chart for your business.

As an additional aid in determining both what needs to be done and who will do it, list each activity that is involved in your business. Next to the activity indicate who will do it. You may do this by name or some other designation such as "worker #1." Remember that a name may appear more than once.

Activity   Name

_____   _____

_____   _____

_____   _____

_____   _____

Put Your Plan into Dollars

At this point, take some time to think about what your business plan means in terms of dollars. This section is designed to help you put your plan into dollars.

The first question concerns the source of dollars. After your initial capital investment, the major source of money is the sale of your services. What dollar volume of business do you expect to do in the next 12 months? $_____.

Expenses. In connection with your annual dollar volume of business, you need to think about expenses. If, for example, you plan to do $100,000 in business, what will it cost you to do this amount of servicing? And even more important, what will be left over as profit at the end of the year? Never lose sight of the fact that profit is **your** pay. Even if you pay yourself a salary for living expenses, your business must make a profit if it is to continue year after year and pay back the money you invested in it.

The following workblock is designed to help you make a quick estimate of your expenses. To use this formula, you need to get only one figure—the cost of sales figure for your line of business. If you don't have this operating ratio, check with your trade association or with sources such as those listed in **Ratio Analysis for Small Business.**

	Expressed in Percentage	Expressed in Dollars	Your Percentage	Your Dollars
1. Sales	100	$100,000	100	$_____
2. Cost of Sales	−61.7*	−61,700	_____	−$_____
3. Gross Margin	38.3*	38,300	_____	$_____

* These figures are taken from **Annual Statement Studies** published by Robert Morris Associates. (See Disclaimer Statement.) These figures related to Automobile Repair Services that have annual sales of less than $250,000. These figures are intended only as a sample. The percentages (costs of sales, advertising, and so on) vary from one line of business to another.

Start-Up Costs. If you are starting a new business, list the following estimated start-up costs:

Fixtures and equipment*	$_____
Starting inventory	$_____
Office supplies	$_____
Decorating and remodeling	$_____
Installation of equipment	$_____
Deposits for utilities	$_____
Legal and professional fees	$_____
Licenses and permits	$_____
Advertising for the opening	$_____
Operating cash	$_____
Owner's withdraw during prep-start-up time	$_____
Total	$_____

Expenses Worksheet

Worksheet

Sample Figures for Repair Services* Percent of Sales	% of Your Sales	Your Dollars JAN	Your Dollars FEB	Your Dollars MAR	Your Dollars APR	Your Dollars MAY	Your Dollars JUN	Your Dollars JUL	Your Dollars AUG	Your Dollars SEPT	Your Dollars OCT	Your Dollars NOV	Your Dollars DEC	Your Annual Sales Dollar
Sales	100%													
Cost of Sales	47.51													
Gross profit	52.49													
Controllable expense														
Operating supplies	1.82													
Gross wages	16.98													
Repairs and maintenance	.38													
Advertising	1.45													
Car and delivery	1.52													
Bad debts	.04													
Administrative and legal	.74													
Outside labor	1.21													
Miscellaneous expense	.81													
Total controllable expense	24.95													
Fixed expense														
Rent	3.35													
Utilities	2.05													
Insurance	.95													
Taxes and licenses	.86													
Interest	.12													
Depreciation	1.25													
Total fixed expenses	8.59													
Total expenses	33.53													
Net profit	18.96													

* These percentages are taken from **Barometer of Small Business,** Accounting Corporation of America. These figures are presented **only as a sample** and refer to repair services with an average annual gross volume of under $50,000. The percentages vary from one business to another.

Estimated Cash Forecast

	Jan.	Feb.	Mar.	April	May	June	July	Aug.	Sept.	Oct.	Nov.	Dec.
(1) Cash in Bank (Start of Month)												
(2) Petty Cash (Start of Month)												
(3) Total Cash (add 1 and 2)												
(4) Expected Cash Sales												
(5) Expected Collections												
(6) Other Money Expected												
(7) Total Receipts (add 4, 5 and 6)												
(8) Total Cash and Receipts (add 3 and 7)												
(9) All Disbursements (for month)												
*(10) Cash Balance at End of Month in Bank Account and Petty Cash (subtract 9 from 8)												

* This balance is your starting cash balance for the next month.

Whether you have the funds (savings) or borrow them, your new business will have to pay back these start-up costs. Keep this fact in mind as you work on the "Expenses" section, and on other financial aspects of your plan.

Break Down Your Expenses. Your quick estimate of expenses provides a starting point. The next step is to break down your expenses so they can be handled over the 12 months. Use the "Expenses Worksheet" form on page 10 to make up an expense budget.

Matching Money and Expenses. A budget helps you to see the dollar amount of your expenses each month. Then from month to month the question is: Will sales bring in enough money to pay the firm's bills on time? The answer is "maybe not" or "I hope so" unless the

owner-manager prepares for the "peaks and valleys" that are in many service operations.

A cash forecast is a management tool which can eliminate much of the anxiety that can plague you if your business goes through lean months. Use the worksheet, "Estimated Cash Forecast," above, or ask your accountant to use it to estimate the amounts of cash that you expect to flow through your business during the next 12 months.

Is Additional Money Needed? Suppose at this point you have determined that your business plan needs more money than can be generated by sales. What do you do?

What you do depends on the situation. For example, the

need may be for bank credit to tide your business over during the lean months. This loan can be repaid during the fat sales months when expenses are far less than sales. Adequate working capital is necessary for success and survival.

Whether an owner-manager seeks to borrow money for only a month or so or on a long-term basis, the lender needs to know whether the store's financial position is strong or weak. Your lender will ask to see a current balance sheet.

A blank current balance sheet is included below. Even if you don't need to borrow, use it, or have your accountant use it, to draw the "picture" of your firm's financial condition. Moreover, if you don't need to borrow money, you may want to show your plan to the bank that handles your store's checking account. It is never too early to build good relations with your banker, to show that you are a manager who knows where you want to go rather than a store owner who **hopes** to make a success.

Control and Feedback

To make your plan work you will need feedback. For example, the yearend profit and loss statement shows whether your business made a profit or loss for the past 12 months.

But you can't wait 12 months for the score. To keep your plan on target you need readings at frequent intervals. A profit and loss statement at the end of each month or at the end of each quarter is one type of frequent feedback. However, the income statement or profit and loss statement (P and L) may be more of a loss than a profit statement if you rely only on it. You must set up management controls which will help you to insure that the right things are being done from day to day and from week to week. In a new business, the record-keeping system should be set up before your business opens. After you're in business is too late. For one thing, you may be too busy to give a record-keeping system the proper attention.

The control system which you set up should give you information about: stock, sales, and disbursements. The simpler the system, the better. Its purpose is to give you current information. You are after facts with emphasis on trouble spots. Outside advisers, such as an accountant, can be helpful.

Stock Control. The purpose of controlling parts and materials inventory is to provide maximum service to your customers and to see that parts and materials are

not lost through pilferage, shrinkage, errors, or waste. Your aim should be to achieve a high turnover on your inventory. The fewer dollars you tie up in inventory, the better.

Current Balance Sheet for

_____

(name of your firm)

As of _____

  (date)

Assets

Current assets:
Cash:
Cash in bank . . . . $ _____
Petty cash . . . . $ _____
Accounts receivable . . . . $ _____
Less allowance for doubtful accounts . . . . . . $ _____
Merchandise inventories . . . . $ _____
Total current assets . . . . $ _____
Fixed assets:
Land . . . . $ _____
Buildings . . . . $ _____
Delivery equipment . . . . $ _____
Furniture and fixtures . . . . $ _____
Less allowance for depreciation . . . . $ _____
Leasehold improvements, less
  amortization . . . . $ _____
Total fixed assets . . . . $ _____
Total assets . . . . $ _____

Liabilities and Capital

Current liabilities:
Accounts payable . . . . $ _____
Notes payable, due within 1 year . . . . $ _____
Payroll taxes and withheld taxes . . . . $ _____
Sales taxes . . . . $ _____
Total current liabilities . . . . $ _____
Long-term liabilities
Notes payable, due after 1 year . . . . $ _____
Total liabilities . . . . $ _____
Capital:
Proprietor's capital, beginning of
  period . . . . $ _____
Net profit for the period . . . . $ _____
Less proprietor's drawings . . . . $ _____
Increase in capital . . . . $ _____
Capital, end of period . . . . $ _____
Total liabilities and capital . . . . $ _____

In a small business, inventory control helps the owner-manager to offer customers efficient service. The control system should enable you to determine what needs to be ordered on the basis of: (1) what is on hand, (2) what is on order, and (3) what has been used.

In setting up inventory controls, keep in mind that the cost of the inventory is not your only cost. You will also have costs such as the cost of purchasing, the cost of keeping control records, and the cost of receiving and storing your inventory.

Sales. In a small business, sales slips and cash register tapes give the owner-manager feedback at the end of each day. To keep on top of sales, you will need answers to questions such as: How many sales were made? What was the dollar amount? What credit terms were given to customers?

Disbursements. Your management controls should also give you information about the dollars your company pays out. In checking on your bills, you do not want to be penny-wise and pound-foolish. You need to know what major items, such as paying bills on time to get the supplier's discount, are being handled according to your policies. Your review system should also give you the opportunity to make judgments on the use of funds. In this manner, you can be on top of emergencies as well as routine situations. Your system should also keep you aware that tax monies such as payroll income tax deductions, are set aside and paid out at the proper time.

Break-Even. Break-even analysis is a management control device because the break-even point shows how much you must sell under given conditions in order to just cover your costs with No profit and No loss.

Profit depends on sales volume, selling price, and costs. Break-even analysis helps you to estimate what a change in one or more of these factors will do to your profits. To figure a break-even point, fixed costs, such as rent, must be separated from variable costs, such as the cost of sales and the other items listed under "controllable expenses" on the expense worksheet, page 10 of this **Aid.**

The formula is:

$$\text{Break-even point (in sales dollars)} = \frac{\text{Total fixed costs}}{1 - \dfrac{\text{Total variable costs}}{\text{Corresponding sales volume}}}$$

An example of the formula is: Bill Jackson plans to open a laundry. He estimates his fixed expenses at about

$9,000, the first year. He estimates his variable expenses at about $700 for every $1,000 of sales.

$$\text{BE Point} = \frac{\$9,000}{1 - \dfrac{700}{1,000}} = \frac{\$9,000}{1 - .70} = \frac{\$9,000}{.30} = \$30,000$$

Is Your Plan Workable?

Stop when you have worked out your break-even point. Whether the break-even point looks realistic or way off base, it is time to make sure that your plan is workable.

Take time to re-examine your plan **before** you back it with money. If the plan is not workable better to learn it now than to realize 6 months down the road that you are pouring money into a losing venture.

In reviewing your plan, look at the cost figures you drew up when you broke down your expenses for one year. If any of your cost items are too high or too low, change them. You can write your changes in the white spaces above or below your original entries on that worksheet. When you finish making your adjustments, you will have a Revised projected statement of sales and expenses for 12 months.

With your revised figures work out a revised break-even point. Whether the new break-even points looks good or bad, take one or more precaution. Show your plan to someone who has not been involved in working out the details.

Your banker, contact man at SBA, or other advisor outside of your business may see weaknesses that failed to appear as you pored over the details of your plan. They may put a finger on strong points which your plan should emphasize.

Put Your Plan into Action

When your plan is as near on target as possible, you are ready to put it into action. Keep in mind that action is the difference between a plan and a dream. If a plan is not acted upon, it is of no more value than a pleasant dream that evaporates over the breakfast coffee.

A successful owner-manager does not stop after he has gathered information and drawn up a plan, as you have done in working through this **Aid.** He begins to use his plan.

At this point, look back over your plan. Look for things that must be done to put your plan into action.

What needs to be done will depend on your situation. For example, if your business plan calls for an increase in sales, one action to be done will be providing funds for this expansion.

Have you more money to put into this business?

Do you borrow from friends and relatives? From your bank? From your suppliers by arranging liberal commercial credit terms?

If you are starting a new business, one action step may be to get a loan for fixtures, employee salaries, and other expenses. Another action step will be to find and hire capable employees.

In the spaces that follow, list things that must be done to put your plan into action. Give each item a date so that it can be done at the appropriate time. To put my plan into action, I must do the following:

Action	Completion Date
_____	_____
_____	_____
_____	_____
_____	_____
_____	_____

Keeping Your Plan Up To Date

Once you put your plan into action, look out for changes. They can cripple the best made business plan if the owner-manager lets them.

Stay on top of changing conditions and adjust your business plan accordingly.

Sometimes the change is within your company. For example, several of your employees quit their jobs. Sometimes the change is with customers; for example, their desires and tastes shift. Sometimes the change is technological as when new raw materials are put on the market introducing the need for new processes and procedures.

In order to adjust your plan to account for such changes, an owner-manager must:

(1) Be alert to the changes that come in your company, line of business, market, and customers.
(2) Check your plan against these changes.
(3) Determine what revisions, if any, are needed in your plan.

The method you use to keep your plan current so that your business can weather the forces of the market place is up to you. Read the trade papers and magazines for your line of business. Another suggestion concerns your time. Set some time—two hours, three hours, whatever is necessary—to review your plan periodically. Once each month, or every other month, go over your plan to see whether it needs adjusting. If revisions are needed, make them and put them into action.

Disclaimer Statement

Robert Morris Associates cannot emphasize too strongly that their composite figures for each industry may **not** be representative of that entire industry (except by coincidence), for the following reasons:
1. The only companies with a chance of being included in their study in the first place are those for whom their submitting banks have recent figures.
2. Even from this restricted group of potentially includable companies, those which are chosen, and the total number chosen, are not determined in any random or otherwise statistically reliable manner.
3. Many companies in their study have **varied** product lines; they are "mini-conglomerates," if you will. All they can do in these cases is categorize them by their **primary** product line, and be willing to tolerate any "impurity" thereby introduced.

In a word, don't automatically consider their figures as representative norms and don't attach any more or less significance to them than is indicated by the unique aspects of the data collection.

Summary

A business plan can provide the owner-manager or prospective owner-manager of a small service firm with a pathway to profit. This **Aid** is designed to help an owner-manager in drawing up a business plan.

In building a pathway to profit you need to consider the following questions: What business am I in? What services do I provide? Where is my market? Who will buy? Who is my competition? What is my sales strategy? What merchandising methods will I use? How much money is needed to operate my firm? How will I get the work done? What management controls are needed? How can they be carried out? When should I revise my plan? Where can I go for help? And many more.

No one can answer such questions for you. As the owner-manager you have to answer them and draw up your **business plan.** The pages of this **Aid** are a combination of text and workspaces so you can write in the information you gather in developing your business plan—a logical progression from a commonsense starting point to commonsense ending point.

A Note on Using this Aid

It takes time and energy and patience to draw up a satisfactory business plan. Use this **Aid** to get your ideas and the supporting facts down on paper. And, above all, make changes in your plan on these pages as that plan unfolds and you see the need for changes.

Bear in mind that anything you leave out of the picture will create an additional cost, or drain on your money, when it crops up later on. If you leave out or ignore enough items, your business is headed for disaster.

Keep in mind, too, that your final goal is to put your plan into action. More will be said about this near the end of this **Aid.**

What's in this for Me?

You may be thinking: Why should I spend my time drawing up a business plan? What's in it for me? If you've never drawn up a plan, you are right in wanting to hear about the possible benefits **before** you do your work.

A business plan offers at least four benefits. You may find others as you make and use such a plan. The four are:

(1) The first, and most important, benefit is that a plan gives you a path to follow. A plan makes the future what you want it to be. A plan with goals and action steps allows you to guide your business through turbulent economic seas and into harbors of your choice. The alternative is drifting into "any old port in a storm."

(2) A plan makes it easy to let your banker in on the action. By reading, or hearing, the details of your plan he will have real insight into your situation if he is to lend you money.

(3) A plan can be a communications tool when you need to orient sales personnel, suppliers, and others about your operations and goals.

(4) A plan can help you develop as a manager. It can give you practice in thinking about competitive conditions, promotional opportunities, and situations that seem to be advantageous to your business. Such practice over a period of time can help increase an owner-manager's ability to make judgments.

Why am I in Business?

Many enterprising Americans are drawn into starting their own business by the possibilities of making money and being their own boss. But the long hours, hard work, and responsibilities of being the boss quickly dispel any preconceived glamor.

Profit is the reward for satisfying consumer needs. But, it must be worked for. Sometimes a new business might need two years before it shows a profit. So where, then, are reasons for having your own business?

Every small business owner-manager will have his or her own individual reasons for being in business. For some, satisfaction comes from serving their community. They take pride in serving their neighbors and giving them quality work which they stand behind. For others, their business offers them a chance to contribute to their employees' financial security.

There are as many rewards and reasons for being in business as there are business owners. Why are you in business?

_____

_____

_____

_____

What Business am I in?

In making your business plan, the first question to consider is: What business am I really in? At the first reading this question may seem silly. "If there is one thing I know," you say to yourself, "it is what business I'm in." But hold on. Some owner-managers go broke and others waste their savings because they are confused about the business they are in.

The changeover of barbershops from cutting hair to styling hair is one example of thinking about what business you're really in.

Consider this example, also. Joe Riley* had a small radio and tv store. He thought of his business as a retail store though he also serviced and repaired anything he sold. As his suburb grew, appliance stores emerged and cut heavily into his sales. However, there was an increased call for quality repair work.

When Mr. Riley considered his situation, he decided that he was in the repair business. As a result of thinking about what business he was really in, he profitably built up his repair business and has a contract to take care of the servicing and repair business for one of the appliance stores.

Decide what business you are in and write your answer in the following spaces. To help you decide, think of the answers to questions such as: What inventory of parts and materials must you keep on hand? What services do you offer? What services do people ask for that you do not offer? What is it you are trying to do better, more of, or differently from your competitors?

_____

_____

_____

_____

Marketing

When you have decided what business you're in, you have made your first marketing decision. Now you are ready for other important considerations.

Successful marketing starts with the owner-manager. You have to know your service and the needs of your customers.

*All names in **Aids** are fictitious.

The narrative and work blocks that follow are designed to help you work out a marketing plan for your firm. The blocks are divided into three sections:

Section One—Determining the Sales Potential
Section Two—Attracting Customers
Section Three—Selling to Customers

Section One—Determining the Sales Potential

In the service business, your sales potential will depend on the area you serve. That is, how many customers in this area will need your services? Will your customers be industrial, commercial, consumer, or all of these?

When picking a site to locate your business, consider the nature of your service. If you pick up and deliver, you will want a site where the travel time will be low and you may later install a radio dispatch system. Or, if the customer must come to your place of business, the site must be conveniently located and easy to find.

You must pick the site that offers the best possibilities of being profitable. The following questions will help you think through this problem.

In selecting an area to serve, consider the following:

population and its growth potential
income, age, occupation of population
number of competitive services in and around your proposed location
local ordinances and zoning regulations
type of trading area (commercial, industrial, residential, seasonal)

For additional help in choosing an area, you might try the local chamber of commerce and the manufacturer and distributor of any equipment and supplies you will be using.

You will want to consider the next list of questions in picking the specific site for your business.

Will the customer come to your place of business?
How much space do you need?
Will you want to expand later on?
Do you need any special features required in lighting, heating, ventilation?
Is parking available?
Is public transportation available?

How much rent must you pay each month?

Estimate the gross annual sales you expect in this location.

When you think you have finally solved the site location question, ask your banker to recommend people who know most about locations in your line of business. Contact these people and listen to their advice and opinions, weigh what they say, then decide.

Attracting Customers

When you have a location in mind, you should work through another aspect of marketing. How will you attract customers to your store? How will you pull business away from your competition?

It is in working with this aspect of marketing that many small retailers find competitive advantages. The ideas that they develop are as good as and often better than those that large companies develop. The work blocks that follow are designed to help you think about image, pricing, customer service policies, and advertising.

Image

A store has an image whether or not the owner is aware of it. For example, throw some merchandise onto shelves and onto display tables in a dirty, dimly lit store and you've got an image. Shoppers think of it as a dirty, junky store and avoid coming into it. Your image should be concrete enough to promote in your advertising and other promotional activities. For example, "home cooked" food might be the image of a small restaurant.

Write out on a worksheet the image that you want shoppers and customers to have of your store.

Pricing

Value received is the key to pricing. The only way a store can have low prices is to sell low-priced merchandise. Thus, what you do about the prices you charge depends on the lines of merchandise you buy and sell. It depends also on what your competition charges for these lines of merchandise. Your answers to the following questions should help you to decide what to do about pricing.

In what price ranges are your line of merchandise sold—High_____, Medium_____, or Low_____ ?

Will you sell for cash only?

What services will you offer to justify your prices if they are higher than your competitor's prices?

If you offer credit, will your price have to be higher than if all sales are for cash? The credit costs have to come from somewhere. Plan for them.

If you use credit card systems, what will it cost you? Will you have to add to your prices to absorb this cost?

Customer Service Policies

The service you provide your customers may be free to them, but you pay for it. For example, if you provide free parking, you pay for your own parking lot or pick up your part of the cost of a lot you share with other retailers.

Make a list of the services that your competitors offer and estimate the cost of each service. How many of these services will you have to provide just to be competitive? Are there other services that would attract customers but that competitors are not offering? If so, what are your estimates of the cost of such services? Now list all the services you plan to offer and the estimated costs. Total this expense and figure out how you can include those added costs in your prices without pricing your merchandise out of the market.

Advertising

Advertising was saved until the last because you have to have something to say before advertising can be effective. When you have an image, price range, and customer services, you are ready to *tell* prospective customers why they should shop in your store.

When the money you can spend for advertising is limited, it is vital that your advertising be on target. Before you think about how much money you can afford for advertising, take time to determine what jobs you want to do for your store. List the strong points of your store. List what makes your store different from your competitors. List the facts about your store and its merchandise that your advertising should tell shoppers and prospective customers.

When you have these facts listed and in hand, you are ready to think about the form your advertising should take and its cost. Ask the local media (newspapers, radio and television, and printers of direct mail pieces) for information about the services and results they offer for your money.

How you spend advertising money is your decision, but don't fall into the trap that snares many advertisers who have little or no experience with advertising copy and media selection. Advertising is a profession. Don't spend a lot of money on advertising without getting professional advice on what kind and how much advertising your store needs.

The following work sheet can be useful in determining what advertising is needed to sell your strong points to prospective customers.

Form of Advertising	Size of Audience	Frequency of Use	Cost of A single ad	Est. Cost
_____	_____	_____ X $	_____ = $	_____
_____	_____	_____ X	_____ =	_____
_____	_____	_____ X	_____ =	_____
_____	_____	_____ X	_____ =	_____

Total $ _____

When you have a figure on what your advertising for the next twelve months will cost, check it against what similar stores spend. Advertising expense is one of the operating ratios (expenses as a percentage of sales) that trade associations and other organizations gather. If your estimated cost for advertising is substantially higher than this average for your line of merchadise, take a second look. No single expense item should be allowed to get way out of line if you want to make a profit. Your task in determining how much to spend for advertising comes down to the question, "How much can I afford to spend and still do the job that needs to be done?"

In-store Sales Promotion
To complete your work on marketing, you need to think about what you want to happen after prospects get inside your store. Your goal is to move stock off your shelves and displays at a profit and to satisfy your customers. You want repeat customers and money in your cash register.

At this point, if you have decided to sell for cash only, take a second look at your decision. Don't overlook the fact that Americans like to buy on credit. Often a credit card, or other system of credit and collections, is needed to attract and hold customers. Customers will have more buying confidence and be more comfortable in your store if they know they can afford to buy. Credit makes this possible.

To encourage people to buy, self-service stores rely on layout, attractive displays, signs and clearly marked prices on the items offered for sale. Other stores combine these techniques with personal selling.

List the display counters, racks, special equipment (something peculiar to your business like a frozen food display bin or a machine to measure and cut cloth), and other fixtures. Figure the cost of all fixtures and equipment by listing them on a worksheet as follows:

Type of Equipment	Number	X	Unit Cost	=	Cost

Draw several layouts of your store and attach the layout that suits you to the cost worksheet. Determine how many signs you may need for a twelve month operation and estimate that cost also.

If your store is a combination of self-service and personal selling, how many sales persons and cashiers will you need? Estimate, I will need _____ sales persons at $_____ each week (include payroll taxes and insurance in this salaries cost). In a year, salaries will cost $ _____.

Personal attention to customers is one strong point that a small store can use as a competitive tool. You want to emphasize in training employees that everyone has to pitch in and get the job done. Customers are not interested in job descriptions, but they are interested in being served promptly and courteously. Nothing is more frustrating to a customer than being ignored by an employee. Decide what training you will give your sales people in the techniques of how to greet customers, show merchandise, suggest other items, and handle customer needs and complaints.

Buying

When *buying* merchandise for resale, you need to answer questions such as:

Who sells the line to retailers? Is it sold by the manufacturer directly or through wholesalers and distributors?

What delivery service can you get and must you pay shipping charges?

What are the terms of buying?

Can you get credit?

How quickly can the vendor deliver fill-in orders?

You should establish a source of supply on acceptable terms for each line of merchandise and estimate a plan for purchasing as follows:

Act of 1970. You may obtain a copy of *Standards for General Industry* from the Superintendent of Documents, U.S. Government Printing Office, Washington, D.C. 20402, or a field office of the Occupational Safety and Health Administration.

Labor Skills. List the labor skills needed to run the equipment:

Skill Classification	Number of Persons Needed	Pay Rate	Availability

List the indirect labor (for example, material handlers, stockmen, janitors, and so on) that is needed to keep the plant operating:

Skill Classification	Number of Persons Needed	Pay Rate	Availability

If persons with these skills are not already on your payroll, where will you get them?

_____

Space. How much space will you need to make the product? Include restrooms, storage for raw material and for finished products, and employee parking facilities if appropriate. Are there any local ordinances you must comply with?

_____

_____

Do you own this space?   Yes _____   No _____

Will you buy this space?   Yes _____   No _____

Will you lease this space?   Yes _____   No _____

How much will it cost you?   _____

Overhead. List the overhead items which will be needed in addition to indirect labor and include their cost. Examples are: tools, supplies, utilities, office help, telephone, payroll taxes, holidays, vacations, and salaries for your key people (sales manager, plant manager, and foreman).

_____

How Much Money is Needed?

Money is a tool you can use to make your plan work. Money is also a measuring device. You will measure your plan in terms of dollars; and outsiders, such as bankers and other lenders, will do the same.

When you determine how much money is needed to start (or expand) your business, you can decide whether or not to move ahead. If the cost is greater than the profits which the business can make, there are two things to consider. Many businesses do not show a profit until the second or third year of operation. If this looks like the case with your business, you will need the plans and financial reserves to carry you through this period. On the other hand, maybe you would be better off putting your money into stocks, bonds, or other reliable investments rather than taking on the time consuming job of managing a small business.

Like most businesses, your new business or expansion will require a loan. The burden of proof in borrowing money is upon the borrower. You have to show the banker or other lender how the borrowed money will be spent. Even more important, the lender needs to know how and when you will repay the loan.

To determine whether or not your plan is economically feasible, you need to pull together three sets of figures:

(1) Expected sales and expense figures for 12 months.
(2) Cash flow figures for 12 months.
(3) Current balance sheet figures.

Then visit your banker. Remember, your banker or lender is your friend, not your enemy. So, meet regularly. Share all the information and data you possess. If the lender is ready to help you, he (or she) needs to know not only your strengths but also your weaknesses.

Expected Sales and Expenses Figures. To determine whether or not your business can make its way in the market place, you should estimate your sales and expenses for 12 months. The form which follows is designed to help you in this task.

Cash Flow Figures. Estimates of future sales will not pay an owner-manager's bills. Cash must flow into the business at the proper times if bills are to be paid and a profit realized at the end of the year. To determine whether your projected sales and expenses figures are realistic, you should prepare a cash flow forecast for the 12 months covered by your estimates of sales and expenses.

The forms that follow were designed to help you estimate your cash situation and to get the appropriate figures on paper.

Projected Statement of Sales and Expenses for One Year

	Total	Jan	Feb	Mar	Apr	May	Jun	Jul	Aug	Sep	Oct	Nov	Dec
A. Net Sales													
B. Cost of Goods Sold													
1. Raw Materials													
2. Direct Labor													
3. Manufacturing Overhead													
Indirect Labor													
Factory Heat, Light, and Power													
Insurance and Taxes													
Depreciation													
C. Gross Margin (Subtract B from A)													
D. Selling and Administrative Expenses													
4. Salaries and Commissions													
5. Advertising Expenses													
6. Miscellaneous Expenses													
E. Net Operating Profit (Subtract D from C)													
F. Interest Expense													
G. Net Profit before Taxes (Subtract F from E)													
H. Estimated Income Tax													
I. Net Profit after Income Tax (Subtract H from G)													

sales bring in enough money to pay the store's bills? The owner-manager must prepare for the financial peaks and valleys of the business cycle.

A cash forecast is a management tool that can eliminate much of the anxiety that can plague you if your sales go through lean months. Use the following format.

Estimated Cash Forecast

	Jan.	Feb.	Mar.	April	May	June	July	Aug.	Sept.	Oct.	Nov.	Dec.
(1) Cash in Bank (Start of Month)												
(2) Petty Cash (Start of Month)												
(3) Total Cash (add 1) and (2)												
(4) Expected Cash Sales												
(5) Expected Collections												
(6) Other Money Expected												
(7) Total Receipts (add 4,5 and 6)												
(8) Total Cash and Receipts (add 3 and 7)												
(9) All Disbursements (for month)												
(10) Cash Balance at End of Month in Bank Acct. and Petty Cash (subtract 9 from 8)*												

*This balance is your starting cash balance for the next month.

Current Balance Sheet*
for

_____
(name of your firm)

As of _____
(date)

Assets			Liabilities and Capital		
Current Assets:			**Current liabilities:**		
Cash:			Accounts payable	$_____	
Cash in bank	$_____		Notes payable due		
Petty Cash	_____	$_____	within 1 year	_____	
Accounts receivable	$_____		Payroll taxes and		
Less allowance for			withheld taxes	_____	
doubtful accounts	_____	_____	Sales taxes	_____	
Merchandise inventories		_____	Total current liabilities		$_____
Total current assets		$_____	**Long-term liabilities:**		
Fixed Assets:			Notes payable, due		
Land	$_____		after 1 year	_____	
Building	_____		Total liabilities		$_____
Delivery equip.	_____		**Capital:**		
Furniture and fixtures	_____	$_____	Proprietor's capital,		
Less allowance			beginning of period	$_____	
for depreciation	$_____	_____	Net profit for		
Leasehold improvements,			the period	$_____	
less amortization		_____	Less proprietor's		
Total fixed assets		$_____	drawings	_____	
Total assets		$_____	Increase in capital		_____
			Capital end of		
			period		$_____
			Total liabilities		
			and capital		$_____

Is Additional Money Needed? Suppose at this point that your business needs more money than can be generated by present sales. What do you do? If your business has great potential or is in good financial condition, as shown by its balance sheet, you will borrow money (from a bank most likely) to keep the business operating during start-up and slow sales periods. The loan can be repaid during the fat sales months when sales are greater than expenses. Adequate working capital is needed for success and survival; but cash on hand (or the lack of it) is not necessarily an indication that the business is in bad financial shape. A lender will look at your balance sheet to see the business's Net Worth of which cash and cash flow are only a part. The sample balance sheet statement format shows a business's Net Worth (financial position) at a given point in time, say as of the close of business at the end of the month or at the end of the year.

Even if you do not need to borrow money, you may want to show your plan and balance sheet to your banker. It is never too early to build good relations and credibility (trust) with your banker. Let your banker know that you are a manager who knows where you want to go rather than someone who merely hopes to succeed.

Control and Feedback

To make your plan work you need feedback. For example, the year-end profit and loss (income) statement shows whether your business made a profit or took a loss for the past twelve months.

Don't wait twelve months for the score. To keep your plan on target you need readings at frequent intervals. An income statement compiled at the end of each month or at the end of each quarter is one type of frequent feedback. Also you must set up management controls that help you insure that the right things are done each day and week. Organization is needed because you as the owner-manager cannot do all the work. You must *delegate work, responsibility, and authority.* The recordkeeping systems should be set up before the store opens. After you're in business it is too late.

The control system that you set up should give you information about stock, sales, receipts and disbursements. The simpler the accounting control system, the better. Its purpose is to give you current useful information. You need facts that expose trouble spots. Outside advisers, such as accountants, can help.

Stock Control. The purpose of controlling stock is to provide maximum service to your customers. Your aim should be to achieve a high turnover rate on your inventory. The fewer dollars you tie up in stock, the better.

In a small store, stock control helps the owner-manager offer customers a balanced assortment and enables you to determine what needs ordering on the basis of (1) what is on hand, (2) what is on order, and (3) what has been sold.

When setting up inventory controls, keep in mind that the cost of the stock is not your only cost. There are inventory costs, such as the cost of purchasing, the cost of keeping stock control records, and the cost of receiving and storing stock.

Sales. In a small store, sales slips and cash register

tapes give the owner-manager feedback at the end of each day. To keep on top of sales, you need answers to questions, such as: How many sales were made? What was the dollar amount? What were the best selling products? At what price? What credit terms were given to customers?

Receipts. Break out your receipts into receivables (money still owed such as a charge sale) and cash. You know how much credit you have given, how much more you can give, and how much cash you have with which to operate.

Disbursements. Your management controls should also give you information about the dollars your company pays out. In checking on your bills, you do not want to be penny-wise and pound-foolish. You should pay bills on time to take advantage of supplier discounts. Your review systems should also give you the opportunity to make judgments on the use of funds. In this manner, you can be on top of emergencies as well as routine situations. Your system should also keep you aware that tax monies, such as payroll income tax deductions, must be set aside and paid out at the proper time.

Break-Even. Break-even analysis is a management control device that approximates how much you must sell in order to cover your costs with NO profit and NO loss. Profit comes after break-even.

Profit depends on sales volume, selling price, and costs. Break-even analysis helps you to estimate what a change in one or more of these factors will do to your profit. To figure a break-even point, fixed costs (like rent) must be separated from variable costs (like the cost of goods sold).
The break-even formula is:

$$\text{Break-even point (in sales dollars)} = \frac{\text{Total fixed costs}}{1 - \frac{\text{Total variable costs}}{\text{corresponding sales volume}}}$$

Sample break-even calculations: Bill Mason plans to open a shoe store and estimates his fixed expenses at about $9,000 the first year. He estimates variable expenses of about $700 for every $1,000 of sales. How much must the store gross to break-even?

$$\text{BE Point} = \frac{\$9,000}{1 - \left(\frac{700}{1,000}\right)} = \frac{\$9,000}{1 - .70} = \frac{\$9,000}{.30} = \$30,000$$

As the company grows to perhaps 50-100 employees, the organization may begin to look something like the chart below.

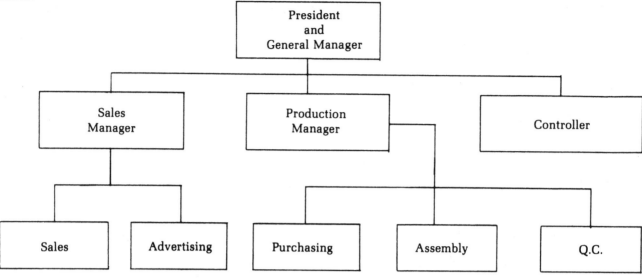

In the space that follows or on a separate piece of paper, draw an organization chart for your business.

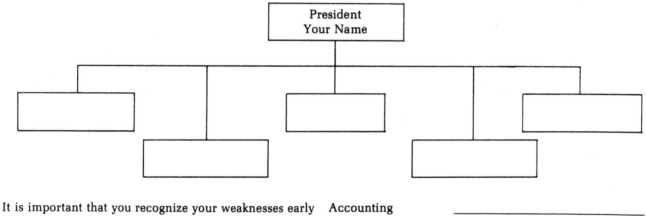

It is important that you recognize your weaknesses early in the game and plan to get assistance wherever you need it. This may be done by using consultants on an as-needed basis, by hiring the needed personnel, or by retaining a lawyer and accountant.

The workblock below lists some of the areas you may want to consider. Adapt it to your needs and indicate who will take care of the various functions. (One name may appear more than once.)

Manufacturing _____

Marketing _____

Research and
Technical Backup _____

Accounting _____

Legal _____

Insurance _____

Other:

_____ _____

_____ _____

_____ _____

_____ _____

Making Your Plan Work

To make your plan work you will need feedback. For example, the year end profit and loss (income) statement shows whether your business made a profit or loss for the past 12 months.

But you can't wait 12 months for the score. To keep your plan on target you need readings at frequent intervals. A profit and loss statement at the end of each month or at the end of each quarter is one type of frequent feedback. However, the P and L may be more of a *loss* than a profit statement if you rely only on it. In addition, your cash flow projection must be continuously updated and revised as necessary. You must set up management controls which will help you to insure that the right things are being done from day to day and from week to week.

The management control system which you set up should give you precise information on: inventory, production, quality, sales, collection of accounts receivable, and disbursements. The simpler the system, the better. Its purpose is to give you and your key people current information in time to correct deviations from approved policies. procedures, or practices. You are after facts with emphasis on trouble spots.

Inventory Control. The purpose of controlling inventory is to provide maximum service to your customers. Your aim should be to achieve a rapid turnover on your inventory, the fewer dollars you tie up in raw materials inventory and in finished goods inventory, the better. Or, saying it in reverse, the faster you get back your investment in raw materials and finished goods inventory, the faster you can reinvest your capital to meet additional consumer needs.

In setting up inventory controls, keep in mind that the cost of the inventory is not your only cost. There are inventory costs, such as the cost of purchasing, the cost of keeping inventory records, and the cost of receiving and storing raw materials.

Production. In preparing this business plan, you have estimated the cost figures for your manufacturing operation. Use these figures as the basis for standards against which you can measure your day-to-day operations to make sure that the clock does not nibble away at profits. These standards will help you to keep machine time, labor man-hours, process time, delay time, and down time within your projected cost figures. Periodic production reports will allow you to keep your finger on potential drains on your profits and should also provide feedback on your overhead expense.

Quality Control. Poorly made products cause a company to lose customers. In addition, when a product fails to perform satisfactorily, shipments are held up, inventory is increased, and a severe financial strain can result. Moreover, when quality is poor, it's a good bet that waste and spoilage on the production line are greater than they should be. The details—checkpoints, reports, and so on—of your quality control system will depend on your type of production system. In working out these details, keep in mind that their purpose is to answer one question: What needs to be done to see that the work is done right the first time? Will you have to do extensive quality control on raw materials? This is an added expense you must consider.

Sales. To keep on top of sales, you will need answers to questions, such as: How many sales were made? What was the dollar amount? What products were sold? At what price? What delivery dates were promised? What credit terms were given to customers?

It is also important that you set up an effective collection system for "accounts receivable," so that you don't tie up your capital in aging accounts.

Disbursements. Your management controls should also give you information about the dollars your company pays out. In checking on your bills, you do not want to be penny-wise and pound-foolish. You need to know that major items, such as paying bills on time to get the supplier's discount, are being handled according to your policies. Your review system should also give you the opportunity to make judgments on the use of funds. In this manner, you can be on top of emergencies as well as routine situations. Your system should also keep you aware that tax monies, such as payroll income tax deductions, are set aside and paid out at the proper time.

Break Even. Break-even analysis is a management control device because the break-even point shows about how much you must sell under given conditons in order to just cover your costs with NO profit and NO loss.

In preparing to start or expand a manufacturing business you should determine at what approximate level of sales a new product will pay for itself and begin to bring in a profit.

Profit depends on sales volume, selling price, and costs. So, to figure your break-even point, first separate your fixed costs, such as rent or depreciation allowance, from your variable costs per unit, such as direct labor and materials.

Part IV
Finding Money for Your Business

Summary

Small businesses never seem to have enough money. Bankers and suppliers, naturally, are important in financing small business growth through loans and credit, but an equally important source of long term growth capital is the venture capital firm. Venture capital financing may have an extra bonus, for if a small firm has an adequate equity base, banks are more willing to extend credit.

This *Aid* discusses what venture capital firms look for when they analyze a company and its proposal for investment, the kinds of conditions venture firms may require in financing agreements, and the various types of venture capital investors. It stresses the importance of formal financial planning as the first step to getting venture capital financing.

What Venture Capital Firms Look For

One way of explaining the different ways in which banks and venture capital firms evaluate a small business seeking funds, put simply, is: Banks look at its immediate future, but are most heavily influenced by its past. Venture capitalists look to its longer run future.

To be sure, venture capital firms and individuals are interested in many of the same factors that influence bankers in their analysis of loan applications from smaller companies. **All** financial people want to know the results and ratios of past operations, the amount and intended use of the needed funds, and the earnings and financial condition of future projections. But venture capitalists look much more closely at the features of the product and the size of the market than do commercial banks.

Banks are creditors. They're interested in the product/market position of the company to the extent they look for assurance that this service or product can provide steady sales and generate sufficient cash flow to repay the loan. They look at projections to be certain that owner/managers have done their homework.

Venture capital firms are owners. They hold stock in the company, adding their invested capital to its equity base. Therefore, they examine existing or planned products or services and the potential markets for them with extreme care. They invest only in firms they believe can rapidly increase sales and generate substantial profits.

Why? Because venture capital firms invest for long-term capital, not for interest income. A common estimate is that they look for **three to five times their investment** in five or seven years.

Of course venture capitalists don't realize capital gains on all their investments. Certainly they don't make capital gains of 300% to 500% except on a very limited portion of their total investments. But their intent is to find venture projects with this appreciation potential to make up for investments that aren't successful.

Venture capital is a risky business, because it's difficult to judge the worth of early stage companies. So most venture capital firms set rigorous policies for venture proposal size, maturity of the seeking company, requirements and evaluation procedures to reduce risks, since their investments are unprotected in the event of failure.

Size of the Venture Proposal. Most venture capital firms are interested in investment projects requiring an investment of $250,000 to $1,500,000. Projects requiring under $250,000 are of limited interest because of the high cost of investigation and administration; however, some venture firms will consider smaller proposals, if the investment is intriguing enough.

The typical venture capital firm receives over 1,000 proposals a year. Probably 90% of these will be rejected quickly because they don't fit the established geographical, technical, or market area policies of the firm—or **because they have been poorly prepared.**

The remaining 10% are investigated with care. These investigations are expensive. Firms may hire consultants to evaluate the product, particularly when it's the result of innovation or is technologically complex. The market size and competitive position of the company are analyzed by contacts with present and potential customers, suppliers, and others. Production costs are reviewed. The financial condition of the company is confirmed by an auditor. The legal form and registration of the business are checked. Most importantly, the character and competence of the management are evaluated by the venture capital firm, normally via a thorough background check.

These preliminary investigations may cost a venture firm between $2,000 and $3,000 per company investigated. They result in perhaps 10 to 15 proposals of interest. Then, second investigations, more thorough and more expensive than the first, reduce the number of proposals under consideration to only three or four. Eventually the firm invests in one or two of these.

Maturity of the Firm Making the Proposal. Most venture capital firms' investment interest is limited to projects proposed by companies with some operating history, even though they may not yet have shown a profit. Companies that can expand into a new product line or a new market with additional funds are particularly interesting. The venture capital firm can provide funds to enable such companies to grow in a spurt rather than gradually as they would on retained earnings.

Companies that are just starting or that have serious financial difficulties may interest some venture capitalists, if the potential for significant gain over the long run can be identified and assessed. If the venture firm has already extended its portfolio to a large risk concentration, they may be reluctant to invest in these areas because of increased risk of loss.

However, although most venture capital firms will not consider a great many proposals from start-up companies, there are a small number of venture firms that will do only "start-up" financing. The small firm that has a well thought-out plan and can demonstrate that its management group has an outstanding record (even if it is with other companies) has a decided edge in acquiring this kind of seed capital.

Management of the Proposing Firm. Most venture capital firms concentrate primarily on the competence and character of the proposing firm's management. They feel that even mediocre products can be successfully manufactured, promoted, and distributed by an experienced, energetic management group.

They look for a group that is able to work together easily and productively, especially under conditions of stress from temporary reversals and competitive problems. They know that even excellent products can be ruined by poor management. Many venture capital firms really invest in management capability, not in product or market potential.

Obviously, analysis of managerial skill is difficult. A partner or senior executive of a venture capital firm normally spends at least a week at the offices of a company being considered, talking with and observing the management, to estimate their competence and character.

Venture capital firms usually require that the company under consideration have a complete management group. Each of the important functional areas — product design, marketing, production, finance, and control — must be under the direction of a trained, experienced member of the group. Responsibilities must be clearly

assigned. And, in addition to a thorough understanding of the industry, each member of the management team must be firmly committed to the company and its future.

The "Something Special" in the Plan. Next in importance to the excellence of the proposing firm's management group, most venture capital firms seek a distinctive element in the strategy or product/market/process combination of the firm. This distinctive element may be a new feature of the product or process or a particular skill or technical competence of the management. But it **must** exist. It **must** provide a competitive advantage.

Elements of a Venture Proposal

Purpose and Objectives — a summary of the what and why of the project.

Proposed Financing — the amount of money you'll need from the beginning to the maturity of the project proposed, how the proceeds will be used, how you plan to structure the financing, and why the amount designated is required.

Marketing — a description of the market segment you've got or plan to get, the competition, the characteristics of the market, and your plans (with costs) for getting or holding the market segment you're aiming at.

History of the Firm — a summary of significant financial and organizational milestones, description of employees and employee relations, explanations of banking relationships, recounting of major services or products your firm has offered during its existence, and the like.

Description of the Product or Service — a full description of the product (process) or service offered by the firm and the costs associated with it in detail.

Financial Statements — both for the past few years and pro forma projections (balance sheets, income statements, and cash flows) for the next 3-5 years, showing the effect anticipated if the project is undertaken and if the financing is secured (This should include an analysis of key variables affecting financial performance, showing what could happen if the projected level of revenue is not attained.).

Capitalization — a list of shareholders, how much is invested to date, and in what form (equity/debt).

Biographical Sketches — the work histories and qualifications of key owners/employees.

Principal Suppliers and Customers

Problems Anticipated and Other Pertinent Information — a candid discussion of any contingent liabilities, pending litigation, tax or patent difficulties, and any other contingencies that might affect the project you're proposing.

Advantages — a discussion of what's special about your product, service, marketing plans or channels that gives your project unique leverage.

Provisions of the Investment Proposal

What happens when, after the exhaustive investigation and analysis, the venture capital firm decides to invest in a company? Most venture firms prepare an equity financing proposal that details the amount of money to be provided, the percentage of common stock to be surrendered in exchange for these funds, the interim financing method to be used, and the protective covenants to be included.

This proposal will be discussed with the management of the company to be financed. The final financing agreement will be negotiated and generally represents a compromise between the management of the company and the partners or senior executives of the venture capital firm. The important elements of this compromise are: ownership, control, annual charges, and final objectives.

Ownership. Venture capital financing is not inexpensive for the owners of a small business. The partners of the venture firm buy a portion of the business's equity in exchange for their investment.

This percentage of equity varies, of course, and depends upon the amount of money provided, the success and worth of the business, and the anticipated investment return. It can range from perhaps 10% in the case of an established, profitable company to as much as 80% or 90% for beginning or financially troubled firms.

Most venture firms, at least initially, don't want a position of more than 30% to 40% because they want the owner to have the incentive to keep building the business. If additional financing is required to support business growth, the outsiders' stake may exceed 50%, but investors realize that small business owner-managers can lose their entrepreneurial zeal under those circumstances. In the final analysis, however, the venture firm, regardless of its percentage of ownership, really wants to leave control in the hands of the company's managers, because it is really investing in that management team in the first place.

Most venture firms determine the ratio of funds provid-

ed to equity requested by a comparison of the present financial worth of the contributions made by each of the parties to the agreement. The present value of the contribution by the owner of a starting or financially troubled company is obviously rated low. Often it is estimated as just the existing value of his or her idea and the competitive costs of the owner's time. The contribution by the owners of a thriving business is valued much higher. Generally, it is capitalized at a multiple of the current earnings and/or net worth.

Financial valuation is not an exact science. The final compromise on the owner's contribution's worth in the equity financing agreement is likely to be much lower than the owner thinks it should be and considerably higher than the partners of the capital firm think it might be. In the ideal situation, of course, the two parties to the agreement are able to do together what neither could do separately: 1) the company is able to grow fast enough with the additional funds to do more than overcome the owner's loss of equity, and 2) the investment grows at a sufficient rate to compensate the venture capitalists for assuming the risk.

An equity financing agreement with an outcome in five to seven years which pleases both parties is ideal. Since, of course, the parties can't see this outcome in the present, neither will be perfectly satisfied with the compromise reached.

It is important, though, for the business owner to look at the future. He or she should carefully consider the impact of the ratio of funds invested to the ownership given up, not only for the present, but for the years to come.

Control. Control is a much simpler issue to resolve. Unlike the division of equity over which the parties are bound to disagree, control is an issue in which they have a common (though perhaps unapparent) interest. While it's understandable that the management of a small company will have some anxiety in this area, the partners of a venture firm have little interest in assuming control of the business. They have neither the technical expertise nor the managerial personnel to run a number of small companies in diverse industries. They much prefer to leave operating control to the existing management.

The venture capital firm does, however, want to participate in any strategic decisions that might change the basic product/market character of the company and in any major investment decisions that might divert or deplete the financial resouces of the company. They will, therefore, generally ask that at least one partner be made a director of the company.

Venture capital firms also want to be able to assume control and attempt to rescue their investments, if severe financial, operating, or marketing problems develop. Thus, they will usually include protective covenants in their equity financing agreements to permit them to take control and appoint new officers if financial performance is very poor.

Annual Charges. The investment of the venture capital firm may be in the final form of direct stock ownership which does not impose fixed charges. More likely, it will be in an interim form—convertible subordinated debentures or preferred stock. Financings may also be straight loans with options or warrants that can be converted to a future equity position at a pre-established price.

The convertible debenture form of financing is like a loan. The debentures can be converted at an established ratio to the common stock of the company within a given period, so that the venture capital firm can prepare to realize their capital gains at their option in the future. These instruments are often subordinated to existing and planned debt to permit the company invested in to obtain additional bank financing.

Debentures also provide additional security and control for the venture firm and impose a fixed charge for interest (and sometimes for principal payment, too) upon the company. The owner-manager of a small company seeking equity financing should consider the burden of any fixed annual charges resulting from the financing agreement.

Final Objectives. Venture capital firms generally intend to realize capital gains on their investments by providing for a stock buy-back by the small firm, by arranging a public offering of stock of the company invested in, or by providing for a merger with a larger firm that has publicly traded stock. They usually hope to do this within five to seven years of their initial investment. (It should be noted that several additional stages of financing may be required over this period of time.)

Most equity financing agreements include provisions guaranteeing that the venture capital firm may participate in any stock sale or approve any merger, regardless of their percentage of stock ownership. Sometimes the agreement will require that the management work toward an eventual stock sale or merger. Clearly, the owner-manager of a small company seeking equity financing must consider the future impact upon his or her own stock holdings and personal ambition of the venture firm's aims, since taking in a venture capitalist as a partner may be virtually a commitment to sell out or go public.

Types of Venture Capital Firms

There is quite a variety of types of venture capital firms. They include:

Traditional partnerships—which are often established by wealthy families to aggressively manage a portion of their funds by investing in small companies;

Professionally managed pools—which are made up of institutional money and which operate like the traditional partnerships;

Investment banking firms—which usually trade in more established securities, but occasionally form investor syndicates for venture proposals;

Insurance companies—which often have required a portion of equity as a condition of their loans to smaller companies as protection against inflation;

Manufacturing companies—which have sometimes looked upon investing in smaller companies as a means of supplementing their R & D programs (Some "Fortune 500" corporations have venture capital operations to help keep them abreast of technological innovations); and

Small Business Investment Corporations (SBIC's)—which are licensed by the Small Business Adminsitration (SBA) and which may provide management assistance as well as venture capital. (When dealing with SBIC's, the small business owner-manager should intially determine if the SBIC is primarily interested in an equity position, as venture capital, or merely in long-term lending on a fully secured basis.)

In addition to these venture capital firms there are individual private investors and finders. Finders, which can be firms or individuals, often know the capital industry and may be able to help the small company seeking capital to locate it, though they are generally not sources of capital themselves. Care should be exercised so that a small business owner deals with reputable, professional finders whose fees are in line with industry practice. Further, it should be noted that venture capitalists generally prefer working directly with principals in making investments, though finders may provide useful introductions.

The Importance of Formal Financial Planning

In case there is any doubt about the implications of the previous sections, it should be noted: **It is extremely**

difficult for any small firm—especially the starting or struggling company—to get venture capital.

There is one thing, however, that owner-managers of small businesses can do to improve the chances of their venture proposals at least escaping the 90% which are almost immediately rejected. In a word—**plan.**

Having financial plans demonstrates to venture capital firms that you are a competent manager, that you may have that special managerial edge over other small business owners looking for equity money. You may gain a decided advantage through well-prepared plans and projections that include: cash budgets, pro forma statements, and capital investment analysis and capital source studies.

Cash budgets should be projected for one year and prepared monthly. They should combine expected sales revenues, cash receipts, material, labor and overhead expenses, and cash disbursements on a monthly basis. This permits anticipation of fluctuations in the level of cash and planning for **short term** borrowing and investment.

Pro forma statements should be prepared for planning up to 3 years ahead. They should include both income statements and balance sheets. Again, these should be prepared quarterly to combine expected sales revenues; production, marketing, and administrative expenses; profits; product, market, or process investments; and supplier, bank, or investment company borrowings. Pro forma statements permit you to anticipate the financial results of your operations and to plan **intermediate term** borrowings and investments.

Capital investment analyses and capital source studies should be prepared for planning up to 5 years ahead. The investment analyses should compare rates of return for product, market, or process investment, while the source alternatives should compare the cost and availability of debt and equity and the expected level of retained earnings, which together will support the selected investments. These analyses and source studies should be prepared quarterly so you may anticipate the financial consequences of changes in your company's strategy. They will allow you to plan **long term** borrowings, equity placements, and major investments.

There's a bonus in making such projections. They force you to consider the results of your actions. Your estimates must be explicit; you have to examine and evaluate your managerial records; disagreements have to be resolved—at least discussed and understood. Financial planning may be burdensome but it's one of the keys to business success.

Now, making these financial plans will not guarantee that you'll be able to get venture capital. Not making them, will virtually assure that you won't receive favorable consideration from venture capitalists.

Summary

Some small businesspersons cannot understand why a lending institution refused to lend them money. Others have no trouble getting funds, but they are surprised to find strings attached to their loans. Such owner-managers fail to realized that banks and other lenders have to operate by certain principles just as do other types of business.

This Aid discusses the following fundamentals of borrowing: (1) credit worthiness, (2) kinds of loans, (3) amount of money needed, (4) collateral, (5) loan restrictions and limitations, (6) the loan application, and (7) standards which the lender uses to evaluate the application.

Introduction

Inexperience with borrowing procedures often creates resentment and bitterness. The stories of three small businesspersons illustrate this point.

"I'll never trade here again," Bill Smith* said when his bank refused to grant him a loan. "I'd like to let you have it, Bill," the banker said,"but your firm isn't earning enough to meet your current obligations." Mr Smith was unaware of a vital financial fact, namely, that lending institutions have to be certain that the borrower's business can repay the loan.

Tom Jones lost his temper when the bank refused him a loan because he did not know what kind or how much money he needed. "We hesitate to lend," the banker said, "to business owners with such vague ideas of what and how much they need."

John Williams' case was somewhat different. He didn't explode until after he got the loan. When the papers were ready to sign, he realized that the loan agreement put certain limitations on his business activities. "You can't dictate to me," he said and walked out of the bank. What he didn't realize was that the limitations were for his good as well as for the bank's protection.

Knowledge of the financial facts of business life could have saved all three the embarrassment of losing their tempers. Even more important, such information would have helped them to borrow money at a time when their businesses needed it badly.

*All names in Aids are fictitious

This **Aid** is designed to give the highlights of what is involved in sound business borrowing. It should be helpful to those who have little or no experience with borrowing. More experienced owner-managers should find it useful in re-evaluating their borrowing operations.

Is Your Firm Credit Worthy?

The ability to obtain money when you need it is as necessary to the operation of your business as is a good location or the right equipment, reliable sources of supplies and materials, or an adequate labor force. Before a bank or any other lending agency will lend you money, the loan officer must feel satisfied with the answers to the five following questions:

1. What sort of person are you, the prospective borrower? By all odds, the character of the borrower comes first. Next is your ability to manage your business.
2. What are you going to do with the money? The answer to this questions will determine the type of loan, short or long-term. Money to be used for the purchase of seasonal inventory will require quicker repayment than money used to buy fixed assets.
3. When and how do you plan to pay it back? Your banker's judgment of your business ability and the type of loan will be a deciding factor in the answer to this question.
4. Is the cushion in the loan large enough? In other words, does the amount requested make suitable allowance for unexpected developments? The banker decides this question on the basis of your financial statement which sets forth the condition of your business and on the collateral pledged.
5. What is the outlook for business in general and for your business particularly?

Adequate Financial Data Is a "Must."
The banker wants to make loans to businesses which are solvent, profitable, and growing. The two basic financial statements used to determine those conditions are the balance sheet and profit-and-loss statement. The former is the major yardstick for solvency and the latter for profits. A continuous series of these two statements over a period of time is the principal device for measuring financial stability and growth potential.

In interviewing loan applicants and in studying their records, the banker is expecially interested in the following facts and figures.

General Information: Are the books and records up-to-date and in good condition? What is the condition of accounts payable? Of notes payable? What are the salaries of the owner-manager and other company officers? Are all taxes being paid currently? What is the order backlog? What is the number of employees? What is the insurance coverage?

Accounts Receivable: Are there indications that some of the accounts receivable have already been pledged to another creditor? What is the accounts receivable turnover? Is the accounts receivable total weakened because many customers are far behind in their payments? Has a large enough reserve been set up to cover doubtfull accounts? How much do the largest accounts owe and what percentage of your total accounts does this amount represent?

Inventories: Is merchandise in good shape or will it have to be marked down? How much raw material is on hand? How much work is in process? How much of the inventory is finished goods?

Is there any obsolete inventory? Has an excessive amount of inventory been consigned to customers? Is inventory turnover in line with the turnover for other businesses in the same industry? Or is money being tied up too long in inventory?

Fixed Assets: What is the type, age, and condition of the equipment? What are the depreciation policies? What are the details of mortgages or conditional sales contracts? What are the future acquisition plans?

What Kind of Money?

When you set out to borrow money for your firm, it is important to know the kind of money you need from a bank or other lending institution. There are three kinds of money: short term, term money, and equity capital.

Keep in mind that the purpose for which the funds are to be used is an important factor in deciding the kind of money needed. But even so, deciding what kind of money to use is not always easy. It is sometimes complicated by the fact that you may be using some of the various kinds of money at the same time and for identical purposes.

Keep in mind that a very important distinction between the types of money is the source of repayment. Generally, short-term loans are repaid from the liquidation of current assets which they have financed. Long-term loans are usually repaid from earnings.

Short-Term Bank Loans

You can use short-term bank loans for purposes such as financing accounts receivable for, say 30 to 60 days. Or you can use them for purposes that take longer to pay off—such as for building a seasonal inventory over a period of 5 to 6 months. Usually, lenders expect short-term loans to be repaid after their purposes have been served: for example, accounts receivable loans, when the outstanding accounts have been paid by the borrower's customers, and inventory loans, when the inventory has been converted into saleable merchandise.

Banks grant such money either on your general credit reputation with an unsecured loan or on a secured loan.

The unsecured loan is the most frequently used form of bank credit for short-term purposes. You do not have to put up collateral because the bank relies on your credit reputation.

The secured loan involves a pledge of some or all of your assets. The bank requires security as a protection for its depositors against the risks that are involved even in business situations where the chances of success are good.

Term Borrowing

Term borrowing privides money you plan to pay back over a fairly long time. Some people break it down into two forms: (1) intermediate—loans longer than 1 year but less than 5 years, and (2) long-term—loans for more than 5 years.

However, for your purpose of matching the kind of money to the needs of your company, think of term borrowing as a kind of money which you probably will pay back in periodic installments from earnings.

Equity Capital

Some people confuse term borrowing and equity (or investment) capital. Yet there is a big difference. You don't have to repay equity money. It is money you get by selling a part interest in your business.

You take people into your company who are willing to risk their money in it. They are interested in potential income rather than in an immediate return on their investment.

How Much Money?

The amount of money you need to borrow depends on the purpose for which you need funds. Figuring the amount of money required for business construction, conversion, or expansion—term loans or equity capital—is relatively easy. Equipment manufacturers, architects, and builders will readily supply you with cost estimates. On the other hand, the amount of working capital you need depends upon the type of business you're in. While rule-of-thumb ratios may be helpful as a starting point, a detailed projection of sources and uses of funds over some future period of time—usually for 12 months—is a better approach. In this way, the characteristics of the particular situation can be taken into account. Such a projection is developed through the combination of a predicted budget and a cash forecast.

The budget is based on recent operating experience plus your best judgment of performance during the coming period. The cash forecast is your estimates of cash receipts and disbursements during the budget period. Thus, the budget and the cash forecast together represent your plan for meeting your working capital requirements.

To plan your working capital requirements, it is important to know the "cash flow" which your business will generate. This involves simply a consideration of all elements of cash receipts and disbursements at the time they occur. These elements are listed in the profit-and-loss statement which has been adapted to show cash flow. They should be projected for each month.

What Kind of Collateral?

Sometimes, your signature is the only security the bank needs when making a loan. At other times, the bank requires additional assurance that the money will be repaid. The kind and amount of security depends on the bank and on the borrower's situation.

If the loan required cannot be justified by the borrower's financial statements alone, a pledge of security may bridge the gap. The types of security are: endorsers; comakers and guarantors; assignment of leases; trust receipts and floor planning; chattel mortgages; real estate; accounts receivables; savings accounts; life insurance policies; and stocks and bonds. In a substantial number of States where the Uniform Commercial Code has been enacted, paperwork for recording loan transactions will be greatly simplified.

Endorsers, Co-makers, and Guarantors
Borrowers often get other people to sign a note in order to bolster their own credit. These **endorsers** are contingently liable for the note they sign. If the borrower fails to pay up, the bank expects the endorser to make the note good. Sometimes, the endorser may be asked to pledge assets or securities too.

A co-maker is one who creates an obligation jointly with the borrower. In such cases, the bank can collect directly from either the maker or the co-maker.

A guarantor is one who guarantees the payment of a note by signing a guaranty commitment. Both private and government lenders often require guarantees from officers of corporations in order to assure continuity of effective management. Sometimes, a manufacturer will act as guarantor for customers.

Assignment of Leases
The assigned lease as security is similar to the guarantee. It is used, for example, in some franchise situations.

The bank lends the money on a building and takes a mortgage. Then the lease, which the dealer and the parent franchise company work out, is assigned so that the bank automatically receives the rent payments. In this manner, the bank is guaranteed repayment of the loan.

Warehouse Receipts
Banks also take commodities as security by lending money on a warehouse receipt. Such a receipt is usually delivered directly to the bank and shows that the merchandise used as security either has been placed in a public warehouse or has been left on your premises under the control of one of your employees who is bonded (as in field warehousing). Such loans are generally made on staple or standard merchandise which can be readily marketed. The typical warehouse receipt loan is for a percentage of the estimated value of the goods used as securtiy.

Trust Receipts and Floor Planning
Merchandise, such as automobiles, appliances, and boats, has to be displayed to be sold. The only way many small marketers can afford such displays is by borrowing money. Such loans are often secured by a note and a trust receipt.

This trust receipt is the legal paper for floor planning. It is used for serial-numbered merchandise. When you sign one, you (1) acknowledge receipt of the merchandise, (2) agree to keep the merchandise in trust for the bank, and (3) promise to pay the bank as you sell the goods.

Chattel Mortgages
If you buy equipment such as a cash register or a delivery truck, you may want to get a chattel mortgage loan. You give the bank a lien on the equipment you are buying.

The bank also evaluates the present and future market value of the equipment being used to secure the loan. How rapidly will it depreciate? Does the borrower have the necessary fire, theft, property damage, and public liability insurance on the equipment? The banker has to be sure that the borrower protects the equipment.

Real Estate

Real estate is another form of collateral for long-term loans. When taking a real estate mortgage, the bank finds out: (1) the location of the real estate, (2) its physical condition, (3) its foreclosure value, and (4) the amount of insurance carried on the property.

Accounts Receivable

Many banks lend money on accounts receivable. In effect, you are counting on your customers to pay your note.

The bank may take accounts receivable on a notification or a nonnotification plan. Under the **notification** plan, the purchaser of the goods is informed by the bank that his or her account has been assigned to it and he or she is asked to pay the bank. Under the **nonnotification** plan, the borrower's customers continue to pay you the sums due on their accounts and you pay the bank.

Savings Accounts

Sometimes, you might get a loan by assigning to the bank a savings account. In such cases, the bank gets an asignment from you and keeps your passbook. If you assign an account in another bank as collateral, the lending bank asks the other bank to mark its records to show that the account is held as collateral.

Life Insurance

Another kind of collateral is life insurance. Banks will lend up to the cash value of a life insurance policy. You have to assign the policy to the bank.

If the policy is on the life of an executive of a small corporation, corporate resolutions must be made authorizing the assignment. Most insurance companies allow you to sign the policy back to the original beneficiary when the assignment to the bank ends.

Some people like to use life insurance as collateral rather than borrow directly from insurance companies. One reason is that a bank loan is often more convenient to obtain and usually may be obtained at a lower interest rate.

Stocks and Bonds

If you use stocks and bonds as collateral, they must be marketable. As a protection against market declines and possible expenses of liquidation, banks usually lend no more than 75 percent of the market value of high grade stock. On Federal Government or municipal bonds, they may be willing to lend 90 percent or more of their market value.

The bank may ask the borrower for additional security or payment whenever the market value of the stocks or bonds drops below the bank's required margin.

What Are the Lender's Rules?

Lending institutions are not just interested in loan repayments. They are also interested in borrowers with healthy profit-making businesses. Therefore, whether or not collateral is required for a loan, they set loan limitations and restrictions to protect themselves against unnecessary risk and at the same time against poor management practices by their borrowers. Often some owner-managers consider loan limitations a burden.

Yet others feel that such limitations also offer an opportunity for improving their management techniques.

Especially in making long-term loans, the borrower as well as the lender should be thinking of: (1) the net earning power of the borrowing company, (2) the capability of its management, (3) the long range prospects of the company, and (4) the long range prospects of the industry of which the company is a part. Such factors often mean that limitations increase as the duration of the loan increases.

What Kinds of Limitations?

The kinds of limitations, which an owner-manager finds set upon the company depends, to a great extent, on the company. If the company is a good risk, only minimum limitations need be set. A poor risk, of course, is different. Its limitations should be greater than those of a stronger company.

Look now for a few moments at the kinds of limitations and restrictions which the lender may set. Knowing what they are can help you see how they affect your operations.

The limitations which you will usually run into when you borrow money are:

(1) Repayment terms.

(2) Pledging or the use of security.

(3) Periodic reporting.

A loan agreement, as you may already know, is a tailor-made document covering, or referring to, all the terms and conditions of the loan. With it, the lender does two things: (1) protects position as a creditor (keeps that position in as protected a state as it was on the date the loan was made and (2) assures repayment according to the terms.

The lender reasons that the borrower's business should **generate enough funds** to repay the loan while taking care of other needs. The lender considers that cash inflow should be great enough to do this without hurting the working capital of the borrower.

Covenants—Negative and Positive

The actual restrictions in a loan agreement come under a section known as covenants. Negative covenants are things which the borrower may not do without prior approval from the lender. Some examples are: further additions to the borrower's total debt, nonpledge to others of the borrower's assets, and issuance of dividends in excess of the terms of the loan agreement.

On the other hand, positive covenants spell out things which the borrower must do. Some examples are: (1) maintenance of a minimum net working capital. (2) carrying of adequate insurance, (3) repaying the loan according to the terms of the agreement, and (4) supplying the lender with financial statements and reports.

Overall, however, loan agreements may be amended from time to time and exceptions made. Certain provisions may be waived from one year to the next with the consent of the lender.

You Can Negotiate

Next time you go to borrow money, thrash out the lending terms before you sign. It is good practice no matter how badly you may need the money. Ask to see the papers in advance of the loan closing. Legitimate lenders are glad to cooperate.

Chances are that the lender may "give" some on the terms. Keep in mind also that, while you're mulling over the terms, you may want to get the advice of your associates and outside advisors. In short, try to get terms which you know your company can live with. Remember, however, that once the terms have been agreed upon and the loan is made (or authorized as in the case of SBA), you are bound by them.

The Loan Application

Now you have read about the various aspects of the lending process and are ready to apply for a loan. Banks and other private lending institutions, as well as the Small Business Administration, require a loan application on which you list certain information about your business.

For the purposes of explaining a loan application, this **Aid** uses the Small Business Administration's application for a loan (SBA Form 4 not included). The SBA form is more detailed than most bank forms. The bank has the advantage of prior knowledge of the applicant and his or her activities. Since SBA does not have such knowledge, its form is more detailed. Moreover, the longer maturities of SBA loans ordinarily will necessitate more knowledge about the applicant.

Before you get to the point of filling out a loan application, you should have talked with an SBA representative, or perhaps your accountant or banker, to make sure that your business is eligible for an SBA loan. Because of public policy, SBA cannot make certain types of loans. Nor can it make loans under certain conditions. For example, if you can get a loan on reasonable terms from a bank, SBA cannot lend you money. The owner-manager is also not eligible for an SBA loan if he or she can get funds by selling assets which his or her company does not need in order to grow.

When the SBA representative gives you a loan application, you will notice that most of its sections ("Application for Loan"—SBA Form 4) are self-explanatory. However, some applicants have trouble with certain sections because they do not know where to go to get the necessary information.

Section 3—"Collateral Offered" is an example. A company's books should show the net value of assets such as business real estate and business machinery and equipment. "Net" means what you paid for such assets less depreciation.

If an owner-manager's records do not contain detailed information on business collateral, such as real estate and machinery and equipment, the bank sometimes can get it from your Federal income tax returns. Reviewing the depreciation which you have taken for tax purposes on such collateral can be helpful in arriving at the value of these assets.

If you are a good manager, you should have your books balanced monthly. However, some businesses prepare balance sheets less regularly. In filling out your "Balance Sheet as of _____, 19 ____,Fiscal Year Ends _____," remember that you must show the condition of you business within 60 days of the date on your loan application. It is best to get expert advice when working up such vital information. Your accountant or banker will be able to help you.

Cash Budget

(For three months, ending March 31, 19 _____)

	January		February		March	
	Budget	Actual	Budget	Actual	Budget	Actual
Expected Cash Receipts:						
1. Cash sales						
2. Collections on accounts receivable						
3. Other income						
4. Total cash receipts						
Expected Cash Payments						
5. Raw materials						
6. Payroll						
7. Other factory expenses (including maintenance)						
8. Advertising						
9. Selling expense						
10. Administrative expense (including salary of owner-manager)						
11. New plant and equipment						
12. Other payments(taxes, including estimated income tax; repayment of loans; interest; etc.)						
13. Total cash payments						
14. Expected Cash Balance at beginning of the month						
15. Cash increase of decrease (item 4 minus item 13)						
16. Expected cash balance at end of month (item 14 plus item 15)						
17. Desired working cash balance						
18. Short-term loans needed (item 17 minus item 16, if item 17 is larger)						
19. Cash available for dividends, capital cash expenditures, and/or short investments (item 16 minus item 17, if item 16 is larger than item 17)						
Capital Cash:						
20. Cash available (item 19 after deducting dividends, etc.)						
21. Desired capital cash (item 11, new plant equipment)						
22. Long-term loans needed (item 21 less item 20, if item 20 is larger than item 20)						

Again, if your records do not show the details necessary for working up profit and loss statements, your Federal income tax returns may be useful in getting together facts for the SBA loan application.

Insurance

SBA also needs information about the kinds of insurance a company carries. The owner-manager gives these facts by listing various insurance policies.

Personal Finances

SBA also must know something about the personal financial condition of the applicant. Among the types of information are: personal cash position; source of income including salary and personal investments; stocks, bonds, real estate, and other property owned in the applicant's own name; personal debts including installment credit payments, life insurance premiums, and so forth.

Evaluating the Application

Once you have supplied the necessary information, the next step in the borrowing process is the evaluation of your application. Whether the processing officer is in a bank or in SBA, the officer considers the same kinds of things when determining whether to grant or refuse the loan. The SBA loan processor looks for:

(1) The borrower's debt paying record to suppliers, banks, home mortgage holders, and other creditors.

(2) The ratio of the borrower's debt to net worth.

(3) The past earnings of the company.

(4) The value and condition of the collateral which the borrower offers for security.

The SBA loan processor also looks for: (1) the borrower's management ability, (2) the borrower's character, and (3) the future prospects of the borrower's business.

Summary

Poor management is the reason why some owner-managers of small firms have trouble when they try to borrow. Those managers often fail to forecast and to plan for cash needs. The resulting business ailment is a "cash crises."

Sound management must be practiced if loans are to be obtained and used profitably. Such management includes: knowing the firm's cash flow, forecasting cash needs, planning to borrow at the appropriate time, and substantiating the firm's payback ability.

This Aid **includes examples of the following: a cash budget forecast, a projection of borrowing requirements, and a cash flow schedule for repaying a loan.**

In spite of respectable sales volumes, many owners of small businesses run into financial trouble. Some get in so deep that they are barely able to pull their heads back above water. Others find themselves only weeks or months away from tacking "out of business" signs on their doors.

Often these owner-managers have three things in common. First, they know their line of business. Their technical ability is first rate. Second, they are poor managers. In many instances, they fail to plan ahead because of their enthusiasm for the operating side of their business. In the third place, most of them feel that additional money will solve their problems. They think that a loan will pull them out of the red.

Lending Officer's Viewpoint

Often a bank lending officer refuses or "declines" that loan request of such manager-owners. It is not that a banker lacks appreciation for the hard work and long hours which these owners put into their businesses. Nor does the bank question their good intentions.

Foremost in the lender's mind is the question: Can the firm pay back this loan? Thus, in many cases, the lender refuses the loan because the owner-manager hastily and haphazardly prepared the loan application under pressuring circumstances. As a result, the lending officer detects an air of instability and lack of planning in the owner-manager's description of his or her affairs. "How is the borrower really going to repay," the lending officer asks, "if the borrower doesn't actually know how much money is needed and how it is going to be used?"

If your request for a loan is turned down, the best bet is to accept the refusal gracefully and look for weaknesses in the presentation. You can correct these weaknesses when applying for a loan in the future.

Pertinent Questions

The lender needs the answers to several pertinent questions to determine whether or not the borrower can repay the loan. One of these questions is: What does the borrower intend to use the money for?

What Kind of Money? When you consider borrowing, determine what kind of money you need. A business uses four basic types of money in its operations. Your purpose in borrowing will determine the type.

1. Trade Credit. This type of "money" is not borrowed. It is money you owe your suppliers who permit you to carry your fast-moving inventory on open account. A good credit experience is proven evidence of your ability to repay borrowed funds.

2. Short-Term Credit. Banks and other lenders will provide this type of money to carry you in your purchases of inventory for special reasons, such as buying inventory for the next selling season. Such loans are self-liquidating because they generate sales dollars. You repay short-term credit in less than a year.

3. Long-Term Credit. Such loans—for more than a year—are used for expansion or modernization of your business. They are repaid out of accumulated profits. Usually, the evidence of this type of loan in a small business is a mortgage or a promissory note with terms.

4. Equity Funds. This type of money is never repaid. You get it by relinquishing a part of your profits to an investor. That is you sell an interest in your business.

Many owner-managers fail to recognize the difference between the four types of money. You should keep in mind that money borrowed for a temporary purpose should be used in the profit producing areas of your business and will be repaid out of that operation. Equity funds are those which remain in the business and increase the net worth for the owner.

Are Your Sales Adequate? Are you asking for a loan to bolster sagging sales volume? To buy additional stocks of high-volume merchandise which you feel has even greater potential? To create a new image by an over-all advertising campaign?

What Is Your Receivables Position? Are your accounts going uncollected and getting old? In effect, do you really need money to carry old accounts?

Is Your Profit Margin Adequate? Are you doing a lot of business and showing a lack of profit thus indicating that expenses are not controlled? Or is your market insufficient? What is your breakeven point for profits?

What Is Your Plan For Repayment? Do you forecast your cash income and expenditures realistically?

The lender scrutinizes the cash flow of the business to determine whether or not the owner-manager is providing sufficient cash to meet the firm's obligations. The lender also has to make sure that cash needed for working capital is not being absorbed by the business into other areas of equity and thereby reducing liquidity.

The "Cash Crisis"

The experience of counsellors, such as members of SCORE (SBA's Service Corps of Retired Executives) volunteers, is that all too often the small business owner feels that his or her needs are financial when they are actually managerial. In such firms, money can ease the pressure temporarily, but further indebtedness only intensifies the basic problem. Money alone cannot provide the sound management needed to continue the business.

Counsellors to small business owners are continually faced with the "cash crisis" problem. This cash deficiency results from the lack of planning.

A mistake many purchasers of a business make is that they buy something beyond their means. They take possession of a business of some value but without one important asset—sufficient operating cash. When a buyer does not put aside working capital (cash), he or she cannot pay current bills and the rest of the story is easy to foretell.

It is the "cash crisis."

Sound management consists of arranging matters so that current liabilities are provided for as they become due and hence paid promptly. When such coordination is not present, the result is a constant "cash crisis."

Without a floating supply of cash, a business will experience occasional convulsions which distort, confuse, embarrass, and alarm everyone concerned with the enterprise. The owner-manager's employees and suppliers are the first to sense the nervousness of the situation. When they do, they begin to consider their futures

in the light of these emergencies.

Lack of cash can drive a firm into bankruptcy even though its products are first rate and its operations are profitable.

Avoid A "Cash Crisis"

To avoid a "cash crisis" you should determine how much cash your firm needs for its normal operations. Then plan your finances to achieve the goal. The amount of cash which a business will need differs because all businesses are not alike. Usually, for comfort, five to ten percent of a firm's working capital should be in cash.

In a sense, financial planning is what you anticipate your financial statements will show on a specific date and how you intend to get there. A cash forecast will indicate whether or not your plan of operation is feasible. A budget will indicate the availability of cash at all points of operations.

Cash Budgeting

When the subject of budgeting comes up, some owner-managers say, "That's for the big fellow. I know what my volume is and my bank account tells me how much money I have." These owners fail to realize that budgeting can help to eliminate errors of judgment made in haste or made on assumptions rather than facts.

The first thing you must know in budgeting is what your anticipated expenses are going to be for the period being budgeted. Then, how much in sales must be generated to pay these expenses? What will be left? You must try to determine the high and low points in your operations in order to provide the adequate amount of cash. A sales analysis of previous periods will indicate when the high and low points occur.

This forecasting helps you to plan for financing the purchase of inventory and for carrying your accounts receivable. Controlling inventory and accounts receivable can help to take the strain off of your working capital.

Uses Of A Cash Budget. The cash budget is the most effective tool for planning the cash requirements and resources of your business. With it you plan your financial operations—the cash you expect to take in and pay out. Your goal in budgeting is to maintain a satisfactory cash position for any contingency. When used to project the cash flow of the business, the cash budget will:

Provide efficient use of cash by timing cash disbursements to coincide with cash receipts. These actions may reduce the need for borrowing temporary additional working capital.

Point up cash deficiency periods so that predetermined borrowing requirements may be established and actual amounts determined to reduce excessive indebtedness.

Determine periods for repayment of borrowings.

Establish the practicability of taking trade discounts or not taking them.

Determine periods of surplus cash for investment or purchase of inventory and equipment.

Indicate the adequacy or need for additional permanent working capital in the business.

Be Factual. The important thing to keep in mind in making a cash budget is the word "cash." Be as factual as you can. Try not to over-estimate sales or under-estimate expenses. Your sales forecase must be as accurate as possible because it is the basis for figuring your cash and expenses.

Use your experience to determine your cash sales. In seasonal businesses and those which have high-ticket merchandise, the percent of sales that are for cash will vary from month to month. Account for these ups and downs in each month if they apply to your business.

A format such as that shown in the example below can help you to be factual. This example of a cash budget forecast uses two columns for each month. The second column allows you to insert the actual figures as they occur and helps in correcting mistakes for future forecasts.

Sound Management - Success Story

With sound management a small firm can often achieve a goal by borrowing only a nominal amount. The experience of two partners in a Southeast business provides an example.

They obtained a contract to manufacture and install kitchen cabinets for a large builder. The contract called for installation in 4 months. To meet this deadline, the partners figured that they needed $56,500 in extra working capital.

Because this amount was more than they wanted to borrow, they asked for help from SBA's SCORE program.

The SCORE counselor helped the partners to come up with a borrowing requirement of only $16,000. This solution was arrived at by:

1. Arranging with their supplier to ship and bill for the materials monthly over a 3-month period.

2. Contracting with the builder to make an initial payment and 4 monthly payments.

3. Agreeing not to take any drawings from the business until the cash flow forecast indicated it was free and available.

Based on these facts, the partners estimated that during the 5 months (July through November) the firm should take in $88,000, pay out $56,500, and have a balance of $31,500 at the end of November. However, the problem was in July and August when expenses would run far ahead of the firm's income. To determine how a loan of $16,000 (including interest) could see the firm through these months, the following estimates were made:

Estimate Of Borrowing Requirements To Take On Additional Contract

	July	August	September	October	November
Cash Requirements					
Inventory	$15,000	$10,000	$ 7,000		
Operating Expenses	4,000	6,000	6,000	$ 4,000	$ 2,000
Extra Equipment	2,500				
Total	$21,500	$16,000	$13,000	$ 4,000	$ 2,000
Cash Available					
Cash on Hand	$ 2,000			$ 2,000	$18,000
Collections	10,000	$10,000	$15,000	20,000	31,000
Total	$12,000	$10,000	$15,000	$22,000	$49,000
Excess Cash Over Receipts	0	0	$ 2,000	$18,000	$47,000
Additional Cash Required	$ 9,500	$ 6,000	0	0	0

According to these estimates, at the end of November, the partners would have cash on hand amounting to $47,000. Certain obligations would be outstanding against this cash. The first one would be the repayment of the loan of $16,000. Other obligations would be those which the partners planned to accumulate during the early months of the contract when cash on hand was at a premium, such as reserve for taxes and the partners' draw.

These estimates convinced the partners that they could perform the contract if they could get a loan. The next step was to convince the bank that their plan was sound.

For the bank lending officer's benefit, as well as their own, the partners projected the loan funds through a cash flow plan for the entire business. The cash flow schedule that was prepared is shown below. It showed: (1) that the amount of money requested would be adequate for the firm's needs and (2) the margin of cash that was expected to be available both during the contract and at the end of the contract.

Keep in mind that records are a reflection of the quality of a firm's management. Nobody knows this fact better or uses it more often than a banker.

The efficiency of an owner-manager portrays itself on the profit and loss statement (income statement). The P&L of an effective operation will show adequate profits for the particular line of business. Sales, promotion, expense control, merchandise turnover, and net profit application are the points on which you will be judged.

To determine trends, the lender looks at your current financial statement and those for the past several years. The current statement also shows the lender the makeup of your net worth.

Cash Budget Forecast

	January Est.	Actual	February Est.	Actual
(1) Cash in Bank (Start of month)	$1,400	$1,400 *	$1,850	$2,090 *
(2) Cash in Register (Start of Month)	100	100	150	70
(3) Total Cash [add (1) and (2)]	$1,500	$1,500	$2,000	$2,160
(4) Expected Cash Sales	1,200	1,420	900	
(5) Expected Collections	400	380	350	
(6) Other Money Expected	100	52	50	
(7) Total Receipts [add (4), (5) and (6)]	$1,700	$1,852	$1,300	
(8) Total Cash and Receipts [add (3) and (7)]	$3,200	$3,352	$2,200	
(9) All Disbursements (For Month)	1,200	1,192	1,000	
(10) Cash Balance at End of Month in Bank Account and Register [Subtract (9) from (8)]	$2,000	$2,160	$2,300	

*The owner-manager writes in these figures as they become available.

Cash Flow Schedule—Period of Contract to Repayment of Loan

	July	August	Sept.	Oct.	Nov.
Estimated Receipts					
Cash Sales	$ 800	$ 600	$ 700	$ 1,200	$ 2,800
Accounts Receivable	10,000	10,200	15,800	20,000	31,600
Other Income	200	400	200	480	250
Total Receipts	$11,000	$11,200	$16,700	$21,680	$34,650
Estimated Disbursements					
Accounts Payable	17,000	11,000	8,200	2,700	2,200
Payroll & Drawing	2,600	4,200	4,200	7,900	5,800
Expenses	1,200	1,800	2,000	2,700	600
Interest Expense	130	130	130	130	130
Plant & Equipment	2,500	460	600	800	100
Reserve for Taxes				3,800 *	3,800 *
Total Disbursements	$23,430	$17,590	$15,130	$18,030	$12,630
Estimated Excess Receipts over Disbursements	($12,430)	($6,390)	$ 1,570	$ 3,650	$22,020
Estimated Cash Balance at Start of Month	$ 4,200	$ 7,770	$ 1,380	$ 2,950	$ 6,600
Borrowings	$16,000				
Loan Repayment					$16,000
Estimated Cash Balance at End of Month	$ 7,770	$ 1,380	$ 2,950	$ 6,600	$12,620

*To be allotted in October and November so that available cash can be kept at the maximum during the months of heavy cash outflows.

Good managers recognize that occasional borrowing is one of the accepted business tools. Your long range plan for borrowing should be based on the fact that each of the various types of money in your business has its specific and appropriate purpose.

Recognizing this fact is important in preventing the misuse of funds. Keep in mind that misuse can cause a shaky financial condition. This point is especially true when operating cash seeps into long term investment in the business. As a result, the business requires a constant renewal of short term borrowings. Such borrowing indicates a capital deficiency in the business and the need for additional permanent capital.

Bear in mind that financial planning is the first step when borrowing. Such planning must be based on facts that come from your records if you are to secure loans and use them profitably.

Part V
Establishing Financial Controls for Your Business

Summary

Accounting services can help the owner-manager of a small service firm keep the business on a sound basis. Among these services are setting up recordkeeping procedures, interpreting a firm's records, and providing financial advice based on such an interpretation.

Sample profit and loss statements are used to illustrate how accounting services can help reveal and correct trouble spots.

Many small service firms seem to have the potential for success. The owner-managers are good craftspeople and offer services which attract customers. And in may cases, sales are good.

Yet, because of poor financial management, some small service firms fail. Others struggle to keep out of the red. Still others stay in the black only because the owner-managers are willing to work for low pay.

In some cases, the poor results are caused by inadequate financial records. In other firms, the records may be good, but the owner-manager lacks the ability or experience to use them.

In achieving effective financial management, the services of a public accountant are helpful. An accountant can design records, set up ways for maintaining them, draw off vital information, and help relate it to a profitable operation.

Bits of Information

Daily bits of information flow into a small service firm. As customers are served, pieces of information are generated about sales, cash, equipment, purchase expenses, payroll, accounts payable, and, if credit is offered to customers, accounts receivable.

To capture these facts and figures, a system is necessary. The accountant can help design one for recording the information which the owner-manager needs to control finances and make profitable decisions.

Such a system usually consists of bookkeeping records which may be set up in journals, ledgers, or other records.

The accountant, with the following basic records, sets up a system according to your particular need.

Cash Receipts—Used to record the cash which the business receives.

Cash Disbursements—Used to record the firm's expenditures.

Sales—Used to record and summarize monthly income.

Purchases—Used to record the purchases of merchandise bought for processing or resale.

Payroll—Used to record the wages of employees and their deductions, such as those for income and Social Security taxes.

Equipment—Used to record the firm's capital assets, such as equipment, office furniture, and motor vehicles.

Inventory—Uses to record the firm's investment in stock which is needed for arriving at a true profit on financial statements and for income tax purposes.

Accounts Receivable—Used to record the balances which customers owe to the firm.

Accounts Payable—Used to record what the firm owes its creditors and suppliers.

Who Keeps the Books?

Once a system of records has been set up, the question is: Who will keep the books?

The public accountant who has set up the books may keep them. But you must weigh the cost because the accountant has to charge for time, operating expenses, and profit. However, his or her professional advice can frequently increase your profits to more than cover these expenses.

If you have the time and inclination, you can keep the books yourself. Another possibility is to hire someone to work part-time.

Drawing the Picture

A set of books is like a roll of exposed film. The latter must be developed before you can see the picture.

Similarly, your books contain facts and figures which make up a picture of your business. They have to be arranged into an order before you see the picture.

The accountant draws such a picture by preparing financial statements, such as a profit and loss statement. The P and L or income statement shows what profit or loss your business had in a certain time period. A sample—"Profit and Loss Statement for OK Appliance Repair Company"* — is shown below.

**Profit and Loss Statement for
OK Appliance Repair Company**

Gross Sales		$70,000
Cost of Sales:		
Opening Inventory	$13,000	
Purchases	25,000	
Total	38,000	
Ending Inventory	14,000	
Total Cost of Sales		24,000
Gross Profit		46,000
Operating Expenses:		
Payroll (not including owner)	26,000	
Rent	3,000	
Payroll Taxes	1,500	
Interest	600	
Depreciation	1,400	
Truck Expense	5,500	
Telephone	2,400	
Insurance	1,000	
Miscellaneous	1,000	
Total		42,400
Net Profit (before owner's salary)		$ 3,600

Analyzing the Picture

Some aspects of the financial picture of a small service firm may stick out like a sore thumb. For example, in the P and L statement on this page the net profit of $3,600 does not warrant the time and effort which the owner-manager puts into the business.

Why is the profit so low?

The reason begins to appear when the accountant analyzes the firm's financial picture. The profit and loss statement on page 4 shows the results of a study where: (1) sales are broken down into two categories: parts and service and (2) expenses are allocated to each category. Such information is easy to

* All names in **Aids** are fictitious.

accumulate when your sales records are set up to capture the breakdown at the time of the sale.

In addition, the example on page 4 uses percentages to show the part of each sales dollar used by each of the various expenses. This method is especially good for comparing current year financial statements with those of prior years to determine the trend of the business. It is also valuable in comparing your figures with those of other firms in your line of business.

Two trouble spots stand out when the expense figures of the OK Appliance Repair Company are broken down into percentages. One is the loss on the sale of parts. The other is an excessive payroll.

The loss on the sale of parts occurred because the owner-manager did not price the parts properly. A careful review indicated the OK Company received a 30 percent discount when it bought the parts. Therefore, the sales price—provided competition allowed it—should have been $34,286 ($24,000 divided by 70 percent equals $34,286) instead of $25,000. This increase in price would have covered costs and would have given a net profit of $6,386 ($10,286 minus operating expenses of $3,900) instead of a loss of $2,900.

Now look at the other trouble spot—payroll. Where more than 57 percent of the service income is spent for payroll, a further study is required. It is even more serious when you recall that this percentage does not include the owner-manager's salary. Therefore, either higher service charges are necessary or a more efficient use of the service person's time is needed.

The reasons for a large payroll cost are difficult to pinpoint. The accountant analyzes the situation by looking for answers to the following kinds of questions: (1) Is an accurate record maintained of time spent on jobs? (2) Is the 8-hour day of each employee accounted for? (For example, is travel time from one job to another charged to either job?), (3) When employees are paid overtime, is the additional expense reflected in the charge to the customer? (4) Is work being done on a guaranteed price basis or is it being billed on an hourly basis? (5) If you bill on a guaranteed price basis, is the actual time spent on the job greater than what was originally estimated? (6) Can employees do their work with minimum wasted effort and time? and (7) Is the percentage spent for payroll appropriate for service activities?

A P and L statement for your firm may reveal various items that need looking into. For example, you may be paying more for rent than is necessary for your type of business. Or there may be a better way to schedule work so that your truck or trucks can be used more efficiently. Perhaps the mails can be used to reduce long distance telephone calls. Or there may be a possibility of increasing inventory turnover.

In the example the average inventory for the 12-month period is $13,500 ($13,000 opening inventory, $14,000 ending inventory, average inventory $13,500). With the cost of sales being $24,000, the firm's average inventory was used less than twice a year. To put it another way, the ending inventory of $14,000 represents a parts supply for approximately 7 months.

When the owner-manager realized this fact, he or she was able to cut the average to $10,000. It depends, of course, on the type of service business, but one of the economies was carrying a small supply of certain parts and relying on immediate delivery from wholesalers for replacements.

Advice and Assistance

In addition to analyzing the profit and loss statement and pointing out areas which need control, your accountant can advise on financial management. He or she can advise on cash requirements, budget forecast, borrowing, business organization, and taxes.

On cash requirements, the accountant can help you work out the amount of cash needed to operate your firm during a certain period—for example, 3 months, 6 months, a year. The accountant considers how much cash you will need for the following: to carry customer accounts receivable, to add to inventory, to pay current bills, to buy equipment, and to repay loans. In addition, the accountant can determine how much of the cash will come from collections of accounts receivables and how much will have to be borrowed.

While working out the cash requirements, the accountant may notice and call to your attention danger spots such as accounts that are in arrears. One firm, for example, allowed a customer to fall $18,000 behind in payments. When the customer went bankrupt, the firm lost $16,000—almost as much as a year's profits.

When you borrow, the accountant can assemble financial information such as a profit and loss statement and a balance sheet. The purpose of such data is to show the lender the financial position of your business and its

OK Appliance Repair Company P AND L Statement Showing Expenses as Percentages of Sales

	Total		Parts		Service	
	Amount	Percent	Amount	Percent	Amount	Percent
Gross Sales	$70,00	100.00	$25,00	100.00	$45,000	100.00
Cost of Sales:						
Opening Inventory	13,000		13,000			
Purchases	25,000		25,000			
Total	38,000		38,000			
Ending Inventory	14,000		14,000			
Total Cost of Sales	24,000	34.29	24,000	96.00		
Gross Profit	46,000	65.71	1,000	4.00		
Operating Expenses:						
Payroll	26,000	37.14			26,000	57.78
Rent	3,000	4.28	1,500	6.00	1,500	3.34
Payroll Taxes	1,500	2.14			1,500	3.34
Interest	600	.86	300	1.20	300	.66
Depreciation	1,400	2.00			1,400	3.11
Truck Expense	5,500	7.86			5,500	12.22
Telephone	2,400	3.43	1,200	4.80	1,200	2.67
Insurance	1,000	1.43	400	1.60	600	1.33
Miscellaneous	1,000	1.43	500	2.00	500	1.11
Total	42,400	60.57	3,900	15.60	38,500	85.56
Net Profit (Loss) —	3,600	5.14	$ (2,900)	(11.60)	$ 6,500	14.44
(Exclusive of owner's salary)						

ability to repay the loan. Using these data, the accountant can advise on whether you need a short-term or long-term loan. The financial data which he or she compiles may include: the assets you will offer for collateral, your present debt obligations, a summary of how you will use the borrowed money, and a schedule of how you intend to repay. In addition, if the owner-manager has never borrowed before, the accountant may help by introducing you to a banker who knows and respects the accountant's reputation.

You, your accountant, and your attorney should work together to decide the type of organization that best fits your need. The accountant can point out the tax advantages and disadvantages of the various types of business organization—proprietorship, partnership, and corporation.

Taxes are another area in which the accountant can provide advice and assistance. Normally, a bookkeeping system which provides the information you need for making profitable decisions will suffice for tax purposes. However, if additional facts are needed because of your type of business, your accountant can bring them to your attention and suggest a method for recording them.

This Aid was edited by SBA staff members. Contributors to the text were Alfred B. Abraham, CPA, Managing Director, Business Diagnostics, New York, NY; William G. Droms, Assistant Dean, School of Business Administration, Georgetown University, Washington, D.C.; James M. Kelly, College of Business, Boise State University, Boise, ID; and Danny S. Litt, Executive Vice President Finance, Century International, Ltd., Los Angeles, CA.

Summary

The prime objective for any business is to survive. That means a firm must have enough cash to meet its obligations. This Aid shows the owner-manager how to plan for the movement of cash through the business and thus plan for future requirements.

Introduction

All businesses, no matter how small or large, function on cash. Many businesses become insolvent because they do not have enough cash to meet their short term obligations; bills must be paid in cash, not profits. Sufficient cash is, therefore, one of the keys to maintaining a successful business. Thus, you must understand how cash moves or flow through the business and how planning can remove some of the uncertainties about future requirements.

Cash Flow

Cash Cycle. In any business there is a continual cycle of events which may increase or decrease the cash balance. The following diagram is used to illustrate this flow of cash.

Cash is decreased in the acquisition of materials and services to produce the finished goods. It is reduced in paying off the amounts owed to suppliers; that is, accounts payable. Then, inventory is sold and these sales generate cash and accounts receivable; that is, money owed from customers. When customers pay, accounts receivable is reduced and the cash account increases. However, the cash flows are not necessarily related to the sales in that period because customers may pay in the next period.

The small business manager must continually be alert to changes in working capital accounts, the cause of these changes, and the implications of these changes for the financial health of the company.

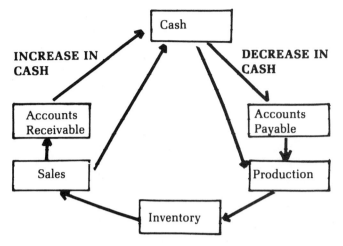

Net Working Capital. Current assets are those resources of cash and those assets which can be converted to cash within one year or a normal business cycle. These include cash, marketable securities, accounts receivable, inventories, etc. Current liabilities are obligations which become due within one year or a normal business cycle. These include accounts payable, notes payable, accrued expenses payable, etc. You may want to consider current assets as the source of funds which reduce current liabilities.

One way to measure the flow of cash and the firm's ability to maintain its cash or liquid assets is to compute *working capital*. It is the difference between current assets and current liabilities. The change in this value from period to period is called *net working capital*. For example,

	19 x 1	19 x 2
Current Assets	$110,000	$200,000
less Current Liabilities	− 70,000	− 112,000
Working Capital	40,000	88,000
Net Working Capital Increase (Decrease)		$48,000

Net working capital increased during the year, but we don't know how. It could have been all in cash or all in inventory. Or, it may have esulted from a reduction in accounts payable.

Cash Flow Statement. While net working capital shows only the changes in the current position, a "flow" statement can be developed to explain the changes that have occurred in any account during any time period. The cash flow statement is an analysis of the cash inflows and outflows.

The ability to forecast cash requirements is indeed a means of becoming a more efficient manager. If you can determine the cash requirements for any period, you can establish a bank loan in advance, or you can reduce other current asset accounts so that the cash will be made available. Also, when you have excess cash, you can put this cash into productive use to earn a return.

The change in the cash account can be readily determined if you know net working capital and the changes in current liabilities and current assets other than cash.

Let:

NWC	be net working capital
CA	be the change in current assets other than cash
CL	change in current liabilities
cash	be the change in cash

Because net working capital is the difference between the change in current assets and current liabilities,

NWC = CA + cash − CL
cash = NWC − CA + CL

This relationship states that if we know net working capital (NWC), the change in current liabilities (CL), and the change in current assets less cash (CA less cash), we can calculate the change in cash. The change in cash is then added to the beginning balance of cash to determine the ending balance.

Suppose you forecast that sales will increase $50,000 and the following will correspondingly change:

Receivables	increase by $25,000
Inventory	increase by $70,000
Accounts Payable	increase by $30,000
Notes Payable	increase by $10,000

Using net working capital of $48,000, what is the projected change in cash?

cash = NWC − CA + CL
     = 48,000 − 25,000 − 70,000 + 30,000 + 10,000
     = − 7,000

Conclusion: Over this time period, under the condition of increasing sales volume, cash decreases by $7,000. Is there enough cash to cover this decrease? This will depend upon the beginning cash balance.

Sources and Application of Funds. At any given level of sales, it is easier to forecast the required inventory, ac-

counts payable, receivables, etc., than net working capital. To forecast this net working capital account, you must trace the sources and application of funds. Sources of funds increase working capital. Applications of funds decrease working capital. The difference between the sources and applications of funds is the net working capital.

The following calculation is based on the fact that the balance sheet is indeed in "balance." That is, total assets equal total liabilities plus stockholders' equity.

$$\text{current atoms} + \text{noncurrent assets} = \text{current liabilities} + \text{long-term liabilities} + \text{equity}$$

Rearranging this equation:

$$\text{current assets} - \text{current liabililties} = \text{long-term liabilities} + \text{equity} - \text{noncurrent assets}$$

Because the left-hand side of the equation is working capital, the right-hand side must also equal working capital. A change to either side is the net working capital. If long-term liabilities and equity increase or noncurrent assets decrease, net working capital increases. This change would be a source of funds. If noncurrent assets increase or long-term liabilities and equity decrease, net working capital decreases. This change would be an application of funds.

Typical sources of funds or net working capital are:

Funds provided by operations

Disposal of fixed assets

Issuance of stock

Borrowing from a long term source

To obtain the item, "funds provided by operations," subtract all expense items requiring funds from all revenues that were sources of funds. You can also obtain this result in an easier manner: add back expenses which did not result in inflows or outflows of funds to reported net income.

The most common nonfund expense is depreciation, the allocation of the cost of an asset as an expense over the life of the asset against the future revenues produced. Adjusting net income with depreciation is much simpler than computing revenues and expenses which require funds. Again, depreciation is not a source of funds.

The typical applications of funds or net working capital are:

Purchase of fixed assets

Payment of dividends

Retirement of long-term liabilities

Repurchase of equity.

The following is an example of how sources and applications of funds may be used to determine net working capital.

Statement of Sources & Applications of Funds

Sources of Funds:	
From Operation	
Net Income	$10,000
Add Back Depreciation (noncash item)	15,000
	25,000
Issuance of Debt	175,000
Issuance of Stock	3,000
	$203,000
Applications of Funds:	
Purchase of Plant	140,000
Cash Dividends	15,000
	155,000
Net Working Capital Increase (Decrease)	$48,000

Statement of Changes in Financial Position. This statement combines two statements previously discussed: the statement of sources and application of funds and the changes in working capital accounts. This statement can be converted into a cash flow statement by solving for cash as the unknown, as shown below.

Cash Flow Statement

Sources of Funds		$203,000
Applications of Funds		155,000
Net Working Capital		$ 48,000
Less:		
Increase in Receivables	25,000	
Increase in Inventory	70,000	– 95,000
		– 47,000
Plus:		
Increase in Accounts Payable	30,000	
Increase in Notes Payable	10,000	40,000
Cash Flow		$ – 7,000

Planning For Cash Flow

Cash flow can be used not only to determine how cash flowed through the business but also as an aid to determine the excess or shortage of cash. Suppose your analysis of cash flow forecasts a potential cash deficiency. You may then do a number of things, such as:

Increase borrowings: loans, stock issuance, etc.

Reduce current asset accounts: reduce receivables, inventory, etc.

Reduce noncurrent assets: postpone expanding the facility, sell off some fixed assets, etc.

By using a cash flow statement you can determine if sufficient funds are available from financing activities, show funds generated from all sources, and show how these funds were applied. Using and adjusting the information gained from this cash flow analysis will help you to know in advance if there will be enough cash to pay

Suppliers' bills

Bank loans

Interest

Dividends.

Careful planning will insure a sufficient amount of cash to meet future obligations on schedule which is essential for the "successful" business.

Planning Aid

The following example is presented to help you develop a cash flow analysis. Of course, all names are fictitious.

During the next month, Irene Smith, owner-manager of Imagine Manufacturing, expects sales to increase to $10,000. Based on past experience, she made this forecast:

Net income to be 9% of sales	$ 900
Income taxes to be 3.2% of sales	320
Accounts receivable to increase	5,000
Inventory to increase	2,000
Accounts payable to increase	3,000

Her beginning cash balance is $3,000 and she plans to purchase a piece of equipment for $1,500. What is her cash flow?

Cash Flow Analysis

Sources of Funds:	
Net Income	$ 900
Add Back Depreciation	1,000
	1,900
Application of Funds:	
Addition to Fixed Assets	$1,500
Payment of Taxes	320
	1,820
Net Working Capital Increase (Decrease)	$ 80
Working Capital Accounts:	
Less Change in	
Inventory	$ – 2,000
Accounts Receivable	– 5,000
Plus Change in	
Accounts Payable	3,000
Cash Flow	$ – 3,920
Plus Beginning Cash Balance	3,000
Equals Ending Cash Balance	$ – 920

Assuming Irene's forecast is correct, she has a cash need of $920 next month. If she cannot borrow the additional funds, she must either reduce sales, which may reduce profits, or find another source of cash. She can now use her cash flow analysis to try to determine a source of funds or a reduction in the application of funds. An easy solution is to postpone the purchase of the equipment. This would increase her cash flow by $1,500, more than enough for a positive cash balance at the end of next month.

Analyzing Your Records for Potential Cash Resources

In addition to the cash flow technique described in the previous section, it is important to know how to analyze your records in order to develop a more efficient business. By eliminating unnecessary cost through increased operating efficiency, the business' cash flow will improve.

Analyzing Your Expenses

Sometimes you cannot cut an expense item. But you can get more from it and thus increase your profits. In analyzing your expenses, you should use percentages rather than actual dollar amounts.

For example, if you increase sales and keep the dollar amount of an expense the same, you have decreased that expense as a percentage of sales. When you decrease your cost percentage, you increase your percentage of profit.

On the other hand, if your sales volume remains the same, you can increase the percentage of profit by reducing a specific item of expense. Your goal, of course, is to do both: to decrease specific expenses and increase their productive worth at the same time.

Before you can determine whether cutting expenses will increase profits, you need information about your operation. This information can be obtained only if you have an adequate recordkeeping system. Such records will provide the figures to prepare a profit and loss statement (preferably monthly for most retail businesses), a cash budget, break-even calculations, and evaluations of your operating ratios compared with those of similar types of business.

Break-even. One useful method for making expense comparisons is break-even analysis. Break-even is the point at which gross profit equals expenses. In a business year, it is the time at which your sales volume has become sufficient to enable your over-all operation to start showing a profit. The two condensed profit and loss statements, in the accompanying example, illustrate the point. In statement "A," the sales volume is at the break-even point and no profit is made. In Statement "B" for the same store, the sales volume is beyond the break-even point and a profit is shown. In the two statements, the percentage factors are the same except for fixed expenses, total expenses, and operating profit.

	A		B	
	Break-Even Amount	Percent of Sales	Profit Amount	Percent of Sales
Sales..............	$500,000	100	$600,000	100
Cost of Sales	300,000	60	360,000	60
Gross Profit.......	200,000	40	240,000	40
Operating Expenses				
Fixed	150,000	30	150,000	25
Variable..........	50,000	10	60,000	10
Total.............	200,000	40	210,000	35
Operating Profit	$ NONE	0	$ 30,000	5

As shown in the example, once your sales volume reaches the break-even point, your fixed expenses are covered. Beyond the break-even point, every dollar of sales should earn you an equivalent additional profit percentage.

It is important to remember that once sales pass the break-even point, the fixed expenses percentage goes down as the sales volume goes up. Also the operating profit percentage increases at the same rate as the percentage rate for fixed expenses decreases—provided, of course, that variable expenses are kept in line. In the illustration, fixed expenses in Statement "B" decreased by 5 percent and operating profit increased by 5 percent. (For a more detailed discussion, see MA 1.019, *Breakeven Analysis: A Decision-Making Tool.*)

Locating Reducible Expenses

Your profit and loss (or income) statement provides a summary of expense information and is the focal point in locating expenses that can be cut. Therefore, the information should be as current as possible. As a report of what *has already been* spent, a P and L statement alerts you to expense items that bear watching in the present business period. If you get a P and L statement only at the end of the year, you should have one prepared more often. At the end of each quarter might be often enough for some firms. Ideally, you get the most recent information from a monthly and P and L.

Regardless of the frequency, for the most information, two P and L statements should be prepared. One statement should report the sales, expenses, profit and/or loss of your operations cumulatively for the current business year to date. The other should report on the same items for the last complete month or quarter. Each of the statements should also carry the following information: (1) this year's figures and each item as a percentage of sales, (2) last year's figures and the percentages, (3) the difference between last year and this year—over or under, (4) budgeted figures and the respective percentages, (5) the difference between this year and the budgeted figures—over and under, (6) average percentages for your line of business (industry operating ratio) when available, and (7) the difference between your annual percentages and the industry ratios—under or over.

This information allows you to locate expense variation in three ways: (1) by comparing this year to last year, (2) by comparing expenses to your own budgeted figures, and (3) by comparing your percentages to the operating ratios for your line of business.

The important basis for comparison is the percentage figure. It represents a common denominator for all three methods. When you have indicated the percentage variations, you should then study the dollar amounts to determine what kind of corrective action is needed.

Because your cost cutting will come largely from variable expenses, you should make sure that they are flagged on your P and L statements. Variable expenses are those which fluctuate with the increase or decrease of sales volume. Some of them are advertising, delivery, wrap-ping supplies, sales salaries, commissions, and payroll taxes. Fixed expenses are those which stay the same regardless of sales volume. Among them are: your salary, salaries for permanent non-selling employees (for example, the bookkeeper), depreciation, rent, and utilities.

Checking Accounts Receivable and Inventory

Accounts receivable represent the extension of credit to support sales. In many lines of business, the types and terms of credit granted by the firm are set by established competitive practices. As an investment, the accounts receivable should contribute to overall Return on Investment (ROI).

Excessive investment in accounts receivable can hurt ROI by tying up funds unnecessarily. One good way to judge the extent of accounts receivable is to compare your average collection period with that of rivals or the industry average. If your average collection period is much higher than your competitors' or the industry norm, your accounts receivable may be excessive.

If they are excessive, it may be that you are not keeping tight control of late payers. You can check this by developing an aging schedule. The aging schedule shows the distribution of accounts receivable with respect to being on time or late.

Failure to closely monitor late payments ties up investment and weakens profits. The more overdue accounts become, the greater is the danger that they will be uncollectable and will have to be written off against profits.

If the aging schedule does not reveal excessive late accounts, your average collection period may be out of line simply because your credit policy is more liberal than most. If so, it should translate into more competitive sales and greater profits; otherwise, you should rethink your credit program.

Inventory also ties up cash. Excessive inventory will reduce your Return on Investment. One way to determine whether your inventory level is excessive is to compare your inventory turnover ratio with the industry norm. If your inventory turnover is much lower than the industry average, your ROI will suffer.

If inventory is much higher than it should be for your level of sales, it may be that you are holding items that are obsolete or that simply do not move fast enough to justify their cost. You may also be speculating on price increases. Or perhaps for competitive reasons you think a full line of inventory items is essential, even if some items are in very low demand. In any case, you should reevaluate your policy and make sure that the gains outweigh the costs of the higher investment.

You must also consider the cost of inventory. There are two basic types of inventory costs: carrying costs and ordering costs.

Carrying costs are the costs associated with inventory storage, handling, and insurance. Ordering costs are the clerical and administrative costs incurred when an order is placed for an item in inventory. If you expect to use 10,000 widgets over the next thirty days, you could simply buy 10,000 now and carry them in inventory until they are all used up. Or you could buy 3,333 units every ten days. The more frequently you place orders for inventory, the less inventory you have to keep on hand and the less carrying costs you have. But more frequent orders also result in greater ordering costs.

Taking Action

When you have located a problem area, the next step obviously is to reduce that cost so as to increase your profit. A key to the effectiveness of your cost-cutting action is the worth of the various expenditures.

As long as you know the worth of your expenditures, you can profit by making small improvements in expenses. Keep an open eye and an open mind. It is better to do a spot analysis once a month than to wait several months and then do a detailed study.

Take action as soon as possible. You can refine your cost-cutting action as you go along.

Be persistent. Sometimes results may be slower than you might like. Keep in mind that only persistent analysis of your records and constant action can keep expenses from eating up profit.

Summary

Budgeting is a tool for dealing with the future. It helps you turn expectations into reality.

An increase in profit should be the first consideration when you think about the prospects for your small service business in the next year. Working up a budget helps you to determine whether or not your profit goal is within reach.

When the figures are all together, you have answers to questions such as: What sales will be needed to achieve the desired profit? What fixed expenses will be necessary to support these sales? What variable expenses will be incurred in producing the services?

Because small business is not a cut-and-dried affair, the first budget often will uncover problems and suggest choices. Working up additional budgets will help you decide what changes to make in order to have a workable plan for next year.

Many owner-managers run their businesses without a planned goal. In trying to survive from week to week and from month to month, such owner-managers overlook an important management tool--budgeting. Whether the plan is for next year, for the next 3 years, or for the next 5 years, budgeting can help just as a map helps you to keep on the right road.

Why Budget

A budget is a plan that enables you to set a goal and list the steps which are necessary to reach that goal. Thus, a budget helps you think about what you want your business to do in the future. By planning, you are in a better position to act to prevent crises.

In its simplest form a budget is a detailed plan of future receipts and expenditures--a projected profit and loss statement. Thus once the period for which you have budgeted is completed, you can compare actual results with anticipated goals. If some of your expenses, for example, are higher than you expected, you can start looking for ways to cut them. Conversely, if you have fallen short of your goal, you may want to look for ways to increase your income.

Budget makers can start either with a forecast of sales and work down or with a forecast of profits and work up. Most small service businesses use the latter method. In other words, you decide what profit you want to make and then list the expenses that you will incur in order to make that predetermined profit.

A Plan For Increased Profit

Before you can use a budget as a plan for increased profit, you have to be sure that your present profit is what it should be. In a service business, the year-end profit should be large enough to make a return on your investment and a return on your own work--pay you a salary.

Value Of Owner's Service. Skilled crafts people who own service businesses are kidding themselves if their firms' profits are less than they can earn working for someone else. Your net profit after taxes should be at least as much as you can earn if you worked at your trade for a weekly pay check.

Return On Investment. The year-end profit is too low if it does not also include a return on the owner-manager's investment. That investment includes the money you put into the firm when you started it and the profit of prior years which you left in the firm--retained earnings. You should check to be sure that the rate of return on your investment is what it should be. Your trade association should be able to provide guidelines about the rate of return on investment in your line of business. Your accountant and banker are also sources of help.

Your Targeted Income. After you know what you made last year, you can set a profit goal for next year. Be sure that your goal includes a return on your services and a return on your investment. Your goal should also include an amount for State and Federal taxes. For example, if you want to make $10,000 after taxes, your goal before taxes should be about $13,333. You have to add this $3,333 to take care of State and Federal taxes. Keep in mind that the larger your goal, the larger the amount which will have to be added to account for taxes. Your accountant can help you determine that amount.

Can You Reach The Goal

Once you have decided on your profit target, the next step in preparing a budget is to determine whether you can achieve it. To do this, you must project your fixed costs and your variable costs. From these three figures--profit, fixed expenses, and variable expenses--you can determine your "hoped for" total income.

In gathering figures, keep in mind that without accurate information planning becomes guessing. The owner-manager who has never budgeted should talk with an accountant about a recordkeeping system. Changes may be needed to provide the necessary budget information. It may be that your present system does not break costs down into fixed and variable expenses, or it may be that you need to have a profit and loss (or income) statement at more frequent intervals to determine the seasonal fluctuations of your revenues and expenses.

Fixed Expenses. Regardless of sales, fixed expenses stay the same. Several examples of fixed expenses are insurance, rent, taxes on property, wages paid to salaried employees, depreciation of equipment, interest on borrowed money, building maintenance costs, office salaries, and office expenses.

Variable Expenses This type of expense varies with sales. In some service businesses, the cost of labor is the biggest factor. Sales commissions, payroll taxes, insurance, advertising, and delivery expenses are other examples of variable expenses.

Determine Your Expected Service Income Your expected service income contribution is the difference between sales and the variable expenses that are necessary to produce these sales. When this difference equals fixed expenses and the desired profit, you have a workable budget.

Lucy's Beauty Shop

Lucy's Beauty Shop* illustrates the principals of budgeting in a small sevice business. The owner-manager is Mrs. Lucy Doe. The shop's income is from two sources: (1) from beauty services which are performed by three operators and (2) from cosmetics and perfumes which are sold by the receptionist. The receptionist also answers the telephone, keep's the shop's daily records, and prepares the checks for Mrs. Doe to sign.

Targeted Income In making a budget, Mrs. Doe decided that she wanted to increase her net profit after taxes. She set the goals at $10,000 for net profit after taxes. This figure meant that the shop's profit before taxes had to be about $13,333 because she figured that her taxes would amount to about $3,333.

This goal was an ambitious one because her previous year's net profit before taxes was $8,390. For details on that year see page four. "Lucy's Beauty Shop—Profit and Loss Statement."

Determining Fixed Expenses. As shown in the table, "Lucy's Beauty Shop–Profit and Loss Statement," the shop's fixed expense items are: depreciation of equipment, receptionist's salary, insurance, rent, interest on equipment obligations, and utilities (heat and air conditioning). In addition, about one half of the laundry and shop maintenance expense is fixed. In budgeting her fixed expenses for next year, Mrs. Doe took into account:

(1) the raise she intended to give the receptionist, (2) a change in amount of interest, and (3) a change in her insurance expense.

She estimated that her fixed expenses for next year would be $11,000.

Determining Variable Expenses. In Mrs. Doe's beauty shop, the variable expenses—those that vary with sales—are cost of cosmetics sold, shop supplies, payroll taxes and costs, utilities (water and electricity), about one-half of laundry and shop maintenance, and operator's salaries. These salaries are variable because each operator receives one-half of the total price charged the customer.

When determining variable expenses, Mrs. Doe uses her trade journals for information on budgeted percentages. For budgeting purposes, all costs are expressed as a percentage of the sales dollar. In her case, the percentages are: beauty shop supplies 10; laundry, including uniforms 3; water and variable utilities 1; and payroll costs 5.

*Names in Aids are Fictitious

Lucy's Beauty Shop
Profit And Loss Statement
For the Year Ended December 31, 19____

Revenue:

Merchandise				$12,000	
Beauty Shop Service				42,000	
Total Revenue				$54,000	
Cost of Merchandise Sold				6,000	

	Variables	Fixed	Total		
Gross Margin					$48,000
Expenses	Variables	Fixed	Total		
Depreciation		300	300		
Salaries and wages	21,000	2,700	23,700		
Supplies	4,200		4,200		
Insurance		110	110		
Rent		4,800	4,800		
Payroll taxes and costs	2,370		2,370		
Interest		250	250		
Utilities	420	1,000	1,420		
Laundry and Shop maintenance	1,260	1,200	2,460		
	29,250	10,360			$39,610
Net Income Before Taxes					$8,390

She estimates her total payroll costs at 5 percent of gross revenue from service or 10 percent of salaries. Payroll taxes both–State and Federal–account for 7.9 percent of the 10 percent, and payment's for workers' compensation and other employee insurance account for 2.1 percent.

Determining Expected Service Income. The next step in preparing a budget for Lucy's Beauty Shop is to determine the expected service income contribution. The basis for estimating this income for next year is the average revenue for each operator's appointment with one customer. This figure is $4. See the following table, "Service Income Contribution."

One half of the $4 belongs to the operator. Other variable expenses take 76 cents. Thus, from each $4 unit of services that is sold, $1.24 is left for service income contribution.

The service revenue for 12 months is shown in the table, "Determination of Total Service Contribution." Mrs. Doe arrived at these estimates as follows:

1. From the appointment book, she learned that each operator averages 15 appointments a day.

2. The shop's income from each operator is $30 a day (15 times $2).

3. Each operator works 5 days a week.

4. Each operator contributes $630 a month to the shop's income (21 days times $30).

Service Income Contribution
Expressed as a Percent of Sales Dollar

Average Service Revenue	$4.00		100%
Variable Expenses			
Operator salaries	$2.00		50%
Beauty supplies	.40		10%
Laundry and uniforms	.12		3%
Water	.04		1%
Payroll costs	.20		5%
Total Variable Expenses		2.76	69%
Income Contribution From Services		$1.24	31%

On this $630, the shop clears $390.60 because 76 cents of each $2 that the shop receives from an operator's work goes for variable expenses (see the table, "Service Income Contribution").

The shop's cosmetic sales contribute a net revenue of 50 cents on the sales dollar. Mrs. Doe estimated, based on past experience, that she could get a 50 percent increase in the sales of cosmetics without additional advertising.

Comparing Revenue and Cost. After Mrs. Doe determines her variable expenses, fixed expenses, and the service income contribution, she is ready to test her budget. She does this by adding her total fixed expenses of $11,000 and the desired gross profit of $13,333. This total comes to $24,333.

But her estimated service revenue (see the table, "Determination of Total Service Contribution,") is only $23,061. It will not cover her fixed expenses and desired profit. Resources will be about $1,300 short of the desired goal.

Determination Of Total Service Contribution

Revenue Per Operator For The Year ($1,260 per month x 12 months)	$15,120
Service Income Contribution Per Operator ($390.60 x 12 months)	4,687*
Total Service Contribution From Beauty Shop (3 operators x $4,687)	14,061
From Cosmetic Sales ($18,000 x 50%)	9,000
Total Service Contribution Based On Present Outlook	$23,061

*Figures are rounded to the nearest dollar.

Where Can She Go?

Because resources are not enough to cover fixed expences and the desired profit, Mrs. Doe has to adjust her budget. She can go in at least three directions. One possibility is to add another operator. Another is to try to increase cosmetic sales. A third solution is to reduce her expected profit. In order to decide what to do, Mrs. Doe needs answers to several questions about each possibility. She may have to work up several tentative budgets to determine what to do.

Add Another Operator. This possibility poses the following questions: Is the relationship between fixed expenses and revenue in line with industry trends? Is there space for an additional booth? What additional fixed expenses will be incurred? Can another operator be kept busy? If so, the additional revenue can help to offset Mrs. Doe's rent which is slightly higher than the average for her line of business. That average is 10 percent of gross beauty service income. The shop has sufficient space for another booth. However, if a booth is added, fixed expenses will increase because equipment for the new booth will mean additional financing costs.

Increase Cosmetic Sales. This possibility seems to be a logical way to increase income because each dollar of sales will increase the revenue by 50 cents. The first question is how much of an increase in cosmetic sales will be needed? Mrs. Doe calculated that these sales must be increased by about 95 percent rather than by 50 percent as she originally planned. Other questions to answer here are: By what method will sales be increased? By what additional advertising? By offering the receptionist and operators a commission on cosmetic sales? By reducing prices? What effect will these methods have on revenue? How much additional inventory will be needed? How will it be financed? Is storage and display space sufficient to accommodate increased sales?

Reduce Expectations. Sometimes the only practical solution is to reduce the expected profit. Mrs. Doe decided that $10,000 net profit after taxes was not in the picture next year. Based on her knowledge of the beauty shop business, she felt that her shop was not quite ready to add another operator. For one thing, she foresaw the possibility of personnel trouble if a new operator was not kept busy.

She also felt that trying to push cosmetic sales up by more than 50 percent could cause customer dissatisfaction. She reminded herself that customers regarded the shop's beauty service highly and decided that any major growth in sales must come from that end of the business. Another operator and $10,000 or more net profit after taxes might be feasible the year after next. She would keep the possibility in mind as she moved into next year.

Periodic Feedback And Control

A budget provides a tool for control. You start building this facility when your budget for 12 months is completed. Break it down into quarters. Such a breakdown allows you to check for any discrepancies that may not show up readily in a 12 month budget. When many items are added together, it is easy for an error to creep into the totals.

During the year, this quarterly division provides a handle for getting a hold on expenses and other activities.

For example, by looking at next quarter's budget you can anticipate peak periods and schedule stock and labor to handle peak sales volume. You can plan vacations, special promotions, and inventory taking for the slow periods.

A monthly or quarterly profit and loss statement allows you to keep the items in your budget in line with operations. Ask your accountant to show the actual and the planned revenues and expenses on the income statement so you can compare them. Thus, you can pinpoint and work on the problems that have occured during the month or the quarter. Your objective is to guide your activities toward the most profitable type of operations.

Summary

Break-even analysis is not a panacea. It doesn't tell you if your costs are out of line. It tells you only what sales volume you need to cover fixed costs.

It is, however, an excellent starting point for finding out where you are and, more importantly, where you can go. It's a good first step to planning.

This *Aid*, presented as a conversation between a business counsellor (C) and the owner-manager of a small store (O-M), discusses a simplified method of calculating the break-even point for a small retail operation. While this method is not appropriate for manufacturers or large retailers, it provides a financial planning takeoff point for small stores.

O-M I'm ready to expand. I've just had a great fourth quarter. I've got a chance to move to a larger store in a good location. I really think I'm on my way. Still, though, I don't want to take any unnecessary chances and lose what I've built up these first three years. What do you think I should do?

C: **Let me answer your question with a question: What's your break-even point now and what will it be if you assume the added expansion cost?**

O-M: I'm not exactly sure, but after that last quarter I've got money in the bank and I'm paying all my bills on time.

What Bank Balances May Not Reveal

C: **I'm glad to hear you're in good shape, but you can't make an intelligent expansion decision based on your bank balance at a given moment.**

O-M: You ought to know, but why not?

C: **Take your balance now, for example. It's a lot better than it was at the end of the first quarter, isn't it?**

O-M: Sure, but the first quarter's usually slow. It' a fact of retail life.

C: **And the fourth quarter is usually good, right?**

O-M: Yes, that's a fact, too. But mine was outstanding—it was the best I've ever had.

C: **I'm sure it was, but it can distort the picture. If you're relying on your bank balance for a feel for your break-even point, you may just be guessing. Many things influence your bank balance that may not necessarily have a direct bearing on the break-even point for you store. Seasonal fluctuation is just one of them.**

O-M: There are more?

C: **Sure, capital expenditures, extraordinary repairs, unusual outlays . . .**

O-M: Okay, I get the point. My bank balance is meaningless. I shouldn't expand.

C: **We don't know that yet. After we find out what sales volume you'll need to break even, then you'll tell me if you ought to expand or not.**

O-M: Some counsellor. First you tell me I don't know what I'm doing and then you expect me to advise me on expansion.

Break-even Analysis Is Not a Substitute for Judgment

C: **You're wrong on the first half of that; I know you know retailing. But, yes, *you'll* decide on the basis of your business knowledge and judgment whether or not expansion now makes sense.**

O-M: I must be doing something right. I'm still in business.

C: **Exactly. You've made it through some of the toughest business years, the first ones. And you're showing a fair profit. I think you've got a real flair for merchandising.**

O-M: Please, you'll make me blush. What about this break-even thing?

What Break-even Means

C: **Break-even is simply the point where costs equal what you're taking in—no profit, no**

loss—over a relevant sales range. To calculate this point you must work with only two factors, fixed expenses (like insurance or rent) and variable costs (like cost of goods or sales commissions).

O-M: I sure wish my costs were fixed. Everything goes up for me. My insurance, for example, looks likes it's going up 25 percent over last year.

Fixed and Variable Costs

C: Well, actually "fixed costs" is something of a misnomer. Sure, rents, property taxes, insurance, even the salary you pay yourself may fluctuate—but on a yearly basis and not in relation to sales. For the purpose of break-even analysis every cost that doesn't vary in relation to sales is call "fixed." *Your rent, for instance, stays the same for the year whether you sell $250,000 or $2.50 worth of goods, though we know some rents are tied to volume and vary. The same is usually true of utilities, depreciation, and similar expense items.*

O-M: I see the point. Variable costs, then, are basically my cost of sales? I have to buy more if I sell more. If I paid commissions, I'd be paying more for more sales, and that sort of thing.

C: That's right. There can be other variable costs, but we're simplifying. In addition, you'll probably find costs that seem to be part variable, part fixed.

O-M: You mean they're "semi-variable" or "semi-fixed?"

C: Yes, they're costs that remain fixed up to a certain sales volume and then jump as that volume is exceeded. For example, office costs, or delivery expenses may fit in this category.

O-M: How do I treat them?

C: Use your good business judgment and split them between fixed and variable costs in what you consider a reasonable proportion. The important thing to hold in mind for simple break-even analysis is to *keep it simple*. Oversimplicity is, of course, a drawback

of this method. But simple break-even analysis really helps you to see your way into a planning problem and to establish its perimeters.

O-M: I like the idea of simplicity, but I don't think break-even sounds simple so far.

C: I think you'll see how easy it is if we work through an example. Here, take a look at this hypothetical income or profit and loss statement for the B-E Retail Store.

B-E Retail Store
Income Statement
For the year ending December 31, 19____

Item	Amount		Percent
Sales	$60,000		100
Cost of Sales	42,000		70
Gross Profit	**18,000**		30
Expenses:			
Rent	$ 1,800		3
Wages	12,600		21
Utilities	2,400		4
Insurance	1,200		2
Taxes	600		1
All Other	600		1
Total Expenses	**19,200**		32
Loss for Period		($ 1,200)	(2)

O-M: B-E doesn't seem to have broken even.

C: Correct. Let's find out what kind of sales volume B-E needed to break even in that year. For simplicity (there's that word again) let's consider cost of sales (which is 70 percent of sales) as the total variable costs and the expense items of $19,200 as the fixed costs. We calculate the break-even point by using an algebraic formula.

O-M: A simple one, I hope.

C: Of course. It's just $S = F + V$, where:
S = Sales at the break-even point,
F = Fixed expenses, and
V = Variable costs and expenses as a percent of sales.

O-M: All right, we know B-E's variable and fixed costs. How do we get sales?

C: Let's plug in the figures:
S = $19,200 + .70S
10S = $192,000 + 7S

O-M: Excuse me, 10S?

C: I multiplied the whole equation by 10 to get rid of the decimal fraction, because I think it's easier to work with whole numbers. Anyway, we get:
10S - 7S = $192,000
3S = $192,000
S = $64,000

O-M: B-E needed $64,000 total sales to break even? Anything less, they'd have a loss; anything more they'd make a profit?

C: You've got it. Let's check it, though, just to confirm it:

Sales	$64,000
Less Cost of Sales	-$44,800 (70% of sales)
Gross Profit	$19,200
Less Expenses	-$19,200
Profit or Loss	$0

O-M: Okay, so B-E has broken even. I think they'd like to make a profit. I know I do.

Calculating Break-even for a Given Profit

C: We can find out what kind of sales B-E needed to make a profit using the formula again. Leaving the other figures the same, let's put in a modest profit—say, $9,000—and see what sales they needed. The formula now looks like this:
Sales = Fixed Expenses + Variable Costs + Profit.

O-M: You just add the desired amount of profit in?

C: Yes, really it affects the break-even point just like a fixed expense:
S = $19,200 + .70S + $9,000 (desired profit)
10S = $192,000 + 7S + $90,000 (multiplied by 10 to eliminate fraction)

3S = $282,000
S = $94,000

O-M: May I check the figures this time?

C: Certainly.

O-M: All right, let's see:

Sales	$94,000
Less Cost of Sales	-$65,800 (70% of sales)
Gross Profit	$28,200
Less Expenses	-$19,000
Profit	$ 9,000

C: Convinced?

O-M: Yes, I can see how this formula can help you find how much you need to sell to break even or make a given profit, but what about my problem?

Break-even Analysis for Planning

C: Break-even analysis is just what you need. It's primarily a planning tool. I've looked at your Income Statement and divided it into fixed and variable costs. As I see it, your cost of sales, which we'll consider as your total variable costs, comes to about 60 percent of sales. Your fixed expenses ran about $60,000. So for last year:
S = $60,000 + .60S
10S = $600,000 + 6S
4S = $600,000
S = $150,000
You had to sell only $150,000 worth of merchandise to break even.

O-M: As you can see, I sold $200,000 worth, but I didn't make a $50,000 profit.

C: Right, you made a $20,000 profit just as the bottom line indicates. Remember, you still had those variable costs on sales even after all of your fixed expenses were covered at the $150,000 level.

O-M: Oh, I see, it's like this:
S = F + V + Profit
S = $60,000 = .60S = $20,000
10S = $600,000 + 6S + $200,000
4S = $800,000
S = $200,000

C: Now you've got it. Let's consider your expansion question. How much will your rent increase?

Using Break-even Analysis to Examine Expansion Feasibility

O-M: It would be about $5,000 more. I figure the utilities for the larger space will be $2,000 more than I paid last years. Taxes, the "fixed" ones, I expect to run about $1,000 more and my insurance will increase about $500. I also think I may need to hire another sales person.

C: **Let's say you do. What do you plan to pay?**

O-M: I'd pay an experienced sales clerk about $9,000. I'm toying with the idea of instituting a 2 percent commission on sales as an incentive, too.

C: **All right. We know it's not as simple as we'll lay it out, but I think the analysis will give you an idea of whether or not to explore the expansion idea more carefully and in greater detail.**

O-M: Fine.

C: **Your fixed expenses will rise by $17,500, if you include hiring another employee. That brings them to $77,500, assuming no other increases from last year's $60,000. For simplicity's sake let's assume your cost of sales (your variable costs) will increase only by the 2 percent commission. That means 62 percent of sales for variable costs. So:**
$$S = \$77,500 + .62S$$
$$100S = \$7,774,000 + 62S \text{ (multiplied by 100 to eliminate fraction)}$$
$$38S = \$7,775,000$$
$$S = \$205,000 \text{ (approximately)}$$

O-M: Only $5,000 more than I did last year? I can do that easily.

C: **And be $20,000 in profits *worse* off than last year. Let's put last year's $20,000 profit in—in an expansion you still might want to do at least as well:**
$$S = \$77,500 + .62S + \$20,000$$
$$100S = \$7,750,000 + 62S + \$2,000,000$$
$$38S = \$9,750,000$$
$$S = \$257,000 \text{ (approximately)}$$

O-M: Hm, that's approximately a 25 percent sales increase just to make the same profit as last year.

Business Judgment Still Necessary

C: **Do you think you can boost sales by that much? Perhaps you see long range benefits from expansion that justify sacrificing some profit for the short run.**

O-M: I'm not sure. I'll have to give it more thought, look at the trends in my business and in this area. My pricing policy may need adjustment. Maybe I can cut some costs. But now at least I've got a starting point, a dollar figure I can work with and from. Most importantly of all, I have a technique to help me attack my problem and help point me toward a rational decision.

C: **That's what break-even analysis is all about.**

Part VI
How to Set Up Effective Security

Curtailing Crime Inside and Out
    Edited by SBA Staff Members
    Contributors to text: Saul D. Aster
                           S. J. Curtis
                           Leonard Kolodny
                           Christopher J. Moran
                           Addison H. Verrill

Small Business Risk Management Guide
    Edited by SBA Staff Members
    Written by: The Travelers' Small Business Program

This publication was edited by SBA staff members. Contributors to the text were **Saul D. Aster**, President, Management Safeguards, Inc., New York, New York; **S.J. Curtis**, Management Consultant, Dayton, Ohio; **Leonard Kolodny**, Manager, Retail Bureau, Metropolitan Washington, Board of Trade, Washington, D.C.; **Christopher J. Moran**, CPA, Partner, A.M. Pullen and Company, Greensboro, North Carolina; and **Addison H. Verrill**, Dale System, Inc., Garden City, New York.

Summary

Positive steps can be taken to curb crime. Some are outlined in this Aid. They include safeguards against employee dishonesty and ways to control shoplifting. In addition, measures to outwit bad-check passing and to prevent burglary and robbery are detailed.

Safeguard Against Employee Dishonesty

Retail theft loss estimates vary by the type of operation and the efficiency of management. They range, for example, from 1.3 percent of sales for a well-managed department store to about 7 percent for the loosely controlled operation. Dishonest employees account for about two-thirds of the retail theft, according to one estimate. You can blame another one-third on shoplifting.

The encouraging thing is that even though you cannot eliminate stealing entirely, you can take positive steps to keep it to a minimum. The key lies in the proper mix of the right controls.

The best profit safeguard you can have in a store is the employee whose integrity is beyond question. The trouble is, too many retailers take integrity for granted. "Innocent until proven guilty" is a meaningful and deep-rooted American principle. But it doesn't preclude the need to install effective theft deterrents and to minimize the chance for dishonesty.

One fact is obvious. The store with the greatest proportion of honest employees suffers the least from theft loss. The trick is to take every precaution to ensure that the people you hire are honest to begin with. Then, take pains to maintain the kind of store climate that will encourage them to stay honest.

Improving the Level of Personnel

Upgrading the level of retail personnel is largely a matter of careful personnel screening and selection, in-

cluding careful reference checks, credit checks, psychological tests, polygraph lie-detector tests, and personal character examinations. Doing these things and sticking to the basic tenets of employee motivation can help you to generate a store atmosphere that discourages employee theft.

Screening Applicants

Just like a book, a job applicant can't be judged by outward appearance alone. Don't let the "front" he or she puts on dull your caution. Appearances, experience, and personality may all be striking points in the applicant's favor. And he or she may still be a thief. Or an alcoholic, drug addict, or other high security risk. Remember that the person you easily pick may just be looking for easy pickings.

One hiring mistake could prove to be a devastating profit drain for months or years to come. No matter how urgently you may need additional personnel, it does not pay to loosen your screening and hiring procedures. When you compromise on your standards of character and integrity, you also compromise on your profit position.

Don't take chances. Run a conscientious reference check on every new employee. No security measure is more important than this.

Lack of knowledge about the store's routine usually restricts new employees' stealing to what they can slip from the cash register or conceal on their persons. You can detect either by closely watching daily receipts and a personal scrutiny of new employees until you are satisfied that you can trust them.

Set the Tone

Checking out new employees is only the beginning of upgrading your personnel. Another important step is setting a tone or atmosphere which will encourage honesty in your store.

In doing it, *shoot for excellence of conduct and performance.* Because people respect high standards, you should not settle for less. They also tend to copy the individuals who set such standards and require that they be met.

It is important to adopt a *"Zero Shortage" attitude.* If you feel that a "reasonable write-off" due to pilferage is all right, keep it a secret and hammer away at shortage control, even when losses diminish.

Owner-managers should *avoid setting a double standard of moral and ethical conduct.* If an employee sees a supervisor in even a minor dishonest act, he or she is encouraged in the same direction. Return overshipments or overpayments promptly. When you set rules, have them apply to everyone. Owner-managers cannot expect their employees to set standards that are any higher than those they set for themselves.

Preserving the dignity of your employees is essential if you expect your people to respect you and the store. Employees should be treated with courtesy and consideration. Show an interest in them as individuals. Then back that interest—to mention an example or two—by keeping restrooms and other areas clean and attractive and, by providing fresh uniforms, if your business uses them. Respecting employees may not reform the hardcore thief. But it will help keep many others from straying.

Finally, owner-managers should not expect their people to achieve the impossible. Giving employees unrealistic goals is an invitation to cheat. When you do, you give no alternative. It is either cheat or admit failure and risk losing their jobs.

Provide the Incentives

A third step in upgrading personnel is to enable employees to live up to your expectations. The following practices can be helpful:

Make certain each person is matched to his or her job. Employees should not be put in positions where they are forced to lie or cheat about performance because they are unable to do their work. Lying and cheating, even on a small scale, are just a step away from theft.

Set reasonable rules and enforce them rigidly. Loosely administered rules are more harmful than no rules at all.

Set clear lines of authority and responsibility. Each employee needs a yardstick by which to measure his or her progress and improve performance. To fill this basic need, duties should be spelled out—preferably in writing. When employees do not know who does what, there will be error, waste, and the kind of indifferent performance that breeds dishonesty.

Employees should be given the resources they need to achieve success. Whether they are buyers, salespeople, or stock clerks, nothing is more frustrating to employees than to see their goals blocked by circumstances beyond their control. To perform well, an employee needs the proper tools, the right information, and guidance when it is required. Denying such support and expecting him or her to produce is a sure way to weaken morale.

Be fair in rewarding outstanding performance. The top producing salesperson who receives the same treatment as the mediocre employee is apt to become resentful. Individuals who make a worthwhile profit contribution are entitled to, and expect, a fair share of ego and financial satisfaction. Honest recognition of merit by the owner-manager triggers more honest effort on the part of the employee.

Finally, you should remove the temptation to steal. One organization of counter service restaurants is noted for its good employee relations. It treats people fairly. It displays faith in their integrity and ability. But it also provides uniforms without pockets.

Remove the opportunity to steal and half the battle is won. There is no substitute for rigid, well-implemented preventive measures.

In addition, owner-managers should use a continuing program of investigation and training. They should train employees on ways to eliminate stock shortage and shrinkage. One small retailer, for example, trains employees to record items, such as floor cleaner, which they take out of stock for use in the store: "Otherwise, it's an inventory loss even though it's a legitimate store expense."

Above all, never stop letting your people know that you are always aware and that you always care. This point must be driven home again and again. And with every restatement of it—whether by a security check, a change of locks, the testing of alarms, a systems audit, a notice on the bulletin board—you can be assured that **you are influencing that moment of decision when an employee is faced with the choice—to steal or not to steal.**

Haphazard Physical Security

Also high on the list of invitations to theft is haphazard physical security. Owner-managers who are casual about issuing keys, locking doors, and changing locks are, in effect, inviting the dishonest employee into the plant or office after work. But intelligent key control and installation of timelocks and alarms are ways of serving notice to crooked workers to play it straight.

The more doors a plant has, the more avenues of theft it offers. For example, one stock clerk parked his car at the receiving dock. He kept the trunk closed but unlocked. At 12:30 p.m., when the shipping-receiving manager was at lunch, the stock clerk threw full cartons of shoes into the trunk and then slammed it locked. Elapsed time: 18 seconds.

The plant that's designed for maximum security will have a minimum number of active doors and a supervisor or guard, if warranted, stationed near each door. Moreover, a supervisor should be present when materials or finished goods are being received or shipped and when trash is being removed. As long as a door stays open, a responsible employee, a supervisor, or a guard should be there.

Central station alarm systems should be used to protect a plant after hours. Their purpose is to record door openings and closings and to investigate unexpected openings. Timelocks are also designed to record all openings.

"Breaking-out"

A record of door openings can be important because the dishonest employee is often a specialist at "breaking-out" (hiding and leaving the plant after closing hours). If your plant is not protected against break-out, you can be hurt badly because this method of operation allows a thief to work pretty much at his or her own speed.

After-hours thieves put out of commission the alarm system that works beautifully against break-in. They can often leave by doors equipped with snap-type locks—doors that do not require keys from the insides. Quickly and easily, they can pass goods outside and then snap doors closed behind them. Thus, they leave no evidence.

A motion detector, electric eye, or central station alarm will deter such thieves. You can also discourage breakouts with locks that need keys on both sides, provided that local or State fire regulations do not prohibit such locks. When goods, materials, or money are missing and evidence of forced entry is lacking, begin to look immediately for the inside thief, the dishonest employee.

Audit Control Methods

Loss prevention controls and procedures by themselves are not enough to protect your assets. Controls and procedures must be audited from time to time or they will break down. No loss-prevention control is stronger than its audit.

One effective auditing method is to commit deliberate errors. What will your people do if, for example, you see that more finished goods than the shipping order calls for reach the platform? Will the shipping clerk return the excess to stock? Will he or she try to divert it for personal use (perhaps in collusion with a truck driver)? Or will the clerk simply ship the order without ever knowing that the excess existed?

If the bookkeeper and the accounts receivable clerk are not dependable, alert, and honest, disaster can result. Check them by withholding an invoice from each of them and watching to see what they do. Will they miss the invoice? Will they realize that a missing invoice means lost revenue and call it to your attention?

Unannounced inspections are another excellent method of checking your preventive procedures. Such inspections are most effective during overtime periods or when the second or third shift is working. For example, one owner-manager popped up on the shipping platform after the second shift left. He noticed a loaded truck parked at the platform and ordered it unloaded. The cartons in the rear were legitimate deliveries, but he found the front half of the truck crammed with stolen goods. The checker, who was hired to see that such stealing did not happen, had gone to sleep and let the accommodating driver load his own truck.

Keep Crooks Off Balance

The employees who are the most successful at their "second trade" are the ones who test the system and are convinced that they can beat it. They can steal you blind. With every "score," their confidence increases and along with it their danger to the company. The best way to stop such crooks is to keep them off balance—keep them from developing the feeling that they can beat your system.

Here's an example of how one owner-manager keeps crooks off balance. When inventory shrinkage became a major problem, he made a loss-prevention survey. To help keep employees honest, he tightened certain existing controls and put in some new ones. He reduced the number of exits employees could use by half. He scheduled "unscheduled" locker inspections for the unlikeliest possible moments. Employees were no longer allowed to take lunch boxes or bags of any kind to their work stations. Packages inspection procedures were tightened.

To date, this owner-manager has caught no thieves. But by simply tightening controls and adding a number of surprise elements to his loss-prevention maintenance system, he reduced his inventory loss drastically.

Don't Play Detective

Dishonest employees, working alone or in collusion with others, can find ways to beat the system no matter how theft-proof you try to make it. "Smart cookies" can devise ways to get away with substantial amounts of money, materials, or goods.

Owner-managers who suspect theft should not attempt to turn detective and try to solve the crimes themselves. Even the best business owner may botch a criminal investigation because it's an area in which the average owner is an amateur.

When you suspect a theft, bring the police or a reliable firm of professional security consultants into the picture without delay. Where dishonest employees are bonded by insurance companies, ironclad evidence of theft must be uncovered before you can file a claim with the insurance company to recover your losses. Professional undercover investigation is among the most effective ways to secure such evidence.

Rules That Can Help

Prosecute employees who are caught stealing. (Settling for restitution and an apology is inviting theft to continue.)

Rotate security guards. (Rotation discourages fraternizing with other employees who may turn out to be dishonest. Rotation also prevents monotony from reducing the alertness of guards.)

Price items by machine or rubber stamp, not by handwriting.

Permit only authorized employees to set prices and mark merchandise.

In cases of returns and refunds, insist on a merchandise inspection and approval by someone other than the person who made the sale.

Pay special attention to cashiers when they are surrounded by clusters of people.

Be alert to the use of over-ring slips to cover up shortages.

Make a dependable second check of incoming materials to rule out the possibility of collusive theft between drivers and employees who handle the receiving. Do not allow a truck to approach the loading platform until it is ready to load or unload.

Do not allow drivers behind the receiving fence. (Discourage drivers from taking goods or materials from the platform by the following devices: installing heavy-gauge wire fencing between bays, with the mesh too fine to provide a toehold; mounting closed-circuit television cameras overhead that will sweep the entire platform; and locating the receiving supervisor's desk or office to afford him or her an unobstructed view of the entire platform.)

At the loading platform, do not permit drivers to load their own trucks, especially by taking goods from stock.

Make sure that every lunchbox, tool box, bag, or package is inspected by a supervisor or guard as employees leave the plant.

Insist that all padlocks be snapped shut on hasps when not in use to prevent the switching of locks.

Control keys to padlocks. Never leave the key hanging on a nail near the lock where a crooked worker can "borrow" it and have a duplicate made while he or she is away from work.

Do not allow trash to accumulate in, or be picked up from, an area near storage sites of valuable materials or finished goods.

Inspect disposal locations and rubbish trucks at irregular intervals for the presence of salable items when you have the slightest reason to suspect collusion between employees and trash collectors.

Supervise trash pickups. (Companies have been systematically drained over long periods by alliance between crooked employees and trash collectors.)

Control receiving reports and shipping orders (preferably by numbers in sequence) to prevent duplication of fraudulent payment of invoices and the padding or destruction of shipping orders.

Make sure that receiving reports are prepared immediately upon receiving a shipment. (Delay in making out such reports can be an invitation to theft or, at best, result in recordkeeping errors.)

Embezzlement

An owner-manager can lose a great deal of money before even suspecting that embezzlement might be going on. That's because by definition this crime is committed by someone in a position of trust. The loss may involve a small amount taken by an employee from the cash register. Or it may be a considerable sum stolen through an elaborate scheme of juggling the books.

Simple controls built into the accounting system can often forestall any such practices in your operation. In any case, the proper internal controls may help document incriminating evidence, without which it is difficult to estimate your loss for insurance purposes or even to prove that it resulted from a crime.

This section offers suggestions on how you can thwart dishonest practices. It also discusses what you should do if it appears that one of your employees has embezzled from your business.

You may not have had any experience with embezzlers but many owner-managers have. Everyday there are newspaper stories about how some dishonest employee has managed to divert company funds to his or her own pocket. It happens often enough to make it worth your while to give the subject some thought and to examine your recordkeeping and auditing procedures to make sure there are no tempting loopholes.

Embezzlement is "the fraudulent appropriation of property by a person to whom it has been entrusted." The key word is "entrusted." That's what makes this crime different from ordinary theft or larceny. The embezzler is someone in your company whom you trust.

You need to have a system of internal control to safeguard money and other property subject to embezzlement. Of course, nobody wants to run a business like an armed camp. But, if you have a built-in control system, administer it tightly, and audit it frequently, you may prevent attempts of embezzlement. At any rate, you will have the means to collect evidence that may expose a crime.

Embezzlers usually think that they are clever—smarter than the owner-manager and cunning enough to beat the system. Before you set about to outwit them, it is a good idea to be familiar with some of their methods of operation.

Some Common Schemes

The embezzler is usually a trusted employee who is taking advantage of the employer's confidence. In many cases the embezzler has been given more authority than the position calls for. Methods of embezzling are limited only by imagination.

In the simplest situation, cash is received and the employee merely pockets it without making a record of the transaction. A theft of this type is difficult to prevent or detect if the transaction is a cash sale and no subsequent entry is necessary in receipt or accounts receivable records. To reduce temptation, prenumbered sales invoices or cash register receipts should be used for all sales regardless of the amount. Spot checks and other monitoring procedures can also help assure you that cash sales are actually being recorded.

A somewhat more complicated type of embezzlement is called lapping. This involves the temporary withholding of receipts such as payments on accounts receivable. Lapping is a continuing scheme which usually starts with a small amount but can run into thousands of dollars before it is detected. For example, take an employee who opens mail or otherwise receives cash and checks as payment on open accounts. The employee holds out a $100 dollar cash payment made by a customer "A" on March 1. To avoid arousing suspicion on "A's" part, $100 is then taken from a $200 payment made by customer "B" on March 5. This is sent on, together with the necessary documentation, for processing and crediting to the account of "A". The embezzler pockets the remaining $100, which increases the shortage to $200.

As this "borrowing" procedure continues, the employee makes away with increasingly larger amounts of money involving more and more accounts. A fraud of this nature can run on for years. Of course, it requires detailed recordkeeping by the embezzler in order to keep track of the shortage and transfer it from one account to another to avoid suspicion. Any indication that an employee is keeping personal records of business transactions outside your regular books of account should be looked into.

Sometimes an embezzler who is carrying on a lapping scheme also has access to accounts receivable records and statements. In this case, he or she is in a position to alter the statements mailed out to customers. Thus the fraud may continue undetected over a long period of time, until something unusual happens. A customer complaint may spotlight the situation. Or the matter may be surfaced through audit procedures such as confirmation of accounts receivable. One embezzler who also handled the customer complaints was able to avoid detection for many years. The amount of the shortage reached such proportions and covered so many accounts that he dared not take a vacation. He even ate lunch at his desk lest some other employee receive an inquiry from a customer concerning a discrepancy in a statement. The owner-manager for whom he worked admired his diligence and loyalty. Fellow workers marveled that his apparent frugality enabled him to enjoy a rather high standard of living. But the inevitable finally happened. This employee was hospitalized with a serious ailment, and in his absence his fraudulent scheme came to light. One reason many firms require regular vacations is to keep some "indispensable man" from dispensing with company funds illegally.

Sometimes company bank accounts are used for check-kiting. In fact, losses from some large check-kiting schemes have been great enough to cause a company to go broke.

In the usual scheme, the check-kiter must be in the position to write checks on and make deposits in two or more bank accounts. One account could be the embezzler's personal account and the other a business checking account. If the embezzler has an accomplice in another business, two business accounts may be used. If your company has more than one checking account at different banks, these accounts may be utilized to carry out the fraud.

The check-kiter is taking advantage of the time period (or "float") which is the number of days between deposit of a check and collection of funds. There may be several days between the date when a kited check drawn on bank "A" is deposited in bank "B" and the date the check is presented to bank "A" for payment. Assuming that it takes 3 business days for checks to clear, a simple kite between two banks could be accomplished as follows:

On December 1, a check in the amount of $5,000 drawn on bank "A" is deposited in bank "B". On December 2, the check kiter cashes a $5,000 check payable to cash and drawn on bank "B" with a teller at bank "B". Since the original kited check will be presented to bank "A" on December 4, the check kiter on or before that date will deposit a $6,000 check drawn on bank "B" in bank "A" not only to insure payment of the original kited check but increase the amount of the kite. As the process is repeated the kited checks become larger, more cash is withdrawn, and the scheme can continue until the shortage is covered—or until the kite "breaks" when one of the banks refuses to honor a kited check because the funds on deposit are uncollected.

A temporary kite may be used by a dishonest employee to conceal cash shortage at the end of a period by depositing a kited check into your company account. This brings the bank balance into agreement with the books. C.P.A.'s will request "cut-off" bank statements to detect frauds of this type.

Payroll frauds are yet another source of loss to management. Occasionally an enterprising embezzler has added the names of relatives or fictitious individuals to the company payroll and thus enjoyed several salary checks each week instead of one.

Sometimes, when a company becomes large enough that the owner-manager can no longer exercise personal surveillance of accounting activities, opportunities arise for a dishonest employee to set up a dummy supplier and falsify documentation of fictitious purchase transactions.

Dishonest employees can figure out any number of ways to defraud their employers. Purchasing agents can accept "kickbacks" from suppliers from purchasing goods at inflated prices. Salespeople and others can pad their expense accounts. Personal items can sometimes be bought and charged to the company. Cashiers in retail firms can undercharge relatives or friends for merchandise. False vouchers can be prepared to conceal thefts from petty cash funds. Overtime can be falsely recorded. Moreover, quite substantial amounts of money may be lost through the cumulative effect of such seemingly minor abuses as personal use of company postage stamps, supplies, and equipment, as well as charging personal long-distance phone calls to the business.

Make Your System Fraud-Proof

The first and one of the most important things an owner-manager should do is to set a good example. Your employees watch what you do and are prone to imitate your habits—good or bad. An employer who dips into petty cash, fudges on an expense account, uses company funds for personal items, or sets other examples of loose business behavior will find employees rationalizing dishonest actions with the attitude "if it's good enough for the boss, it's good enough for me."

Another important way an owner-manager can discourage embezzlement is by establishing a climate of accountability. Employees should know their jobs and feel trusted. But they should also realize that they are held accountable for their actions. To some people, management indifference in financial administration is a license to steal. That's why it is important for you to examine your procedures and determine what controls can be added to forestall any dishonest practices. And, just as important, the system should be designed to help document evidence in the event someone does try to embezzle your funds. One problem in fidelity loss claims is that of proving the amount that was stolen. The owner-manager has to support a loss claim with evidence—facts and figures that you get from your records.

Reliance for prevention and detection of fraud must be placed principally upon an adequate accounting system with appropriate internal controls that safeguard your assets. Your public accountant can be of great help in setting up a good recordkeeping system. Then it must be tested and evaluated at least annually by the auditor. The purpose of periodic examination is to make sure that there are no loopholes through which an embezzler can manipulate your funds.

One fundamental control is separation of the duties of employees. For example, persons concerned with receiving checks and cash should not also be responsible for the entries in the accounts receivable records. No one person should handle a transaction from beginning to end. If you do not exercise tight control over invoices, purchase orders, discounts, customer credits, you are asking for trouble.

You should insist that your accounting system provide you with operating statements issued at least monthly. These will inform you of the operations to date and the firm's financial condition. You can use these documents to compare the figures with prior periods. Any unusual or unexplained variations should be discussed with your public accountant to determine the reason.

Look For Clues

You know how in medicine the symptoms of one disease often resemble those of another. Likewise in business the symptoms, or danger signs, of an embezzlement are often cause by other factors. Here are a few clues which indicate that either an embezzler is at work in your company or certain aspects of the business need more of your attention.

Increase in overall sales returns could be caused by defective merchandise—or it might represent a concealment of accounts receivable payments.

Unusual bad-debt write-offs can be due to a number of business reasons—or they could be covering up a fraudulent scheme.

A decline or usually small increase in cash or credit sales might mean that business has not been good—or it could mean that some sales were not being recorded.

Inventory shortage can be caused by error or mismanagement—or they could indicate fictitious purchases, unrecorded sales, or employee pilferage.

Profit declines and/or increases in expenses can be entirely legitimate—or they could be a sign that cash is being siphoned off illegitimately.

Slow collections can be caused by business conditions—or they can be a device to mask embezzlement.

Ounces Of Prevention

There are many steps an owner-manager can take to cut down on the possibility of losses through embezzlement. Do you take the following precautions?

1. Check the background of prospective employees. Sometimes you can satisfy yourself by making a few telephone calls or writing a few letters. In other cases, you may want to turn the matter over to a credit bureau or similar agency to run a background check. (Keep in mind that the rights of individuals must be preserved in furnishing, receiving, and using background information.)

2. Know your employees to the extent that you may be able to detect signs of financial or other personal problems. Build up rapport so that they feel free to discuss such things with you in confidence.

3. See that no one is placed on the payroll without authorization from you or a responsible official of the company. If you have a personnel department, require that it approve additions to the payroll as a double check.

4. Have the company mail addressed to a post office box rather than your place of business. In smaller cities, the owner-manager may want to go to the post office to collect the mail. In any event, you or your designated keyperson should personally open the mail and make a record at that time of cash and checks received. Don't delude yourself that checks or money orders payable to your company can't be converted into cash by an enterprising embezzler.

5. Either personally prepare the daily cash deposits or compare the deposits made by employees with the record of cash and checks received. Make sure you get a copy of the duplicate deposit slip or other documentation from the bank. Make it a habit to go to the bank and make the daily deposit yourself as often as you can. If you delegate these jobs, make an occasional spot check to see that nothing is amiss.

6. Arrange for bank statements and other correspondence from banks to be sent to the same post office box, and personnally reconcile all bank statements with your company's books and records. The owner-manager who has not reconciled the statements for some time may want to get oriented by the firm's outside accountant.

7. Personally examine all canceled checks and endorsements to see if there is anything unusual. This also applies to payroll checks.

8. Make sure that an employee in a position to mishandle funds is adequately bonded. Let employees know that fidelity coverage is a matter of company policy rather than any feeling of mistrust on your part. If would-be embezzlers know that a bonding company also has an interest in what they do, they may think twice before helping themselves to your funds.

9. Spot check your accounting records and assets to satisfy yourself that all is well and that your plan of internal control is being carried out.

10. Personally approve unusual discounts and bad-debt write-offs. Approve or spot check credit memos and other documentation for sales returns and allowances.

11. Don't delegate the signing of checks and approval of cash disbursements unless absolutely necessary and never approve any payment without sufficient documentation or prior knowledge of the transaction.

12. Examine all invoices and supporting data before signing checks. Make sure that all merchandise was actually received and the price seems reasonable. In many false purchase schemes, the embezzler neglects to make up receiving forms or other records purporting to show receipt of merchandise.

13. Personally cancel all invoices at the time you sign the check to prevent double payment through error or otherwise.

14. Don't sign blank checks. Don't leave a supply of signed blank checks when you go on vacation.

15. Inspect all prenumbered checkbooks and other prenumbered forms from time to time to insure that checks or forms from the backs of the books have not been removed and possibly used in a fraudulent scheme.

16. Have the preparation of the payroll and the actual paying of employees handled by different persons, especially when cash is involved.

If You Suspect A Crime

First of all, be sure that you do not jump to any unwarranted conclusions. What may appear to be an obvious embezzlement may, on further investigation, turn out to have a perfectly valid explanation. A false accusation could result in serious civil liability. There have been cases where employees have been charged by management with embezzlement, dismissed from their positions, and later found to be entirely innocent.

But if you have good reason to suspect embezzling, contact your attorney immediately. Be guided by legal advice on how to proceed. Discuss the necessity of notifying the bonding company and appropriate law enforcement authorities. Follow legal advice in matters regarding prosecution so that you will not subject yourself or your company to charges of false arrest.

Don't subject yourself to criminal charges by helping conceal the commission of a crime. Embezzlers should be prosecuted when the facts so warrant and when there is a sufficiency of evidence. These and other legal questions are best left to your attorney.

Computer-Related Embezzlements

The news media have given a lot of publicity to computer-assisted frauds and embezzlements. The computer crimes receiving this publicity are usually complex and give the impression that computer-related frauds can be committed only by highly skilled technicians using sophisticated computer systems. This could create a false feeling of security for owner-managers who use less sophisticated systems or service centers for processing their records.

A recent study by the U.S. General Accounting Office of Computer-Related Crimes in Federal Programs disclosed that most computer-related crimes were committed by people with limited knowledge of computer technology. Most cases resulted from preparation of false input data to computer-based systems. Neglect of control on input is a weakness. You should have your outside accountant review your controls and strengthen them if needed.

To Sum Up

The following are three principal ways in which you can minimize the possibility of embezzlement losses. None is completely effective without the others.

Internal controls are perhaps the most effective safeguards against fraud, but even the best precautions can't make it absolutely impossible.

Independent audits discourage fraud and may uncover it. But they can't, as some people mistakenly believe, guarantee disclosure of all irregularities.

Fidelity coverage can help you recover what may be lost in spite of your best efforts to prevent embezzlements.

Shoplifting

Petty thievery may not seem like major crime to the casual crook who pockets a ball-point pen here, a pocket calculator there. But to the small business fighting for survival, it's murder.

Just to cover a yearly loss of $1,000 in thefts, a retailer would have to sell each day over 900 candy bars, or 130 packs of cigarettes, or 380 cans of soup. Faced with such unreasonable selling volumes most small business people are forced instead to raise their prices and lower their ability to compete.

This section contains practical advice on how to spot, deter, apprehend, and prosecute shoplifters.

Who's Robbing You Blind?

What does a shoplifter look like? Like you. Or like me. Shoplifters can be male or female, any race or color, as young as five or well into their 80's. Anyone who deliberately takes merchandise from a store without paying for it is a shoplifter, whether the theft is large or small, premeditated or impulsive.

Fortunately for business people, most shoplifters are amateurs rather than professionals. To the wary eye, they are not difficult to spot and, with the right kind of handling, they may never try petty thievery again. Here are the various types of shoplifters.

Juvenile offenders. Young people account for about 50 percent of all shoplifting. They may steal on a dare or simply for kicks. Frequently they expect that store owners and courts will go easy on them because of their youth. They may enter stores in gangs in an attempt to intimidate management further. You simply cannot permit this kind of manipulation. Youth is no excuse for crime, and the adult who lets it slip by is not doing the youngsters any favor. Shoplifting is usually the first type of theft attempted by juveniles, and it may lead to more serious crimes. Juvenile theft should be pursued and prosecuted through the proper legal channels.

Impulse shoplifters. Many ''respectable'' people fall into this category. They have not premeditated their thefts but a sudden chance (such as an unattended dressing room or a blind aisle in a supermarket) presents itself, and the shopper succumbs to temptation. The retailer can combat impulse shoplifting most effectively by simple prevention: building deterrents into the store layout and training employees to be aware of the problem and effective in dealing with it.

Alcoholics, vagrants and drug addicts. Abnormal physical need can drive people to theft, as well as to other crimes. These criminals are often clumsy or erratic in their behavior and may be easier then other types of shoplifters to detect. The store owner should remember, however, that people under the influence of drugs or with an obsessive physical need may be violent. They may be armed as well. It is best to leave the handling of such people to the police.

Kleptomaniacs. A driving psychological need can have similar effects. Kleptomaniacs are motivated by a compulsion to steal. They usually have little or no actual use for the items they steal and in many cases could well afford to pay for them. It is not up to the business person to make a psychological diagnosis. Shoplifting is shoplifting. It is no less costly simply because it is involuntary.

Professionals. Since the professional shoplifter is in the business of theft, he or she is usually highly skilled and hard to spot. Professionals generally steal items which will quickly be resold to an established fence. They tend to concentrate on high-demand, easily-resold consumer goods such as televisions, stereos, and other small appliances. The pro, or ''booster,'' may case a store or department well in advance of the actual theft. While professionals may be hard to prosecute (they may belong to underworld organizations which are very effective in raising bail and providing defense in court), they can be deterred from theft by effective layout and alert personnel.

How Do They Do it?

Shoplifters may work alone or in groups. While it's impossible to give an infallible rule of thumb, experience has shown that juveniles and professionals tend to work in groups, while the impulse shoplifter is a loner.

Working in a group, the shoplifter may use confederates to be concealed. One member of the gang may also distract sales help while the thieves do their work. Gang members may also start an argument with store personnel or among themselves, or even feign a fainting spell to draw attention, giving a cohort the opportunity to steal merchandise from another part of the store.

Shoplifters don't like crowds. They keep a sharp eye out for other customers or store personnel; quick, nervous glances may be a giveaway. They also tent to ''shop'' during hours when store staff is lighter than usual— during lunch hours, early morning, or just before closing.

Shoplifters also have their own arsenal of professional tools. Articles as innocent as bulky packages, pocketbooks, baby carriages, knitting bags, shopping bags, umbrellas, newspapers and magazines can be used to carry stolen goods. Even an oversized arm sling can help the shoplifter conceal merchandise.

Specially-constructed devices such as coats or capes with hidden pockets and zippered hiding places are useful to the more experienced shoplifter. Some thieves use booster boxes (large boxes with a hinged end, top, or bottom). Booster boxes may be gift-wrapped to frustrate detection.

Unsupervised dressing rooms offer excellent opportunities for theft. Shoplifters may simply pile on layers of pilfered clothing, or they may exchange new items for the clothes they were wearing and return the originals to the rack.

Price tickets can often be too easily switched, particularly in grocery stores or drugstores where prices are written on gummed labels and—often carelessly— stuck to the item.

How Can You Deter Shoplifters

Your time and money are better spent in preventing crime than prosecuting it. There are three major areas in which deterrence efforts pay off royally for the store owner:

1. **Educate your employees.** Train your sales help to be alert to the shoplifter's early warning signals. They should be on the lookout for customers carrying the concealment devices mentioned earlier in this Aid. They should watch for shoppers walking with short or unnatural steps, tipoffs that the customers may be concealing items between their legs.

Clothing store employees should be alert to groups of shoppers who enter the store together, then break up and go in different directions. A customer who attempts to monopolize a sales person's time may be covering for a confederate stealing elsewhere in the store.

Sales help should remember that ordinary customers want attention; shoplifters do not. When busy with one customer, the sales person should acknowledge waiting customers with polite remarks such as, ''I'll be with you in a minute.'' This pleases legitimate customers, while making a shoplifter feel uneasy.

Sales people should watch for a customer who handles a lot of merchandise, but who takes an unusually long time to make a decision. They should watch for customers lingering in one area, loitering near stock rooms or other restricted areas or wandering aimlessly though the store. They should try to be alert to customers who consistently shop during hours when staff is low.

Cashiers should be trained to check the lower racks of shopping carts, to watch for switched price labels, to inspect containers such as garbage cans or tool boxes which could conceal stolen items.

Local police often conduct training seminars for store personnel. They can instruct your employees in spotting potential shoplifters, as well as in what to do when they observe a theft. Periodic review sessions, at least once every three months, will help keep employees aware.

You can help your employees help you. Schedule working hours to allow an adequate number of clerks to be on hand at all times. Discourage ''coffee-klatching'' on the selling floor. A group of employees in one spot means inadequate coverage somewhere else.

2. **Plan store layout with deterrence in mind.** Maintain adequate lighting in all areas of the store. Keep protruding ''wings'' and end displays low, not more than two or three feet high. Set display cases in broken sequences. If possible, run them for short lengths with spaces in between.

Keep small items of high value (film, cigarettes, small appliances) behind a counter or in a locked case with sales clerk on duty. Keep displays neat; it's easier to spot an item missing from an orderly array.

Attach noise alarms to unlocked exits. Close and block off unused checkout aisles. If you are involved in store design, plan to have entrances and exits in a common vestibule.

3. Use protective personnel and equipment. Protective devices may not be cheap, but shoplifting is costlier. You can get an idea of how much you can expect to lose to thieves by multiplying the number of shoplifters apprehended last year in your store by the average value of the stolen merchandise, then multiplying that figure by 50 weeks. The total is usually far greater than the cost of deterrence systems.

Some of the most widely-used devices are two-way mirrors, peep-holes, closed-circuit television, convex wall mirrors, and detectives posing as customers. To be valuable, surveillance devices must be properly placed and monitored.

Uniformed guards are powerful visual deterrents to the shoplifter.

There are several ways to identify merchandise as having been legitimately paid for. One is to instruct cashiers to staple receipts to the outside of the packages. Electronic tags may be attached to soft articles such as clothing. They can be removed only by a cashier with special shears, and they trigger an alarm if the shoplifter tries to carry the article from the store.

If you see electronic sensing devices, be sure cashiers are diligent in their use. If your employee forgets to remove the device and the customer is falsely accused, you could be liable.

Two-way radios make it easy to stay close to suspected shoplifters and to alert security personnel.

Ticket-switching can be discouraged through the use of tamper-proof gummed labels, hard-to-break plastic string, multiple price tickets concealed on items, or special staple or punch patterns on price tags.

Price labels marked by rubber stamps or pricing machines are better than pencilled or felt-markered price tags.

What About Apprehension, Arrest and Prosecution?

While good deterrent systems will greatly reduce shoplifting, there are always people who are too dumb or too "smart" to be deterred. They'd try to steal the teeth out of a tiger's mouth if they thought the tiger wasn't looking.

These people could force you to the last line of defense for your store. Remember, to give your charges a chance of sticking, you must be able to:

See the person take or conceal merchandise,

Identify the merchandise as yours,

Testify that it was taken with the intent to steal,

Prove that the merchandise was not paid for.

If you are not able to meet all four criteria, you leave yourself open to countercharges of false arrest. False arrest need not mean police arrest; simply preventing a person from conducting normal activities can be deemed false arrest. Furthermore, any physical contact, even a light touch on the arm, may be considered unnecessary and used against you in court.

Check the laws in your state. Many states have passed shoplifting laws which deal with apprehension. Your lawyer or local police can advise you. Also, always consider your safety and that of your employees first and foremost.

In general, store personnel should never accuse customers of stealing, nor should they try to apprehend suspected shoplifters. If they observe suspicious behavior or an apparent theft in progress, they should alert the store owner, manager, store detective, or police.

It is wisest to apprehend shoplifters outside the store. You have a better case if you show that the shoplifter left the store with stolen merchandise. Outside apprehension also eliminates unpleasant scenes which might disrupt normal store operation.

You may prefer to apprehend a shoplifter inside the store, if the merchandise involved is of considerable value or if you feel that the thief may be able to elude you outside the store premises.

In either case, avoid verbal accusation of the suspect. One recommended procedure is to identify yourself, then say, "I believe you have some merchandise which you have forgotten to pay for. Would you mind coming with me to straighten things out?"

When cornered, the first thing most shoplifters—impulse thieves or pros—will say is, "I've never done this before." In general, this is all the more reason, if your evidence is sufficient, to call the police and proceed with prosecution. Failure to prosecute first offenders encourages them to try it again. Word also gets around that your store is an "easy hit."

Some organizations have control files on shoplifters who have been caught. Your retail merchants' association can inform you about the services available in your area. You can check these files to see whether the person you catch has a prior record. A shoplifter who claims to be a first offender is likely to remain a "first offender" unless you get positive identification and file his or her name with the police and local retail merchants' association.

Naturally, each situation must be handled differently and your good judgement is required. You may wish to release elderly or senile shoplifters and not press charges where there's some indication that the person could honestly have forgotten to pay for the merchandise.

In most cases, however, prosecution is in order. It is essential if the shoplifter is violent, if he or she lacks proper identification and you suspect a prior record, if he or she appears to be under the influence of alcohol or other drugs, if the theft involves merchandise of great value, or if the shoplifter appears to be a professional.

Juvenile shoplifters require special handling. A strict, no-nonsense demeanor often makes a lasting impression on the young offender and may deter future theft. While many stores choose to contact the parents of young shoplifters rather than the police, remember that juveniles account for half of all shoplifting that goes on in this country. The parents of troubled youngsters may be ineffective in handling the situation. Whom are you helping if you let the young shoplifter go to steal again?

Bad Check Passing

Time was when a man's word was as good as his bond. But nowdays, even the signatures of many persons are worthless—especially to retailers who are stuck with bad checks.

This section offers suggestions that should be helpful in keeping bad checks out of the cash registers of small stores. For example, the key items on a check should be examined closely because they can tip off the owner-manager to a worthless check. Your

procedures should also include a dollar limit on the size of checks you will accept and the type of identification necessary to back up the the the signature or endorsement. In addition, it is profitable to review with employees the checks which the bank refuses to honor.

A neatly dressed stranger pays for her groceries with a payroll check issued by a company in a nearby city. In the next few hours, she does the same thing in several other food stores.

In another community, a middle-aged man pays for a pair of shoes with a Government check. He moves to other stores and cashes several more Government Checks.

In a third city, a well-dressed woman pays for an expensive dress with a blank check. "I need a little pocket cash," she says. "May I make the check for $20 more?" The salesclerk agrees, never suspecting that the customer does not have an account in any bank.

Tomorrow, these three con-artists will work in other communities.

The specialist in payroll checks will fill out blank ones which she has stolen. The passer of Government checks is also a thief. He steals Social Security checks, tax refund checks, and so on from individual mail boxes. "Blank check" Bessie will hit her victim after the banks have closed.

These three, and others who pass worthless checks, are clever. They live by their wits and are often glib talkers. But they are not so clever that you can't outwit them.

Types of Checks

Winning the battle of wits against bad-check passers is largely a matter of knowledge and vigilance. You have to know what you're up against, pass the information on to your employees, and be constantly on guard when accepting checks.

You are apt to get seven different kinds of checks; personal, two-party, payroll, Government, blank, counter, and traveler's. And some customers may offer money orders.

A personal check is written and signed by the individual offering it. The individual makes it out to you or your firm.

A Two-Party Check is issued by one person, the maker, to a second person who endorses it so that it may be cashed by a third person. This type of check is susceptible to fraud because, for one thing, the maker can stop payment at the bank.

A Payroll Check is issued to an employee for wages or salary earned. Usually the name of the employer is printed on it, and it has a number and is signed. In most instances "payroll" is also printed on the check. The employee's name is printed by a check writing machine or typed. In metropolitan areas, you should not cash a payroll check that is handprinted, rubber stamped or typewritten as a payroll check, even if it appears to be issued by a local business and drawn on a local bank. It may be a different story in a small community where you know the company officials and the employee personally.

A Government Check can be issued by the Federal Government, a State, a county, or a local government. Such checks cover salaries, tax refunds, pensions, welfare allotments, and veterans benefits, to mention a few examples.

You should be particularly cautious with government checks. Often they are stolen and the endorsement has been forged.

In some areas, such thievery is so great that some banks refuse to cash Social Security, welfare, relief, or income tax checks, unless the customer has an account with the bank. You should follow this procedure also. In short, know your endorser.

A Blank Check, sometimes known as a universal check, is no longer acceptable to most banks due to the Federal Reserve Board regulations that prohibit standard processing without the encoded characters. This universal check may be used, but it requires a special collection process by the bank and incurs a special cost.

A Counter Check is still used by a few banks and is issued to depositors when they are withdrawing funds from their accounts. It is not good anywhere else. Sometimes a store has its own counter checks for the convenience of its customers. A counter check is not negotiable and is so marked.

A Traveler's Check is a check sold with a preprinted amount (usually in round figures) to travelers who do not want to carry large amounts of cash. The traveler signs the checks at the time of purchase and should counter-sign the check only in the presence of the person who cashes them.

In addition, a Money Order can be passed as a check. However, a money order is usually sent in the mail. Most stores should not accept money orders in face-to-face transactions.

Some small stores sell money orders. If yours does, never accept a personal check in payment for money orders. If the purchaser has a valid checking account, why does he or she need a money order? The check is possibly no good.

Look For Key Items

A check carries several key items such as name and location of bank, date, amount (in figures and spelled out), and signature. Close examination of such key items can sometimes tip you off to a worthless check. Before accepting a check, look for:

Nonlocal Banks. Use extra care in examining a check that is drawn on a nonlocal bank and require positive identification. List the customer's local and out-of-town address and phone number on the back of the check.

Date. Examine the date for accuracy of day, month, and year. Do not accept the check if it's not dated, if it's post-dated, or if it's more than 30 days old.

Location. Look first to be sure that the check shows the name, branch, town and State where the bank is located.

Amount. Be sure that the numerical amount agrees with the written amount.

Legibility. Do not accept a check that is not written legibly. It should be written and signed in ink and must not have any erasures or written-over amounts.

Payee. When you take a personal check on your selling floor, have the customer make it payable to your firm. Special care should be used in taking a two-party check.

Amount of Purchase. Personal checks should be for the exact amount of the purchase. The customer should receive no change.

Checks Over Your Limit. Set a limit on the amount—depending on the amount of your average sale—you will accept on a check. When a customer wants to go beyond that limit, your salesclerk should refer the customer to you.

Low Sequence Numbers. Be more cautious with low sequence numbers. Experience indicates that there seems to be a higher number of these checks that are returned. Most banks who issue personalized checks begin the numbering system with 101 and numbering sequence when a customer reorders new checks.

$$$ Amount of Check. Most bad-check passers pass checks in the $25.00 to $35.00 range on the assumption that the retailer will be more cautious when accepting a larger check.

Types of Merchandise Purchased—Be watchful of the types of merchandise purchased. Random sizes, selections, lack of concern about prices by customers should indicate to you that a little more caution should be exercised when a check is offered as payment.

Require Identification

Once you are satisfied that the check is okay, the question is, ''Is the person holding the check the right person?'' Requiring identification helps you to answer the question.

But keep in mind that no identification is foolproof. A crook is a crook no matter what type of identification you ask to see. If the person wants to forge identification, he or she can.

Some stores demand at least two pieces of identification. It is important to get enough identification so the person presenting the check can be identified and located if and when the check turns out to be worthless.

The following types of identification should be useful in determining the type to use in your store.

Current Automobile Operators License. If licenses in your State do not carry a photograph of the customer, you may want to ask for a second identification.

Automobile Registration Card. Be sure the name of the State agrees with the location of the bank.

If it doesn't, the customer should be able to explain why they don't agree. Also make sure that the signatures on the registration and check agree.

Shopping Plates. If they bear a signature or laminated photograph, shopping plates or other credit cards can be used as identification. The retail merchants'

organization in some communities issues lists of stolen shopping plates to which you should always refer when identifying the check passer.

Government Passes can also be used for identification in cashing checks. Picture passes should carry the name of the employing department and a serial number. Building passes should also carry a signature.

Identification Cards, such as those issued by the armed services, police departments, and companies, should carry a photo, a description, and a signature. Police cards should also carry a badge number.

Several types of cards and documents are not good identification. Some of them (for example, club cards) are easily forged, and others (for example, customer's duplicate saleschecks) were never intended for identification. Unless they are presented with a current automobile operator's license, do not accept the following:

Social Security Cards	Letters
Business Cards	Birth Certificates
Club or Organization Cards	Library Cards
Bank Books	Initialed Jewelry
Work Permits	Unsigned Credit Cards
Insurance Cards	Voter's Registration Cards
Learner's Permits	Customer's Duplicate Cards

Some large stores photograph each person who cashes a check along with the identification. This procedure is a deterrent because bad-check passers don't want to be photographed.

Some stores, when in doubt about a check, will verify an address and telephone number in the local telephone directory or with the information operator. Someone intending to pass a bad check will not necessarily be at the address shown on the check. If the address and telephone number cannot be verified, the check should be considered a potentially bad check.

Compare Signatures

Regardless of the type of identification you require, it is essential that you and your employees compare the signature on the check with the one on the identification.

You should also compare the person standing before you with the photograph and or description on the identification.

Set A Policy

You should set a policy for cashing checks, write it down, and instruct your employees in its use. Your policy might require your approval before a salesclerk can cash a check. When all checks are handled alike, customers have no cause to feel that they are being treated unfairly.

Your procedure might include the use of a rubber stamp. Many stores stamp the lower reverse side of a check and write in the appropriate information. Here is a sample of such a stamp.

Print			
Salesperson-Name and No.			
Auth. Signature			
Customer's Address			
Home Phone		Business Phone	
Ident. No. 1			
Ident. No. 2			
Dept. No.		Amount of Sale	
Take	Send	COD	Will Call

Your policy might also include verifying a check through the bank that issued the check. Some banks will do this only if you are a depositor in the bank. It might be helpful to establish business accounts in several banks, particularly where many of your customers have accounts.

You may want to verify a check through a check verification service. Should you contract with such a service or if you receive lists of bad-check passers, ask the service to show you proof from the Federal Trade Commission that their service is in compliance with the Fair Credit Reporting Act.

Employee apathy toward accepting checks is a big reason why stores get stuck with bad checks. The bigger the store, the more difficult it is to keep employees interested in catching bad checks. One effective way is to show employees your bad checks.

Refusing A Check

Review your policy and procedure on check cashing frequently with your employees. Remind them of what to look for to spot bad checks.

You are not obligated to take anyone's check. Even when a stranger presents satisfactory identification, you do not have to accept the check.

In most cases, you accept a check when the customer has met your identification requirements. You want to make the sale. But never accept a check if the person presenting it appears to be intoxicated.

Never take a check if the customer acts suspiciously. For example, the customer may try to rush you or your employees while you are checking identification.

Never take a check that is dated in advance.

Never discriminate when refusing a check. Don't tell a customer that you can't accept a check because he or she is a college student or lives in a bad neighborhood. If you do, you may be in violation of a State or Federal law on discrimination.

What Can You Recover?

Whether or not you recover any money lost on a bad check depends on the person who gave it to you. He or she may be one of your best customers who inadvertently gave you a check when the funds in his or her bank account were insufficient. On the other end of the scale, he or she may be a forger. Once you are stuck with a bad check, here are some of the situations you face.

Insufficient Funds. Most checks returned because of insufficient funds clear the second time you deposit them. Notify the customer that his or her account is overdrawn and that you are redepositing the check. But if the check is returned a second time, in some localities, it is the retailer's collection problem and you must try to get the maker to honor the check by paying immediately.

You should check the practices of your bank. In some areas, for example, after a second return for insufficient funds, the bank will not let you re-deposit the check. It is your collection problem. Some stores prosecute if the customer does not redeem such a check within a week of the second return. Stores with a reputation for being easy-going about insufficient funds checks usually get plenty of them.

The procedure for prosecution depends on the State. In one jurisdiction, for example, a merchant must send the check writer a certified or registered notice of an intention to prosecute. The bad-check writer then has five days from date of receipt of that notice to comply before the merchant can prosecute. In another jurisdiction, the maker has five days after the date of notice to make the check good. In a third, a resident has ten days to make good on the check.

No Account. Usually you've lost when the bank returns a check marked "no account." Such a check is evidence of a swindle or a fraud unless there has been an extraordinary error. In rare instances, a customer may issue a check on the wrong bank or on a discontinued account. You should quickly determine what the circumstances are. If the person is known in the community, proceed with your collection efforts. If you find yourself "stuck" with the check, call your police department.

Closed Account. A check marked "closed account" is a warning of extreme carelessness or fraud. Accounts are closed by both individuals and by banks. The latter may close an account because of too many overdrafts. An individual may open a new account by removing funds from an old account. In such case, the individual may forget that he or she has issued a check that is still outstanding against the old account.

If you don't get your money back within a reasonable time, you should consider prosecuting the check writer.

Forgery. Forged checks are worthless—a total loss to you.

Watch out for smudged checks, misspelled words, poor spacing of letters or numbers indicating that changes may have been made. Payroll checks with the company's name and address typed in could be fraudulent. Most payroll checks are printed.

When you suspect forgery, call the police. Thus, you can help yourself and others against further forgery. Refer a U.S. Government check to the field office of the U.S. Secret Service.

Check with your lawyer about court collection practices in your area. In the Washington, D.C. area, for example, merchants cannot collect through the courts on bad checks used to pay an open account. The reason is: The merchant still has the account and no injury was suffered through the issuance of the check. The account may be collectable through the usual civil procedures used for collection purposes.

Any alteration, illegal signature(s) of the maker of the check, a forgery of the endorsement, an erasure or an obliteration on a genuine check is a crime.

A bad check issued to pay for merchandise is not a theft but a misdemeanor. It is an exchange—the checks for goods. A misdemeanor carries a lighter penalty than a theft since a check may be collectable through civil procedures. Criminal action may be taken through signing a formal charge with the police.

A forged check transported in interstate commerce is a Federal offense.

Get Evidence. You cannot prosecute bad-check passers without good evidence. The person who cashed the bad check should be positively identified and connected with the receiving of money for it.

Burglary and Robbery

Small stores are prime targets for burglars and robbers. Seeking dark and easy-to-enter stores, burglars usually operate at night. Attracted by careless displays of cash, robbers often strike at opening or closing time or when customer traffic is light.

Because you may be the next victim of a robbery or a burglary in your area, you should be aware of the precautionary measures that are available to lessen the impact of these two crimes.

Burglary

Burglary is any unlawful entry to commit a felony or a theft, even though no force was used to gain entrance.

Retailers whose stores have been broken into know that burglaries are costly. What these business owners may not be aware of is that the number of burglaries has doubled in the past several years and, therefore, they may be two-, three-, or four-time losers if the trend is not reversed.

Moreover, few burglars are caught. Almost 80 percent of all burglaries go unsolved. Police prevention and detection are difficult because of lack of witnesses or evidence to identify the criminal.

Prevention must start with the small merchant—you. You can use a combination of measures to protect your store from burglars. Among the things you can use are: (1) suitable locks, (2) an appropriate alarm system, (3) adequate indoor and outside lighting, and (4) a secure store safe.

In addition, the owners of high-risk stores—ones in areas with a reputation for rampant crime—should also consider using: (1) heavy window screens, (2) burglar-resistant glass windows, (3) private police patrols, and (4) watchdogs.

Locks. Be sure to use the right kind of lock on your doors. In addition to being an obstacle to unwanted entry, a strong lock requires a burglar to use force to get into the store. Under standard burglary insurance policies, evidence of a forced entry is necessary to collect on burglary insurance.

Most experts on locks agree that the **pin-tumbler cylinder lock** provides the best security. It may have from 3 to 7 pins. Locksmiths caution, however, that a burglar can easily pick a lock with less than 5 pins.

(There are a few non-pin tumbler locks that give high security, but you should check with a locksmith before you use one.)

Dead bolt locks should be used. They cannot be opened by sliding a piece of flexible material between the door edge and door jamb. (Dead bolt is a lock bolt that is moved positively by turning the knob or key without action of a spring.)

When you use a double cylinder dead lock, the door cannot be opened without a key on either side. This fact means that on a glass door there is no handle for a burglar to reach by merely breaking the glass. Such a lock also provides protection against "break-outs"—a thief being concealed before closing time and breaking out with stolen goods.

Safeguarding entrance ways, especially the rear door, cannot be over emphasized. Bar the rear door, in addition to locking it, because many burglars favor back doors.

Installing Locks. The best lock is ineffective if it is not properly installed. For example, if a lock with a ⅝″ long latch bolt is installed in a door that is separated from the door-jamb by ½″, the effective length of the bolt is cut to only ⅛″. Have a locksmith check the locks on your exterior doors to be sure that your locks give you the right protection.

Key Control. To keep keys from falling into the hands of burglars, issue as few keys as possible. Keep a record on the keys you issue. Exercise the same care with keys as you would a thousand dollar bill. Do the following:

1. Avoid the danger of key duplication. Caution employees not to leave store keys with parking lot

attendants, or in a topcoat hanging in a restaurant, or lying about the office or stockroom.

2. Keep your records on key distribution up-to-date so that you know what keys have been issued to whom.

3. Whenever a key is lost or an employee leaves the firm, without turning in his or her key, re-key your store.

4. Take special care to protect the "master key" used to remove cylinders from locks.

5. Have one key and lock for outside doors and a different key and lock for your office. Don't master-key because it weakens your security.

6. Have a code for each key so that it does not have to be visibly tagged and only an authorized person can know the specific lock that key fits. Don't use a key chain with a tag carrying the store's address.

7. Take a periodic inventory of keys. Have employees show you each key so you will know it has not been lost, mislaid, or lent.

Burglar Alarms. The silent central-station burglary alarm system gives your store the best protection. The reason: It does not notify the burglar as does the local alarm—such as a siren or bell—outside the store. A silent alarm alerts only the specialists who know how to handle burglaries.

In large cities, central alarm systems are available on a rental basis from private firms in this business; in small cities, they are often tied directly into police headquarters. Part of the cost for installing a silent alarm system will sometimes be defrayed by a reduction in your burglary insurance premium.

Although a building-type local alarm is cheaper and easier to install, it too often only warns the thief and is not considered by specialists to be as effective as a central station alarm. Of course, if no central alarm service system is available, or such an alarm is not economically feasible, then by all means install a building alarm.

Whether your alarm is central or local, you have a wide choice of alarm sensing devices. Among them are radar motion detectors, invisible photo beams, detectors that work on ultrasonic sound, and vibration detectors. Also there is supplemental equipment, such as an automatic phone dialer. This phones the police and the store owner, and gives them verbal warning when an alarm is breached.

Each type of alarm has advantages in certain situations. For example, proximity alarms are often used on safe cabinets. You should seek professional guidance to get the best alarm for your needs.

Flood Your Store With Lights. Outdoor lighting is another way to shield the store from burglary. Almost all store break-ins occur at night. Darkness conceals the burglar and gives him or her time to work.

By floodlighting the outside of your store on all sides you can defeat many burglars. All sides include alley entrances and side passageways between buildings where entry might be made.

Mercury and metallic vapor lamps are good for illuminating the exterior walls of a store. They are designed to withstand vandalism and weather—wind velocities up to 100 miles per hour. Some have a heat-tempered lens that cannot be broken with less than a 22 calibre rifle.

Indoor lighting is also important. When a store is lighted inside, police officers can see persons in the store or notice the disorder which burglars usually cause. When the store is left dark, a burglar can see the police approaching, but they can't see the burglar.

Police get to know the lighted stores and will check the premises when, and if, the light is off.

It is also important to arrange window display so police patrols can see into the store.

Your Safe. Be sure the safe in which you keep your money and other valuables is strong enough to deter burglars. Police remind merchants that a file cabinet with a combination lock is not a money safe. Store money should be protected in a **Burglar-resistant Money Chest**—as such safes are properly called.

Insurance companies recognize the E Safe as adequate for most merchant risks (except, in a few cities, where torch and explosive attacks on safes are common). Insurance companies give a sizeable reduction in premiums for use of the E Safe. Over the years, the saving can pay the added cost of an E Safe.

Locating Your Safe. Putting a safe in the back of the store or where it is not visible from the street, invites burglary. Police recommend that the safe be visible to the outside street. Also the safe area should be well-lighted all night.

But visibility and lighting will be wasted effort if your safe can be carted off by a burglar. Weight is no guarantee that the safe can't be stolen. Safes weighing 2,000 pounds have been taken out of stores.

No matter what the safe weights, bolt it to the building structure.

Leave the "Cupboard Bare." Even when you use an "E" rated burglar-resistant money box, it is a good idea to keep on hand the barest minimum of cash. Bank all excess cash each day.

Leave your cash register drawer empty and open at night. A burglar will break into a closed one, and the damage to your register can be costly.

In addition to leaving the "cupboard" as bare as possible, use a silent central station alarm on your safe cabinet. When closing your safe at night, be sure to do the following:

1. Check to see that everything has been put into the safe.

2. Make a note of the serial numbers on large bills taken in after your daily deposit.

3. Check to be sure that your safe is locked.

4. Activate the burglar alarm.

Make it a practice never to leave the combination of your safe on store premises. Change the combination when an employee who knows it leaves your firm.

High-risk Locations. Some stores are in high-risk locations. These areas have a reputation for crime. Night after night, people break display windows and help themselves or force their way into stores.

Because many windows are smashed on impulse, you should minimize the chance of loss. If possible, remove attractive and expensive merchandise from the window at night. Many jewelry stores protect items left in the display window by secondary glass—a piece of heavy glass hanging on chains from the window's ceiling. Being non-fixed, the secondary glass is difficult to break even if the burglar smashes the display window.

If your store is in a high-risk location, you need to consider using heavy window screens, burglar-resistant glass, watch dogs, or private police patrols.

Heavy Window Screens. Heavy metal window screens or grating are an inexpensive way for protecting show windows. You store them during business hours, at closing time, you put the screens up and lock them in place.

Burglar-resistant Glass. When used in exterior doors, windows, display windows, and in interior showcases, this type of glass deters burglars. It has a high tensile strength that allows it to take considerable beating. It is useful in areas with vandalism problems.

Burglar-resistant glass is a laminated sandwich with a sheet of invisible plastic compressed between two sheets of glass. It mounts like ordinary plate glass and comes in clear, tinted, and opaque.

Of course, this type of glass can be broken with continual hammering—as with a baseball bat or sledge hammer. But it will not shatter. The burglar who is patient enough to bang a hole in the glass will find it bordered by a barrier of jagged glass icicles.

Even in prestige locations, burglar-resistant glass offers protection. It can be used in stores selling high value merchandise, such as cameras, furs, and jewelry.

Watchdogs. In larger cities, agencies offer watch dog service on a nominal hourly basis. An owner-manager can use these dogs on a spot check basis one or two nights a week to deter burglars. Word soon gets around that a store is using watchdogs, and burglars cross the store off their list. The sight and sound of an angry watchdog makes them afraid.

Private Police Patrols. A private police patrol can be used to supplement the public police force when it is undermanned and overworked. A private patrol can discourage burglars by checking the store during the night. Sometimes private police may catch a burglar in the act; other times they can discover the break-in shortly after it occurs. In either case, their prompt notice to the police increases the likelihood of catching the culprit and recovering your merchandise and money.

A private patrol is also qualified to testify on the store conditions prior to a crime. This sort of testimony expedites the payment of insurance claims. In disaster, such as a flood or riot, private police can initiate emergency measures.

Private patrol can also help you train your employees, reveal unlocked doors, open windows, and other signs of employee carelessness which they can help correct.

Robbery

Robbery is stealing or taking anything of value by force, or violence, or by use of fear.

Retailers who have been robbed several times are not surprised to learn that police call robbery the fastest growing crime in the Nation. Moreover, the greatest increase is in retail stores. Holdups there have increased 75 percent in the past several years.

Only about one third of the robberies in the United States are solved by identification and arrest. Even when robbers are caught almost none of the cash or property is recovered.

Robbery is a violent crime. The robber always uses force or the threat of force, and the victims are often hurt. In 65 percent of store holdups, the robber uses a weapon.

What can you do to reduce losses from robbery in your store?

Your first line of defense is training your people. How you handle your cash is also important. Two other vital defense actions are: (1) you should use care in opening and closing your store and (2) you should use care when answering after-hours emergency calls.

Training to Reduce Risk. You should let each of your employees know what may happen if a robbery occurs. Train them on how to act during a holdup.

Emphasize the protection of lives as well as money. Warn each person that you want no "heroes." The heroic action by an employee or customer may end as a deadly mistake. The robber is as volatile as a bottle of nitro-glycerine. Handle him or her with the same care your would use with any explosive.

Instruct your people to the following when, and if, they face a robber:

(1) Reassure the robber that they will cooperate in every way.

(2) Stay as calm as possible.

(3) Spend their time making mental notes on the criminal's build, haircolor, complexion, voice, what he or she is wearing, and anything that would make it possible to indentify him or her. A calm accurate description of the robber can help bring him or her to justice. (Police advise that employees should not discuss or compare descriptions with each other but wait until the police arrive.)

You can provide a reference point to make descriptions accurate. Mark the wall or the edge of the door jamb in such a way that later the employee will be able to give a more accurate estimate of the robber's height. Often the person who has been held up compares the criminal's height with that of another person in the store. The clerk ends up unconsciously describing this innocent person used for comparison, rather than the robber.

Instruct your employees not to disclose the amount of loss. The police and news reporters should receive such information only from you. When talking to reporters, play down the theft. Don't picture your store as being an easy mark with a great deal of cash on hand.

Don't Build Up Cash. Cash on hand is the lure that attracts a robber. The best deterrent is to keep as little cash in the store as possible. Another deterrent is camera equipment that photographs robbers.

Make bank deposits daily. During selling hours, check the amount of cash in your register or registers. Remove all excess cash from each register several times a day.

Do not set up cashier operations so that they are visible to outsiders. The sight of money can trigger crime. Balance your register an hour or two before closing—not at closing time. Make it a rule to keep your safe locked even during business hours.

When making bank deposits, use an armored car service, if practical. If not, you should take a different route to the bank each day and vary the time of the deposit. Obviously, the best time to make deposits is during daylight hours.

You should also vary the routes you travel between the store and your home. Keep your store keys on a separate key ring. At least then, you won't be stranded by the loss of your car and personal keys.

Opening and Closing Routine. Opening or closing the store is a two-man job. When opening your store, station one person—an employee or your assistant—outside where he or she can observe your actions. You enter the store, check the burglar alarm to be sure it is still properly set, then move around in the store and look for any signs of unwanted callers.

You and your assistant should have an agreement on the length of time this pre-opening check is to take. Then if you do not reappear at the scheduled time, your assistant should phone the police.

The outside person should always know where the nearest phone is located. He or she should have a card in his or her wallet with the police phone number typed on it and coins taped to the back side of the card so that he or she has the right change to make the call.

When calling the police, calmly:

1. Give his or her name.

2. Give the name and address of the store.

3. Report that a holdup is in progress at the store.

Under normal conditions, the owner-manager would return to the entrance after finishing the store inspection and give the outside person a predetermined "all clear" signal.

Your night closing should be a similar routine. A few minutes before closing, you make a routine check of stockrooms, furnace room, storeroom, and other places where a thief might hide. A second employee should wait just outside the store until you have finished your inspection. If you drive to work, he or she should bring your car to a location near the exit door. He or she should watch while you set the burglar alarm and lock the doors and windows.

Be Cautious of Night Calls. Whenever you receive an emergency call to return to the store at night, be careful.

First, never return to the store without first notifying someone that you are returning.

Second, if it is a burglar-alarm break, phone the police department and ask that a police car meet you at the store.

Third, if it is a repair problem, phone the repair company and have the service truck sent out before you leave home.

Fourth, if you arrive at the store and do not see the police car, or the repair truck, do not park near the store. And do not enter the store.

Fifth, make it a habit to verify *all* phone calls you receive after store hours, no matter where they originate. A careless slip on your part may be all the criminal is waiting for.

Following these precautions can mean the difference between life and death.

Bibliography

Information presented here is necessarily selective and no slight is intended toward material not mentioned. Publishers are invited to notify the SBA of relevant publications and other sources of information for possible inclusion in future editions. Prices of publications and their availability are subject to change. Management Aids may be reprinted but not used to indicate approval or disapproval by the SBA of any private organization, product or service.

Books

Crime Prevention Manual for Business Owners and Managers, Margaret Kenda. AMACOM, 1982.

Protecting Your Business, Egan W. Loffel. David McKay Company, Inc., 1977.

Security and the Small Business Retailer, National Institute of Law Enforcement and Criminal Justice, Law Enforcement Assistance Administration. U.S. Dept of Justice, 1979.

The Small Business Security Handbook, James E. Keogh. Prentice-Hall, Inc., 1981.

Periodicals

Security. Cahners Publishing Company, P.O. Box 5080, Cahners Plaza, 1350 E. Touhy Ave., Des Plaines, IL 60018. $50.00 per year.

Security Management. American Society for Industrial Security, 1655 N. Ft. Meyer Dr., Arlington, VA 22209. $27.00 per year.

Security Systems Administration. PTN Publishing Corporation, 101 Crossways Park West, Woodbury, NY 11797.

Staff members of the Small Business Administration edited this publication, which was written by staff members of The Travelers' Small Business Program.

INTRODUCTION

The subjects discussed in this guide should heighten your awareness of business insurance and encourage you to consider carefully the various insurance programs and options available on the market.

It is imperative that all small business owners and managers understand the various aspects of insurance and how it can help a firm be more successful.

Your Independent Agent is your key to protecting your business and ultimately, contributing to your success. Multiline agencies can provide a comprehensive range of employee benefits, property/casualty and financial services to small businesses.

In addition to helping you identify, minimize and in some instances eliminate business risks, this Aid includes a Checklist to help you strengthen your insurance program and provide guidelines for discussions you should have with a qualified insurance professional. A Glossary of Insurance Terms is also included to provide simple definitions for the highly technical terms you will encounter when selecting insurance for your business.

RISK AND THE SMALL BUSINESS

Is your business a risky business? You bet! Every small business is. Just think for a minute about the hundreds of things that most business owners worry about. A few are predictable or, at the very least, are items that you can plan for and perhaps even control to a certain extent, such as:

- expected sales volume
- salary costs
- taxes
- overhead expenses

- equipment and supply costs
- the price you charge for the goods or services you offer to your customers

Others are unpredictable, largely beyond your control. Examples of these unpredictable risks include:

- actions your competitors may take
- changing tastes and trends
- the effect they have on your market and your customers
- the local economy and its impact on your customer base (plant closings or unemployment, for example).

And then there are the events that can and do happen to small businesses all the time. They could directly affect your day-to-day operations, impact profits, and result in unexpected financial losses that may be serious enough to cripple your business or even bankrupt it. You've probably already considered the most obvious risks and have bought insurance to protect against the financial losses that could result from them. Most business owners recognize the loss potential from fire and injury.

- Fire could damage or destroy the building your firm occupies and turn the building's contents into a pile of smoking rubbish. Whether you rent or own, your place of business and your ability to continue to do business may both be seriously affected.

- If someone is injured on business premises, or injured by a product you manufacture or market, or because of the way your firm performed a service, your firm may be held responsible for that person's medical bills, lost wages or even loss of future income.

Loss of property from fire and liability for injury to another person (or another person's property) are familiar exposures. But there are hundreds of other losses and liabilities that every small business faces, many of which are often overlooked or ignored.

Large corporations often employ a full-time "risk manager" to identify and analyze possible exposures to loss or liability. The risk manager then takes steps to protect the firm against accidental and preventable loss and to minimize the financial consequences of losses that cannot be prevented or avoided. But most small businesses can't afford the services of a risk manager, even part-time, so the business owner often has to take on that responsibility.

WHAT IS "RISK MANAGEMENT"?

Regardless of who does it, risk management consists of:

1. Identifying and analyzing the things that may cause loss.

2. Choosing the best way of dealing with each of these potentials for loss.

You've worked hard to build your business, and you've poured a lot of time, effort and money into identifying loss exposures.

IDENTIFYING AND ANALYZING EXPOSURES TO LOSS

Identifying exposures is a vital first step: until you know the scope of all possible losses, you won't be able to develop a realistic, cost-effective strategy for dealing with them. The last thing you want to do is come up with a superficial Band-Aid approach that may cause more problems than it solves.

It is not easy to recognize the hundreds of hazards, or perils that can lead to an unexpected loss. Unless you've experienced a fire, for example, you may not realize how extensive fire loss can be. Damage to the building and its contents are obvious exposures, but you should also consider:

- the damage or destruction that smoke or water from dozens of fire hoses can create.

- damage to employees' property (coats, tools and personal belongings) and to property belonging to others (data-processing equipment you lease or customers' property left with you for inspection or repair, for example).

- the amount of business you'll lose during the weeks (or months) it takes to get back to normal again.

- the loss to competitors of customers who may not return when you reopen for business.

You begin the process of identifying exposures by taking a close look at each of your business operations and asking yourself:

1. "What could cause a loss"? If there are dozens of exposures you may find dozens of answers.

For each exposure you identify, ask yourself:

2. "How serious is that loss"? (This question helps you focus on the possible severity of each exposure. What kind of price tag, in dollars and cents, applies to that exposure?) The purpose here is not to determine where the money will come from, but how costly the loss could be.

Many business owners use a "risk analysis" questionnaire or survey as a checklist. These are available from insurance agents, most of whom will provide the expertise to help you with your analysis. With their expertise and experience, you're less likely to overlook any exposures. They'll also be available to answer your questions when you try to determine how serious a loss from a given exposure may be.

WHAT KINDS OF EXPOSURES SHOULD I LOOK FOR?

In general, most questionnaires and surveys address the potential for:

- property losses
- business interruption losses
- liability losses
- key person losses
- automobile losses

PROPERTY LOSSES

Property losses stem from one of the following:

- physical damage to property
- loss of use of property
- criminal activity

Physical Damage

Property damage can be caused by many common perils: fire, windstorm, lightning and vandalism may be the first that come to mind. And it's a rare business that doesn't buy insurance to protect against these. But to cope effectively with the possibility of physical damage to property, the business owner should consider more than just damage to or destruction of the building itself.

Contents may be even more susceptible: manufacturers might lose both raw materials and finished goods that were ready to be shipped. Merchants may lose valuable inventories and fixtures. Any business might lose valuable accounting records (making it difficult to bill customers or collect from customers who owe money). Vital machinery or equipment may become inoperable because of fire and, if replacements can't be found and installed immediately, the business may even be forced into a temporary shutdown. (A detailed discussion of business interruption is provided later in this booklet.)

Loss of Use

Your business could lose the use of property without suffering any physical damage. A government agency can close a manufacturer for violating health and safety regulations. The local health department may close a restaurant because of unsanitary conditions. A gas-main break or downed utility lines may shut down an entire block for one or more days.

Criminal Activity

Small businesses may also be susceptible to crimes committed by others. Burglary and robbery are obvious perils, but don't overlook possible exposure to white-color crime, employee theft, embezzlement or forgery. Merchants, in particular, may need protection against losses caused by acceptance of forged checks or unauthorized use of credit cards.

Obviously, the property exposures a bank faces are different from those that a painting contractor, a delicatessen or a bookstore faces. An experienced insurance agent is familiar with exposures to property loss in many different kinds of business. Just as you rely on an accountant to guide you through the maze of tax regulations and record-keeping requirements, you can rely on an experienced insurance professional to help you identify the exposures to loss that your business may face.

The four kinds of exposure we've examined are only part of the story of risk and business. Another major exposure is business interruption.

BUSINESS INTERRUPTION LOSSES

You have already seen how a direct loss from fire can shut down a business temporarily. Although property insurance provides money for repairing or rebuilding physical damage that is a direct result of a fire, most property policies do not cover indirect losses, such as the income that is lost while the business is interrupted for the repairs.

A special kind of insurance *will* cover indirect losses that occur when a direct loss (that results from a covered peril, such as fire) forces a temporary interruption of business. For example:

- Tornado damage to a toy store in October was repaired by late November and stocks replenished. But by then, it was too late in the Christmas selling season for the store to approach normal sales. Instead of earning the usual 55 percent of its annual volume in December, it earned only 15 percent. A 40 percent loss!

- If a prep school that burns down in August can't reopen until November, the school may lose half, or even all, of a school year's tuition.

Business interruption insurance would reimburse policyholders for the difference between normal income and the income that is earned during the enforced shutdown period.

Not only is income reduced or cut off completely during such interruptions, but also many business expenses continue such as taxes, loan payments, salaries to key employees, interest, depreciation and utilities. Without income to pay for these expenses, the business is forced to dip into reserves.

Interruption often triggers **extra expenses**. For example, a business may authorize overtime to shorten the interruption period, or it may reopen with a skeleton staff (additional payroll) in temporary quarters (additional rent) using leased furniture and equipment (additional overhead). These extra expenses put an additional strain on finances at a time when little if any income is being produced.

A firm can even buy business interruption insurance to protect against interruptions triggered by direct loss on someone else's property.

- If a **key supplier** is shut down by a fire and can't deliver critical raw materials to a manufacturer, the manufacturer's business may be interrupted just as effectively as if the supplier's factory has burned to the ground.

- Property damage at the **key customer's** business may have the same effect. If you depend upon the customer for most of your volume, and that firm's interruption causes them to suspend purchasing, you may be left holding the bag. Their interruption has caused you to lose income.

Every year hundreds of businesses that carry adequate insurance against direct loss of property fail because they overlook the possibility of indirect loss. Don't forget to protect your business against loss of income and unusual expenses that may result if direct loss forces you to close temporarily.

LIABILITY LOSS

Every business also faces exposures to liability loss. A business may become legally liable (i.e., responsible for payment) for bodily injury suffered by another person or persons, or for damage to or destruction of the property of others. This liability may be the result of:

- A court decision (as in a lawsuit charging negligence)

- Statutory provisions (such as a state's workers' compensation law)

- Violation of contract provisions (a contract that makes one party responsible for certain kinds of losses)

PUBLIC LIABILITY

A business may be held liable for injuries or other losses suffered by a member of the general public as the result of the firm's (or its employees') negligence or fault.

- A customer in the firm's building trips on a broken step.

- A defect in a product causes injury to its user.

- A workman who installs a ceiling fan a customer has purchased fails to secure it properly. The fan falls, injuring the customer.

- A secretarial firm rents one floor in an office building and signs a lease that holds the tenant (rather than the building owner) responsible for any third party claims for injury or property damage occurring in or on the rented space.

Your daily paper will provide dozens of other examples. A firm that is found legally liable for harming a third party will have to pay damages to compensate the injured party. Sometimes the court also imposes punitive damages. In cases involving violation of a statute that protects the community as a whole, the court may also award a fine in hopes of discouraging future violations.

Regardless of who wins or looses such a suit, litigation is time-consuming and expensive. No matter how ridiculous or unfounded the suit may be, productive business hours are still lost, lawyers still have to be retained and paid and other related cost have to be met.

Liability to Employees

Every state has enacted some sort of legislation that protects the interest of employees who are injured or who contract a disease as a result of job-related activities.

Workers' compensation laws require most employers to compensate employees for loss of income or medical expenses that are a result of work-related disease or injury (except for certain self-inflicted injuries). Should an employee die, as a result of a job-related accident or disease, the employee's family also collects a specified amount.

Although workers' compensation in some states does not apply to all kinds of businesses or to all small businesses, a suit may trigger court action that requires a normally exempt firm to compensate employees for losses that result from work-related injury or disease.

So far, the exposures we have looked at have all been more or less external to the business. There are, however, several major exposures that have to do with the business itself.

KEY PERSONS LOSSES

What would happen to your business if an accident or illness made it impossible for you to work? What if one of your partners or your sales manager were to die suddenly? Most of us would rather not think about such a "what if." Nevertheless, it is important for you to prepare your business for survival, long before a key person dies or is disabled. Unfortunately, it is a step that is often overlooked.

The following questions address a few problems that may occur.

How will the business survive if the owner becomes seriously ill or disabled?

- What will the owner's source of income be? How will it be treated for tax purposes?

- Who would "take over" so that the business can continue?

- What if that person is not qualified or is a minor?

Suppose the owner dies?

- If a will is *not* in place before the owner's death, what happens to the business? Does it close? Does someone inherit? Who?

- If the owner's life savings have been invested in the business, will the surviving family have to watch those savings go down the drain because no one knows what to do or how to do it?

- What will the surviving family's source of income be while the future of the business is being decided?

- If the business is to be sold, where will working capital come from for the transition period?

- How is the fair market value of the business to be determined?

- Would the fair market value be apt to change because of the loss of a key person?

- If the business forms the bulk of the estate, what are the income and inheritance tax implications for the surviving spouse and heirs?

- Is there some pre-death strategy that could minimize that tax liability?

The answers to these questions can best be determined with the help of the professionals on your business's planning team: your attorney, accountant and insurance agent. Their expertise in estate planning, financial planning, current legal and tax codes will help you develop a plan for your business's survival and a way of implementing it.

Suppose the business is a partnership and one of the partners dies?

- Unless the partners have prepared some other binding arrangement, that is already in place, their partnership is dissolved when one of them dies.

- The duties of the surviving partner(s) are limited to winding up the affairs of the partnership.

- The surviving partner(s) will be personally liable for losses that the business's assets are insufficient to cover.

The partners may have to set up agreements that provide for the surviving partner's purchase of a deceased partner's interest at a prearranged valuation. Business life insurance of each partner could provide the fund the survivors need to purchase the deceased partner's interest.

- Who should pay the premium? The business? Each partner?

- What are the pros and cons of these alternatives?

- What are the tax implications of each?

- How would each affect the firm's cash flow?

There are many plans and many ways to set them up. Your planning team can suggest a wide range of options compatible with your needs, your firm's cash position and local and federal tax implications.

What if the business is incorporated?

In most small incorporated businesses there are only a few stockholders, and most of them take an active part in running the business.

- Death of a major stockholder often throws a spotlight on the survivors' differences. Conflict or major personality clashes can seriously threaten the survival of the firm. Dissension also damages employee morale, can lead to a loss of business and may even harm the firm's credit rating.

- Unless otherwise provided for, the deceased major stockholder's shares will become part of his or her estate. While the estate is being settled, the estate administrator can vote (i.e., exercise the right to control) the stock. If a controlling interest in the firm is involved, he or she could name a new board of directors and take over full control of the corporation.

- What if the heirs decide to get involved in the business? If they decide to retain the stock, will it provide enough income for them to live on?

- If the heirs decide to sell, would they be required to offer the other major stockholders first refusal? Could some plan be set up that would allow the surviving stockholders to finance a buy-out of the heirs' holdings?

- Without such a plan, would the remaining stockholders' search for buy-out funds have any impact upon the firm's credit?

Once again, planning is essential. Your attorney, accountant and insurance agent can develop a legally binding strategy to prevent outsiders from unexpectedly coming into the business and to ensure an orderly "changing of the guard" should a major stockholder die.

The Key Person Exposure

Do not overlook what would happen if you were to suddenly lose the services of a key person (who is not an owner, partner or major stockholder) because of illness, disability or death (e.g., a sales manager or the office manager/bookkeeper).

- What impact would that person's absence have on sales volume? Costs? Productivity? Efficiency? The firm's credit?

- How would you reassign duties to cover the missing person's functions?

- What extra costs would you have to incur to recruit a replacement?

- How long would it take before the replacement is trained and productive?

The way you answer these questions depends on many factors, such as the kind of employee benefits already in place.

SMALL GROUP BENEFITS

We've already touched briefly on some legally required employee benefits:

- Social Security
- Workers' compensation
- Unemployment insurance
- Temporary disability benefits

Let's look at some others. Few small businesses offer all of these benefits, but most firms recognize that employees expect basic benefits. As an employer, you are one of several businesses competing for the most qualified individuals in the local labor pool. Unless you offer minimal benefits, at the very least, attracting and keeping qualified employees may be very difficult.

The firm that provides a good employee benefits program is usually known as a good place to work (which may enhance the company's reputation in the community). A good benefits program often affects employee morale which, in turn, affects employee productivity. In most instances, the firm's contributions to an employee benefits plan qualify as a business tax deduction.

You may want to consider one or more of the following to help you attract and retain the very best people you can:

- Pensions

- Group health protection either as a traditional group plan or in the health maintenance organization format. Health benefits may include life, medical, dental, vision care, prescription drugs and major medical expenses.

- Other group benefits (life, travel, accidental death and dismemberment, personal auto and homeowners).

Other plans offer medical self-care and health-promotion programs to help employees make informed decisions regarding healthy lifestyles. These can significantly reduce the cost to you, the employer. Increased awareness of general health care and preventative medicine can foster greater productivity, reduce absenteeism and increase morale.

As you can see from what you have read about identifying and analyzing risks and the kinds of exposures a business may face, many possibilities have to be considered. Once exposures have been identified and analyzed for severity, and employee benefits have been reviewed, the next step is to decide upon the risk management measures that will best protect your business.

LOSS EXPOSURES AND RISK MANAGEMENT

The next two steps of the risk management process are similar to those we face in managing our personal finances.

1. Loss control: What can be done to prevent or limit exposure to loss?

2. What techniques can be used to assure that funds will be available for losses that cannot be avoided or prevented?

Loss Control

Preventing or Limiting Exposure to Loss

One principle of loss prevention and control is the same in business as it is in your personal life: avoid activities that are too hazardous. For example:

A merchant may decide not to sell a particular product because it is likely to injure customers; thereby, the firm avoids a product-liability exposure. For example:

If you can't avoid an exposure completely, minimize it.

An apartment owner may decide against constructing a new building on a rural hillside site that has a long history of brush fires. Instead, he builds on suburban, level land, which is supplied by town water and is two minutes from a fire station. While exposure of loss from fire can seldom be elminated completely, this owner has reduced the possible severity of loss by choosing a safer site closer to the fire-fighting services.

Look again to see if the extent of possible loss can be further reduced.

That same apartment owner, for example, may decide to build using fire-resistant construction and materials, thereby reducing the chance of fire spreading. He may also decide to install smoke detectors, fire alarms and automatic extinguishing systems throughout the building to further reduce the severity and spread of fire.

Risk Retention

A business owner may decide that the firm can afford to absorb some losses, either because the frequency and probability of loss are low or because the dollar value of loss is manageable.

— A firm owns several business vehicles. The drivers have an excellent safety record, and exposure to collision is low because these vans cover uncongested rural routes. Because these are older vehicles, their book value has decreased substantially.

— Rather than continue to pay for collision insurance on the vans, the firm decides to drop the collision coverage completely. If an accident damages one or more of the vans, the firm will pay for collision damage with company funds. In effect, the firm has decided to retain the risk itself rather than transfer the risk to an insurance company by paying for collision insurance.

— Or the firm could decide to retain part of the risk and insure the rest.

Transferring Risk

Another method of managing exposure to loss is by transferring the risk. Although most businesses do this by buying insurance (which transfers some or all of the risk to the insurance company), there are other noninsurance options.

— The firm may decide to eliminate the collision exposure completely by selling the firm's vans and hiring a local delivery service. This solution eliminates not only the collision exposure, but also the exposures associated with owning and maintaining the vans. In effect, the firm has transferred all of the expenses to the local delivery service.

— To reduce exposure to property damage, a retailer may decide to cut in-store inventories and to handle certain items only on a special-order basis. The owner will place small reorders with suppliers more frequently. The result? Lower inventory values in the store, therefore a lower exposure. The retailer is actually transferring much of the exposure of property loss to the suppliers.

Insurance as a Risk Strategy

The most common method of transferring risk is insurance. By insuring your home and your car, you have transferred much of the risk of loss to the company that issued the policy. You pay a relatively small amount in premium rather than run the risk of not protecting yourself against the possibility of a much larger financial loss.

In business insurance, as in personal insurance, only you can decide which exposures you absolutely must insure against. Some decisions, however, are already made for you:

• those required by law (such as workers' compensation)

• those that others require. For example, you cannot register or operate a business vehicle in most locations unless you can prove that it is insured. Similarly, few lenders will finance property acquisition or construction unless it is adequately insured, and unless they are named on the policy as having an insurable interest.

Today, very few businesses or individuals have sufficient cash or financial reserves to protect themselves against the hundreds of property and liability exposures that most businesses face.

What those exposures are, what their dollar value is and how much protection is enough, are thorny questions. When you add the need for an employee benefits program, the need to protect the business when its ownership or management changes, the picture becomes increasingly complex. That is why the experience and professional knowledge of an insurance agent are so important in helping you cover all the bases.

The Role of the Insurance Professional

The agent is the insurance industry's primary client representative. Typically, the independent agent is a small-business owner and manager. By using this distribution system, insurance companies are represented by agents who receive a com-

mission for selling the companies' products and services. An agent may represent more than one insurance company.

The professional independent insurance agent has been trained in risk analysis. He or she is familiar with the insurance coverages and financial strategies available in your state, and with the regulations that govern them. With this expertise, the agent can point out exposures you may otherwise overlook.

Finally, your insurance professional can help you develop possible solutions. You make the final decisions, but your agent can suggest options from a vast menu of risk-management strategies. He or she has the technical knowledge to amend a basic policy by adding special coverages and endorsements. The resulting policy will be custom-tailored to your business's unique protection needs.

Your agent can also recommend noninsurance strategies to meet your needs. Where appropriate, he or she will suggest that your accountant and attorney be brought into the decision-making process to review the legal and tax implications of suggested strategies.

Other Services Insurers Provide

You may not be aware of some of the other services that insurance companies provide to policyholders.

• *Legal defense.* Liability insurance coverages (particularly for property damage and bodily injury) usually include legal defense at no additional charge when the policyholder is named a party to a lawsuit that involves a claim covered, by the policy. Litigation is costly, whether the claimant's suit is valid or ridiculous. The legal defense provision greatly reduces those costs.

• *Rehabilitation.* Insurance companies that write a lot of workers' compensation insurance may have extensive rehabilitation services available. Generally, these services help return injured workers to useful employment and, in some cases, may even help train the worker for a different job.

• *Inspection services.* Many cities require businesses to conduct regular inspections of the steam boilers in commercial buildings. Boiler and machinery insurance policies not only protect against certain kinds of damage to energy equipment but also provide for inspection by the insurance company's specialists. The insurance company issues a certificate of inspection to the policyholder as proof that the inspection requirement has been met.

- *Loss control services.* Some commercial insurance policyholders may also qualify for consulting services of the insuring company's Loss Control (or Engineering) Department. This department is staffed with engineers and safety experts who specialize in inspecting business premises, identifying hazards, perils and possible trouble spots and in recommending possible solutions.

INSURANCE CHECKLIST FOR SMALL BUSINESS

In addition to helping you identify, miminize and in some instances eliminate business risks, this checklist will help you strengthen your insurance program and provide guidelines for discussions you should have with a qualified insurance professional.

The points covered are grouped under three general headings: 1) coverages that are essential for most businesses; 2) coverages that are desirable for many firms; and 3) coverages for employee benefits.

This checklist is followed by a brief discussion of four basic steps that are necessary for good insurance management: 1) Recognize the risks to which you are exposed. 2) Follow the guides for buying insurance economically. 3) Have a plan. 4) Get professional advice.

Some small-business owners look on insurance as if it were a sort of tax. They recognize that it is necessary but consider it a burdensome expense that should be kept at a minimum. Is this view justified?

Not if you take a more conservative approach. You can use insurance to get many positive advantages, as well as the negative one of avoiding losses. Used correctly, insurance can contribute a great deal to your success by reducing the uncertainties under which you operate. It can reduce employee turnover, improve your credit at the bank, make it easier to sell customers on favorable terms and help keep your business going in case an insured peril interrupts operations. The potential benefits of good insurance management make it well worth your study and attention.

CHECKLIST

The points covered in the checklist are grouped under three general classes of insurance: 1) coverages that are essential for most businesses, 2) coverages that are desirable for many firms but not absolutely necessary and 3) coverages for employee benefits. For each of the statements, put a check in the first answer column if your understand the statement and how it affects your insurance program. Then study your policies with these points in mind and discuss with your agent questions you still have.

ESSENTIAL COVERAGES

Four kinds of insurance are essential: fire, liability, automobile, and workers' compensation insurance. In some areas and in some kinds of business, crime insurance, which is discussed under "Desirable Coverage," is also essential.

Are you certain that all the following points have been given full consideration in your insurance program?

FIRE INSURANCE

	No action needed	Look into this
1. You can add other perils—such as windstorm, hail, smoke, explosion, vandalism and malicious mischief—to your basic fire insurance at a relatively small additional fee.	___	___
2. If you need comprehensive coverage, your best buy may be one of the all-risk contracts that offer the broadest available protection for the money.	___	___
3. The insurance company may indemnify you—that is, compensate you for your losses—in any one of several ways: (1) It may pay actual cash value of the property at the time of loss. (2) It may repair or replace the property with material of like kind and quality. (3) It may take *all* the property at the agreed or appraised value and reimburse you for your loss.	___	___

	No action needed	Look into this

4. You can insure property you don't own. You must have an insurable interest—a financial interest—in the property *when a loss occurs* but not necessarily at the time the insurance contract is made. For instance, a repair shop or drycleaning plant may carry insurance on customers' property in the shop, or you may hold a mortgage on a building and insure the building although you don't own it. ___ ___

5. When you sell property, you cannot assign the insurance policy along with the property unless you have permission from the insurance company. ___ ___

6. Even if you have several policies on your property, you can still collect only the amount of your actual cash loss. All the insurers share the payment proportionately. Suppose, for example, that you are carrying two policies— one for $20,000 and one for $30,000—on a $40,000 building, and fire causes damage to the building amounting to $12,000. The $20,000 policy will pay $4,800, that is. ___ ___

$\frac{20,000}{50,000}$, or $\frac{2}{5}$ of $12,000.

The $30,000 policy will pay $7,200;

that is $\frac{30,000}{50,000}$, or $\frac{3}{5}$ of $12,000.

7. Special protection other than the standard fire insurance policy is needed to cover the loss by fire of accounts, bills, currency, deeds, evidence of debt and money and securities. ___ ___

8. If an insured building is vacant or unoccupied for more than 60 consecutive days, coverage is suspended unless you have a special endorsement to your policy canceling this provision. ___ ___

	No action needed	Look into this

9. If, either before or after a loss, you conceal or misrepresent to the insurer any material fact or circumstance concerning your insurance or the interest of the insured, the policy may be voided. ___ ___

10. If you increase the hazard of fire the insurance company may suspend your coverage even for losses not originating from the increased hazard. (An example of such a hazard might be renting part of your building to a cleaning plant.) ___ ___

11. After a loss, you must use all reasonable means to protect the property from further loss or run the risk of having your coverage canceled. ___ ___

12. To recover your loss, you must furnish within 60 days (unless an extension is granted by the insurance company) a complete inventory of the damaged, destroyed and undamaged property showing in detail quantities, costs, actual cash value and amount of loss claimed. ___ ___

13. If you and the insurer disagree on the amount of loss, the question may be resolved through special appraisal procedures provided for in the fire-insurance policy. ___ ___

14 You may cancel your policy without notice at any time and get part of the premium returned. The insurance company also may cancel at any time with a 5-day written notice to you. ___ ___

15. By accepting a coinsurance clause in your policy, you get a substantial reduction in premiums. A coinsurance clause states that you must carry insurance equal to 80 or 90 percent of the value of the insured property. If you carry less than this, you cannot collect the full amount of your loss, even if the loss is small. What percent of your loss you can collect will depend on what percent of the full value of the property you have insured it for. ___ ___

	No action needed	Look into this

16. If your loss is caused by someone else's negligence, the insurer has the right to sue this negligent third party for the amount it has paid you under the policy. This is known as the insurer's right of subrogation. However, the insurer will usually waive this right upon request. For example, if you have leased your insured building to someone and have waived your right to recover from the tenant for any insured damages to your property, you should have your agent request the insurer to waive the subrogation clause in the fire policy on your leased building. ___ ___

17. A building under construction can be insured for fire, lightning, extended coverage, vandalism and malicious mischief. ___ ___

Liability

1. Legal liability limits of $1 million are no longer considered high or unreasonable even for a small business. ___ ___

2. Most liability policies require you to notify the insurer immediately after an incident on your property that might cause a future claim. This holds true no matter how unimportant the incident may seem at the time it happens. ___ ___

3. Most liability policies, in addition to _bodily_ injuries, may now cover _personal_ injuries (libel, slander and so on) _if_ these are specifically insured. ___ ___

4. Under certain conditions, your business may be subject to damage claims even from trespassers. ___ ___

5. You may be legally liable for damages even in cases where you used ''reasonable care.'' ___ ___

6. Even if the suit against you is false or fraudulent, the liability insurer pays court costs, legal fees and interest on judgments in _addition to_ the liability judgments themselves. ___ ___

7. You can be liable for the acts of others under contracts you have signed with them. This liability is insurable. ___ ___

8. In some cases you may be held liable for fire loss to property of others in your care. Yet, this property would normally not be covered by your fire or general liability insurance. This risk can be covered by fire legal liability insurance or through requesting subrogation waivers from insurers of owners of the property. ___ ___

Automobile Insurance

1. When an employee or a subcontractor uses a car on your behalf, you can be legally liable even though you don't own the car or truck. ___ ___

2. Five or more automobiles or motorcycles under one ownership and operated as a fleet for business purposes can generally be insured under a low-cost fleet policy against both material damage to your vehicle and liability to others for property damage or personal injury. ___ ___

3. You can often get deductibles of almost any amount—say $250 or $500—and thereby reduce your premiums. ___ ___

4. Automobile medical-payments insurance pays for medical claims, including your own, arising from automobile accidents regardless of the question of negligence. ___ ___

5. In most States, you must carry liability insurance or be prepared to provide other proof (surety bond) of financial responsibility when you are involved in an accident. ___ ___

<table>
<tr><td></td><td>No action needed</td><td>Look into this</td></tr>
</table>

6. You can purchase uninsured-motorist protection to cover your own bodily-injury claims from someone who has no insurance. ___ ___

7. Personal property stored in an automobile and not attached to it (for example, merchandise being delivered) is not covered under an automobile policy. ___ ___

Worker's Compensation

1. Federal and common law requires that an employer (1) provide employees a safe place to work, (2) hire competent fellow employees, (3) provide safe tools and (4) warn employees of an existing danger. ___ ___

2. If an employer fails to provide the above, the employer is liable for damage suits brought by an employee and possible fines or prosecution. ___ ___

3. State law determines the level or type of benefits payable under workers' compensation policies. ___ ___

4. Not all employees are covered by workers' compensation laws. The exceptions are determined by State law and therefore vary from State to State. ___ ___

5. In nearly all States, you are now legally *required* to cover your workers under workers' compensation. ___ ___

6. You can save money on workers' compensation insurance by seeing that your employees are properly classified. ___ ___

7. Rates for workers' compensation insurance vary from 0.1 percent of the payroll for "safe" occupations to about 25 percent or more of the payroll for very hazardous occupations. ___ ___

<table>
<tr><td></td><td>No action needed</td><td>Look into this</td></tr>
</table>

8. Most employers in most States can reduce their workers' compensation premium cost by reducing their accident rates below the average. They do this by using safety and loss-prevention measures. ___ ___

Desirable Coverages

Some types of insurance coverage, while not absolutely essential, will add greatly to the security of your business. These coverages include business-interruption insurance, crime insurance, glass insurance and rent insurance.

Business Interruption Insurance

1. You can purchase insurance to cover fixed expenses that would continue if a fire shut down your business—such as salaries to key employees, taxes, interest, depreciation and utilities—as well as the profits you would lose. ___ ___

2. Under properly written contingent business-interruption insurance, you can also collect if fire or other peril closes down the business of a supplier or customer and this interrupts your business. ___ ___

3. The business-interruption policy provides payments for amounts you spend to hasten the reopening of your business after a fire or other insured peril. ___ ___

4. You can get coverage for the extra expenses you suffer if an insured peril while not actually closing your business down, seriously disrupts it. ___ ___

5. When the policy is properly endorsed, you can get business-interruption insurance to indemnify you if your operations are suspended because of failure or interruption of the supply of power, light, heat, gas or water furnished by a public utility company. ___ ___

	No action needed	Look into this

Crime Insurance

1. Burglary insurance excludes such property as accounts, fur articles in a showcase window and manuscripts. ___ ___

2. Coverage is granted under burglary insurance only if there are visible marks of the burglar's forced entry. ___ ___

3. Burglary insurance can be written to cover, in addition to money in a safe, inventoried merchandise and damage incurred in the course of a burglary. ___ ___

4. Robbery insurance protects you from loss of property, money and securities by force, trickery or threat of violence on or *off* your premises. ___ ___

5. A comprehensive crime policy written just for small business owners is available. In addition to burglary and robbery, it covers other types of loss by theft, destruction and disappearance of money and securities. It also covers thefts by your employees. ___ ___

6. If you are in a high-risk area and cannot get insurance through normal channels without paying excessive rates, you may be able to get help through the federal crime insurance plan. Your agent or State Insurance Commissioner can tell you where to get information about these plans.

Glass Insurance

1. You can purchase a special glass-insurance policy that covers all risk to plate-glass windows, glass signs, motion-picture screens, glass brick, glass doors, showcases, countertops and insulated glass panels. ___ ___

2. The glass-insurance policy covers not only the glass itself, but also its lettering and ornamentation, if these are specifically insured, and the costs of temporary plates or boarding up when necessary. ___ ___

3. After the glass has been replaced, full coverage is continued without any additional premium for the period covered. ___ ___

Rent Insurance

1. You can buy rent insurance that will pay your rent if the property you lease becomes unusuable because of fire or other insured perils and your lease calls for continued payments in such a situation. ___ ___

2. If you own property and lease it to others, you can insure against loss if the lease is canceled because of fire and you have to rent the property again at a reduced rental. ___ ___

Employee Benefit Coverages

Insurance coverages that can be used to provide employee benefits include group life insurance, group health insurance, disability insurance and retirement income.

Key-man insurance protects the company against financial loss caused by the death of a valuable employee or partner.

Group Life Insurance

1. If you pay group-insurance premiums and cover all employees up to $50,000, the cost to you is deductible for Federal income tax purposes, and yet the value of the benefit is not taxable income to your employees. ___ ___

	No action needed	Look into this

2. Most insurers will provide group coverages at low rates even if there are 10 or fewer employees in your group. ⎯ ⎯

3. If the employees pay part of the cost of the group insurance, State laws require that 75 percent of them must elect coverage for the plan to qualify as group insurance. ⎯ ⎯

4. Group plans permit an employee leaving the company to convert group-insurance coverage to a private plan, at the rate for his/her age, without a medical exam, within 30 days after leaving the job. ⎯ ⎯

Group Health Insurance

1. Group health insurance costs much less and provides more generous benefits for the worker than individual contracts would. ⎯ ⎯

2. You pay the entire cost. Individual employees cannot be dropped from a group plan unless the entire group policy is canceled. ⎯ ⎯

3. Generous programs of employee benefits, such as group health insurance, tend to reduce labor turnover. ⎯ ⎯

Disability Insurance

1. Workers' compensation insurance pays an employee only for time lost because of work injuries and work-related sickness— not for time lost because of disabilities incurred off the job. But you can purchase, at a low premium, insurance to replace the lost income of workers who suffer short-term or long-term disability not related to work. ⎯ ⎯

	No action needed	Look into this

2. You can get coverage that provides employees with an income for life in case of permanent disability resulting from work-related sickness or accident. ⎯ ⎯

Retirement Income

1. If you are self-employed, you can get an income tax deduction for funds used for retirement for you and your employees through plans of insurance or annuities approved for use under the Employees Retirement Income Security Act of 1974 (ERISA). ⎯ ⎯

2. Annuity contracts may provide for variable payments in the hope of giving the annuitants some protection against the effects of inflation. Whether fixed or variable, an annuity can provide retirement income that is guaranteed for life. ⎯ ⎯

Key-Man Insurance

1. One of the most serious setbacks that can come to a small company is the loss of a key employee. But your key employee can be insured with life insurance and disability insurance owned by and payable to your company. ⎯ ⎯

2. Proceeds of a key-man policy are not subject to income tax, but premiums are not a deductible business expense. ⎯ ⎯

3. The cash value of key-man insurance which accumulates as an asset of the business, can be borrowed against and the interest and dividends are not subject to income tax as long as the policy remains in force. ⎯ ⎯

Organizing Your Insurance Program

A sound insurance protection plan is just as important to the success of your business as good financing, marketing, personnel management or any other business function. And like the other functions, good risk and insurance management is not achieved by accident, but by organization and planning. A lifetime of work and dreams can be lost in a few minutes if your insurance program does not include certain elements. To make sure that you are covered, you should take action in four distinct ways:

1. Recognize the various ways you can suffer loss.
2. Follow the guides for buying insurance economically.
3. Organize your insurance-management program.
4. Get professional advice.

Recognize the risks. The first step toward good protection is to recognize the risks you face and make up your mind to do something about them. Wishful thinking or an it-can't-happen-to-me attitude won't lessen or remove the possibility that a ruinous misfortune may strike your business.

Some businesses will need coverages not mentioned in the checklist. For example, if you use costly professional tools or equipment in your business, you may need special insurance covering loss or damage to the equipment or business interruption resulting from not being able to use the equipment.

Study insurance costs. Before you purchase insurance, investigate the methods by which you can reduce the costs of your coverage. Be sure to cover the following points:

1. Decide what perils to insure against and how much loss you might suffer from each.

2. Cover your largest loss exposure first.

3. Use as high a deductible as you can afford.

4. Avoid duplication in insurance.

5. Buy in as large a unit as possible. Many of the "package policies" are very suitable for the types of small businesses they are designed to serve, and often they are the only way a small business can get really adequate protection.

6. Review your insurance program periodically to make sure that your coverage is adequate and your premiums are as low as possible yet consistent with sound protection.

Have a plan. To manage your insurance program for good coverage at the lowest possible cost, you will need a definite plan that undergirds the objectives of your business. Here are some suggestions for good risk and insurance management:

1. Write down a clear statement of what you expect insurance to do for your firm.

2. Select only one agent to handle your insurance. Having more than one may spread and weaken responsibility.

3. If an employer or partner is going to be responsible for your insurance program, be sure he/she understands the responsibility.

4. Do everything possible to prevent losses and to keep those that do occur as low as possible.

5. Don't withhold from your insurance agent important information about your business and its exposure to loss. Treat your agent as a professional helper.

6. Don't try to save money by underinsuring or by not covering some perils that could cause loss, even though you think the probability of their occuring is very small. If the probability of loss is really small, the premium will also be small.

7. Keep complete records of your insurance policies, premiums paid, losses and loss recoveries. This information will help you get better coverage at lower costs in the future.

8. Have your property appraised periodically by independent appraisers. This will keep you informed of what your exposures are, and you will be better able to prove what your actual losses are if any occur.

Get professional advise about your insurance. Insurance is a complex and detailed subject. A professionally qualified agent, broker or consultant can explain the options, recommend the right coverage and help you avoid financial loss.

For more information on the products and services discussed here, contact your local Independent Agent.

GLOSSARY of INSURANCE TERMS

ADJUSTER. A person who settles insurance claims. An adjuster may be a Travelers employee or an independent operator.

ADJUSTMENT. The settlement of a claim; final premium determination.

AGENT'S AUTHORITY. The authority placed in the agent by the insurance company; the extent to which the agent may act on behalf of the company. This authority is defined by a contract between the agent and the company.

ALL-RISK. A term commonly used to describe broad forms of Property or Liability coverages. It is misleading because no Property or Liability Policy is truly an ALL-RISK coverage. A Policy will invariably contain some exclusions.

APPRAISAL. An estimate of value, loss or damage.

ASSIGNED RISK. A risk that has been declined by one or more companies. Such a risk may be assigned to designated companies by a recognized authority. The operation is called an Assigned Risk Plan.

ASSURED. The insured; the one for whom insurance is written.

BASIC BENEFITS. Basic benefits, generally, are all the benefits offered by a group health plan except major medical. Basic benefits may include hospital, surgical and medical expense insurance; supplemental accident, diagnostic lab and X-ray, radiation therapy and dental expense insurance.

BENEFICIARY. A person who will receive policy benefits.

BENEFIT FORMULA. A benefit formula defines the amounts of life insurance that may be purchased for employees in a specific classification (salary, occupation, length of service).

BENEFIT. That amount payable under an insurance policy because of an accident, injury or illness.

BINDER. An agreement, usually written, whereby one party agrees to insure another party pending receipt of a final action upon the application.

BUSINESS INTERRUPTION. Insurance covering the loss of earnings resulting from the destruction of property: called Use and Occupancy Insurance.

CANCELLATION. The terminating of an insurance contract by either the insurance company or the insured.

CARRIER. An insurance company.

CASH DEDUCTIBLE. The amount of money an insured must pay for covered expenses before certain benefits can begin.

CASH VALUE. The value, in cash, of a life insurance policy.

CASUALTY. An accident, occurrence or event; the person to whom it happens; the general insurance term applied to insurance coverages for an accident, occurrence or event.

CERTLET. A booklet that describes the benefits and all the provisions of a group policy that affect the insured. The certlet becomes a certification of insurance when the person is eligible for the insurance. It is then the legal document that proves the person is actually insured.

CLAIM. A request by an insured for benefits under an insurance policy.

COINSURANCE. Two or more entities providing insurance protection and sharing in losses.

COMPENSATION. Wages, salaries, awards, fees, commissions; any return in payment for a financial loss.

COMPREHENSIVE. A loosely used term signifying broad or extensive insurance coverage.

CONTRIBUTORY. A group insurance plan that is paid partly by employees' contributions and partly by the employer's contributions.

CONTRIBUTORY NEGLIGENCE. Partial responsibility for one's own injury or damage.

COVERAGE. The insurance potection provided by the policy.

DECLARATIONS. That part of an insurance policy containing the information about the applicant that the applicant listed on the application for insurance.

DEDUCTIBLE. An amount the insured must pay before insurance benefits may be paid.

DISCOUNT. A reduction applied to an insurance premium because of good experience, for example.

DRAFT. A financial instrument similar to a check frequently used by insurance companies to pay losses.

EFFECTIVE DATE. The date the policy is put in force; the inception date.

ENDORSEMENT. A written amendment affecting the declarations, insuring agreements, exclusions or conditions of an insurance policy; a rider.

EVIDENCE OF INSURABILITY. Medical proof, from either a questionnaire or a physical examination, that an applicant, employee or dependent is healthy and, therefore, insurable.

EXAMINER. An individual who reviews, evaluates and processes claims.

EXCLUSION. That which is expressly eliminated from the coverage of an insurance policy.

EXPIRATION DATE. The date an insurance policy terminates.

EXPOSURE. Person or property, injury to whom or damage to which will cause an economic loss.

FACE AMOUNT. In life insurance, the amount of basic coverage stated on the face of the policy.

GRACE PERIOD. A period beyond the premium-due date, during which the premium may be paid and the insurance will be continued in force.

GROUP INSURANCE. Insurance covering a group of employees.

HAZARD. A condition that creates or increases the probability of a loss.

HEALTH INSURANCE. Commonly called Accident and Health Insurance, protection against financial loss from a personal accident or illness.

INCURRED LOSS. A loss that, while not yet paid, has been sustained and for which reserves have been established to pay in the future.

INDEMNITY. Insurance protection that will place the insured in the same financial position as before a loss was sustained.

INSPECTION. An examination by those having authority. An insurance company usually reserves the right to inspect any property it insures.

INSURANCE. Protection against loss. The insured sacrifices a small certain loss (the premium) for protection against a large uncertain loss (an accident, fire, death). The insurance company assumes the risk by employing the law of large numbers and the principle of risk spreading.

INSURED. The entity whose life or property is protected by the insurance. The one for whom insurance is written.

LAPSE. To fail to continue an insurance policy; to cease to provide insurance protection.

LIABILITY. Being bound by law and justice to do something that may be enforced by the courts.

LIMITS. The value or amount of a policy; the greatest amount that can be collected under the policy.

LOSS. In insurance, the amount the insurer is required to pay because of an insured's loss.

MULTI PERIL. An insurance policy that provides coverage against many perils. Sometimes called a ''package'' policy.

OCCURRENCE. A continuance of a repeated exposure to conditions which result in injury.

PERIL. Anything that may cause a loss (cause of a possible loss).

POLICY. A legal contract of insurance.

POLICYHOLDER. The owner of the policy; the one who purchases the policy and pays the premiums.

POLICY PERIOD. The term for which insurance remains in force, sometimes definite, sometimes not.

PREMIUM. The cost of an insurance policy. The charge the policyholder pays for the insurance protection.

PROPERTY. The thing owned; real property is real estate and things attached to it; anything else is personal property.

PROPERTY DAMAGE. Physical damage to property.

PROVISIONS. The terms or conditions of an insurance policy.

RATE. Cost per unit of insurance.

REINSTATE. To restore coverage after it has been canceled or suspended.

REINSURANCE. Insurance placed by an underwriter in another company to reduce the amount of the risk his or her company has assumed.

RENEW. To continue; to replace as with a new policy.

RIDER. An endorsement.

SCHEDULE OF BENEFITS. The amount of insurance for which each classification of employees is eligible. (Classifications can be based on salary, wage, occupation or length of service.)

SELF-INSURANCE. An arrangement where, instead of purchasing an insurance policy, a party maintains a reserve fund to protect it against a loss.

SETTLEMENT OPTION. The way in which money for the death benefit of an insurance policy will be paid to a beneficiary.

SURETY. A guarantee that a person, normally called the principal, will perform according to a statute or a contract. Surety offers protection to a third party, normally called an obligee.

UNDERWRITER. The insurance company; a party assuming the risk; the person performing the underwriting function.

VOID. Of no force; null.

WAITING PERIOD. A period immediately after the inception of the policy, during which no benefits will be paid even if a loss occurs. Pertains to health insurance.

WAIVER OF PREMIUM. In life insurance, a provision which states that, if the insured becomes disabled and the disability appears total and permanent, the insurance policy will continue in full force without further payment or premium.

Part VII
Using Computers to Improve Your Business

How to Get Started with a Small Business Computer
  Michael M. Stewart
  Alan C. Shulman

A Small Business Guide to Computer Security
  Edited by SBA Staff Members
  Principal author: Stuart W. Katzke
  Insurance Section: David Kaiser
  Legal Section: James Smiddy
  Computer Selection Section: William Murray
  Self-audit Checklist: Steven Levin
  Other Contributors: Donald L. Adams
                      John R. Bjork
                      Peter S. Browne
                      Donald Foster
                      Diane Fountaine
                      Robert A. Krell
                      Dennis Steinauer

Summary

The purpose of this *Aid* is to help you forecast your needs, evaluate the alternative choices, and select the right computer system for your business.

Introduction

Micro or Personal computers (PC's) make it economically possible for (even very) small businesses to acquire electronic data processing equipment. With its business applications, a microcomputer system gives you professional management planning and control capability that can maximize your personal management abilities and goals and your company's growth and profit potentials. To grasp this opportunity, you must use your best analysis and judgment when choosing a computer for your small business.

What Can Computerization Do For You?

To answer this question, you must have a clear understanding of the long and short range goals of your firm, the advantages and disadvantages of all of the alternatives to a computer and, specifically, what you want to accomplish with a computer. Compare the best manual system you can develop using your present resources with the computer system you hope to get. It may be possible to improve your existing manual system to do the job.

Generally a business that is reasonably well organized and staffed may benefit from computerization if it has large volumes of detailed or repetitious information that needs to be handled with great speed and precision. A complete computer system can:

(1) **Organize and store many similarly structured pieces of information** (i.e., addresses having NAME, STREET, CITY, STATE and ZIP);

(2) **Retrieve a single piece of information from many stored ones** (i.e., the address of John Smith);

(3) **Perform complicated mathematical computations quickly and accurately** (i.e., the terms of a loan amortized over many years);

(4) **Print information quickly and accurately** (i.e., sales report);

(5) **Perform the same activity almost indefinitely and precisely the same way each time** (i.e., print a hundred copies of the same form letter).

Managers use these computer capabilities to solve many business problems. Some of the most common business applications are keeping transaction records (such as a Cash Receipts Journal, Receivables Ledger, and General Journal) and preparing statements and reports (such as a Balance Sheet, Income Statement, or Inventory Status Report).

Look at the following situations. These manual operations have areas that could definitely be improved by computerization.

Accounts Receivable—Even if properly organized and maintained, a large volume of active accounts receivable customers can cause your staff to spend many hours posting sales, receipts and, especially, preparing statements. Unfortunately, as the volume of information to be handled goes up, the number of errors often increases.

Advertising—Using only manual systems, it is costly and complicated to have special sales programs directed toward particular customers. Manually prepared mass mailings are time consuming and expensive.

Inventory—A large number of items or high volume turnover can cause major errors in tracking inventory. Errors in inventory control can result in lost sales and in the maintenance of unnecessarily high quantities of slow moving products.

Payroll—Calculating and writing checks are tedious operations in payroll administration. It can also be extremely difficult to effectively implement any kind of employee incentive plan using manual procedures.

Planning—Manual systems or procedures make planning for the future time-consuming and difficult. *"What If"* situations such as—If sales increase, to what extent will expenses increase?—are not easy to simulate with a manual system.

The general areas of computer business applications are:

Financial Modeling programs prepare and analyze financial statements.

Word Processing programs compile statistics, plot trends and markets, do market analysis, modeling, graphs and forms. Can combine all these functions, interchange and evaluate data from four programs simultaneously.

Critical Path Analysis programs divide large projects into smaller, more easily managed segments or steps, targeting goals and ultimate completion.

Legal programs track cases and tap information from databases.

Payroll system programs keep all payroll records, calculate pay, benefits and taxes, and prepare pay checks.

File Management programs enable you to create and design forms, then store and retrieve the forms and the information obtained on them.

The business applications for PC's are available in packaged software programs that enable you to interact with the computer, entering, manipulating, and processing complex evaluations and computations of voluminous quantities of data.

After analyzing your application needs, consider 1) the investment decision (pay back period, depreciation, tax impact, etc.) and 2) the potential increase in your management capability.

There are, however, some things you should **not** expect your computer to do.

• Don't expect a computer to clean up a mess in the office. The mess will only get worse if you attempt to computerize it.

• Don't put in a computer because you don't have the right people to do the jobs in your organization. At least initially, the computer will make more demands on your organization, not fewer.

• Don't install a computer with the idea that any information you want will be instantly available. Computers require structured, formal processing that may not produce some information as fast as an informal system could.

• Don't expect the installation of a computer to help define the jobs that must be done. The computer is a tool to get those jobs done, but the jobs must be well-defined first.

• Don't expect a computer installation to occur like magic. Computer selection and installation will be successful only through a lot of hard work.

• Don't expect any computer system to exactly fit your present methods of getting jobs completed. If you are not willing to listen to new ideas on solving problems.

you will not be able to install a computer successfully or at a reasonable cost.

• Don't acquire a computer to generate information you will not use. Growing companies may benefit from structured management information systems, but many owner-managers of small companies already have their fingers on the pulse of their businesses and do not need a formal, electronic system.

Selecting The Right Computer System For Your Business

Two options for your own in-house computer system are the **Minicomputer** and the **Microcomputer.**

A *Minicomputer* is a general purpose computer that can be programmed to do a variety of tasks and is generally designed so input can be entered directly into the system. For example, data such as a sales order is put into the computer at the same time the order is written. A minicomputer can be operated by users who don't have special computer knowledge. The costs for minicomputer equipment begin around $25,000, and range to above $200,000. However, costs are decreasing rapidly, so inquire for the latest estimates.

The *Micro or Personal Computer* is a household word if not quite yet a universal household system. It is inexpensive, small, lightweight and can be set on a desk. Such computers run programs that do an astonishing variety of tasks and can be easily operated by personnel who do not have special computer knowledge. Prices for personal computers begin at $1,500. They can satisfy the needs of many small business owners. The micro or PC usually handles one task at a time. Some may have modest capabilities for multi-tasking and multi-user applications (more than one program and terminal at one time). There are supermicros with multi-tasking and networking capabilities. These cost $5,000 and up and can be used by multi-departmented companies.

Choosing The Right Computer

To "computerize" your business you will have to choose the right programs, select the right equipment, and implement the various applications. This involves training personnel, keeping up security, maintaining equipment, supplies, and day to day operation. If you follow a well laid out plan and make well informed choices, your computer system should provide the information and control intended.

Computer Components:

Hardware:

Component	Function
Central Processing Unit (CPU)	The CPU performs logic calculations, manages the flow of data within the computer, and executes the program instructions.
Main Memory	Memory is measured in the "K" you'll often hear mentioned—for example 32K (32,000 positions). It is simply a storage area readily accessible to the CPU.
Mass Storage	This storage is simply "non-main." There are a number of devices available, such as disk, diskette, and magnetic tape.
Input Device(s)	These units are used to enter data into the system for processing. An input device commonly used with computers is a combination keyboard and television-like display screen called a CRT (cathode ray tube).
Output Device(s)	These display the data. The most common output device is a printer.

Software:

Component	Function
Operating System Software	Software that tells the hardware how to run.
Applications Programs	Software written to perform a particular function, such as word processing, accounts receivable, payroll, or inventory control "applications."
Compilers and Interpreters	Special software that translates programs into machine language that the CPU can execute.

Choosing The Right Programs (Software)

A program is a set of instructions that tells the computer to do a particular task. Programs are written in a language (such as FORTRAN, COBOL, BASIC) that is easy for people to work with. These programs are usually referred to as *software.*

The software determines what data or information is to be entered into the computer and what output or report is to be returned by the computer after it has performed as instructed by the program. The act of entering information into a computer is called inputing the data.

Generally, there are three types of software:

Compilers and Interpreters—special software that translates programs written in people language (such as FORTRAN, COBOL, BASIC) into machine language that the CPU can execute.

Operating System Software—the programs that control all the separate component parts of the computer, such as the printer and disk drives, and how they work together. Systems software generally comes with the computer and must be present before the application software can work.

Application Software—software composed of programs that make the computer perform particular functions such as payroll check writing, accounts receivable posting or inventory reporting. Application software programs, particularly the more specialized ones, are normally purchased separately from the computer hardware.

Because the application software provides the features that will assist you and your business, it should always be evaluated and decided upon before you look at computer equipment. Before beginning your search for application software that is right for you, identify *what the software will have to accomplish.* Your time will be well spent if you research and write down your requirements.

Determine Your Requirements

To help you determine your requirements, prepare a list of all functions in your business in which speed and accuracy are needed for handling volumes of information. These are called applications. For each of these applications make a list of all reports that are currently (or will need to be) produced. You should also include any preprinted forms such as checks, billing statements or vouchers. If they don't exist, develop a good idea of what you want—a hand-drawn version will help. For each report list the frequency with which it is to be generated and the number of copies needed.

In addition to printed matter, make a list of information you would like to see displayed on the computer video screen (CRT). Again, design a hand-drawn version. List the circumstances under which you would like to see this information displayed.

For each application make a list of all materials that are used as input into your manual system. These may include items such as time cards, work orders, receipts, etc. Describe the time period in which these items are created, who creates them and how they get into the system. Also, describe the maximum and average expected number of these items generated in the appropriate time period. As with the reports, include copies of the input items or drawn drafts.

For all files you are keeping manually or expect to computerize (customer files, employee files), list the maximum and average expected number of entries in an appropriate time period, such as 10 employees per year, 680 customers per year. Normally a file, manual or otherwise, is cleaned out after a specified time and the inactive entries are removed. The maximum number should reflect the number expected to be in the file just before the cleaning out process is begun.

Identify how you retrieve a particular entry. Do you use account numbers or are they organized alphabetically by name? What other methods would you like to use to retrieve a particular entry? Zip code? Product purchased?

Note which of your requirements are a *"must"* and on which you will compromise. The more detailed you are, the better your chance of finding application software that will be compatible with your business. It is also true that the more detailed you are, the more time it will take to research and evaluate each alternative application software package.

Evaluate Your Choices

If after compiling all of your information, you find your needs are fairly complex, you may wish to engage the services of a small business consultant to assist you in evaluating your software requirements. Or you can submit the list to software retailers, custom software vendors, or mail order software houses. They, in turn, should provide you with software that meets as many of your requirements as possible.

At this point you will have to review the software and verify for yourself the extent to which it actually meets your needs. Ask yourself these questions: Does it cover all of my *"musts"*? How many of my other requirements

does it fulfill? Does it provide me with additional features I had not thought of earlier but now believe to be important?

After you have found one or more software packages that fit your needs, there are other general features you should check out before you make your final decision to buy a computer.

• **Does it come with effective documentation? Is the operating manual written for the novice? Is the information organized so you can use it effectively after you become an experienced user?**

• How easy is the software to use (user-friendly)? Does the information that is displayed on the computer screen make sense? Is there a *"help"* facility?

• How easy is it to change? Can you change data that has already been processed? Can you yourself change the "program" instructions such as payroll withholding rates, or will you have to pay the vendor to change these for you? If yes, what will it cost?

• Will you be required to change any of your business practices? If so, are these changes that you should make anyway? Will it provide the accounting and management information you need?

• How well is the software documented? You should be able to understand the general flow of information: which program does what and when.

• Does it have security features such as passwords, or user identification codes? Can it prevent unauthorized access to private information?

• Is it easy to increase the size of files?

• Will the software vendor support the software? Does the vendor have a good track record? Will the vendor make changes, and if so, how much will the changes cost?

• How long has the vendor been in business? What are the vendor's prospects for staying in business?

Ready-made Software

If you find a ready-made software package that fits your system needs and price range, take it. You may still have to do a lot of work adapting your procedure, but generally you will be better off than if you design your own software system.

Although some different manufacturers' software and hardware can be adapted to work together compatibly, such standardization is not yet prevalent. That is why it is so important that first you find the right software and then select the hardware that can handle it.

Preparing a Request For Proposal

If you can't find software packages that fit your needs, prepare a request for proposal (RFP) to send to selected hardware vendors and turnkey systems houses. (Turnkey systems houses are companies that put together complete hardware and software systems.)

The form of your RFP depends upon the kind of proposals you are soliciting—turnkey system with custom software, a turnkey system with packaged software, or hardware and/or software in separate packages.

Because most first-time users get turnkey systems, the following guidelines apply to RFP's for this method:

1. Give a brief description of your company.

2. Describe the business operation to be computerized.

3. Submit the materials you designed and accumulated earlier.

4. Describe the criterion that will be used to evaluate proposals, and request a response for each criteria (i.e., maintenance, technical support, training).

5. Specify which of your requirements must be met exactly and which must be met only in substance. Distinguishing between discretionary and nondiscretionary requirements is important when dealing with software packages.

6. Request a detailed price quotation that includes all charges to meet your needs, including one-time charges for equipment, set up training, applications and systems software, and ongoing charges such as maintenance and technical support. Request financing alternatives such as lease-purchase and direct or third party lease.

Selecting The Right Equipment (Hardware)

Choosing the software is by far the most difficult job in deciding upon the computer system that is right for you. Because most software is written for one, or several specific computers, you will probably have narrowed your equipment choices down considerably by the time you have selected your software.

You should review the choices and ask the same questions about potential computer hardware vendors that

you asked when evaluating software vendors. Don't forget to check the cost of shipping, installation and equipment maintenance.

The computer and associated equipment known as hardware consists of a number of components, each doing a different job. They include:

Processor—The *"thinking"* part of the computer is known as the processor, or Central Processing Unit (CPU) and is designed to execute software instructions, perform calculations, control the flow of data to and from the memory, and control other hardware components.

Computer Memory—Computer memory usually is measured in bytes (which is a grouping of binary digits or bits). Roughly speaking, each byte of memory holds one character of data, either a letter or a number. A 2K (2,000 bytes) memory in practical terms holds about one double spaced typed page. There are two kinds of memory, *ROM (Read-Only Memory)* and *RAM (Random Access Memory)*.
ROM is a program stored in the computer memory and cannot be changed by the user or an externally entered program.

RAM—Random Access Memory is located in the Central Processing Unit (CPU) and is normally measured in "K's" or 1000's (64K = approximately 64,000 characters or about 32 pages of information). RAM is used to store all the information necessary for the CPU to do its job: the program running the portion of data that is currently being processed and some portion of the system software. **Information stored in RAM lasts only as long as the power is on.** Once the power is turned off, all RAM information is erased.

DOS is software that controls the interactions among the CPU, disk drive, keyboard, video monitor and printer. These two, the DOS and applications program, may need about 55K.

Storage—Just as a company retains its relatively permanent records in a file cabinet, so a computer must rely on a relatively permanent method of maintaining its information. Disks are the most common form of storage for small business computers. They resemble a small phonograph record. They may be *"floppy"* or *"hard."* A floppy disk is made of soft, thin plastic encased in a stiff paper envelope and comes in 3½, 5¼, and 8 inch diameters. Hard disks are made of metal, have faster access and have more storage capacity. Hard disks are also much more expensive than "floppies", but their greater storage capacity and speed usually make up for the difference in cost. Information on the disk is recorded, retrieved and erased through a disk drive which is controlled by the system and application software.

Terminal—In order for a computer to perform useful work, you must be able to communicate with it. Most often this two-way communication is carried out with the help of a terminal consisting of a typewriter-like keyboard used to enter data into the computer and a CRT display screen (cathode ray tube). The video display should be able to display 24 lines of 80 characters on the screen at one time. For some users, 16 lines of 64 characters may be adequate. Some monitors (video screen) can handle color and graphics more readily than character display. Color graphics quality is determined somewhat by "*pixels*" or picture elements. If a display is "280 by 192 pixels", the screen is divided into 280 rows and 192 columns. The larger the number of pixels, the finer or more precise the picture display will be.

Printer and Drives—The main output of a computer system is usually printed material—reports, checks, invoices, etc. As with all other hardware choices you make, you must choose a printer that can do the job for you. The print quality of various printers ranges from dot-matrix to typewriter quality. Disc drives are single or double sided and discs come in 8-inch standard, 3½ inch or 5¼ inch diskettes.

Warmware—*Warmware* is the critical after-the-sale service and support you will require, particularly for the software. If you choose wisely, the combined software and hardware packages can become an invaluable tool to enable you to better manage your business. However, without the qualified people to train your staff, install the system and be available to answer future questions, your system may never get off the ground, Once up, running and relied upon, a computer system failure without the necessary vendor warmware support can make it very hard for you to carry on your business.

Evaluating the Computer System—The most important step in judging a minicomputer system is to visit a few companies using the minicomputer system you think you'll get. Visit these companies without the sales representative for the system, and try to find companies with configurations and applications as close to yours as possible.

Use the following criteria, listed in order of importance, to evaluate a minicomputer system.

1. Software Developer's Past Performance Record	Software developer should have prior experience with similar applications for the same equipment configuration.
2. Commitment of Hardware Vendor	Where will your commission sales rep be after the contract is signed? How many systems engineers does the vendor have in your local area?
3. Hardware Capacity	Does the hardware have adequate processing capability to meet your requirements within the acceptable time frames?
4. Quality of Systems Software	The quality of the system software (operating systems and utilities) dramatically affects how difficult the system is to program and use.
5. Systems Documentation	What kind of systems documentation does the vendor provide and how is it updated? Can it be understood at some basic level by the user? Is it designed so other experts can understand how things were done and change them when necessary?
6. Service and Maintenance Support	When your system breaks down, how long will it take to get it fixed? Who will do it? Will it be subcontracted? Are there any provisions for backup during down time?
7. Expandability & Compatibilities	What are the technical limits of your system and how close to those limits is your current configuration? Is there software compatibility among the vendor's product lines?
8. Security	What security features will your system have to prevent unauthorized use of the system or unauthorized program modifications?
9. Financial Stability of Vendors	Satisfy yourself about the financial stability of your vendor.

10. Environmental Requirements

Mini and Microcomputers do not require special environments such as raised floors, special wiring or special air conditioning. Some may, however, and it pays to find out in advance.

11. Price

With computers you generally get what you pay for. Low price alone should not be a prime evaluation criterion.

Contracting For a Turnkey System

If you have decided to purchase a turnkey system rather than the software and hardware separately, you should have a contract or agreement.

Examine the standard contract supplied by the vendor. Be aware that it may not protect your interests. If you have any questions, have your lawyer review the contract and suggest changes that will help you implement the system.

An important part of the contract is when do you pay. Do you have to pay before the installation or after the installation is completed? Or will you pay for the installation periodically on a draw schedule? The more money held back until the installation is complete, the more power you have to insure that the vendor satisfactorily completes all that has been promised and contracted for.

The contract should include detailed references to the following:

Description of equipment and software

Installation responsibilities

Provisions for additional equipment

Performance guarantees

Responsibility for training

Software rights

Provisions for default, bankruptcy of vendor, or termination of contract

Software documentation

Systems Documentation

Responsibility for freight charges and sales tax for hardware

Acceptance testing

Conversion responsibilities (from manual system to computer)

Upgrading privileges and trade-in rights

Restart (what is required to restart system from failure).

If the contract is for software developed specifically for you, the contract should include by reference your Request For Proposal and the Vendor's responding proposal.

Recognize the importance of the contract and how it forces all parties to plan and to agree on objectives. A good contract will help you prepare for the system's installation and will make the whole experience a more satisfactory business transaction.

Points to consider when selecting your personal/micro computer system:

• *Reputation* of manufacturer and vendor.

• *Reliability*—How qualified are the manufacturer and the vendor?

• What is the incidence of repair on the system equipment?

• *Resources*—How long have the manufacturer and vendor been in business?

• How strong are their financial positions and credit ratings?

• *Services*—Is ongoing consulting, training, supply and repair available?

• *Rates*—Are charges competitive? What terms are offered?

• *Backup*—What happens if your system fails?

Implementation

As was suggested before, successful computer applications for your business depend heavily on the implementation process. Problems are inevitable but proper planning can help avoid some of them and mitigate the effects of others.

After the software and hardware choices have been made, you will need to prepare your business for the new system. One vital point to keep in mind: successful implementation of a computer system in a small business requires intense involvement of the owner-manager from the initial decision to acquire a computer through system specification, selection and implementation. Also the success of the new computer system will be directly related to the cooperation of a number of your employees; therefore it is important to involve them as early as possible with the steps to be taken. Explain to each affected employee how his or her position will change. To those unaffected, explain why their jobs will remain unchanged.

Set target dates for key phases of the implementation (especially the last date for format changes).

Prepare the installation site. Check the hardware manual to be sure the location where you will keep your new computer meets the system's requirements for temperature, humidity and electrical power.

Prepare a prioritized list of applications to be converted from manual to computer systems. It is very important to plan on converting them one at a time, not all at once.

Prepare a list of all your business procedures that will be changed so the computer system will fit into the regular work flow. Develop new manual procedures to interface with the computer system.

Train, or have the vendors train, all people who will be using the system.

When the above steps are complete, the computer system can be installed. Each application on the conversion list should be entered (files set up, historical data entered, and the system prepared for new transactions) and run parallel with the pre-existing, corresponding manual system for a number of processing periods. This means that two complete systems will be running, placing a great deal of pressure on your employees and yourself. However, until you have verified that the new system does its job, it will be worth the effort.

Insist on progress reports from everyone involved in the change over of systems.

At the same time you are converting each application, you must begin dealing with the long term issues that will keep your computer operation successful.

• *System Security*—If you consider confidential some information that is critical to your business, you will want to implement a system of safeguards to keep unauthorized users from stealing, modifying or destroying data. These safeguards can include simply locking up the equipment, or more advanced schemes that use User Identification and Password software. Other safeguards include:

☐ Control access to your computer, disks, and reports.

☐ Label all disks to identify their contents. Verify correct labeling.

☐ Don't let computer operators initiate original accounting transactions, adjustments or corrections.

☐ Rotate computer employees or schedule their vacations to expose possible unauthorized practices.

☐ Require dual signature authorizations to control software modifications.

• *Data Safety*—Data, confidential or otherwise, can be destroyed by unexpected disasters (fire, water, power fluctuations, magnetic fields, etc.) or employee tampering and could result in high costs to recreate. The best and cheapest insurance against the high cost of lost data is to keep back-up copies of all data and programs. The information on each diskette should be backed up regularly and as often as necessary to minimize the cost of recreating lost information. Copies should be kept in a safe place away from the business.

☐ Have and test a disaster recovery plan.

☐ Identify all data, programs, and documents that are needed for essential tasks during recovery from a disaster.

• *Employee Cross-Training*—Just as with a manual system, it is important to have more than one employee know how to operate a system. Once your business relies upon the computer system, the absence (sickness, termination, etc.) of a computer operator can be devastating unless another person is prepared to fill in.

• *Management Controls*—Although computer systems allow small businesses to process more data more accurately than ever before, there is a chance that the same system can cause greater problems if left unsupervised. All systems, manual or otherwise, must be continually monitored to insure the quality of the data that goes into and comes out of it.

If all this seems like a lot of work, it is. The use of a computer, like any tool, requires learned skills in order to fulfill its purpose. If you believe that you and your business need a computer, plan to spend the time and the money it takes to make its installation and operation successful.

You can hire a consultant to advise and guide you if you don't have the confidence or time to select the software and hardware yourself. If you prefer, some full-service firms and manufacturers will assist you in developing your computer system. Make sure your advisors understand your specific needs. Have a contract specifying the exact nature and cost of such services.

With no prior knowledge of computers, you can buy a personal computer with applications for your business. With some guidance, self-study, and experience you can develop computer based management planning and control expertise. By taking advantage of the speed and complex capabilities of a computer, you can tap the potential of growth and profit in yourself and your business.

A Quick Review: What To Consider When Buying

Needs
Business operations to be done

Costs
Comparative cost vs. comparative capabitities

Memory
Capacity of RAM
Capacity of ROM

Disk Drives
Bit capacity
Multiple drives

Keyboard
Typewriter style

Software
Disk and cartridge
Number of programs written for or compatible with the PC you are interested in

Display
Color or black and white
Resolution quality
Graphics capability

Expandability
Connections for add-ons and attachments
Compatibility with other manufacturers' equipment

Supplies
Custom forms
Printer paper
Furniture
Accessories
  Disks
  Dust Covers

Repair and Training
Compare service contracts
Training provided, how much

I. INTRODUCTION

The computer has become a valuable and often essential part of every business, large or small. Computers offer many benefits, however, they also bring many risks. Do you, as a small business owner-manager, understand these risks, their potential impact on your business, and how to minimize them? Do you take the necessary steps to avert potential catastrophe while realizing the potential benefits of computer technology?

Computer security procedures are simply a form of good management. Because computer technology is still fairly new to most small business persons, you may believe that security measures are beyond your resources or are difficult to understand and implement. In fact, protecting your computer-based assets deserves as much attention as protecting against theft, embezzlement, or fire. The concepts are the same.

Computer-related losses are similar to other threats a small business confronts; the probability of any given incident may be small, but the cost of that incident may be devastating. You need to weigh the potential for catastrophic loss against the cost of protective measures then select and implement those measures that provide a net benefit to the business—just as in your other business decisions. The purpose of this guide is to help you understand the nature of computer security risks and the controls that help reduce those risks.

This guide is written for people who own or manage small businesses or are responsible for their firm's information processing systems. Its primary focus is the small business which uses small to medium-sized, general-purpose computer systems (i.e., microcomputers and minicomputers). However, much of the discussion applies equally well to components of larger organizations which have separate computer resources.

The guide addresses:

• Why you should be concerned about computer security;

• What can happen, and how; and

• What steps you can take to reduce the risks.

Also included are sections dealing with the insurance and legal aspects of owning and purchasing computers. Appendices contain a self-audit checklist, suggested readings, and a list of additional sources of information and assistance.

II. WHY SHOULD YOU BE CONCERNED ABOUT COMPUTER SECURITY?

What is computer security?

Computer security includes policies, controls, and/or procedures designed to ensure:

• **Integrity and Accuracy** of data and the processing systems that handle it;

• **Confidentiality** of personal, proprietary, or otherwise sensitive data;

• **Availability** of the systems, data, computer applications, and the services they support.

Why is computer security important?

Inadequate computer security exposes a business to accidental or intentional events that can cause serious losses. Such events include:

• **Environmental Hazards** such as damage from fire, flooding, static electricity, dust, or electrical storms;

• **Hardware and Equipment Failure** such as mechanical or electrical failure of the computer, its storage capacity, or its communications devices;

• **Software Errors** ranging from programming bugs to simple typos in spreadsheet formulas;

• **Accidents, Errors, and Omissions** by anyone using your computers or the information they process; and

• **Intentional Acts** including fraud, theft, sabotage, and misuse of information by competitors, clients, vendors, and employees.

Unfortunately, many people in small business still think that computer security is a concern only for big business, banks, and the military. Actually, inadequate computer security can be more threatening to your business than it is to a large corporation.

How is my business more threatened than a large organization?

While a small business may see fewer incidents of computer-related losses, it may lack the resiliency and resources to spring back from them. A similar loss in a large corporation, on the other hand, rarely results in the firm's failure. Large firms usually have the capital and other resources necessary to reduce the impact of computer-related business problems. In addition, large businesses can command the expertise necessary to ensure that sophisticated computer security procedures and equipment are implemented and used. Few small business persons lead such a comfortable existence.

Is it really that much of a concern?

Small businesses are learning the many advantages of using computers in every aspect of their operations. It is not unusual now for a small business to install a microcomputer and rapidly automate all of its business records and controls. The entire business becomes dependent on computerized data. Personnel records, tax records, inventories, receivables, payables, shipments, bank accounts, and all other vital records are all contained on small diskettes that easily fit in your pocket.

In such a concentrated form, your business records are extremely vulnerable to removal or destruction. If something were to happen to those diskettes, it could have the same effect as the sudden disappearance of significant business records and files. A tipped coffee cup, a misplaced magnet, an inadvertent scratch, or an accumulation of dust or dirt can leave valuable corporate records inaccessible.

Crime may also be facilitated when computers are involved. People with access to your computerized data have the very pulse of your business at their fingertips. Dishonest employees can, and have, diverted funds and goods for their personal gain. Furthermore, if adequate security procedures are not followed, you may find your business ruined before you are aware that anything is amiss. Your entire business may be at risk, and fraud can be difficult to detect or trace until it is too late. If a disgruntled

employee or intruder gains access to your unprotected computer files, it takes only seconds to destroy them. Similarly, if a malicious person destroys your diskettes, perhaps as simply as with a pair of scissors, he or she also destroys or seriously impairs your business.

Among the benefits of new technologies are the capacity to use your computers to transfer funds, control inventory, or process customers' orders. These same technologies, however, increase opportunity for unauthorized access to business data. "Hackers," people who use their own computers and telephones to gain access to your computerized data, may become an extremely serious problem for your organization. If you do not take elementary security measures, you can become their target; if they gain access to your business records, they can steal valuable proprietary information, divert your money or goods, or destroy your records—with a surprisingly small chance of being caught.

If I am faced with this risk, why should I even consider using a computer?

Despite the risks, the advantages that computers offer usually outweigh the disadvantage. Computers can provide you with a strong competitive advantage. They usually offer cost-effective means to maintain your records, analyze your operations, and establish control procedures that would be otherwise impossible.

The same characteristics of a computer system that expose your organization to large risks can offer significant business protection. Using computers will increase control much more than risk. The risks inherent in the use of a computer in your business can be reduced to a minimum with procedures that are usually quite simple.

Can I have too much computer security?

Surprisingly, the answer is yes. Computer security, like other business controls, is not a free commodity. Typically, each degree of security has a cost associated with it in terms of dollars, effort, reduced system access, or flexibility for those who need to use the system. A balance must be struck between the threats to which a system is exposed and the costs of addressing those threats. Security measures beyond those necessary to appropriately protect the system result in "overkill" and a waste of valuable corporate resources.

III. WHAT CAN HAPPEN AND WHY?

Computer applications support business functions. Examples include word processing, spreadsheet programs, inventory control, accounts payable/receivable, and customer mailing lists. The real objective, then, is not computer security, but information security. The loss or destruction of the computer itself, while certainly of concern, is less likely to be as devastating to your operations as loss or destruction of key business information and functions that the computer supports.

What causes computer-related losses?

The primary threats to computer applications are:

Environmental and Natural Hazards
- flood, fire, earthquake, tornadoes
- power fluctuations that damage/destroy the computer or the data contained in the computer
- dirt, dust, or other particles that damage magnetic media

Hardware and Equipment Failure
- disk head crashes
- defective power supplies

Software Errors
- failure to perform intended functions
- incorrect results, even when intended functions are performed

Accidents, Errors and Omissions
- erroneous data collection or entry
- improper handling of magnetic media
- software errors or failures
- accidental destruction of business records
- failure to backup vital data and programs
- failure to maintain current documentation

Intentional Acts
- alteration of financial records for monetary gain
- malicious destruction of business records "to get even"
- insertion of unauthorized code into commonly used software to perform unintended and unauthorized functions
- unauthorized use of the computer system for personal gain
- theft of computer equipment, data, or programs

These events generally result in a loss of confidentiality, integrity, or availability of data or computer applications. While direct effects can immediately disrupt

the business, the longer term, indirect effects can have the most disastrous impact on your business. For example:

- Disclosure of proprietary business plans, product designs, costs, market data, or customer lists can lead to a loss of competitive advantage in the marketplace, financial loss, and lost opportunities.

- Fraudulent modification of inventory or other financial records for personal gain; malicious modification of critical business data by disgruntled employees; and unintentional errors introduced into source data which then propagate throughout the entire business' records, can result in significant losses.

- Unavailability of business information on computer resources can be a major cause of business disruption. Most businesses understand the impact on day-to-day operations of a key individual not reporting to work for several days or of the unavailability of important support equipment (e.g., the lifts in an automobile service station). However, many small businesses underestimate (or fail to recognize) their dependence on computerized information and their requirements for continuity of computer processing capability. The impact of these situations can result in lost customers, loss of competitive advantage, and, ultimately, failure.

Is a centralized or decentralized computer system more secure?

In general, a centralized computer system is more secure than a decentralized one. The advantages are lower costs for physical and operational controls and reduced threats to data communications links. However, adequate security measures can be developed for both centralized and decentralized systems.

What types of vulnerabilities increase the risk of a computer-related loss?

Vulnerabilities exist when control measures are absent, weak, or flawed. In lieu of attempting to identify all vulnerabilities in all computer applications, you should concentrate on those applications that have a high loss potential. Section IV presents a method for identifying such applications, as well as an approach for selecting controls.

IV. HOW CAN YOU REDUCE THE RISKS?

How do I achieve an acceptable level of computer security?

The following steps outline a systematic approach to computer security in your organization:

Step 1: Establish information security as a management priority.

Step 2: Identify your information resources and determine your sensitivity to and the potential impact of losses.

Step 3: Select and implement control measures to reduce potential losses.

Step 4: Audit and monitor results.

STEP 1: ESTABLISH INFORMATION SECURITY AS A MANAGEMENT PRIORITY

It is imperative that management give priority and direct attention to information security. As with other important concerns of the small business (cash flow, production schedules, and regulatory compliance, for example), once it has been established that the issue is being adequately addressed, less direct attention is needed. Developing an information security policy, implementing it, then communicating it properly to employees significantly aids this process.

Develop an Information Security Policy

An information security policy is a prerequisite for addressing computer security concerns because it establishes a uniform and consistent framework for handling and protecting all information. The policy can be as formal or detailed as your business requires, but without such a policy, employees cannot be held wholly responsible for computer-related accidents and misuse. In many organizations, existing security policies that apply to traditional "hard copy" documents need to be reviewed and expanded to include information in automated form.
An information security policy should:

- Assign responsibility for managing and monitoring information security;

- Identify the information that needs protection (e.g., trade secrets, product plans, financial records, and customer lists) and the degree to which it must be protected.

Communicate Your Computer Security Program

Your security program needs to be clearly stated in writing and readily accessible to those who need it. You should introduce it in person to new users of the system and review it in person with those who are regular or permanent users. When you do this, you should:

- Clearly state that information resource security is a major goal and that all employees must play a part in achieving that goal;

- Require that all persons involved in information processing activities be fully aware of their responsibilities for implementing and following the information security policy.

STEP 2: IDENTIFY YOUR INFORMATION RESOURCES AND DETERMINE SENSITIVITY TO AND POTENTIAL IMPACT OF LOSSES

Develop an Inventory and Identify Applications

Since computer security requirements will vary for different computer applications, you must first identify which of your business computer applications or uses require additional protection. To do this, begin with each hardware system (i.e., each computer) and determine the following:

- System identification and location

- User responsible for the system (i.e., the "owner")

- Other users

- General categories of information used

- General description of physical access and environmental conditions

- Specific, identifiable applications that use the hardware system, their purpose, and the individual responsible for each application

Be sure to include all uses of your system, even those that involve routine or mundane activities that are associated with word processing and spreadsheet programs. These are important because the data files generated and processed by these programs often contain valuable or sensitive information.

Determine Sensitivity to Loss of Confidentiality, Integrity, and Availability

Ask yourself the following questions:

• If the business information, software, or hardware of this application were modified, would it harm my business or my customers? Is the application related to customer service, product, or cash flow?

• Does the application store, process, or transmit any information that I would not like disclosed to the general public, my competitors, my customers, or my employees?

• Would it matter if the information or service provided by the application was not available for one minute, one hour, eight hours, one day, several days, one week, several weeks, one month?

A "yes" to any of these questions for a particular application indicates a sensitivity in that area and possible requirements for some additional computer security controls. Such so-called "sensitive applications" may include those that:

• Are necessary for continued operation of the business;

• Contain personnel data, proprietary client data, trade secrets, business plans, product designs or composition, or information that must be protected by law;

• Control real-time processing (e.g., automated manufacturing, automated inventory tracking and reordering);

• Control or account for business, financial, or material resources.

For these applications, you must estimate the potential impact on your business should harmful events occur in the identified sensitive area(s).

If you did not answer "yes" to any of the above questions, then you may want to consider whether the application is, in fact, needed. If it is, then your main concern should be to make sure that the application is not over-protected, thereby costing more or using more resources than necessary.

Estimate Potential Impact Due to a Loss of Confidentiality, Integrity, and Availability

This task may be difficult since it is often hard to quantify information losses in dollars. For example, the disclosure of confidential information about your business' clients could have a range of impacts on your business, depending on how many clients are affected, who they are, and how the information is used. It is frequently useful to use dollars as a measurement. When this is difficult or impossible, use qualitative judgments to make relative comparisons of loss or importance, such as "high," "medium," and "low" categories.

Once you have identified your potential losses, divide them into the following categories (or others that suit your situation):

• Those that you cannot possibly live with (i.e., would ruin you);

• Those that you can live with, but would have significant negative impact on your business;

• Those that you do not like, but would have a minor impact on business operations.

Within each category, list the items in decreasing order of impact on your business. The items in the first category are the ones you must protect as soon as possible. Some of the items in the second category you may choose to remedy within a reasonable time frame (six months or a year). You should take care of the items in the last category as time and resources permit.

STEP 3: SELECT AND IMPLEMENT CONTROL MEASURES TO REDUCE POTENTIAL LOSSES

Descriptions of rigorous, formal methods for selecting computer security controls are beyond the scope of this guide and are probably not needed for most small businesses. You can significantly improve your computer security by implementing a subset of controls from the five major areas described below. Additionally, you can take advantage of shared effort and resources to solve your problems by using high-level automated programs and industry standards and guidelines.

Administrative Controls are procedural in nature and generally the easiest and least costly to implement. They ensure that employees understand how to perform their jobs correctly, accurately, and effectively. In particular, administrative controls protect against employee accidents, errors, and omissions; disgruntled employees; computer-related fraud and embezzlement; mishandling of data during entry and distribution; and insufficient insurance coverage. These controls center on establishing policies and procedures which assign management and individual responsibilities; guide employee selection, evaluation, and termination; offer computer security training; and provide for proper handling of information resources.

Physical and Equipment Controls protect against loss of business information and processing capability due to fire, water damage, electric power outages and fluctuations, physical damage, theft, heat and humidity, and air contaminants. These controls address limiting physical access to information resources to authorized personnel; protecting computer hardware and supplies from water and fire damage; maintaining appropriate environmental conditions; and protecting against power outages and fluctuations.

Information and Data Controls incorporated into the hardware and software of computer systems prevent unauthorized individuals from using the computer. They also prevent individuals from accessing or modifying information (including computer programs) that they are not authorized to see or change; incorporated controls also record user activities so that individuals are held accountable for their actions. Such controls include authenticating users, establishing and enforcing authorization rules for what information and programs users can access and why, and maintaining a record of user actions.

Software Development and Acquisition Controls ensure that software developed in-house or under contract performs intended functions correctly and does not produce any results that would adversely affect security; that purchased, off-the-shelf software

is a legitimate, licensed copy that has not been tampered with (i.e., no unauthorized modifications, deletions, or insertions made) prior to its purchase; and that all software used by your organization is also protected from tampering and illegal copying. These controls include purchasing off-the-shelf software from reputable vendors establishing rigorous controls over the development and use of programs and data for sensitive applications and applying caution when using software that is in the public domain which may be not fully tested and documented and may contain codes (sometimes known as "worms") that destroy or modify your data and software files.

Backup and Contingency Planning Controls are essential for small businesses since they provide the last line of defense against events that can contribute to the demise of your organization. These procedures make sure that your organization can continue critical business activities which depend on computer applications. The procedures include training employees to respond to emergency conditions maintaining backup copies of information and computer programs for critical applications assuring that alternative computer processing equipment and software (especially copy-protected software) is available planning for the restoration or replacement of the primary equipment and cross-training of employees for critical functions.

STEP 4: AUDIT AND MONITOR RESULTS

After appropriately selecting and implementing the above controls, you should conduct some post-implementation reviews and periodic audits. These assure not only that the controls are in place and operating but also that they remain effective and relevant as the organization and information environment change.

V. INSURANCE CONSIDERATIONS

Computer systems can be insured under coverages designed for general office contents, however, special policies designed specifically for computer system exposure are preferable and often less expensive. In general, the greater the investment in the computer system, the greater the need for special coverage. This type of insurance can be an important safeguard for a small business that depends heavily on computers because it can help the business survive a major loss.

What should I insure?

There are three basic coverages in specialized computer systems policies:

1) **Hardware**, including all peripheral equipment which is owned, leased or rented;

2) **Data and Media**, including all software programs;

3) **Extra-expense** (over and above normal expenses) to continue to operate your business or recreate data lost due to a covered loss.

A fourth type of insurance—business interruption—is available if your business may lose income in the event that the computer system suffers loss or damage.

What locations do the policy cover?

Insurance for your computer system may be limited to your office or other specified locations. If you have portable hardware or have hardware, data, and media at employees home, these exposures may need to be added to the insurance policy.

What types of losses are covered?

Insurance coverages are broadly divided into two categories: "named peril" and "all risk." A "named peril" policy specifically details the types of losses that are covered. An "all risk" policy covers all losses unless specifically excluded. "All risk" policies are more favorable for the policy holder.
Both policies cover the most common types of losses—fire, wind, lightning, explosion, and vandalism.

General business contents policies are usually written on an "all risk" basis, as are computer system policies. The specialized policies are generally broader because they contain fewer exclusions.

What policy limitations should I look for?

In comparing insurance policies, review the limitations on what is covered. Some common limitations are:

- Only hardware that is specifically listed and reported to the company is covered.
- Coverage for electronic recordings is limited.
- Time period limitations are placed on extra expenses due to damaged electronic recordings.
- Property in transit or property away from the place of business is not covered.

The following types of losses are often excluded under standard "all risk" policies:

- Electrical surge, short circuit, brown-out, or other electrical damage
- Mechanical breakdown, faulty materials or workmanship, and errors in design

- Water damage, sewer back-up, flood
- Earthquake, landslide, mud slide, or other earth movement
- Breakage, including fragile items such as VDTs
- Accidental or unintentional erasure of data
- Corrosion, rust or other damage caused by changes in temperature
- Mysterious disappearance or inventory shortage
- Magnetic damage to electronic recordings
- Theft of property from an unlocked vehicle
- Theft or burglary
- Employee theft.

These losses often can be covered under specialized computer system policies. (You can use this list to compare insurance policies.)

How much insurance should I buy?

Most insurance policies cover hardware for its replacement cost. Often, the cost of hardware decreases over a relatively short period of time, especially as newer models are introduced. Monitor the cost of new equipment each year before renewing insurance coverage. If you rent or lease equipment, you may not be responsible for the replacement cost of the equipment. Check the lease or rental agreement carefully to determine the proper amount of insurance to buy.

If duplicate copies of all software and the operating manual are kept in another location, software does not have to be insured, except for the value of the media on which it is stored. If, as often happens, these duplicates are not kept current or in a separate location, or if the software publisher does not allow copies to be made, the cost of the software should be insured.

The value of data is equal to the loss your business may incur as a result of unauthorized disclosure, modification, or destruction of data. You must assess your data in each area to determine your insurance coverage needs. As a minimum, the value of data (other than software) is equal to the cost of reproducing the data. If data is backed-up regularly and stored in a separate location, the value of the data need not be insured as it can be reproduced inexpensively from the backups.

Determining the proper amount of extra-expense insurance to purchase requires careful thought and some research. The costs of temporary space, rented or time-shared equipment, overtime, rush installation of communications lines and the proper computer room environment, and general additional administrative expenses need to be considered.

How do I get the best price for the broadest coverage?

When purchasing your insurance, compare the coverage forms and the prices. Be sure your agent or company knows the price differences and all the safeguards you employ to protect your computer system. A business with a well-protected system may be able to justify higher deductibles at a reduced rate or buy less insurance. Coordination of alternate facilities with another company will reduce your need for extra-expense insurance.

What else should I know?

An insurance policy is not a substitute for maintenance agreements or proper maintenance and protection of your computer system. Even with the best insurance program, any loss is disruptive and potentially damaging to the health of a business.

VI. LEGAL CONSIDERATIONS

The following questions and answers are intended to help you avoid some of the legal risks involved in installing a computer system. The list also points out some of the protections and remedies available should you become engaged in a dispute that involves computer hardware or software. For more detailed advice, consult an attorney.

Do I need the assistance of an attorney when acquiring computer hardware or software?

Probably not when licensing off-the-shelf software or when purchasing standard hardware, such as a personal computer from an established computer vendor. In these situations, you should review the terms of the contract and, if not satisfied, consider another vendor. When purchasing larger systems or custom software, it may be helpful to get the advice of an attorney who is experienced in these matters. The attorney will be able to assist you in structuring an agreement that will more fully protect your legal rights.

When acquiring computer hardware or software, is it a good practice to sign the vendor's "standard form contract"?

Although the impression is sometimes created that the terms of the contract cannot be altered, vendors may modify the contract if the buyer's requests are reasonable.

Standard, off-the-shelf software, however, frequently comes with a license agreement in a clean plastic wrapper ("shrink-wrap agreement"). Merely opening the package binds the purchaser to the terms of the agreement. These shrink-wrap agreements rarely can be altered by the purchaser.

Why should I alter the terms of the contract?

Contracts are sometimes biased or weighted in favor of the person who drafted them. Therefore, as the buyer, you may be at a disadvantage when signing a contract that was prepared by the vendor. For example, a software contract prepared by a vendor may disclaim certain warranties and may limit the vendor's liability. This means that you may be without a legal remedy if the software is defective. You also need to understand that any verbal or written statements are usually not considered part of the contract. Such statements, therefore, may not be enforceable under the contract.

How do I modify a contract?

Simply draw a line through the part of the contract that you want to delete and write your initials opposite the deletion in the margin. If you want to change something, write the changes clearly on the document and initial them. If there is not room to make the changes, write an asterisk (*) at the point that you want to make the changes, initial it, and, at the bottom or on a separate page, add the change and initial it. After both parties have signed the contract in the space provided, make a copy for yourself and send the original to the vendor. Make certain that the other party initials the contract each place you do and that the person who signs the contract is authorized to do so.

Do I have any legal duties or responsibilities for the computer system after its installation?

Yes. You have a duty to exercise reasonable care when operating the system. For example, the records in one finance company's computer system showed that a customer had not made a payment on an automobile, while the customer insisted the payment had been made. The company repossessed the automobile, and the customer subsequently proved that the payment had in fact been made. The customer sued and recovered actual and punitive damages because of the finance company's negligence in the operation of the computer.

You should also maintain reasonable security procedures when operating the system. If a company keeps sensitive data, such as employee records, in the computer, some protection procedures should be installed in the system. If someone inside or outside the company gains unauthorized access to the computer records and harms someone else in the process, the company could be held liable for negligence. These cases frequently involve invasion of someone's privacy or alteration of financial records.

If I acquire off-the-shelf software, what are my rights regarding the use of that software (e.g., can the software be copied; can the software be used on multiple machines; can the software be modified)?

Most software is accompanied by a license agreement. If you sign the license, you are bound by its terms. If, on the other hand, it is a shrink-wrap license agreement, you are probably bound by the terms of the license if you open the package, even though you may not sign the agreement. These licenses typically limit the number of copies the purchaser can make (except backup copies), and prohibit using or modifying the software on more than one machine. Furthermore, if the software contains a copyright notice, you are prevented under penalty of the Federal copyright statutes from making unauthorized copies.

When I hire someone to write a custom software program, who owns the software that is created?

This depends on whether you consider the person hired an employee or an independent contractor. If the person writing the software is considered an employee, the software belongs to the employer, i.e., you own the copyright. If, however, the person is an independent contractor, then he or she owns the copyright. You can be protected in these situations by specifying in a software development or employment agreement that all software developed as a result of the agreement belongs to you.

How can I protect confidential information that is valuable to my business?

There are various ways to protect valuable, confidential information (sometimes called trade secrets). This means you must make sure it is not generally known outside the company. Furthermore, you should make this information available only within the company to people who need to know it. The information should be stamped "confidential" and should be stored in a locked area when not being used. You should also have signed confidentiality agreements with all employees who come in contact with this confidential information.

How can I protect the business if the computer hardware or software does not perform the functions it is supposed to perform?

Protection may be provided for in the contract between you and the vendor. The contract should contain a detailed description of the functions that the hardware or software is to perform (the functional specifications). These functional specs should be attached to and made a part of the contract; it may be of little value in a legal dispute if the specs are contained in a separate letter or advertising brochure. You are further protected if the contract contains warranties that the hardware or software will perform those functions described in the functional specs.

Moreover, the contract should specify remedies, such as money damages, in the event the warranties are breached. You can also exert pressure on the vendor to fix any problems that may exist if the contract specifies the completion of an "acceptance period" before making the final payment. The acceptance period should commence when the hardware or software is installed on your premises. During testing, you should run the system while using your own data. The acceptance period ends when you are reasonably satisfied that the hardware and software perform the functions specified in the contract. These concessions depend on the bargaining strength of you and the vendor. It never hurts to ask.

If the vendor's "form contract" contains no warranties and no damages, what remedies are available if the system fails to perform as promised?

If you can prove fraud on the part of the vendor, you can sue for damages based on fraud instead of breach of contract. In this situation, you may ignore the disclaimer of warranties and the limitation of damages specified in the contract. In order to prove fraud, however, you must show that the vendor made false statements, that the vendor knew the statements were false and that you relied on these statements to your detriment.

Are there any State or Federal statutes that protect small businesses from fraud or abuse with regard to computer systems?

Currently, 47 States have enacted laws that specifically make certain activities involving computers a criminal and/or civil offense. Moreover, Congress has enacted a Computer Fraud and Abuse Act. This Federal statute makes fraud and relative activities in connection with certain computers and computer access devices punishable. These State and Federal computer crime statutes add to existing, traditional statutes that protect businesses from fraud and abuse

(i.e., destruction and theft of property, invasion of privacy, trespass, and embezzlement). Statutes enacted specifically to protect against computer-related crimes make it easier for prosecutors to convict wrongdoers, thus providing more protection for business persons.

Some activities that are specifically prohibited under these computer crime statutes are: unauthorized access to computers, theft of computer services, interruption of computer services, misuse of computer system information, destruction of computer equipment, trafficking in computer passwords with the intent to defraud, and committing an offense by the use of two or more computers if the computers are located in different States. Since many small businesses attach their computers to public telephone lines, this last prohibition could provide important federal protection against unauthorized access by persons using a computer located in another State. Many State statutes provide similar protection against unauthorized access of a computer by use of another computer located in the same State.

APPENDIX A

WHERE YOU CAN GO FOR HELP

The following organizations, groups, and professionals can provide valuable assistance in evaluating and satisfying your computer security requirements:

THE SMALL BUSINESS ADMINISTRATION. The SBA maintains a large network of expert business counseling services and co-sponsors a wide range of small business courses, workshops, and conferences throughout the country. You can obtain assistance for your computer security or other business problems by calling the nearest office or the SBA answer desk at 1–800–368–5855. SCORE, the Service Corps of Retired Executives (202–634–6200), may also be of assistance.

VENDORS AND SERVICE PROVIDERS. Most manufacturers and vendors of computer equipment and software can provide valuable advice on computer security techniques and can often refer you to other information sources. Consultants, especially those who specialize in computer security or the automation of small businesses, will likely have experience in achieving the level of protection you need.

OTHER PROFESSIONALS. Your business insurance agent can usually advise you on computer security issues. Some insurance firms offer coverage not only for computer losses from fire, flood, theft, and electrical problems, but also from losses resulting from computer crime, damages to third parties resulting from computer negligence and many other possible

risks and hazards. Your accountant is usually a good source for information on protecting your vital records and on the requirements for the proper audit trails of computerized records. Your attorney will be able to discuss the tax and other legal considerations for the maintenance and retention of certain files and restrictions on the access to and disclosure of information subject to privacy considerations.

BUSINESS ASSOCIATIONS, PROFESSIONAL ASSOCIATIONS, AND USER GROUPS. There are a number of professional associations and user groups that can provide information on computer usage and security considerations. Computer equipment and software firms can put you in touch with these organizations. The Association for Computing Machinery (ACM) and the Institute for Electrical and Electronics Engineers Computer Society have publications, special interest groups (SIG's), and technical advisory committees (TAG's) that address issues of concern. Similarly, the American Bankers Association and the Bank Administration Institute have related publications and programs. Also contact the American Institute of CPAs, and the EDP Auditors Association.

THE NATIONAL BUREAU OF STANDARDS. The NBS Institute for Computer Sciences and Technology establishes standards and guidelines, including computer security issues, for the effective use of computers. The Institute has a number of publications on computer security. Some of these are listed in the Reference section. To obtain a complete list of available computer security publications, contact: National Bureau of Standards, Computer Security Division, Technology Building, Gaithersburg, MD 20899.

NBS also provides information on computer security through its Microcomputer Electronic Information Exchange, an electronic bulletin board available to the public. The data lines for the board are 301–948–5717 and 301–948–5718. Additional information can be obtained by calling 301–975–3359.

NATIONAL COMPUTER SECURITY CENTER. The National Computer Security Center provides computer security assistance to those firms processing classified and national security-related information for the Government. The Center also publishes an Evaluated Products List (EPL) of approved computer products which provide various degrees of security. The EPL includes products for personal computers as well as large computer systems. If your computer is operating under or for any government contract or contractor meeting these criteria, contact the Center at (301) 688–6311.

APPENDIX B
A SELF-AUDIT CHECKLIST

1. Management Issues

1.1 Organization and Policy

- Develop policies and procedures which address the handling of sensitive and proprietary information.
- Clearly state policies regarding personal use of computer equipment and software.
- Implement computer protection procedures that are consistent with sensitive information policies currently used in the organization.
- Assign accountability for a significant event to a single individual.
- Make sure that sensitive transactions are independently originated, approved, authorized and reconciled.
- Assign duties so that an individual cannot default and conceal.

1.2 Security Planning

- Make information security a management priority.
- Identify your information resources; determine sensitivity to and potential impact of losses.
- Establish a security policy. It should include the following:
  - A statement that information resource security is a major goal
  - A description of the functions of a computer systems security office
  - A list of the types of information that need protection
  - A requirement that all persons involved be fully aware of their responsibilities

1.3 Security Awareness

- Develop and implement a company-wide security awareness program.

1.4 Technical Training

- Ensure that management has the technical background for understanding and analyzing the programs used.

1.5 Legal Considerations

- Be aware that you are responsible for damages resulting from unauthorized access or employee errors.
- Determine ownership before a custom software program is written for you.
- Draft signed confidentiality agreements with employees who come in contact with confidential information.
- Determine whether or not your purchase requires the advice of an attorney.
- Understand that you are not forced to sign a "standard form" contract.
- Make sure warranties are included in contracts; statements made verbally or in letters are usually not enforceable under contract.
- Make sure the contract is modified specific to your business.
- Make sure your contract contains a detailed description of the functions that the hardware or software is to perform.

1.6 Insurance

- Carefully determine the proper amount of insurance you need for your system.
- Be aware of coverage limited to specific locations.
- Discuss with your insurance agent which losses are and are not covered under your policy.
- Keep your insurance policy current with additions and deletions to your computer system.

2. Security Considerations in Equipment And Software Acquisition

2.1 Equipment Selection

2.1.1 Lockability

- Lock any system that contains permanent secondary storage (hard disk) or that is used in an open environment.

2.1.2 Backup facilities

- Establish backup facilities that allow the business to continue to operate long enough to replace lost computers or data.

2.1.3 Environmental Protection

- Take steps to ensure electrical power quality.
- Maintain acceptable levels of temperature and relative humidity.
- Protect equipment from airborne contaminants (smoke, dust).

2.2 Business Application Software

- Ensure that software is developed in an organized fashion, with frequent management reviews and user "sign-offs".
- Have an independent technical person review all software before it is placed in service.
- Demand a detailed test plan for the software.
- Test all combinations of data and operating conditions.
- Ensure that all software updates are logged and managed under a control system that tracks changes to the system configuration.

3. Physical and Environmental Controls

3.1 Hazard Protection

Fire
- Fire-proof the premises with appropriate alarms, extinguishers, fire-walls, and exits.
- Clear the area of combustibles.

Water
- Give proper attention to potential overhead leaks.
- Know where to shut off the water supply to any pipes in the overhead.
- Be prepared to cover or move computers and equipment to a safer place.

3.2 Access Control

- Limit access to sensitive areas and resources through locks, separate rooms, or other controls.

3.3 Control of Storage Media

- Establish procedures for external labeling of sensitive materials.
- Maintain adequate storage facilities for security-sensitive media (hard copy, removable magnetic media).
- Establish procedures to ensure the proper handling and storage of magnetic media to reduce physical or magnetic damage.
- Enforce procedures for the proper disposal of sensitive media (e.g., shredding of paper, degaussing of diskettes).

4. Personnel Controls

4.1 Hiring and Termination

- Carefully check credentials and references of new employees.
- Take measures to ensure that terminated employees cannot affect sensitive information.

4.2 Supervision

- Be sensitive to changes in employee situations, life-style, behavior, attitudes, or morale that might affect continuing reliability and integrity.
- Properly schedule vacations and assignment rotations.

4.3 Separation of Duties

- Separate the following duties in user departments:
  - initiation and authorization of source documents
  - entry of data into the system
  - operation of the computer
  - use of output reports

4.4 User Training

- Ensure that users are adequately trained to operate the system.
- Promote a security awareness program that emphasizes employee responsibility to protect the company from malicious or inadvertent damage.

5. Business Transaction Controls

5.1 Segregation of Functions

- Separate critically related functions (e.g., printing and signing of checks).

5.2 Accountability

- Clearly communicate your expectations to all employees.
- Instruct employees that they are responsible for the protection and proper use of all assets, including data.
- Indicate that employees are accountable for the correct result.
- Ask users to report dangerous conditions and suspicious or unusual activity to management.
- Explain to employees that you own all of the data they use or produce.
- Advise employees that they are accountable for ensuring that data is appropriate for the intended use.

5.3 Auditability

- Ensure that business procedures provide sufficient audit trails to establish how a record came to look as it does now and how it looked at specific times in the past.

- Make sure that audit trails reliably determine which employees are responsible for which data.
- Ensure that users are prevented from making unauthorized modifications or destroying audit trail data.

5.4 Standard Accounting Controls

6. Technical Issues

6.1 Data and System Integrity

- Protect common-use (shared) software from undetected modification.
- Provide adequate procedures to validate results when important decisions are based on data produced by a PC.

6.2 Use of Utility Programs

- Maintain independent control over transaction and master file changes, such as item count, control total, and hash totals.
- Limit access to utilities.
- Remove utilities from system when practical to do so.

6.3 System and Data Access Controls

- If a system has a limited number of users, provide adequate methods (physical or otherwise) to prevent unauthorized use.
- If there are multiple users of a system using a fixed disk, provide adequate mechanisms to ensure needed file access control.
- If access control hardware or software is used:
  - Constrain user interface to prevent users from circumventing the control mechanisms.
  - Establish a method to prevent use of unauthorized copies of the operating system.
- If cryptography is used, establish adequate key selection and management procedures.
- Determine whether users should be provided with utilities (or training) to overwrite sensitive disk files or system memory.
- If only authorized users can use the system, make certain the system can identify and authenticate users before granting access.

6.4 Passwords

- If passwords are used:
  - Change them frequently.
  - Protect them like the data they access.
  - Select them carefully so they are not guessed.

6.5 Remote Access

- Limit connection to your computers to authorized individuals.
- Ensure that you are talking to whom you intend.
- Initiate all calls or limit incoming calls to those that you expect.
- Request confirming data.
- Restrict remote access to intended applications and data.

7. Contingency Planning

7.1 Emergency Plans

- Regularly schedule drills, rehearsals, and tests for likely scenarios.
- Plan to protect your employees, property, and data from natural and man-made disasters.
- Provide for the timely recognition and communication of emergency conditions.
- Train and drill all employees in appropriate responses to emergency situations.
- Make sufficient copies of all data necessary for the continued operation of the business.
- Ensure that emergency copies are safe.

7.2 Backup Procedures

- Ensure that the business can continue to operate long enough to replace lost computers or data.

7.3 Recovery Plans

- Confirm that suppliers can replace computers and data fast enough for the continued health of the business.
- Maintain sufficient funds from reserves or insurance to pay for restoring required resources.

APPENDIX C

SUGGESTED READING

Trudy E. Bell, "Your Insurance Can Ruin You," *Personal Computing*, Aug. 1983, pp.115–119.

Ivan Berger, "Hard-Disk Backup," *Popular Computing*, May 1984, pp. 131–134.

Security Evaluation For Small Computer Centers, The Chantico Technical Management Series, Wellesley, MA: QED Information Sciences, Inc., 1985.

Arielle Emmet, "Thwarting The Data Thief," *Personal Computing*, Jan. 1984, pp. 98–1055ff.

Thomas B. Freeman, "Clean Power," *Small Systems World*, Dec. 1983, pp. 41–44.

Collen Gillard and Jim Smith, "Computer Crime: A Growing Threat," *BYTE*, Oct. 1983, pp. 398–424.

Microcomputer and Office System Security, Washington, DC: GSA, 1983.

James V. Hansen, "Audit Considerations In Distributed Processing Systems," *Communications of the ACM*, Aug. 1983, pp. 1–10.

Tom Henkel and Peter Bartolid, eds., "Special Rep,VL4ort: Protecting The Corporate Data Resource," Computerworld, Nov. 18, 1983.

Richard A. Immel, "Data Security," Popular Computing, May 1984, pp. 65–68.

Avery Jenkins, "Firms Need Data-Protection Policies," *PC Week*, Mar. 13, 1984, pp. 38–41.

Howard A. Karten, "Stress Test For Floppies" PC Magazine, Jul. 10. 1984, pp. 196–202.

Carolyn J. Mullins, "IBM PCs Need a Clean Environment," PC Week, Mar. 13, 1984, pp. 40–42.

William H. Murray, "Good Security Practice For Personal Computer," Computer Security Journal, Fall/Winter 1983, pp. 77–83.

William E. Perry, "Auditing the Small Business Computer," EDP Auditor Update, Sep./Oct. 1983, pp. 7–8.

Microcomputers: Their Use and Misuse in Your Business, Price Waterhouse, Jan. 1983, p. 31.

Alan M. Riegland, "Before You Sign: Negotiating and Structuring Computer Contracts," *Small Systems World*, Feb. 1984.

Schweitzer, James A., "Managing Information Security: A Program For the Electronic Information Age," Boston, MA: Butterworth, Inc., 1982.

"Computer Insurance: How Much Do You Need?" Small Systems World, Feb. 1984, pp. 22–23.

Eric Stanford, "Control Issues In Personal Computing Systems," Auerbach Publishers, Inc., 1984.

Dennis Steinauer, "Security of Personal Computers: A Growing Concern," Computer Security Journal, 1984.

Dennis Steinauer, "Security In Small Computer Systems," Auerbach Publishers, Inc., 1984.

Rein Turn, "Privacy and Security Bibliography," Washington, DC: Privacy and Security Committee CBEMA, Oct. 1982, p. 51.

Gerald M. Ward and William M. Perkins, "Security and Control of Microcomputers," Auerbach Publishers, Inc., 1984.

Part VIII
Developing New Products

Summary

Sometimes the only way a small manufacturer can expand sales is by introducing a new product. The products made have reached their sales peak. Moreover, they cannot be modified to generate additional sales.

It becomes a question of where to look for a new product that can be made and sold at a profit. This *Aid* **speaks to that question. It discusses a practical approach to the selection of a suitable new product and suggests sources that can be helpful to finding such a product.**

A systematic approach is the best way to find a new product. In such an approach, your first action should be to set a new product policy. Before you start to search for a new product, set guidelines for that search.

These guidelines should help to provide answers to questions, such as: Can the new product be made on present equipment? Will it be sold to your present market? What is the profit potential of the new product?

The second major action involves responsibility for finding a new product. Will you personally handle the project? Or will you delegate it? Either way, the person who looks for the new product should have a clear understanding of the resources available for this project. In addition, he/she should be authorized to make decisions for your company.

Defining a New Product for Your Company

Although there are thousands of products available on a reasonable basis to any company that will manufacture and market them, the question is: Which ones can be made at a profit? In fact, so many exist and are being generated, it would consume all the resources of a small company to examine each one of them only briefly. On the other hand, too brief a search or a hasty decision can result in costly mistakes, if not outright disaster. It is thus imperative to define the product you are seeking.

Your task is to get on paper some facts about the kind of new product you want to produce in your factory. These facts consist of your requirements in general terms which will be applicable to the new product. The following questions, though not all inclusive, should

stimulate your thinking in defining a product or establishing criteria by which you can judge potential products. When you have set such criteria, you can write a "profile of product interest."

Your Company's Strengths

	Yes	No
1. Is manufacturing your company's strength?	——	——
2. Do you prefer a highly automated production line?	——	——
3. Do you prefer a product with a high ratio of labor to production costs?	——	——
4. Are your production personnel highly skilled?	——	——
5. Are your industrial product designers exceptionally skilled?	——	——
6. Does your present equipment have a long usable life?	——	——
7. Is your present equipment largely under utilized?	——	——
8. Do you have a strong sales force?	——	——
9. Is your sales force hampered by too narrow a product?	——	——
10. Do you have strong capability in a particular technology?	——	——
11. Does your company have cash or credit resources not used in your present operation?	——	——
12. Does your company have a reputation for high quality products?	——	——
13. Does your company have a reputation for low cost production?	——	——

Market Preference

	Yes	No
14. Do you prefer a particular industry?	——	——
15. Do you prefer a product sold to retail consumers?	——	——
16. Do you prefer a product sold to industrial users?	——	——
17. Do you prefer a product sold to the government?	——	——
18. Do you prefer a product with long usage?	——	——
19. Will you accept a product that may be a fad item?	——	——
20. Do you prefer a consumable item?	——	——
21. Is there a distribution system (trade practice) you prefer?	——	——
22. Would you consider a product limited to a given locality? (Or a product in		

demand largely in overseas markets?)

Yes   No

23. Is a product that requires specialty selling desirable?
24. Is a product that needs mass merchandising suitable?
25. Do you intend overseas distribution?
26. Must your present sales department be able to sell a new product?
27. Are you willing to create a new or separate marketing department to sell a new product?

Sales Volume Desired

Yes   No

28. Have you determined the optimum annual volume from the product over the next 3 years?
29. Do you have any preference for a unit price range in a product?
30. Do you have 5 and 10 year volume objectives for a new product?
31. Will this product have to support its own sales organization?
32. Will the product support its own manufacturing equipment?
33. At what volume does a product exceed your company's capability?

Product Status

Yes   No

34. Will you accept an idea for a product?
35. Will you accept an unpatentable product?
36. Is a non-exclusive license of a patent acceptable?
37. Are you willing to develop an idea to a patentable stage?
38. Will you develop a patent without acceptable prototype?
39. Will you accept a product that has been on the market but is not yet profitable?
40. Will you license a patent?
41. Do you insist on owning the product's patent?
42. Will you enter a joint venture for a new product with another company?
43. Would you merge with or buy a company that has good products but needs your company's strengths in

manufacturing, sales, finances, or management?

Yes   No

The Product Configuration

Yes   No

44. Are there any maximum size limitations to a product you can manufacture?
45. Would weight of a product be a factor?
46. Do warehousing facilities or yard space impose size limitation?
47. Does length of production time influence the desirability of a product?
48. Have you determined your equipment tolerance?
49. Do you have adequately trained personnel to do the job?
50. Would you prefer that a product be made of certain materials?
51. Are there manufacturing processes that should constitute the major portion of a new product?
52. Are there any manufacturing processes that the product should not have?
53. Would a product requiring extensive quality control costs be desirable?

Finance

Yes   No

54. Has an overall budget been established for the new product?
55. Have separate budgets been established for finding, acquisition, development, market research, manufacturing, and marketing the new product?
56. Has a time period been established by which a new product must become self-supporting, profitable, or capable of generating cash?
57. Does the new product require a certain profit margin to be compatible with your financial resources or company objectives?
58. Has external long-range financing been explored for your new product?
59. Is the length of the sales cycle for the new product known?

	Yes	No
60. Do trade practices require you to furnish financial assistance, such as floor planning or dating plans, for distribution of your product?	___	___
61. Have you determined average inventory to sales ratio for the new product?	___	___
62. Have you determined average aging of accounts receivable for your new product?	___	___
63. Does the product have seasonal aspects?	___	___

Profile of Product Interest

Your answers to the 63 questions above can lead to a well thought-out guide as to the acceptability of any potential new product. A short condensed profile helps communicate your needs. Such a profile also indicates a high degree of professional management which sources of new products will welcome. For illustrative purposes a fictitious sample profile follows:

The XYZ company, a defense-aerospace oriented precision metal stamping and machine shop, desires to acquire a product or product line to the following specifications:

Market
The product desired is one used by industrial or commercial firms of a specific industry but not by the government or general public except incidentally.

Product
The product sought is one in which 60 percent of the total direct manufacturing cost consists of metal stamping and/or machining processes.

Price Range
Open, but preferably the unit price to the user will be in the $100 to $400 range.

Volume
Open, but preferably a product which aggressively marketed will produce $500,000 in sales the first year with an annual potential sale of 3 to 5 million dollars.

Finance
Initial resources to $150,000 in addition to present plant capacity are available for manufacturing a new product.

Type of Acquisition
Prefer royalties to a patent but will consider purchse of a patent, joint venture, merger, or purchase of a company outright.

Having read the sample profile, it is suggested that you review the preceding questions. It will become apparent that the answer to almost any single question could completely change the profile of the product being sought. This stresses the importance to you of a thorough analysis of your firm's objectives and strengths as the basis for a profile of a product in which you would be interested. For example, suppose you are interested in a product at the patent or development stage. Can your company afford to take the risks involed? Are you prepared to meet the high costs of development? Or does your analysis indicate you should be looking for a fully developed product?

Suggested Sources for New Products

After having developed your Profile of Product Interest, you will have a practical gauge against which to measure new products. Where do you look for the products? A good idea for a new product can originate from almost any individual. However there are a number of sources that continually generate new products. A systematic search of these sources will almost certainly develop a choice from a number of products, any one of which could meet your needs. Suggested sources are:

Government-owned patents. Generally any U.S. Government owned patent is available on a nonexclusive royalty-free basis. Some government agencies will issue a license with some degree of exclusivity if no license has been requested after 2 years from the date of publication of the patent. Information on government-owned patents may be obtained from your local Small Business Administration office, the field office of the U.S. Department of Commerce nearest you, or by writing to the U.S. Patent Office, Department of Commerce, Washington, D.C. 20231.

Patent Abstract Bibliography (PAB) is a semiannual publication listing NASA-owned patents and applications for patents as a service for those seeking new licensable products for the commercial market. PAB may be ordered from the National Technical Information Service (NTIS), U.S. Department of Commerce, Springfield, Virginia 22151.

AEC-NASA Tech Briefs are 1- or 2-page descriptions of ideas, concepts, or patents for new products, innovations, applications, or processes. They are the result of work peformed by or under contract to the Atomic Energy Commission or the National Aeronatuics and Space administration. These ideas and products are available to the general public. *AEC-NASA Tech Briefs* are available from NTIS. Your local SBA office can give you additional information on them.

Government Reports Announcements and Index are current awareness announcements published semimonthly. These announcements may be ordered from NTIS.

Private Patents. The *Official Gazette* of the U.S. Patent Office is published weekly and lists all the patents granted by the U.S. Patent Office. Annual subscriptions are available from the Superintendent of Documents, Government Printing Office, Washington, D.C. 20402. The *Gazette* contains a section that lists, one time only, patents available for sale or licensing.

There are a number of private publications in which patents available for licensing or sale are listed. Your local library should be able to give you a complete listing of all such private publications.

The patent attorneys in your area are another source of new products.

Large Corporations. Most large corporations, especially aerospace companies, develop many new products. Because of company policy, many of these products although highly desirable are not suitable for their own manufacturing or marketing operations. Usually the large company will maintain a separate department or subsidiary company for the sole purpose of finding suitable licensees. In some cases these new product licenses include marketing studies, manufacturing know-how, and other pertinent information or services, which reduce the risk to the firm seeking a new product. This is considered one of the finest sources of new products.

Inventors Shows. The Chambers of Commerce in large metropolitan areas generally sponsor an annual "Inventors Show." The purpose of these shows is to enable manufacturers and inventors to get together to put new products on the market. Check with your local Chamber of Commerce for the dates for their next show or write to the Office of the Inventions and Innovations, National Bureau of Standards, Washington, D.C. 20234, for a lisiting of the major inventors shows scheduled throughout the United States.

Commercial Banks. One way to obtain a new product is to acquire all or part of another business. Many small companies with fine products may need the strengths of your company to become successful. These strengths may consist of equipment, facilities, personnel, or knowhow in manufacturing, marketing, or management, as well as money.

Small Business Investment Company's (SBIC'S) and Investment Bankers. In the very nature of such companies, they continually are examining existing and potential businesses. Contacts with these firms could very well lead to a new product or an equity position in a business with desirable products. Your local SBA office can furnish you with a list of licensed SBIC's in your area.

Licensing Brokers. A new type of consultant is the licensing broker. They generally have a wide range of acquaintences in the licensing field. Usually they represent companies seeking licensees (including foreign companies) as well as those searching for a product to license. Often they also have wide experience in developing fair and reasonable licensing agreements and can advise their clients accordingly.

Foreign Licenses. The U.S. Department of Commerce publishes weekly *The International Commerce Magazine*. This contains a "Licensing Oportunities Section" in which are listed products for which foreign manufacturers are seeking U.S. firms to manufacture and sell these products to the U.S. market. This may be ordered through the Department of Commerce local field office which will also have previous issues available for public inspection.

Also you may write a letter to your local Department of Commerce field office and enclose a copy of your firm's brochure and your "Profile of Product Interest." This information will be handled by their International Investment Section which will make every effort to put you in touch with a suitable foreign product licensor.

In large metropolitan areas, you should contact the local Commercial Attaches at each country's embassy or consulate. They, too, are looking for appropriate licensee for products developed in their countries.

A word of caution is in order though in such instance. You should consult an attorney experienced in foreign licensing to prevent possible legal complications in the licensing procedure.

New Product Advertising. Trade or industry periodicals and financial newspapers often carry ads of new products available to a manufacturer. These ads could very well lead you to a new product. However, looking through such ads is a passive form of search. You might consider advertising in these publications as an active, aggressive form of search. A very condensed version of your "Profile of Product Interest" should make an ideal ad.

Your Company's Brochure. Before finding a new product, you may enter into negotiations with a number of people. To assist you in establishing a sound relationship with new product sources, it is suggested that you prepare a brochure on your firm. It may be very simple or as elaborate as you wish, but it should contain: a brief history of your firm's legal structure; information on your key personnel, plant, and equipment; descriptions of jobs or products handled and, if they are agreeable, some of your best customers; and financial statements and financial resources available.

Summary

Innovative ideas are essential to business progress. It is very difficult, however, for innovators to get the kind of financial and management support they need to realize their ideas.

This *Aid,* **aimed at idea people, inventors, and innovative owner-managers of small companies, describes the tests every idea must pass before it makes money.**

You've Got an Idea? Great!

So, you've had an idea for an invention or an innovative way of doing something that will boost productivity, put more people to work, and make lots of money for you and anyone who backs you? As you've probably heard, you're the kind of person your country needs to compete in world markets and maintain its standard of living. You're the cutting edge of the future.

You are another of those individuals on whom progress has always depended. We all know that it hasn't been huge corporations that have come up with the inventions that have revolutionized life. As the discoverer of penicillin, Sir Alexander Flemming, said, "It is the lone worker who makes the first advance in a subject: The details may be worked out by a team, but the prime idea is due to the enterprise, thought and perception of an individual." Innovators like you are business's lifeblood.

Owner-managers who have started companies on new ideas know first hand about the innovation process. They also know that you can expect to hear....

You've Got an Idea? So What?

In the first place, the chances that you are the first to come up with a particular innovation are somewhere between slim and none. Secondly, even if you have come up with the better mouse trap, nobody — but nobody — is going to beat a path to your door. In fact, in the course of trying to peddle your BMT, you'll beat up plenty of shoe leather wearing paths to other people's doors. You'll stand a good chance of wearing out your patience and several dozen crying towels as well.

Why is it so hard to find backers for your brainchildren? One consultant put it: "Nobody wants unproven ideas. Nobody wants to be first. Everybody wants to be second." Why this fear of the new?

Well, new product failure rates are estimated conservatively to be between 50 and 80 percent. One survey of major companies with millions of dollars to spend on R & D, market research, and product advertising, and with well-established distribution systems found that of 58 internal proposals only 12 made it past initial screening. From these 12 only *one* successful new product emerged.

Another group set up to help innovators has found that of every 100 ideas submitted 85 have too many faults to bother with. They can be eliminated immediately. Of the remaining 15, maybe five will ever be produced. One of those might — only might — make money.

With odds like 99 to 1 against an idea being a monetary success, is it any suprise that your idea is greeted with a chorus of yawns? People — companies, investors, what have you — are basically conservative with their money. Ideas are risky.

Does that mean you should forget about your idea? Of course not. It merely means that now you're beginning to see what Edison meant, when he said, "Genius is one per cent inspiration and ninety-nine percent perspiration."

Again, those of you who own small firms started on innovations are well aware of the truth of Edison's words. You've been through the hard work.

Can You Exploit Your Idea?

Although coming up with what you think is a sure-fire idea is the biggest step, it's still only the first one. You've got the other thousand miles of the journey to success still ahead of you.

Many things remain to be done before you can expect to realize the first dollar from your invention or other innovation. You should be prepared for the unhappy discovery that the end of the line for your idea may turn up well before the point you needed to reach to make money from it.

At a bare minimum, your idea will have to pass the following tests:

Is it original or has someone else already come up with it?

Can someone produce and distribute it if it's an invention or other product, or use it if it's a marketing innovation, a new use for an existing product, or the like?

Will it really make money? (Will someone buy it?)

Can you protect your idea?

That seems to be a modest enough list, and it is. The problems arise from the dozens of underlying questions that must be answered before the major questions can be resolved. Here, for example, are the 33 areas that the University of Oregon's Innovation Center runs each submitted idea through to detemine if it has commercial merit:

Legality	Development Status
Safety	Investment Costs
Environmental Impact	Trend of Demand
Societal Impact	Product Line Potential
Potential Market	Need
Product Life Cycle	Promotion
Usage Learning	Appearance
Product Visibility	Price
Service	Protection
Durability	Payback Period
New Competition	Profitability
Functional Feasibility	Product Interdependence
Production Feasibility	Research and Development

Stability of Demand
Consumer/
User Compatibility
Marketing Research
Distribution
Perceived Function
Existing Competition
Potential Sales

Now that is *not* a modest list. However, for the moment let's ignore the 33 and look at the four broad questions.

Is Your Idea Original?

Obviously, if somebody has already come up with and produced as good an item or a better one, if would be pointless for you to pursue a similar idea any further. You'd only be wasting your time and money.

There are lots of places to look to find out. If your idea is for a consumer product, check stores and catalogs. Check trade associations and trade publications in the field into which your invention or innovation fits. Visit trade shows relevant to your idea. Look in the business and popular press. (Here, you can consult *The Reader's Guide to Periodical Literature* to help you in your search. Your public library has a copy.)

Don't be afraid to ask people in the field if they've ever heard of anything along the lines of your idea. In the pure idea stage it's not very likely that somebody will steal your idea—all the hard work still has to be done. Besides, you can ask general sorts of questions and keep the details of your idea to yourself if you're really anxious that your idea will be pirated. Patent rights to an idea in major foreign countries will be jeopardized by uncontrolled disclosure prior to filing a patent application in the United States.

Obviously, if what you've come up with is an invention or an idea that can be put into patentable form, you'll eventually have to make a patent search. You could do that in this early stage, but it's probably a better idea to hold off until you've taken a look at your idea in the light of the next two questions.

How Will the Invention Be Produced and Distributed?

The first thought many innovators have is to take their ideas to a big national company. Provide the dazzling idea, they think, and let the giant work out the details. After all, the national company has the money, the production capability, and the marketing know-how to make this surefire profit maker go.

Unfortunately, the big companies are almost never interested in ideas from outsiders. Whether that's because, as one innovation broker has suggested, that outside technology is "a risk, a threat," or simply because large corporations need potential sales of an item to be in the tens of millions of dollars, doesn't matter. The cold fact is that selling a big firm on your idea is in the 100,000 to 1 shot range.

On the other end of the scale, you may be able to produce some items yourself, working out of your home and selling by mail order. This method can be a good way to get started, but after a while you may find yourself getting tired of having 200,000 better mouse traps stashed in your bedroom.

To be sure, if you can start (or already have) your own company, you will be better off. It's easier to sell a company than a patent, even if the company is losing money.

Many potential buyers understand a company much better than they understand the technology of an invention. Business people usually look at the profit-and-loss possibilities differently from the way an innovator does.

Many of these business people follow what one innovator has called "the 'Anyhow' theory of economics": We have a plant anyhow. We have a sales force anyhow. We advertise anyhow. We're smarter anyhow." Such business people also know that by the time they purchase a company most of the bugs are out of the technology and customers exist.

Between the extremes of starting your own company or having big business buy you out is taking your idea to small and medium-sized businesses. Such firms would be happy to produce an item producing sales in amounts that simply don't interest large companies. Smaller firms may lack marketing and distribution expertise, but again your major problem is even finding one that can help you realize your idea and is interested in trying.

Will Your Idea Make Money?

This is the question that worries everybody. Here is where the risk arises that makes it so difficult to interest people in backing your idea.

It's a question that's really impossible to answer with any assurance. After all, major corporations even with massive market studies hit clinkers all the time. Remember the Edsel? On the other hand, an idea so seemingly stupid that you'd think it was somebody's idea of a silly joke might make millions. Don't you wish you'd thought of the pet rock?

So many factors need to be considered to answer this queston. Is there a market? Where is it? Is it concentrated or dispersed? Could the size of the market change suddenly? Will competition drive you out? These questions are by no means the bottom of the iceberg. Yet, answering the money question to the satisfaction of potential backers is the key to the other questions.

Can You Protect Your Idea?

Once you've come up with tentatively satisfying answers to the originality, production and distribution, and salability questions, it's time to consider protecting your idea. After all, it looks like you may have something.

If you do have a patentable item, it's time to look into trying to protect it under the patent laws. Here briefly are the steps you'll need to follow:

Get a close friend (who understands your invention) to sign his or her name on a dated diagram or written description of the invention. Or, you can file a "disclosure document" with the Patent Office. Taking one to these measures will provide evidence of the time you came up with your invention in case of a dispute with other inventors over who conceived it first. Sending yourself a registered letter describing the invention is useless as evidence. Filing a disclosure document does not give you any protection. Get patent protection as soon as possible.

Make a patent search to see whether or not the invention has already been patented in as good or better a version. You can make a search yourself. The only place to make such a search efficiently is at the Patent and Trademark Office in Arlington, Virginia. The staff at the Office will help you. You may find, however, that the only practical way to proceed from patent search on is with the help of a patent attorney.

If the invention has not been patented, prepare a patent application and file it with the Patent and Trademark Office.

Again, you can do this yourself, following the pattern you find in similar, recent patents, though, again, a patent attorney will be helpful. If you have an attorney prepare your application, go through the exercise yourself, anyway. Compare your application with your attorney's. Make sure all of the points you regard as important are covered and that the attorney has written what you want to say. Work out differences together.

Promptly file amendments or additional patent applications with the Office if you make important changes in your invention.

Having a patent won't mean you have absolute protection. In fact, one survey found that in over 70% of the infringement cases brought by patent holders to protect their patents, the patent itself was held invalid.

Defending your patent can be very expensive. If you don't have a patent, however, the probability of successfully protecting your invention approaches zero.

Mere ideas or suggestions can't be patented. Some of these you may be able to be put in patentable form, but for those that you can't it's pretty much do-it-yourself. Consult with a patent attorney or the Patent Office about the classes of patentable subject matter.

Say, for example, you think you have a great gimmick for selling more of Company A's products. Leaving aside the likelihood that Company A won't be interested, how do you approach Company A with your idea with any assurance they won't simply use it without paying you a cent?

About the best you can do is write them a letter telling them you have a promotional (or whatever) idea and, without giving them any details, offer to send it to them. Include in your letter a statement to be signed and returned by a Company A representative promising they won't divulge your idea or make use of it without compensation (to be negotiated between them and you), if they'd like to know the details of your plan. They'll probably say thanks but no thanks or that they can't promise any such things without seeing the idea, but it's the only course open to you.

Is There Any Hope?

Each section of this *Aid* seems to be packed with bad news, but the *Aid* wouldn't be doing you any favors by raising false hopes. The point is, you need to be more than an idea person to make money out of an invention or other innovation.

Many small businesses have been doomed from the start because of false hopes. Those of you who already operate going firms have avoided wishful thinking in other business areas. You need to avoid it where innovation is concerned, too.

What *are* potential idea and invention backers looking for? If you read around in the subject, you'll run across many comments to the effect that:

What we want is an entrepreneur, someone who cannot only invent a product but find capital and a way of getting the product on the market.

It's better to have a fair new product and a great manager than the other way around.

Management is the most important element for success of an invention.

Edison wasn't only an inventing genius. He was also a promoting genius, a publicity genius, a capital-raising genius, a genius at seeing potential markets for inventions.

Have you ever heard of Joseph Swan? A strong case could be made for saying he invented the electric light eight months before Edison. Who got the patents? Who got the bulb to the market? Edison. Who invented the electric light bulb? Edison.

Few of us are Edisons. We may have brilliant product ideas, but we aren't usually knowledgeable, let alone brilliant, in all the of the areas that need to be covered. We need help.

Where Can you Go for Help?

While you probably still have to invest considerable perspiration yourself, you can get help with some of the sweating. Even Edison had some help.

Patent Attorneys and Agents. Attorneys and agents can help you make patent searches and applications, if you can't do them yourself. The U.S. Patent Office has geographical and alphabetical listings of such people, but doesn't make recommendations or assume any responsibility for your selection from their lists. You can also find attorneys and agents by looking in the classified section of your telephone directory under "Patents."

Invention Promotion Firms. Also likely to be listed in the "Patents." section of the directory are firms that offer — for a fee — to take on the whole job of protecting and promoting your idea. Caution is necessary in dealing with such promoters.

Federal Trade Commission investigations found that one firm, which charged fees ranging from $1,000 to $2,000, had ten clients who made money on their inventions — that was out of a total of 35,000. Another firm with 30,000 clients had only three with successful inventions. If you elect to use an idea promotion firm, make sure:

They can provide you with solid evidence of their track record — not just a few flashy success stories, but verifiable statistics on the number of clients they've had and the number who have actually made money.

They don't collect the entire fee in advance.

They will provide you with samples of their promtional materials and lists of companies to whom they've sent it. (Then check with those companies yourself.)

You check the promotion firm's reputation with the local Better Business Bureau, Chamber of Commerce, a patent attorney, or a local inventors or innovators club.

Invention Brokers. Brokers work for a portion of the profits from an invention. They may help inventors raise capital and form companies to produce and market their inventions. They often provide sophisticated management advice. In general, you can expect these brokers to be interested in more complex technology with fairly large sales potential.

University Innovation/Invention/Entrepreneurial Centers. These centers, some funded by the National Science Foundation, show promise for helping inventors and innovators. The best known one, the University of Oregon's Experimental Center for the Advancement of Invention and Innovation (The Innovation Center no longer exits), for example, evaluated an idea for a very modest fee. The Center evaluated an idea on 33 criteria (listed earlier in the Aid) to help inventors weed out bad ideas so they won't waste further time and money on them.

The Center also indentified trouble spots that required special attention in planning the development or commercialization of a potential new product. If an idea looked like it had merit and was commercially feasible, the Center tried to link the innovator with established companies or referred him or her to sources of funds.

The Small Business Administration. The SBA's Small Business Institutes (SBI's) are located at more than 450 colleges and universities around the country. While currently few SBI schools can provide much help with the technical R & D aspects of innovations, they certainly can provide the market research, feasibilty analysis, and business planning assistance necessary to make an innovation successful.

SBA field offices (see your local telephone directory under "U.S. Government") can provide you with information about the SBI program. You may find other management assistance programs offered at the field offices of help in realizing your idea as well.

National Bureau of Standards. The Office of Energy-Related Inventions in the U.S. Department of Commerce's National Bureau of Standards will evaluate non-nuclear energy-related inventions and ideas for devices, materials, and procedures without charge. If the office finds that the invention or idea has merit, it will recommend further study by the Department of Energy. The Department of Energy may provide support for the invention if it shows promise. This process may take from nine months to a year.

Inventor's Clubs/Associations/Societies. You may have such clubs in your locality. You can share experiences with kindred spirits and get good advice, low cost evaluation, and other help.

Talking with other inventors is probably the most helpful thing you can do. Find someone who has been through the entire routine of patents, applied R&D, and stages of financing. It doesn't matter if the end result was a financial success or failure. Getting the nitty-gritty of the process is what's important.

Are You Being Unreasonable About Your Chances?

If you have read this *Aid* and still think you can make money with your idea, some people might think you've missed the point. If you continue to believe in your idea after looking at the odds and obstacles, you *are* being unreasonable.

That's exactly what you should be. You're in good company.

All progress is made by unreasonable people, George Bernard Shaw observed. Reasonable people adapt to the world around them; unreasonable people try to change it.

Summary

Because of the tremendous development and complexity of technology, products, and processes, manufacturers should be familiar with patent protection and procedures. It is important to understand patent rights and the relationships among a business, an inventor, and the Patent and Trademark Office to assure protection of your product and to avoid or win infringement suits. This *Aid* gives some basic facts about patents to help clarify your rights in this important legal area. The U.S. Department of Commerce, Patent and Trademark Office and the courts are the final authorities in this field.

To understand the details of patent procedure you should at the start know what a patent is and distinguish among patents, trademarks, and copyrights.

What is a Patent?

A **patent** is an exclusive property right to an invention and is issued by the Commissioner of Patents and Trademarks, U.S. Department of Commerce. It gives an inventor the right to exclude others from making, using or selling an invention for a period of seventeen years in the United States, its territories, and possessions. A patent cannot be renewed except by act of Congress. **Design patents** for ornamental devices now are granted for 14 years. You will find many useful facts in the booklet *General Information Concerning Patents*, available from the Government Printing Office, Washington, D.C. 20402. You may also want to request a leaflet entitled *Publications Obtainable from the United States Patent and Trademark Office*.

Trademarks are also registered by the Commissioner of Patents and Trademarks on application by individuals or companies who distinguish, by **name** or **symbol**, a product used in commerce subject to regulation by Congress. They can be registered for a period of twenty years.

Copyrights, administered by the Copyright Office (Libary of Congress, Washington, D.C.), protect authors, composers, and artists from the "pirating" of their **literary** and **artistic** work.

First Steps

When you get an idea for a product or process that you think is mechanically sound and likely to be profitable, write down your idea. Consider specifically what about your new device is original or patentable and superior to similar devices already on the market (and patented). Your idea should be written in a way that provides legal evidence of its origin because your claim could be challenged later. Next you need help to determine your device's **novelty** and to make a proper application for a patent.

Professional Assistance. Professional assistance is recommended strongly because patent procedures are quite detailed. Also, you may not know how to make use of all the technical advantages available. For instance, you may not claim broad enough protection for your device. As a rule therefore, it is best to have your application filed by a patent lawyer or agent.

Only attorneys and agents who are **registered** with the Patent Office may prosecute an application. That Office has geographical and alphabetical listings of more than 11,000 such people. It will not, however recommend any particular attorney or agent, nor will it assume responsibility for your selection.

Establishing Novelty. This is one of the most crucial and difficult determinations to make, involving two things: 1) analyzing the device according to specified standards and 2) seeing whether or not anyone else has patented it first. The only sure way of accomplishing this is to make a search of Patent Office files.

Analyzing your device. This should be done according to the following standards of what is **patentable:**

(1) Any **new, useful,** and **unobvious** process (primarily industrial or technical); machine; manufacture or composition of matter (generally chemical compounds, formulas, and the like); or any new, useful, and unobvious improvement thereof;

(2) Any new and unobvious original and ornamental design for an article of manufacture, such as a new auto body design, (Note that a design patent may not always turn out to be valuable because a commercially similar design can easily be made without infringing the patent);

(3) Any distinct and new variety of plant, other than tubes-propagated, which is asexually reproduced.

Another way of analyzing your product is to consider it in relation to what is **not** patentable, as follows:

(1) An idea (as opposed to a mechanical device);

(2) A method of doing business (such as the assembly line system); however, any structural or mechanical innovations employed might constitute patentable subject matter;

(3) Printed matter (covered by copyright law);

(4) An inoperable device;

(5) An improvement in a device which is obvious or the result of mere mechanical skill (a new assembly of old parts or an adaptation of an old principle—aluminum window frames instead of the conventional wood).

Applications for patents on machines or processes for producing fissionable material can be filed with the Patent and Trademark Office. In most instances, however, such applications might be withheld if the subject matter affects national security and for that reason should not be made public.

The invention should also be tested for novelty by the following criteria:

(1) Whether or not known or used by others in this country before the invention by the applicant;

(2) Whether or not patented or described in a printed publication in this or a foreign country before the invention by the applicant;

(3) Whether or not described in a printed publication more than one year prior to the date of application for patent in the United States.

(4) Whether or not in public use or on sale in the country more than one year prior to the date of application for patent in the United States.

These points are important. For example, if you describe a new device in a printed publication or use it publicly or place it on sale, you must apply for a patent before one year has gone by; otherwise you lose any right to a patent.

Although marking your product "patent pending" after you have applied has no legal protective effect, it often tends to ward off potential infringers.

Search of existing patents and technical literature. It is not necessary for you or your attorney to travel personally to Arlington, VA to make a search of Patent and Trademark Office files. Arrangements can be made with associates in Arlington, VA to have this done.

Only the files of patents granted are open to the public. Pending applications are kept in strictest secrecy and no access is given to them except on written authority of the applicants or their duly authorized representatives. Existing patents may be consulted in the Search Room of the Patent and Trademark Office where records of over 4,000,000 patents issued since 1836 are maintained. In addition, over 9,000,000 copies of foreign patents may also be seen in the Patent Library. That library contains a quantity of scientific books and periodicals which may carry a description of your idea and thus affect its patentability.

A search of patents, besides indicating whether or not your device is patentable, may also prove informative. It may disclose patents superior to your device but not already in production which might profitably be manufactured and sold by your company. A valuable business association may result.

Points of Caution

While the advantages of obtaining a patent are fairly obvious, it must be recognized that a number of pitfalls and obstacles lurk in the path of every applicant. For example, a patent by no means guarantees immunity from lawsuits, but rather sometimes seems to attract challenges to its legality. As one patent lawyer has said. "A patent is merely a fighting interest in a lawsuit."

Interference. One of these snags is interference (occurring in about only one percent of the cases) when two or more applicants have applications pending for substantially the same invention. Because a patent should be granted to only one applicant, the parties in such a case must give proof of the date the invention was made. Ordinarily, the applicant who proves that he or she was the first to conceive the invention and produce a working device will be held to be the prior inventor. If no other evidence is submitted, the date of filing the applications is used to settle the controversy. Priority questions are determined on evidence submitted to a board of examiners.

Infringement. Unauthorized manufacture, use, or sale of subject matter embraced by the claims of a patent constitutes infringement. The patent owner may file suit in a Federal court for damages and/or an injunction prohibiting the continued use or manufacture of the patented article. If an item is not marked "patented," the holder of the patent may sue for damages on account of infringement but no damages can be received covering the period before the infringer is so notified.

Moreover, no recovery of damages is possible for any infringement occurring more than six years before the filing of the complaint. There is no established method of learning of any infringement. A clipping service and a sharp eye for reference in trade literature may be helpful, but the responsiblity lies entirely with the patentee (patent holder).

Foreign Patents. If you wish to market your patented product in a foreign country, you should apply for patent protection in the particular country to prevent infringement. See **General Infomation Concerning Patents** for further details, or consult a patent attorney or agent who can assist in getting you foreign patents.

Selling Part Interest. Once you get a patent, consider how to make the best use of it. You have several choices of action. If you have the facilities and money, you can manufacture and sell the article. Alternatively, you can sell all or part of the patent or you can license or assign it to someone else.

Probably the trickiest operation of all is selling part interest in a patent. Remember that joint ownership holds many pitfalls unless restricted by a contract. A joint owner, no matter how small his or her interest, may use the patent as the original owner. He may make use of or sell the item for his own profit, without regard to any other owner, and he may also sell his interest in it to someone else. A new part owner is responsible for making sure that any such transfer is recorded within three months at the Patent and Trademark Office.

This is what could happen. An inventor offers to sell this patent for $100,000, but the prospective buyer, claiming this is too expensive, proposes to buy part interest of say $10,000 or ten percent interest in it. If the sale were concluded, the new part owner—unless specifically restrained from doing so by contract — could go ahead and manufacture and sell the item as if he owned it 100 percent, without accounting to the other part owner (who is the original investor and patent holder).

Assignments and Licenses. A patent is personal property and can be sold or even mortgaged. You can sell or transfer a patent or patent application. Such a transfer of interest is an **assignment;** and the assignee then has the rights to the patent that the original patentee had. A whole or part interest can be assigned.

Like an assignment, a **grant** conveys an interest in a patent but only for a specified area of the United States.

A mortgage of patent property gives ownership to the lender for the duration of the loan.

You can license your patent which means someone pays you for the right to your patent according to the conditions of the license.

All assignments, grants, licesnses, or conveyances of any patent or application for a patent should be notarized and must be recorded with the Patent and Trademark Office within three months of the transfer of rights. If not, it is void against a subsequent buyer unless it is recorded prior to the subsequent purchase.

All references and documents relating to a patent or a patent application should be identified by the number, date, inventor's name and the title of the invention. Adequate identification will lessen the difficulties of determining ownership rights and what patents and applications are in issue.

Other Problems You Confront as an Inventor. Even though your invention passes the expert, impartial judgment of a patent examiner as to novelty and workability, it still must be commercially acceptable if you are to make money from it. In this respect you should expect no help for the Patent and Trademark Office, as it can offer no advice on this point.

Also, you should realize that, in modern technology, the vast majority of patents granted are merely improvements or refinements on a basic invention. The claims allowed on an improvement patent are narrow, as compared with those of a basic invention. Because the claims allowed on an improvement patent are narrow as compared with those of a basic patent, the inventor therefore runs a proportionately greater risk of infringement if a basic patent is in force.

Here is an example: Inventor George Westinghouse patented an entirely new device—the air brake. For this he was granted **broad protection** by the Patent and Trademark Office. Suppose that later, inventor "B" devised a structural improvement, such as a new type of valve for the compressed air. Inventor "B" would have received relatively **narrow** protection on the valve and would not have been able to manufacture the complete air brake without infringing Westingouse's patent. Nor could anyone else to whom "B" licensed the patent make the whole brake.

Also, be aware that United States patent laws make no discrimination with respect to the citizenship of an inventor. Regardless of citizenship, any inventor may apply for a patent on the same basis as an American citizen.

Finally, purchasing is an important aspect of all business and touches upon patents. Purchase orders can have clauses dealing with patent infringement. Practice, type of goods, and many factors affect the clause; but such a clause could be as follows:

Seller shall indemnify and save harmless the buyer and/or its vendees from and against all cost, expenses, and damages arising out of any infringement or claim of infringement of any patent or patents in the use of articles or equipment furnished hereunder.

Application for a Patent

If you find, after preliminary search, that your invention appears to be patentable, the next step is the preparation of a patent application covering your invention. File it with the **Commissioner of Patents and Trademarks, Wahington, DC 20231.** All subsequent correspondence should also be addressed to the Commissioner.

The Patent Application. With few exceptions the patent application must be filed in the name of the inventor. Even the application for a patent on an invention by a company's researcher must be filed in the inventor's name. If there is more than one inventor, a joint application is made. The patent application can be assigned, however, to an individual or a corporation, and then the patent will be granted to the assignee, although filed in the inventor's name.

Often employment agreements require an employee to assign to the employer any invention relating to the employer's business. Even without such an agreement, the employer may have a "shop right" to use (free) an invention developed on the job by an employee.

Application for a patent is made to the Commissioner of Patents and Trademarks and includes:

(1) A written document that comprises a petition, a specification (descriptions and claims), and an oath;

(2) A drawing in those cases in which a drawing is possible; and

(3) The filing fee of $150 for small entities and $300 for corporations.

The exacting requirements of the Patent and Trademarks Office for a patent application are described in **Title** 37, **Code of Federal Regulation,** which may be purchased from the **Superintendent of Documents, Government Printing Office, Washington, DC 20402.** The construction of the invention, its operation, and its advantages should be accurately described. From the "disclosure" of the application, any person skilled in the field of the invention should be able to understand the intended construction and use of the invention. Commercial advantages, which would be attractive to a prospective manufacturer, need not be discussed.

The claims at the end of the specification point out the patentably new features of the invention. Drawings must be submitted according to rigid Patent and Trademark Office regulations.

The filing fee is normally paid by check, payable to the Commisssioner of Patents and Trademarks or by a money order sent by registered mail. The Patent and Trademark Office assumes no responsibility for its safe arrival.

What Happens to Your Application in the Patent Office. When your application is received in the Patent and Trademark Office, it is given a preliminary examination to determine whether or not all requirements are met. If The application is in order, you will be notified of that fact and your application assigned a serial number and filing date. These govern its position on the docket. If there is some very minor deficiency, such as some irregularity in the drawings, the date and number will be assigned and the necessary revision requested later. If the application is incomplete, you will be notified and your application will be held up until you supply the required information to correct the deficiency.

After your application is filed, it is examined by an examiner trained and experienced in the field of your invention. Frequently, the examiner finds existing patents showing inventions enough like yours that revision of the application claims will have to be make. Sometimes several revisions and arguments by your patent attorney (or agent) are necessary to overcome successive objections raised by the examiner. Each objection constitutes an **action** by the Patent and Trademark Office; and if no response is made to an action within a prescribed period, the application is considered **abandoned.** An abandoned application is dropped from further consideration. Because each application must ordinarily await its turn to be considered or reconsidered, it generally takes on the average of nineteen months to get a patent.

If the examiner finally refuses to grant a patent on the basis of the claims requested, the application may be appealed to the Board of Appeals of the Patent Office on payment of $57.50 for small entities and $115 for corporations plus the same fee amount if a brief in support of an appeal is filed. A brief for this appeal must be filed within sixty days after the date of the appeal.

When all the examiner's objections are satisfied, a patent may be obtained by payment of a final fee: $250 for small entities and $500 for corporations plus certain printing charges. A brief description of each patent issued is published weekly in the **Official Gazette of the U.S. Patent Office**. At the same time, specifications and drawings of current issuances are published separately, and copies are generally available to the public for fifty cents each.

Making Applications Special. Only under limited conditions may a petition be filed requesting that an application be given **special** treatment; that is, taken up for examination before its normal turn is reached. These requirements are of particular importance to small business owners who are eager to obtain a patent before starting a manufacturing program. If you ask for special treatment for that reason, you must state under oath:

(1) That you have sufficient capital available and facilities to manufacture the invention in quantity. If you are acting as an individual, there must also be a corroborating affidavit from an officer of a bank, showing that you have obtained sufficient capital to manufacture the invention.

(2) That you will not manufacture unless it is certain that the patent will be granted.

(3) That you will obligate yourself or your company to produce the invention in quantity as soon as patent protection has been established. A corporation must have this commitment agreed to in writing by its board of directors.

(4) That if the application is allowed, you will furnish a statement under oath within three months of such allowance, showing (a) how much money has been expended, (b) the number of devices manufactured, and (c) labor employed.

Your attorney must file an affidavit to show that he or she has made a careful and thorough search of the **prior art** and believes all the claims in the application are allowable. The attorney will also be expected to make sure that the last sworn statement described above is properly filed.

As distinguished from mechanical patents, there are also available patents to protect ornamental designs for articles of manufacture. The filing fee on each application is $87.50 for small entities and $115 for corporations. Issue fees for design patents are $62.50 for small entities and $125 for corporations. Design patents are in effect for fourteen years. Printed copies of issued design patents may be purchased by the public for twenty cents each.

Plant Patents

Plant patents were introduced in 1930. A plant patent is granted to an inventor (or his heirs or assigns) who has invented (or discovered) and asexually reproduced a distinct and new variety of plant. Plant seedlings discovered, propagated asexually, and proved to have new characteristics distinct from other known plants are patentable. Tuber-propagated plants (such as potatoes and artichokes) or plants found in the uncultivated state are not patentable. Tuber-propagated plants are excluded because, among asexually reproduced plants, they are propagated by the same part of the plant that is sold as food.

The grant is the right to exclude others from asexually reproducing the plant, or selling, or using the plant so reproduced. Patented plants must have new characteristics which distinguish them from others, such as resistance to drought, cold, or heat. They must also not have been introduced to the public nor placed on sale more than one year before the filing of a patent application. Application papers must be made out in duplicate and sent to the Commissioner of Patents and Trademarks.

Index

Other Bestsellers of Related Interest

THE SMALL BUSINESS TAX ADVISOR: Understanding The New Tax Law—Cliff Roberson, LLM, Ph.D

The most extensive changes ever in the history of American tax laws were made in 1986. And to help you better understand these changes, Cliff Roberson has compiled the information every small business operator, corporate officer, director, or stockholder needs to know into a manageable and readily understandable new sourcebook. 176 pages. Book No. 30024, $12.95 paperback only

GREAT AD!: Low-Cost, Do-It-Yourself Advertising for Your Small Business—Carol Wilkie Wallace

If you have big plans but a small budget, this book will help you to produce an effective, professional, and economical advertising campaign. It takes a hands-on approach and walks you step-by-step through research, media planning, and creative strategy. *Great Ad!* helps you research the competition, assess your business image, analyze the market, target your audience, schedule sales, and develop a media calendar. You also get hints on sources for artwork and music, and methods for effective copy. 352 pages, 36 illustrations. Book No. 3467, $19.95 paperback, $32.95 hardcover

SITE SELECTION: Finding and Developing Your Best Location—Kay Whitehouse, CCIM

"I highly recommend it . . ."

—**Roger B. Baumgartner, Realtor, CCIM**

"This book is long overdue . . . much needed guidance and information . . . a must for anyone preparing to . . . invest in real estate"

—**A. J. West, Director of Franchising Development, Denny's Incorporated**

Whether you're a businessowner, investor, or real estate professional responsible for locating potential business sites, this book will help you spot the pitfalls that can turn a seemingly beautiful piece of property into a financial disaster. 192 pages. Book No. 30053, $21.95 hardcover only

GETTING OUT: A Step-by-Step Guide to Selling a Business or Professional Practice
—Lawrence W. Tuller

A management consultant and former business owner, the author brings 25 years of buyout and acquisition experience to bear on the problems of establishing a "getting-out" position. He offers a complete and authoritative treatment of the subject for owners of any size business—as well as doctors, lawyers, accountants, and other professionals in private practice. 320 pages, 30 illustrations. Book No. 30063, $24.95 hardcover only

FRANK CAPPIELLO'S NEW GUIDE TO FINDING THE NEXT SUPERSTOCK—Frank Cappiello

"Frank Cappiello is one of America's most brilliant securities analysts . . . he has few peers as a super stock picker."—**Louis Rukeyser**

Investors today still marvel at the huge profits made in superstocks of the past such as Xerox, IBM, and Hewlett Packard. For savvy investors, such opportunities still exist. In this new guide, Frank Cappiello reveals his own successful approach to uncovering the superstocks of the future. He shows readers how to sift through the thousands of available stocks and pick out the few that are poised for hypergrowth. 208 pages, 102 illustrations. Book No. 30041, $12.95 paperback, $18.95 hardcover

INSTANT LEGAL FORMS: Ready-to-Use Documents for Almost Any Occasion—Ralph E. Troisi

By following the clear instructions provided in this book, you can write your own will, lend or borrow money or personal property, buy or sell a car, rent out a house or apartment, check your credit, hire contractors, and grant power of attorney—all without the expense or complication of a lawyer. Author-attorney Ralph E. Troisi supplies ready-to-use forms and step-by-step guidance in filling them out and modifying them to meet your specific needs. 224 pages, illustrated. Book No. 30028, $16.95 paperback only

CREDIT AND COLLECTIONS FOR YOUR SMALL BUSINESS—Cecil J. Bond

Here's a practical guide for busy entrepreneurs and credit managers that tells how to set up or overhaul a small credit department. Includes forms, applications, letters, and reports ready to be copied and put to use. 192 pages, 66 illustrations. Book No. 30035, $18.95 paperback, $28.95 hardcover

SUCCESSFUL BUSINESS PRESENTATIONS—Joseph A. Quattrini

This sourcebook shows you how to become more effective at communicating orally at all levels—with your peers, superiors, subordinates, and customers. Quattrini shows you how to plan, organize, and deliver information in every conceivable speaking situation: proposals, demonstrations, lectures, committees, oral briefings, interviews, negotiations, discussion groups, debates, telephone sales, and more. 200 pages. Book No. 30055, $15.95 paperback, $24.95 hardcover

WHY EMPLOYEES DON'T DO WHAT THEY'RE SUPPOSED TO DO AND WHAT TO DO ABOUT IT—Ferdinand F. Fournies

"...honest, concise, and immediately applicable methods"

—Chris Marlin, Training Director, Buick-Oldsmobile-Cadillac Group

Getting employees to do what they are supposed to do is probably the biggest challenge for any manager. Ferdinand F. Fournies, internationally known business consultant and author, here shares innovative, yet practical ideas on how managers can prevent the most common reasons for employee nonperformance by preventive management. 120 pages. Book No. 30064, $14.95 hardcover, $8.95 paperback

COACHING FOR IMPROVED WORK PERFORMANCE—Ferdinand F. Fournies

"... a sorely needed guide/help book for sales-marketing managers."—**The Sales Executive**

Over 70,000 copies sold in hardcover; now available for the first time in paperback! By one of the nation's best-known business training consultants and specialist in coaching procedures, this book shows you face-to-face coaching procedures that allow you to obtain immediate, positive results with your subordinates. Filled with examples, case studies, and practical problem-solving techniques. 224 pages. Book No. 30054, $12.95 paperback only

UNDERSTANDING WALL STREET—2nd Edition—Jeffrey B. Little and Lucien Rhodes

"An excellent introduction to stock market intricacies"

—American Library Association Booklist

This bestselling guide to understanding and investing on Wall Street has been completely updated to reflect the most current developments in the stock market. The substantial growth of mutual funds, the emergence of index options, the sweeping new tax bill, and how to keep making money after the market reaches record highs and lows are a few of the things explained in this long awaited revision. 240 pages, 18 illustrations. Book No. 30020, $9.95 paperback, $19.95 hardcover

MAKING YOUR SMALL BUSINESS A SUCCESS —G. Howard Poteet

An ideal companion to G. Howard Poteet's Starting Up Your Own Business: Expert Advice from the U.S. Small Business Administration (Book No. 3548), this volume concentrates on strategies new and established business owners should follow to make their enterprises competitive and profitable. Once again, Poteet has compiled into one volume the work of more than 50 leading business experts, commissioned specifically by the SBA to produce a series of management aids for the growing entrepreneurial community. Available April 1991. 224 pages. Book No. 3718, $17.95 paperback only

Prices Subject to Change Without Notice.

Look for These and Other TAB Books at Your Local Bookstore

To Order Call Toll Free 1-800-822-8158
(in PA, AK, and Canada call 717-794-2191)

or write to TAB BOOKS, Blue Ridge Summit, PA 17294-0840.